MINI HINDI DICTIONARY

HINDI-ENGLISH
ENGLISH-HINDI

Richard Delacy

TUTTLE Publishing

Tokyo | Rutland, Vermont | Singapore

CONTENTS

Hindi in Contemporary South Asia

Hindi, or Modern Standard Hindi as it is also known, is the joint official language of the Republic of India, along with English. Modern Standard Hindi is based on the dialect spoken in and around Delhi known as Khari Boli, or "standing speech." In reality, however, Hindi may be considered an umbrella term for a multitude of spoken and literary registers employed by over 450 million people throughout the north of the Indian subcontinent, from Rajasthan in the west to Bihar in the east, and from the border with Nepal in the north to the border of Maharashtra in the middle of the country. It is quite difficult to pin down the tremendous number and variety of registers that exist in the northern states, even as Modern Standard Hindi is officially privileged as their standardized form. It is also true that the ways in which people speak are changing rapidly. For this reason, it is better to think of language as operating on a continuum across the length and breadth of north India, particularly when it comes to spoken forms, as well as the registers that are used in the burgeoning media.

The modern name of the language comes originally from Persian, and is related to "Sindhu," a Sanskrit term for river and particularly the Indus River that flows through the state of Punjab in Pakistan. Both the words Hindi and Hindu were used by Persian speakers to describe the people and the languages on the east of the Indus River in the second millennium of the Common Era. Other words that were also in currency included Hindavi and Hindui. While Hindi has been associated with a tremendous number of spoken registers that have existed in a state of constant flux in north India for at least a millennium, the evolution of the language has been traditionally understood in terms of literature (both devotional and courtly) produced over the second millennium across this region. In histories of Hindi literature produced from the 19th century onwards, historians frequently underlined the importance of an impressive number of compositions by poets patronized in royal courts and in the form of devotional texts produced by Hindu saints, often in regional registers, as critical to the development of the modern language. At the same time, a modern literary style, predominantly written in the Devanagari script, came to be privileged as a medium of education and for some administrative tasks at lower levels of the bureaucracy during the colonial period. Gradually this form came to be standardized and to gain further official recognition, in addition to being used in the emerging print media as well.

Over the 19th and 20th centuries however, descriptions of Hindi came to be infused with a particular language politics, especially in regard to its relationship to Urdu and English. At the level of everyday speech, Hindi and Urdu are conventionally understood to be more or less mutually intelligible. At the literary level, however, Urdu ordinarily draws much more of its vocabulary from Persian and Arabic, and is conventionally written in a modified form of the Arabic script. English has occupied a contentious place in India since the colonial period, when it represented the language of colonial power and, over time, the language of the colonized elite classes.

Given the vast number of different registers, and the pace at which languages are changing in contemporary South Asia, Hindi learning materials understandably focus more on written forms of language, such as those found in the media and in literary texts. Over the years Hindi writers have conventionally drawn most heavily from Sanskrit, the classical language of Indian antiquity, for their vocabulary needs. Indeed, it is commonly accepted that the structure of Hindi and its core vocabulary emerged out of classical Sanskrit and later registers. In addition to this, many literary registers in Hindi have also drawn on a rich store of words from Persian and Arabic in particular. It is interesting to note that the influence of languages originating outside of South Asia on the languages of India tells us much about the fascinating history of contact between different peoples over the second millennium of the Common Era.

This dictionary has been prepared from the perspective that the English-speaking learner of Hindi is more likely to need to consult such a resource when reading literary texts to look up the meaning of words that came into Hindi over the centuries from languages such as Sanskrit, Persian, Arabic, Turkish, etc. Of these by far the largest number of words come from Sanskrit. Words of Sanskrit origin in Hindi appear broadly in two forms. The first is in the form that they occur in Sanskrit. In Hindi these words are known as tatsama words, that is, words in the same form as their Sanskrit originals. The second group is known as tadbhava words, that is, words that have the same meaning but a slightly different form to their Sanskrit originals.

It is with this in mind that an effort has been made to include in this dictionary as many words as possible that may be encountered in the first years of learning Hindi, particularly in literary texts. The vast majority of these, for the reasons mentioned above, have come into Hindi from Sanskrit. Perhaps the fewest number of words are included here from English, which does not reflect an effort to ignore or shun these words and their growing usage in Hindi, but recognizes that to be as practical as possible, this dictionary should include as many words as it can in order to read texts. An effort has been made to be as comprehensive as possible, following on from earlier dictionaries such as R. S. McGregor's *Hindi-English Dictionary* (OUP), and Mahendra Chaturvedi and Bola Nath Tewari's wonderful *A Practical Hindi-English Dictionary* (National Publishing House, Delhi).

How to Use This Dictionary

Each character in Hindi represents a single syllable, and the dictionary order of these is arranged according to the point of articulation, from the back of the mouth to the front. The vowels appear first, followed by the consonants.

VOWELS

अ	आ	इ	ई	उ	ऊ	ऋ	ए	ऐ	ओ	औ
a	*ā*	*i*	*ī*	*u*	*ū*	*ṛ*	*e*	*ai*	*o*	*au*

CONSONANTS

Velar	क/क़ *ka/qa*	ख/ख़ *kha/ <u>kh</u>a*	ग/ग़ *ga/<u>gh</u>a*	घ *gha*	ङ *ṅa*
Palatal	च *ca*	छ *cha*	ज/ज़ *ja/za*	झ *jha*	ञ *ña*
Retro-flex	ट *ṭa*	ठ *ṭha*	ड (ड़) *ḍa (ṛa)*	ढ (ढ़) *ḍha (ṛha)*	ण/ण *ṇa*

Dental	त *ta*	थ *tha*	द *da*	ध *dha*	न *na*
Labial	प *pa*	फ/फ़ *pha/fa*	ब *ba*	भ *bha*	म *ma*
Liquids	य *ya*	र *ra*	ल *la*	व *va/wa*	
Sibilants and fricatives	श *śa*	ष *ṣa*	स *sa*		
aspirate	ह *ha*				

The same order is followed for every syllable in the word. For example, all words that begin with क *[ka]* will then be followed by all words that begin with:

का	कि	की	कु	कू	कृ	के	कै	को	कौ
kā	*ki*	*kī*	*ku*	*kū*	*kṛ*	*ke*	*kai*	*ko*	*kau*

The vowels here appear in their modified forms (*mātrā forms*) when combined with a consonant, replacing the inherent अ a vowel that occurs with each consonant. This order is repeated for every syllabus in the word.

Syllables in which there appears nasalization (ँ) or a nasal consonant without its inherent 'a' vowel (most often represented by a dot above the line at the top of the word), or the symbol that represents the reduplication of the vowel (:), appear at the beginning of that syllable.

For example:

चं precedes च	चंचल *[cañcal]* ADJ fickle precedes चकमा *[cakmā]* M trick
गाँ precedes गा	गाँव *[gā̃v]* M village precedes गाड़ी *[gāṛī]* F vehicle
दुः precedes दु	दुःख *[du-hu-kh]* M sorrow precedes दुआ *[duā]* F prayer

In the orthography occasionally the forms of consonants are modified and they are written together (conjunct consonants) to represent that a vowel is not pronounced with the first consonant. Syllables with conjunct consonants appear after syllables with the final vowel.

For example:

कौन *[kaun]* INTER PRO who *is followed by* क्या *[kyā]* INTER what

Conjunct Consonants

These can be divided into six groups, depending on the particular modification to the consonant that takes place. In all cases, conjunct clusters are read from left to right and then top to bottom.

1. The first group of conjunct forms includes only the

consonants क and फ. Both of these end in a short, horizonal half-stroke.

क्या *[kyā]* what? (also question marker)
शक्कर *[śakkar]* F sugar
रफ़्तार *[raftār]* F speed
मुफ़्त *[muft]* free

2. The second group consists of consonants that lose the vertical line when they are joined to the following consonant. This includes the majority of the consonants in the syllabary.

ख ग घ च ज त थ ध प
ब भ य ल व श ष स

विख्यात *[vikhyāt]* famous
ग्यारह *[gyārah]* eleven
अच्छा *[acchā]* good
छज्जा *[chajjā]* M balcony
त्याग *[tyāg]* M renunciation
पृथ्वी *[pṛthvī]* F earth
ध्यान *[dhyān]* M attention
प्यास *[pyās]* F thirst
शब्द *[shabd]* M word
अभ्यास *[abhyās]* M practice
अय्यर *[ayyar]* a name

ख़्याल *[khyāl]* M idea, thought
बग्घी *[bagghī]* F buggy
बच्चा *[baccā]* M child
राज्य *[rājya]* M state, province
कुत्ता/कुत्ता *[kuttā]* M dog
तथ्य *[tathya]* M fact
अध्यापक *[adhyāpak]* M teacher
चप्पल *[cappal]* F sandal
ब्याह *[byāh]* M marriage
सभ्य *[sabhya]* ADJ civilized

जल्दी *[jaldī]* F haste

व्यवहार *[vyavahār]* M behavior

नाश्ता *[nāśtā]* M snack, breakfast

शिष्य *[śiṣya]* M disciple

नमस्कार *[namaskār]* M greeting

दिल्ली *[dillī]* F Delhi

व्यापार *[vyāpār]* M business

चश्मा *[caśmā]* M spectacles, eyeglasses

कष्ट *[kaṣṭ]* M difficulty, pain

पुस्तक *[pustak]* F book

3. The third group of conjunct characters contains all of the nasal consonants: ङ, ञ, ण/ण, न, म. When they appear as the first member of a consonant cluster, they may either be written in a modified form and joined to the following consonant or as a dot above the horizontal line. Nasal conjuncts will only occur with a consonant of the series to which they belong in the syllabary.

ङ (combines with क, ख, ग, घ)
शङ्कर/शंकर *[śaṅkar]* M Shiva
कङ्घी/कंघी *[kaṅghī]* F comb
पङ्खा/पंखा *[paṅkhā]* M fan

ञ (combines with च, छ, ज, झ)
सञ्जय/सञ्जय/संजय *[sañjay]* Sanjay
चञ्चल/चञ्चल/चंचल *[cañcal]* ADJ restless, fickle

ण/ण (combines with ट, ठ, ड, ढ)
अण्डा/अण्डा/अंडा *[aṇḍā]* M egg

ठण्डा/ठण्डा/ठंडा *[ṭhaṇḍā]* cold
घण्टा/घण्टा/घंटा *[ghaṇṭā]* M hour, bell

न* (combines with त, थ, द, ध)
सुन्दर/सुंदर *[sundar]* beautiful
सन्त/संत *[sant]* M saint

a) When न combines with त, थ, द or ध, it may be written as a dot or in the modified form.

b) When न combines with र, श and स, it should be written as a dot. When it combines with म etc. it should be written in the modified form न्.

मुन्नी/मुन्नी *[munnī]* F child
नन्हाँ *[nanhā̃]* tiny, wee, small (as in child)

म** (combines with प, फ, ब, भ)
चम्मच *[cammac]* M spoon
कम्बल/कंबल *[kambal]* M blanket
तुम्हारा *[tumhārā]* your (from तुम)

4. The fourth group consists of the consonants that have a rounded shape: ट, ठ, ड, ढ, द and ह. As the first member of a consonant cluster, these characters may be represented in two ways. The consonants can be joined

---

* न may also combine with म, य, र, व, श, स, and ह.

** When म combines with प, फ, ब, or भ, it may be written as a dot but when it combines with म, न, य, ल, and ह the conjunct form म् is employed.

one on top of the other, or the symbol ् (हलंत *[halant]*) may be written under the first consonant to represent the omission of the अ vowel.

चिट्ठी/चिट्‌ठी *[ciṭṭhī]* F letter
छुट्टी/छुट्‌टी *[chuṭṭī]* F holiday
पाठ्य-पुस्तक/पाठ्‌यपुस्तक *[pāṭhya-pustak]* F textbook
लड्डू/लड्‌डू *[laḍḍū]* M (an Indian sweet)
धनाढ्य/धनाढ्‌य *[dhanāḍhya]* wealthy
कद्दू/कद्‌दू *[kaddū]* M pumpkin
चिह्न/चिह्‌न *[cihn]* M sign
ब्राह्मण/ब्राह्‌मण *[brāhmaṇ]* M Brahman

5. The fifth group consists only of the consonant र, which takes three forms depending on whether it occurs as the first member or the final member of the conjunct cluster and the character with which it is combined.

a) When र occurs as the first member of the cluster it is written above the line *after* the consonant to which it is joined.

धर्म *[dharm]* M justice, duty, religion
सर्दी *[sardī]* F cold, winter

b) When र occurs as the second member of the consonant cluster it is written as a diagonal stroke at the bottom of the consonant it follows.

चक्र *[cakra]* M circle
ग्राहक *[grāhak]* M customer

c) When र is the second member after any of the rounded consonants, ट, ठ, ड, ढ, द, ह, ळ, it is written under the consonant thus ‸ or ⸝ (or in the case of ह, in the consonant).

ट्रेन *[ṭren]* F train
राष्ट्र *[rāṣṭra]* M nation
द्रव्य *[dravya]* M substance, money
ह्रास *[hras]* M decay

6. The final group consists of the exceptional conjunct consonants.

क् + ष	=	क्ष/क्ष	परीक्षा *[parīkṣā]* F examination
क् + र	=	क्र	क्रिया *[kriyā]* F action, verb
क् + त	=	क्त	भक्त *[bhakt]* M devotee
ज् + ञ	=	ज्ञ	ज्ञान *[jñān]* M knowledge (pronounced *[gyān]*)
त् + त	=	त्त	पत्ता *[patta]* M leaf
त् + र	=	त्र	मित्र *[mitra]* M friend
द् + ध	=	द्ध	शुद्ध *[śuddh]* pure
द् + भ	=	द्भ	अद्भुत *[adbhut]* wonderful, astonishing
द् + य	=	द्य	विद्या *[vidya]* F knowledge
द् + व	=	द्व	द्वार *[dvār]* M door
न् + न	=	न्न	मुन्ना *[munnā]* M baby
श् + ऋ	=	शृ	शृंगार *[śṛṅgār]* M beautification, adornment*
श् + च	=	श्च/श्च	निश्चय *[niścay]* M decision

श्‌ + र	=	श्र	श्री *[śrī]* ADJ, M Mr.
श्‌ + व	=	श्व/श्व	ईश्वर *[īśvar]* M God
ह्‌ + ऋ	=	हृ	हृदय *[hṛday]* M heart*
ह्‌ + व	=	ह्व	ह्वाइट *[hvāiṭ]* white
ह्‌ + य	=	ह्य	असह्य *[asahya]* unbearable

* These are not actually conjunct consonants but the consonant together with the *mātrā* form of the vowel ऋ.

The definitions of words in the dictionary are arranged in the following manner. First there is the head word in Hindi. This is followed by its phonetic description in roman characters. Then there is the grammatical description of the word. Finally the English definition appears, together with any secondary words and colloquial expressions that include the head word or related words. For example:

कवि *[kavi]* M poet; कविराज *[kavirāj]* M a king of poets

Words are given in their basic form. Nouns and adjectives appear in their singular, uninflected form and verbs appear in the infinitive form. The infinitive forms of verbs are made up of the stem of the verb together with the infinitive suffix ना *[nā]*.

For example:

जा *[jā]* go (stem) + ना *[nā]* (infinitive marker) = जाना *[jānā]* to go

The student of Hindi is advised to pay particular attention to the gender of nouns (masculine and feminine), and whether verbs are transitive or intransitive. There is no absolutely precise way to tell the gender of many nouns based on their form and so the gender of each and every noun must be memorized. Gender is critical in Modern Standard Hindi, particularly because feminine nouns decline differently to masculine nouns and particular nouns decline differently according to what occurs in a word-final position. Adjectives with particular endings also must be declined to agree with the gender, number and case of the noun they qualify. Verbs also must often be conjugated for the gender and number of a particular noun in the sentence. Whether a verb is transitive is important when the perfective form is employed. In such cases, the verb is conjugated for the number and gender of the object of the sentence, if it is not followed by a postposition. If there is no object stated, the verb is most often conjugated in its masculine, singular perfective form.

The following grammatical abbreviations have been employed in this dictionary:

M	noun, masculine	CONJ	conjunction
F	noun, feminine	PL	plural
ADJ	adjective	PP	postposition
ADV	adverb	INTER	interrogative
V.T.	verb, transitive	PRO	pronoun
V.I.	verb, intransitive	VOC	vocative

Guide to Pronunciation

a like the 'a' in "b*u*t"
ā like the 'a' in "f*a*ther"
i like the 'i' in "b*i*t"
ī like the 'ee' in "n*ee*d"
u like the 'oo' in "b*oo*k"
ū like the 'oo' in "s*oo*n"
ṛ like the 'ri' in "*ri*p" (the 'r' sound is trilled)
e like the 'ay' in "b*ay*"
ai like the 'a' in "b*a*d" or the 'ei' in "h*ei*ght"
o like the 'o' in "b*o*th"
au like the 'aw' in "s*aw*"
ka/qa like the 'k' in "*k*ing" (*qa* is pronounced further back in the throat)
kha/k͟ha like the 'kh' in 'bloc*kh*ead' (*k͟ha* pronounced with partial closure of air passage)
ga/g͟ha like the 'g' in "*g*o" (*g͟ha* is pronounced further back in the throat)
gha like the 'gh' in "lo*gh*ouse"
ṅa like the 'n' in "ki*n*g"
ca like the 'ch' in "*ch*urch"
cha like the 'ch' in "chur*chh*ill"
ja/za like the 'j' in "*j*azz" (*za* like 'z' in "*z*ebra")
jha like the 'dgeh' in "he*dgeh*og"
ña like the 'n' in "cru*n*ch"

ṭa a 't' sound where the tongue touches the top of the mouth
ṭha a 'th' sound where the tongue touches the top of the mouth and a breath is released with the sound
ḍa (ṛa) a 'd' sound where the tongue touches the top of the mouth (*ṛa* the tongue touches the top of the mouth and flaps down)
ḍha (ṛha) a 'd' sound where the tongue touches the top of the mouth and a breath is released with the sound (*ṛha* is the aspirated form of *ṛa*)
ṇa a 'n' sound where the tongue touches the top of the mouth
ta a 't' sound where the tongue touches the back of the top teeth
tha a 'th' sound where the tongue touches the back of the top teeth and a breath is released with the sound
da a 'd' sound where the tongue touches the back of the top teeth
dha a 'dh' sound where the tongue touches the back of the top teeth and a breath is released with the sound
na a 'n' sound where the tongue touches the back of the top teeth
pa like the 'p' in "s*p*it"
pha/fa like the 'p' in "*p*it" (*fa* like the 'f' in "*f*ather")
ba like the 'b' in "*b*ut"
bha like the 'bh' in "clu*bh*ouse"
ma like the 'm' in "*m*other"

ya like the 'y' in "*y*oung"
ra like the 'r' in "*r*un"
la like the 'l' in "*l*ung"
va/wa like the 'v' in "*v*an" (this is sometimes closer to a 'v' sound and sometimes closer to a 'w' sound)
śa like the 'sh' in "*sh*ave"
ṣa like the 'sh' in "flu*sh*"
sa like the 's' in "*s*un"
ha like the 'h' in "*h*unt"

In Hindi the rules for pronunciation are fairly straightforward. Each consonant is pronounced with an inherent 'a' vowel (like 'a' in the word "sun") unless it is replaced by the abbreviated form of another vowel.

क *[ka]*
का *[kā]*

However, in particular positions in a word the inherent 'a' vowel is sometimes elided, or its pronunciation is modified by surrounding consonants. The following is a guide to help you pronounce words in Devanagari and match them with their Romanization in this Dictionary:

1. The inherent 'a' vowel is not pronounced with consonants in a word final position.

   काम *[kām]* M work

2. An inherent 'a' vowel may be omitted unless it is being omitted twice in a row.

   कलसा *[kalsā]* M a metal pitcher
   नमक *[namak]* M salt

3. The presence of the character ह *[ha]* may impact the pronunciation of a preceding inherent 'a' vowel. If there is no full vocalic sound pronounced with the ह *[ha]*, a preceding 'a' vowel is often pronounced as an 'e' sound.

   बहन *[behan]* F sister

   but

   महीना *[mahīnā]* M month

(N.B. The system of Romanization employed in this dictionary reflects this shift from a short 'a' to an 'e' sound.)

Hindi–English

अ

अंक *[aṅk]* M number; numeral, figure
अंकुर *[aṅkur]* M sprout, an off-shoot; अंकुरित ADJ sprouted, grown
अंग *[aṅg]* M limb; a member; body, part
अंगरेज़ *[aṅgrez]* M English person
अंगरेज़ी *[aṅgrezī]* F English; English language; अंगरेज़ी भाषा *[aṅgrezī bhāṣā]* F the English language
अँगूठा *[ãgūṭhā]* M thumb
अँगूठा दिखाना *[ãgūṭhā dikhānā]* V.T. to defy, to evade in defiance
अंगूठी *[aṅgūṭhī]* F ring
अंगूर *[aṅgūr]* M grape
अँगौछा *[ãgauchā]* M towel, any piece of clothing for wiping the body dry
अंग्रेज़ी *see* अंगरेज़ी
अंचल *[añcal]* M fringe of the sari; region, frontier
अंजाम *[añjām]* M conclusion; end result; completion
अंजीर *[añjīr]* M fig
अंजुमन *[añjuman]* M association; a society
अंडा *[aṇḍā]* M egg
अंत *[ant]* M end
अंतड़ी *[antaṛī]* F intestines
अंतर *[antar]* M difference; distance; interval; heart
अंतरात्मा *[antarātmā]* F soul, inner self
अंतर्देशीय *[antardeśīya]* ADJ interstate, inland
अंतर्धान *[antardhān]* M disappearance; invisibility
अंतर्मुख *[antarmukh]* intro-vertive
अंतर्मुखी *[antarmukhī]* ADJ introverted
अंतर्राष्ट्रीय *[antarrāṣṭrīya]* ADJ international
अंतिम *[antim]* ADJ last, final; ultimate, concluding
अंदर *[andar]* ADV inside
अंदरी *[andarī]* ADJ internal; intrinsic; inherent

अंदरूनी *[andarūnī]* ADJ internal; intrinsic; inherent; internecine
अंदाज़ *[andāz]* M mode; style; characteristic manner; an estimate
अंदाज़ा *[andāzā]* M estimate; guess
अंदेशा *[andeśā]* M misgiving; suspicion, misapprehension
अंध *[andh]* PREFIX an allomorph of; अंधा used as the first member of a compound, such as
अंधकार *[andhakār]* M darkness; gloom
अंधविश्वास *[andhviśvās]* M superstition, blind faith
अंधविश्वासी *[andhviśvāsī]* ADJ superstitious
अंधा *[andhā]* ADJ blind, irrational; unenlightened
अंधेरा *[andherā]* ADJ, M dark; black; darkness
अंबर *[ambar]* M the sky; cloth/ clothes, garment
अंबार *[ambār]* M heap; pile
अंश *[añś]* M part, share; division; fragment
अकड़ *[akaṛ]* F stiffness; rigidity; intractability; airs
अकड़ना *[akaṛnā]* V.I. to be stiff, rigid, intractable; to assume airs; to be affected; to be conceited
अकड़ू *[akṛū]* ADJ stiff-necked; haughty
अकस्मात् *[akasmāt]* ADV suddenly; unexpectedly
अकादेमी *[akādemī]* F academy
अकारण *[akāraṇ]* ADV, ADJ needlessly, causelessly; without any reason or cause, without any pretext
अकाल *[akāl]* M famine; scarcity; ADJ premature, untimely
अकृतज्ञ *[akṛtajña]* ADJ ungrateful
अकृतज्ञता *[akṛtajñatā]* F thanklessness
अकेला *[akelā]* ADJ alone;
अकेलापन *[akelāpan]* M solitude; loneliness;
अकेलापन लगना *[akelāpan lagnā]* V.I. to feel alone
अकेले *[akele]* ADV alone
अक्खड़ *[akkhaṛ]* ADJ headstrong, rude and rough
अक्खड़पन *[akkhaṛpan]* M haughtiness, rudeness
अक़्ल *[aql]* F common sense; intellect, wits; अक़्ल मोटी

होना *[aql moṭī honā]* V.I. for one's intellect to be dull
अक़्लमंद *[aqlmand]* ADJ prudent; sensible, wise; intelligent; intellectual
अक्षर *[akṣar]* M letter (of the alphabet); character, symbol
अक्स *[aks]* M shadow; reflection, reflected image;
अक्स करना/लेना *[aks karnā/lenā]* V.T. to trace
अक्सर *[aksar]* ADV often
अकसरियत *[aksariyat]* F majority
अखंड *[akhaṇḍ]* ADJ whole; complete; undivided
अखंडता *[akhaṇḍtā]* F completeness, wholeness, integrity
अखंडित *[akhaṇḍit]* ADJ unbroken, undivided, unimpaired
अख़बार *[akhbār]* M newspaper
अख़बारनवीस *[akhbārnavīs]* M journalist
अख़बारनवीसी *[akhbārnavīsī]* F journalism
अख़रोट *[akhroṭ]* M a walnut
अखाड़ा *[akhāṛā]* M arena; wrestling arena; a place for exercise; a congregation of *sadhus* or their abode
अखिल *[akhil]* ADJ whole; entire, all
अगणित *[agaṇit]* ADJ unnumbered
अगर *[agar]* CONJ if
अगरचे *[agarce]* CONJ although, though
अगरबत्ती *[agarbattī]* F incense, an incense stick
अगर-मगर *[agar magar]* F if and but; wavering; dilly-dallying
अगल-बग़ल *[agal-baghal]* ADV on both sides; side by side, nearby
अगला *[aglā]* ADJ next; following
अगली बार *[aglī bār]* ADV next time
अगले हफ़्ते *[agle hafte]* ADV next week
अगुआ *[aguā]* M leader; pioneer, guide
अगुआई *[aguāī]* leadership; guidance
अगूढ़ *[agūṛh]* ADJ intelligible, apparent; simple
अग्नि *[agni]* F fire; the god of fire

अग्रसर *[agrasar]* ADJ forward; ahead; अग्रसर करना *[agrasar karnā]* V.T. to move forward; to advance
अघोरी *[aghorī]* ADJ, M filthy; uncouth and unclean (man); detestable; one who eats indiscriminately
अचंभा *[acambhā]* M wonder; surprise; astonishment
अचंभित *[acambhit]* ADJ surprised
अचकचाना *[ackacānā]* V.I. to be surprised/astonished, to be confounded
अचकचाहट *[ackacāhaṭ]* F astonishment
अचकन *[ackan]* F a kind of tight-fitting, long coat
अचरज *[acraj]* M surprise; astonishment; wonder
अचल *[acal]* ADJ immovable/immobile; stationary, motionless
अचल *[acal]* ADJ still
अचलता *[acaltā]* F immovability; inertia
अचानक *[acānak]* ADV suddenly
अचार *[acār]* M pickles
अचेत *[acet]* ADJ unconscious; senseless
अचेतनता *[acetantā]* F unconsciousness, the state of being inanimate
अच्छा *[acchā]* ADJ good; fine; excellent; pleasant; righteous ADV well; correctly; अच्छा-ख़ासा *[acchā khāsā]* ADJ fairly good, reasonable; अच्छा करना *[acchā karnā]* V.T. to fix, to cure; (x को) अच्छा लगना *[(x ko) acchā lagnā]* V.I. (x) to like
अच्छी तरह *[acchī tarah]* ADV well, in a good manner
अच्छाई *[acchāī]* F goodness; virtue; merit
अच्छाई-बुराई *[acchāī-burāī]* F virtue and vice, good and bad
अछूत *[achūt]* ADJ untouchable
अजगर *[ajgar]* M python
अजनबी *[ajnabī]* ADJ unknown; unfamiliar; alien
अजनबी *[ajnabī]* M stranger
अजब *[ajab]* ADJ strange; peculiar
अजायबघर *[ajāyabghar]* M museum
अजित *[ajit]* ADJ unvanquished; undefeated
अजीब *[ajīb]* ADJ strange; peculiar

अज्ञान *[ajñān]* M ignorance
अटकना *[aṭaknā]* V.I. to get stuck; to be held up
अटकल *[aṭkal]* F conjecture; guess
अटपटा *[aṭpaṭā]* ADJ odd; incongruous; absurd
अटूट *[aṭūṭ]* ADJ unbreakable; firm; resolute; incessant; अटूट संबंध *[aṭūṭ sambandh]* M a firm relationship
अट्टालिका *[aṭṭālikā]* F mansion
अट्ठाईस *[aṭṭhāīs]* ADJ twenty-eight
अट्ठानवे/अट्ठानबे *[aṭṭhānve/aṭṭhānbe]* ADJ ninety-eight
अट्ठावन *[aṭṭhāvan]* ADJ fifty-eight
अट्ठासी *[aṭṭhāsī]* ADJ eighty-eight
अट्ठारह/अठारह *[aṭṭhārah/aṭhārah]* ADJ eighteen
अट्ठारहवाँ *[aṭṭhāhvā̃]* ADJ eighteenth
अठहत्तर *[aṭhhattar]* ADJ seventy-eight
अड़तालीस *[aṛtālīs]* ADJ forty-eight
अड़तीस *[aṛtīs]* ADJ thirty-eight
अड़ना *[aṛnā]* V.I. to insist; to stick (to a position)
अड़सठ *[aṛsaṭh]* ADJ sixty-eight
अड्डा *[aḍḍā]* M stand; base; meeting place; haunt; resort
अणु *[aṇu]* M molecule; atom; minute particle
अतल *[atal]* ADJ bottomless; fathomless
अति *[ati]* PRE a prefix expressing extremity, beyond, over, surpassing, intense, excessive, etc.
अतिथि *[atithi]* M guest; अतिथिगृह *[atithigrh]* M guesthouse; अतिथि देवो भव *[atithi devo bhava]* the guest is like god
अतिरिक्त *[atirikt]* ADJ additional; extra; spare; auxilary
अतीत *[atīt]* M, ADJ past
अतुल *[atul]* ADJ unparalleled; unequalled; immense
अत्यंत *[atyant]* ADJ, ADV much; excessively, exceedingly
अत्याचार *[atyācār]* M atrocity; tyranny; excess; outrage
अत्याचारी *[atyācārī]* M a tyrant, despot

अथक *[athak]* ADJ untiring; unceasing

अथवा *[athvā]* CONJ or; that is

अथाह *[athāh]* ADJ unfathomable; bottomless; very deep

अदब *[adab]* M respect; politeness; literature

अदबी *[adabī]* ADJ literary, pertaining to literature

अदरक *[adrak]* F ginger

अदला-बदली *[adlā-badlī]* F exchange; interchange; mutual transfer

अदा *[adā]* F graceful manner or mein; coquetry, blandishment; performance

अदाकार *[adākār]* M actor, performer

अदाकारा *[adākārā]* F actress

अदाकारी *[adākārī]* F acting; performance

अदालत *[adālat]* F court of law

अदृढ़ *[adṛṛh]* ADJ loose, not firm

अदृश्य *[adṛśya]* ADJ invisible; imperceptible

अदृश्यता *[adṛśyatā]* F invisibility, imperceptibility

अद्भुत *[adbhut]* ADJ marvellous; fantastic

अद्वितीय *[advitīya]* ADJ unique; unparalleled

अद्वितीयता *[advitīyatā]* F uniqueness; exceptionality

अद्वैत *[advait]* M absence of duality; negation of duality

अद्वैतवाद *[advaitvād]* M monism

अधकहा *[adhkahā]* ADJ half-expressed; semi-explicit

अधखिला *[adhkhilā]* ADJ semi-bloomed; half-open; half-burnt

अधपका *[adhpakā]* ADJ half-ripe; half-backed

अधमरा *[adhmarā]* ADJ half-dead

अधर *[adhar]* M underlip; lip; midair, empty space

अधर्म *[adharm]* M vice; wrong; sin, sinful act

अधर्मी *[adharmī]* ADJ sinful; vicious N sinner

अधार्मिक *[adhārmik]* ADJ irreligious; unrighteous

अधार्मिकता *[adhārmiktā]* F irreligosity; unrighteousness

अधिक *[adhik]* ADJ more, too much

अधिकांश *[adhikānś]* ADJ more than half; a major portion

अधिकार *[adhikār]* M right; authority; command; possession
अधिकारी *[adhikārī]* M official, officer
अधिवास *[adhivās]* M domicile
अधिवासी *[adhivāsī]* M settler, domicile ADJ settled
अधिवेशन *[adhiveśan]* M session, meeting
अधीर *[adhīr]* ADJ restive, impatient, petulant, nervous
अधीरता *[adhīrtā]* F impatience; nervousness
अधूरा *[adhūrā]* ADJ incomplete, unfinished
अधूरापन *[adhūrāpan]* incompleteness; imperfection
अधेड़ *[adheṛ]* ADJ middle-aged
अध्यक्ष *[adhyakṣ]* ADJ president, chairman; head
अध्यक्षता *[adhyakṣtā]* F presidentship; chairmanship
अध्ययन *[adhyayan]* M study; अध्ययन-अध्यापन *[adhyayan-adhyāpan]* M studying and teaching
अध्यात्म *[adhyātma]* M spiritual contemplation
अध्याय *[adhyāya]* M chapter
अध्यापक *[adhyāpak]* M teacher, educator, lecturer
अध्यापिका *[adhyāpikā]* F (female) teacher, educator, lecturer
अनकहा *[ankahā]* ADJ untold; implicit; unspoken
अनखुला *[ankhulā]* ADJ not open; covered, closed
अनगिनत *[anginat]* ADJ innumerable; numberless; countless
अनचाहा *[ancāhā]* ADJ unwanted, undesired, undesirable
अनजान *[anjān]* ADJ unknown, unacquainted; ignorant
अनजाने *[anjāne]* ADV unknowingly, unwittingly; अनजाने में *[anjāne mẽ]* unknowingly
अनदेखा *[andekhā]* ADJ unseen, unforeseen
अनधिकार *[anadhikār]* ADJ unauthorized
अनधिकृत *[anadhikṛt]* ADJ unauthorized; unoccupied
अनन्नास *[anannās]* M pineapple tree and its fruit
अनपचा *[anpacā]* ADJ undigested
अनपढ़ *[anpaṛh]* ADJ illiterate; unlettered

अनबन *[anban]* M discord, estrangement, rift
अनमना *[anmanā]* ADJ out of sorts; indisposed, in low spirits
अनमनापन *[anmanāpan]* M absentmindedness
अनमेल *[anmel]* ADJ inharmonious, discordant; dissimilar, heterogeneous
अनमोल *[anmol]* ADJ invaluable, precious, priceless
अनर्थ *[anarth]* M calamity; absurdity, grievous wrong
अनर्थकर/अनर्थकारी *[anarthkar/anarthkārī]* ADJ calamitous, devastating
अनशन *[anśan]* M a fast
अनसुना *[ansunā]* ADJ unheard; अनसुना करना *[ansunā karnā]* V.T. to ignore
अनहोनी *[anhonī]* F improbable, impossible occurrence ADJ unusual; improbable
अनाज *[anāj]* M grain, corn
अनाड़ी *[anāṛī]* ADJ inexperienced M unskilled; a novice
अनाथ *[anāth]* M an orphan ADJ orphaned
अनाथालय *[anāthālay]* M orphanage
अनादर *[anādar]* M insult, disrespect, disregard
अनायास *[anāyās]* ADJ without effort; with ease, spontaneous
अनार *[anār]* M pomegranate
अनावश्यक *[anāvaśyak]* ADJ unnecessary, unimportant
अनावश्यकता *[anāvaśyaktā]* F absence of necessity
अनिच्छुक *[anicchuk]* ADJ reluctant
अनियम *[aniyam]* M lawlessness, disorder
अनिल *[anil]* M wind, breeze
अनिवार्य *[anivārya]* ADJ inevitable, unavoidable; compulsory
अनिश्चय *[aniścay]* M indecision
अनिश्चित *[aniścit]* ADJ uncertain, undecided, indefinite
अनीति *[anīti]* F impropriety, inequity
अनुकरण *[anukaraṇ]* M imitation, emulation; mimicry
अनुकूल *[anukūl]* ADJ favorable, agreeable; befitting; well-disposed; comfortable; x के

अनुकूल *[x ke anukūl]* PP befitting x

अनुकूलता *[anukūltā]* F favorableness, agreeability; conformity

अनुग्रह *[anugrah]* M obligation, favor; kindness

अनुचित *[anucit]* ADJ improper, unbecoming, unseemly; wrong

अनुच्छेद *[anucched]* M paragraph; an article (of the constitution etc.)

अनुदान *[anudān]* M grant

अनुदेश *[anudeś]* M instruction

अनुनासिक *[anunāsik]* ADJ nasal M a nasal sound

अनुपम *[anupam]* ADJ matchless, unparalleled; out and away

अनुपलब्ध *[anupalabdh]* ADJ unachieved; unacquired

अनुपलब्धि *[anupalabdhi]* F unavailability

अनुपस्थित *[anupasthit]* ADJ not present; absent

अनुपस्थिति *[anupasthiti]* F absence

अनुपात *[anupāt]* M proportion

अनुबंध *[anubandh]* M contract; addendum; appendage; stipulation

अनुबंधित *[anubandhit]* M contracted; signed (a contract)

अनुभव *[anubhav]* M experience

अनुभवी *[anubhavī]* ADJ experienced, veteran, seasoned

अनुभूति *[anubhūti]* F emotional experience; realization; sensibility

अनुमति *[anumati]* F assent; approval; leave

अनुमान *[anumān]* M guess, estimate, surmise; supposition

अनुयायी *[anuyāyī]* M follower, adherent

अनुराग *[anurāg]* M love; affection; attachment; fondness

अनुरागी *[anurāgī]* ADJ affectionate, loving, fond

अनुरूप *[anurūp]* ADJ like; fit, conforming, according to; analogous

अनुरोध *[anurodh]* M solicitation, entreaty

अनुरोधी *[anurodhī]* ADJ one who entreats

अनुवाद *[anuvād]* M translation; repetition

अनुवादक *[anuvādak]* M translator

अनुशासन *[anuśāsan]* M discipline

अनुशासक *[anuśāsak]* M disciplinarian

अनुशासित *[anuśāsit]* ADJ disciplined

अनुष्ठान *[anuṣṭhān]* M ritural ceremony, religious performance; undertaking; exercise

अनुसंधान *[anusandhān]* M research, investigation

अनुसरण *[anusaraṇ]* M following, pursuance; x के अनुसरण *[x ke anusaraṇ]* PP following x

अनुसार *[anusār]* M according; x के अनुसार *[x ke anusār]* PP according to x

अनुसूचित *[anusūcit]* ADJ scheduled; अनुसूचित जाति *[anusūcit jāti]* F scheduled caste

अनुसूची *[anusūcī]* F schedule

अनुस्वार *[anusvār]* M after sound; the nasal sound which is marked by a dot above the line and always follows the preceding vowel

अनूठा *[anūṭhā]* ADJ unique; unparalleled; unprecedented

अनूप *[anūp]* ADJ unequalled; unparalleled; singular; unique

अनेक *[anek]* ADJ many, numerous; several

अनेकता *[anektā]* F diversity, varied character

अनैतिक *[anaitik]* ADJ immoral; depraved; अनैतिकता *[anaitiktā]* F immorality; depravity

अनैतिहासिक *[anaitihāsik]* ADJ unhistorical; legendary; अनैतिहासिकता *[anaitihāsiktā]* F unhistoricality

अनोखा *[anokhā]* ADJ unique, peculiar

अनौपचारिक *[anaupcārik]* ADJ unofficial; unceremonious

अनौपचारिकता *[anaupcāriktā]* F informality; unofficial way

अन् *[an]* IND a Sanskrit prefix signifying negation

अन्न *[anna]* M corn; food (usually cooked)

अन्न-जल *[anna-jal]* M subsistence

अन्य *[anya]* ADJ other, another; different

अन्यतम *[anyatam]* ADJ foremost; best

अन्यथा *[anyathā]* F otherwise; contrary, against

अन्याय *[anyāy]* M injustice, wrong, inequity

अन्यायी *[anyāyī]* ADJ unjust, inequitable M a wrong-doer; persecutor

अपंग *[apaṅg]* ADJ crippled, maimed

अप *[ap]* PREFIX a Sanskrit prefix denoting down, away, off, base, deterioration or inferiority

अपकार *[apakār]* M harm; ill-turn; damage

अपकारी *[apakārī]* ADJ detrimental; hurtful/harmful; damaging M one who inflicts harm

अपक्व *[apakva]* ADJ unripe, raw; immature

अपच *[apac]* M indigestion, dyspepsia

अपचार *[apacār]* M evil deed; aberration

अपना *[apnā]* ADJ one's own

अपनापन *[apnāpan]* M cordiality; affinity

अपनाना *[apnānā]* V.T. to adopt; to appropriate

अपमान *[apamān]* M insult, disgrace; affront; x का अपमान करना *[x kā apamān karnā]* V.T. to insult; disgrace x

अपमानित *[apamānit]* ADJ insulted, disgraced

अपराजित *[aparājit]* ADJ unvanquished; undefeated

अपराध *[aprādh]* M crime; offence; fault

अपराधी *[aprādhī]* ADJ, M criminal; guilty; offending

अपरिचित *[aparicit]* ADJ unacquainted N a stranger

अपरिपक्व *[aparipakva]* ADJ immature; unmatured, unripened

अपरिपक्वता *[aparipakvatā]* F immaturity

अपरिपुष्ट *[aparipuṣṭ]* ADJ unconfirmed, uncorroborated

अपरिपुष्टता *[aparipuṣṭtā]* F the state of being unconfirmed

अपरिहार्य *[aparihārya]* ADJ unavoidable, indispensable; inevitable

अपरोक्ष *[aparokṣ]* ADJ direct, visible; tangible

अपर्याप्त *[aparyāpt]* ADJ inadequate, insufficient

अपलक *[apalak]* ADJ, ADV without a blink, unblinking
अपवचन *[apavacan]* M slander, calumny
अपवाद *[apavād]* M exception; slander, calumny
अपवित्र *[apavitra]* ADJ unholy, impure; desecrated, profane
अपवित्रता *[apavitratā]* F impurity, profanity
अपशब्द *[apaśabd]* M abuse, abusive language or word
अपहरण *[apaharaṇ]* M abduction, kidnapping
अपहर्ता *[apahartā]* M abductor, kidnapper
अपांग *[apāṅg]* ADJ disabled; crippled, maimed
अपार *[apār]* ADJ boundless; shoreless, immense
अपारदर्शी *[apārdarśī]* ADJ opaque
अपाहिज *[apāhij]* M, ADJ disabled, crippled, maimed
अपि *[api]* IND also; and; though, although
अपितु *[apitu]* IND but, on the other hand
अपील *[apīl]* F appeal
अपुष्ट *[apuṣṭ]* ADJ unconfirmed; stunted
अपुष्टता *[apuṣṭatā]* F lack of confirmation; malnourishment
अपूर्ण *[apūrṇ]* ADJ incomplete; unfinished; imperfect
अपूर्णता *[apūrṇtā]* F incompleteness, deficiency
अपूर्व *[apūrva]* ADJ unprecedented, novel; unique
अपूर्वता *[apūrvatā]* F uniqueness
अपेक्षा *[apekṣā]* F expectation, requirement
अपेक्षाकृत *[apekṣākṛt]* ADV comparatively; comparatively speaking
अप्रकाशित *[aprakāśit]* ADJ unpublished; undisclosed
अप्रत्यक्ष *[apratyakṣ]* ADJ invisible; indirect
अप्रत्याशित *[apratyāśit]* ADJ unexpected; hidden
अप्रसन्न *[aprasanna]* ADJ unhappy; displeased;
अप्रसन्नता *[aprasannatā]* F displeasure
अप्राकृतिक *[aprākṛtik]* ADJ unnatural; abnormal; uncommon
अप्राकृतिकता *[aprākṛtiktā]* F abnormality

अभ्यास *[abhyās]* M practice
अमंगल *[amaṅgal]* M inauspiciousness, evil; disaster
अमन *[aman]* M peace, tranquillity; अमन-चैन *[aman-cain]* M peace and happiness
अमनपसंद *[amanpasand]* ADJ peace-loving; अमनपसंदी *[amanpasandī]* F pacifism, the state of liking peace
अमर *[amar]* ADJ immortal, eternal; अमरता *[amartā]* F immortality
अमरीका *[amrīkā]* M America
अमरीकी *[amrīkī]* ADJ American
अमरूद *[amrūd]* M guava
अमल *[amal]* M action, execution; application; addiction
अमांगलिक *[amāṅgalik]* ADJ inauspicious, ominous
अमानक *[amānak]* ADJ non-standard; not conforming to the prescribed standard
अमानत *[amānat]* F something given in trust; deposit
अमानवीय *[amānvīya]* ADJ inhuman; beastly; cruel
अमानवीयता *[amānvīyatā]* F inhumanity; cruelty
अमावस/अमावस्या *[amāvas/ amāvasyā]* F the last day of the dark fortnight; new moon
अमिट *[amiṭ]* ADJ indelible; indestructible; unmeasured; boundless; immense, enormous
अमिताभ *[amitābh]* ADJ possessing unlimited brilliance M a name of Lord Buddha
अमीर *[amīr]* ADJ wealthy
अमीरी *[amīrī]* F wealthiness, richness
अमूल्य *[amūlya]* ADJ priceless, valuable
अमृत *[amṛt]* M nectar
अमौलिक *[amaulik]* ADJ not original; not fundamental
अम्माँ *[ammā̃]* F mother
अम्मी जान *[ammī jān]* F dear mother
अयोग्य *[ayogya]* ADJ incompetent; unworthy; unqualified; unfit
अयोग्यता *[ayogyatā]* F incompetence; unworthiness
अरण्य *[araṇya]* M forest, wilderness

अरब *[arab]* ADJ billion M Arab
अरबी *[arabī]* F Arabic language ADJ Arabian; pertaining to the land of Arabs
अरमान *[armān]* M aspiration, longing
अरसठ *[arsaṭh]* ADJ *see* अड़सठ
अरसा *[arsā]* M period, interval, duration
अराजक *[arājak]* ADJ chaotic; anarchical; bereft of a ruler
अराजकता *[arājaktā]* F anarchy; chaos
अरी *[arī]* F, VOC hey!
अरुण *[aruṇ]* ADJ reddish brown, ruddy M the dawn
अरुणाचल *[aruṇācal]* M the eastern state of Arunachal
अरूप *[arūp]* ADJ formless
अरे *[are]* M, VOC hey!; अरे वाह *[are vāh]* VOC Oh wow!
अर्चन/अर्चना *[arcan/arcanā]* M, F worship, adoration
अर्चनीय *[arcanīya]* ADJ worthy of being worshipped; adorable
अर्ज़ *[arz]* F request, supplication
अर्ज़ी *[arzī]* F application, petition; अर्ज़ी देना *[arzī denā]* V.T. to apply
अर्थ *[arth]* M meaning; import, sense; wealth, money
अर्थनीति *[arthnīti]* F economic policy
अर्थव्यवस्था *[arthvyavasthā]* F economy; economic system
अर्थशास्त्र *[arthśāstra]* M economics
अर्थात् *[arthāt]* IND that is, that is to say, namely
अर्थी *[arthī]* F a bier M a petitioner ADJ desirous
अर्ध *[ardh]* ADJ semi-, demi-, half; अर्ध-विराम *[ardh-virām]* M semicolon
अर्धचंद्र *[ardhcandra]* M half moon, crescent
अर्धनारीश्वर *[ardhnārīśvar]* M Lord Shiva as envisaged in fusion with Goddess Parvati
अलंकार *[alaṅkār]* M embellishment; ornament; figure of speech
अलग *[alag]* ADJ different; अलग-अलग *[alag-alag]* ADJ separate; different
अलगाना *[algānā]* V.T. to set apart, to separate; to isolate; to segregate
अलगाव *[algāv]* M isolation, separation; segregation

अलबत्ता *[albattā]* IND nevertheless; of course
अलबम *[albam]* M album
अलमारी *[almārī]* F an *almirah*; cupboard
अलार्म *[alārm]* M an alarm; अलार्म-घड़ी *[alārm gharī]* F an alarm clock
अलाव *[alāv]* M a campfire
अलावा *[alāvā]* IND besides; in addition to; apart from; except; x के अलावा *[x ke alāvā]* PP besides x; in addition to x; apart from x; except x
अलौकिक *[alaukik]* ADJ unearthly, heavenly, celestrial
अलौकिकता *[alaukiktā]* F unearthliness
अल्प *[alp]* ADJ a little, small; minute; short
अल्लाह *[allāh]* M Allah, God
अवकाश *[avakāś]* M leisure; leave of absence, recess
अवतार *[avatār]* M incarnation
अवतारी *[avatārī]* ADJ incarnate
अवधारणा *[avadhāraṇā]* F concept
अवरुद्ध *[avaruddh]* ADJ obstucted, hampered
अवरोध *[avarodh]* M obstruction
अवरोहण *[avarohaṇ]* M descending
अवरोही *[avarohī]* ADJ descending, falling
अवशेष *[avaśeṣ]* M remnant, remains, residue; vestige
अवश्य *[avaśya]* ADV certainly, definitely; necessarily
अवसर *[avasar]* M opportunity, chance; occasion
अवसरवाद *[avasarvād]* M opportunism
अवसरवादी *[avasarvādī]* M opportunist
अवसाद *[avasād]* M lassitude; languor; dejection
अवस्था *[avasthā]* F condition; state; age; stage; phase
अवहेलना *[avahelnā]* neglect, distain, contempt
अवाक् *[avāk]* ADJ speechless, stunned
अवाम *[avām]* M the people, common man
अविकास *[avikās]* M absence of growth or development
अविचल *[avical]* ADJ steady; motionless; firm

अविचारी *[avicārī]* ADJ thoughtless; injudicious
अविच्छिन्न *[avicchinna]* ADJ uninterrupted; continuous
अविच्छिन्नता *[avicchinnatā]* F the state of being uninterrupted
अविच्छेद *[avicched]* M absence of interruption; continuity
अविजित *[avijit]* ADJ unconquered, unvanquished
अविनाशी *[avināśī]* ADJ immortal; indestructible
अविलंब *[avilamb]* ADV at once, without delay; forthright
अविवाहित *[avivāhit]* ADJ unmarried, bachelor
अविवेक *[avivek]* M absence of reason; indiscretion; imprudence
अविश्वसनीय *[aviśvasnīya]* ADJ unreliable, untrustworthy, unbelievable
अविश्वसनीयता *[aviśvasnīyatā]* F unreliability
अविश्वस्त *[aviśvast]* ADJ unreliable; untrustworthy
अविश्वास *[aviśvās]* M distrust, disbelief, suspicion
अविश्वासी *[aviśvāsī]* ADJ distrustful, suspicious M unbeliever
अवैज्ञानिक *[avaijñānik]* ADJ unscientific; unsystematic
अवैज्ञानिकता *[avaijñāniktā]* F lack of systematicness
अवैध *[avaidh]* ADJ illegal, unlawful; illegitimate, illicit
अव्यक्त *[avyakt]* ADJ not manifest, not apparent; imperceptible
अव्वल *[avval]* ADJ foremost
अशक्त *[aśakt]* ADJ weak, feeble; unable; incompetent; invalid
अशांत *[aśānt]* ADJ restless, agitated, unquiet
अशांति *[aśānti]* F unrest, agitation
अशिक्षित *[aśikṣit]* ADJ uneducated; unlettered
अशुद्ध *[aśuddh]* ADJ erroneous, wrong; impure
अशुभ *[aśubh]* ADJ inauspicious; ill-omened; evil
असल *[asal]* ADJ real, true; असल में *[asal mẽ]* ADV in reality; दर असल *[dar asal]* ADV in reality
असलियत *[asaliyat]* F reality
अस्पताल *[aspatāl]* M hospital

अस्सलाम अलैकुम *[assalām alaikum]* Peace be upon you! (an Urdu greeting)
अस्सी *[assī]* ADJ eighty

आ

आँकड़े *[ā̃kṛe]* M statistics, figures
आँकना *[ā̃knā]* V.T. to assess; to reckon; to appraise
आँख *[ā̃kh]* F eye
आँगन *[ā̃gan]* M courtyard
आँच *[ā̃c]* F flame, fire, harm
आँचल *[ā̃cal]* M part of a sari that covers the upper portion of a woman's body; region ADJ regional
आंदोलन *[āndolan]* M movement, agitation; campaign
आँधी *[ā̃dhī]* F storm, dust-storm
आँध्र *[ā̃dhra]* M Telugu-speaking southern state of the Indian Union; आँध्र प्रदेश *[ā̃dhra pradeś]* M the state of Andhra Pradesh
आँसू *[ā̃sū]* M tear
आइंदा *[āindā]* ADV in the future ADJ future
आइना *[āinā]* M mirror
आकर्षक *[ākarṣak]* ADJ attractive, charming, alluring
आकर्षण *[ākarṣaṇ]* M attraction, charm, alllurement
आकर्षित *[ākarṣit]* ADJ attracted, charmed, allured
आकस्मिक *[ākasmik]* ADJ sudden, abrupt; contingent
आकांक्षा *[ākāṅkṣā]* F aspiration
आकांक्षी *[ākāṅkṣī]* ADJ aspirant
आकार *[ākār]* M form; shape; size
आकाश *[ākāś]* M sky; space; आकाश-गंगा *[ākāś- gaṅgā]* F the Milky Way
आकाशवाणी *[ākāśvāṇī]* F an oracle; the Hindi name for All India Radio
आकुल *[ākul]* ADJ restless, uneasy, distracted
आकुलता *[ākultā]* F restlessness, uneasiness; mental distress
आकृति *[ākṛti]* F shape, figure; form, structure; appearance; features; contour
आक्रमण *[ākramaṇ]* M attack, assault; incursion; invasion; आक्रमण करना *[ākramaṇ karnā]*

आक्रामक *[ākrāmak]* M invader, attacker; aggressor ADJ aggressive
आख़िर *[ākhir]* M end ADV finally, in the end
आख़िरी *[ākhirī]* ADJ last, final, ultimate
आख्यान *[ākhyān]* M tale, legend; fable; description; communication
आग *[āg]* F fire
आगमन *[āgaman]* M arrival; approach
आगे *[āge]* ADV ahead; in front; before; in the future
आग्रह *[āgrah]* M insistence, persistence
आघात *[āghāt]* M blow, stroke, hit; shock; impact; trauma
आचरण *[ācaraṇ]* M conduct; behavior; practice
आचार *[ācār]* M conduct; custom practice; ethos; behavior; आचार-व्यवहार *[ācār-vyavahār]* M conduct and morals
आचार्य *[ācārya]* M teacher, preceptor; professor
आज *[āj]* M, ADV today
आजकल *[ājkal]* ADV these days
आज़माना *[āzmānā]* V.T. to try; to test (to put to a test)
आज़ाद *[āzād]* ADJ independent
आज़ादी *[āzādī]* F independence, freedom
आजीवन *[ājīvan]* ADV life-long, for one's entire life
आज्ञा *[ājñā]* F command, order
आज्ञाकारी *[ājñākārī]* ADJ obedient
आटा *[āṭā]* M flour
आटे दाल का भाव मालूम होना *[āṭe dāl kā bhāv mālūm honā]* V.I. to discover a harsh truth
ऑटो(रिक्शा) *[āṭo(rikśā)]* M auto(rickshaw)
आठ *[āṭh]* ADJ eight
आठवाँ *[āṭhvā̃]* ADJ eighth
आड़ू *[āṛū]* M a peach
आढ़त *[āṛhat]* F commission; commission agency
आतंक *[ātaṅk]* M terror; panic
आतंकवाद *[ātaṅkvād]* M terrorism
आतंकवादी *[ātaṅkvādī]* M terrorist
आतिश *[ātiś]* M fire
आतिशबाज़ी *[ātiśbāzī]* F fireworks
आतुर *[ātur]* ADJ rash, hasty; restless

आतुरता *[āturtā]* F rashness; hastiness; restlessness
आत्म *[ātma]* M self, pertaining to oneself
आत्मकथा *[ātmakathā]* F autobiography
आत्म-केंद्रित *[ātma-kendrit]* ADJ self-centered
आत्मचरित *[ātmacarit]* M an autobiography
आत्मज्ञान *[ātmajñān]* M self-realization, self-knowledge
आत्मनियंत्रण *[ātmaniyantraṇ]* M self-restraint
आत्मनिर्भर *[ātmanirbhar]* ADJ self-sufficient
आत्म-मोह *[ātma-moh]* M narcissism
आत्म-विश्वास *[ātma-viśvās]* M self-confidence
आत्म-संयम *[ātma-sanyam]* M self-control
आत्म-समर्पण *[ātma-samarpaṇ]* M surrender (of oneself)
आत्म-सम्मान *[ātma-sammān]* M self-respect
आत्मसात् *[ātmasāt]* ADJ assimilated
आत्मसात् करना *[ātmasāt karnā]* V.T. to assimilate
आत्म-हत्या *[ātma-hatyā]* F suicide
आत्म-हत्या करना *[ātma-hatyā karnā]* V.T. to commit suicide
आत्मीय *[ātmīya]* ADJ pertaining to self, one's own; intimate
आत्मीयता *[ātmīyatā]* F cordiality; close relationship
आदत *[ādat]* F habit
आदमियत *[ādmiyat]* F gentlemanliness; humanity; humanness
आदमी *[ādmī]* M man
आदर *[ādar]* M respect, esteem, honor; (x का) आदर करना *[(x kā) ādar karnā]* V.T. to respect (x)
आदर्श *[ādarś]* M ideal model, norm; pattern
आदर्शवाद *[ādarśvād]* M idealism
आदाब *[ādāb]* M manners, salutation ("greetings")
आदि *[ādi]* M beginning IND etcetera
आदित्य *[āditya]* M sun
आदिवासी *[ādivāsī]* M an aborigine ADJ aboriginal; first settler
आदी *[ādī]* ADJ accustomed, habituated; (x का) आदी

होना *[(x kā) ādī honā]* V.I. (x) to be accumstomed to
आदेश *[ādeś]* M command
आधा *[ādhā]* ADJ one half
आधार *[ādhār]* M base, foundation; basis
आधारित *[ādhārit]* ADJ based
आधुनिक *[ādhunik]* ADJ modern
आधुनिकता *[ādhuniktā]* F modernity
आध्यात्मिक *[ādhyātmik]* ADJ spiritual, pertaining to the soul or the Supreme Spirit
आध्यात्मिकता *[ādhyātmiktā]* F spirituality; spiritualism
आनंद *[ānand]* M bliss, happiness; joy, pleasure, delight
आनंदमय *[ānandmay]* ADJ blissful; filled with happiness; delightful
आना *[ānā]* V.I. to come
आप *[āp]* PRO you (plural; polite)
आप ही *[āp hī]* ADV (by) oneself
आपका *[āpkā]* ADJ your
आपको *[āpko]* PRO oblique form of आप + को
आपत्ति *[āpatti]* F objection; predicament
आपस *[āpas]* PRO each other, one another; आपस में *[āpas mẽ]* ADV mutually, with one another
आपसी *[āpasī]* ADJ mutual, reciprocal
आपूर्ति *[āpūrti]* F fulfilment
आप्रवास *[āpravās]* M settling in a foreign country, immigration
आफ़त *[āfat]* F distress; trouble; calamity
ऑफ़िस *[āfis]* M office
आब *[āb]* F luster, brilliance M water
आबरू *[ābrū]* F honor, chastity
आबरूदार *[ābrūdār]* ADJ honorable; respected
आबहवा *[ābhavā]* F climate; *see* आबोहवा
आबादी *[ābādī]* F population
आभार *[ābhār]* M gratitude; obligation; indebtedness; burden
आभारी *[ābhārī]* ADJ obliged; grateful; indebted
आभास *[ābhās]* M inkling; glimpse; semblance; fallacious appearance; phenomenon; effect

आमंत्रण *[āmantraṇ]* M invitation; a call; solicitation
आमंत्रित *[āmantrit]* ADJ invited; solicited
आम *[ām]* M mango ADJ general; ordinary
आम तौर पर *[ām taur par]* ADV generally
आमदनी *[āmdanī]* F income; revenue
आमना-सामना *[āmnā-sāmnā]* M an encounter; confrontation; coming face-to-face
आमने-सामने *[āmne-sāmne]* ADV face to face, opposite one another
आमीन् *[āmīn]* IND Amen! Be it so!
आय *[āya]* F income; revenue
आयकर *[āyakar]* M income-tax
आया *[āyā]* F *ayah*, a female attendant V.I. came
आयु *[āyu]* F age
आयुक्त *[āyukt]* M commissioner
आयुर्वेद *[āyūrved]* M the Indian medical system; the science of health and longevity
आयोग *[āyog]* M commission
आयोजक *[āyojak]* M convener; a sponsor
आयोजन *[āyojan]* M convening; sponsoring, organizing
आयोजित *[āyojit]* ADJ convenied; sponsored; organized
आरंभ *[ārambh]* M start, beginning; outset; commencement; inception
आरंभिक *[ārambhik]* ADJ initial, preliminary; related to the beginning
आरज़ू *[ārzū]* F desire, yearning
आरती *[ārtī]* F ceremony performed in front of a deity or a guest by moving a lighted lamp in a circular motion in front of the person
आरती उतारना *[ārtī utārnā]* V.T. to perform this motion
आर-पार *[ār-pār]* ADV across M the two banks of a river
आराधना *[ārādhnā]* F worship; adoration
आराम *[ārām]* M rest, relaxation
आराम से *[ārām se]* ADV comfortably

आरामतलब *[ārāmtalab]* ADJ indolent; slothful; easy-going
आराम-प्रिय *[ārām-priya]* ADJ a person who likes to relax
आरोप *[ārop]* M allegation, charge; imputation; imposition
ऑर्डर *[ārḍar]* M order
आर्थिक *[ārthik]* ADJ economic
आर्थिक-स्थिति *[ārthik-sthiti]* F economic state, condition
आर्य *[ārya]* ADJ, M noble; Aryan
आलथी-पालथी *[ālthī-pālthī]* F sitting with one's legs crossed over and with the right ankle resting on the left thigh and the left on the right thigh
आलम *[ālam]* M world; state
आलय *[ālay]* M abode; a dwelling place
आलस *[ālas]* M laziness; slothfulness; lethargy
आलसी *[ālsī]* ADJ lazy, lethargic
आलिंगन *[āliṅgan]* M embrace
आलू *[ālū]* M potato
आलोचना *[ālocnā]* F criticism
आवश्यक *[āvaśyak]* ADJ necessary
आवश्यकता *[āvaśyaktā]* F necessity
आवाज़ *[āvāz]* F voice; noise
आवारा *[āvārā]* M vagabond; loafer ADJ vagrant, wandering; loitering
आवास *[āvās]* M residence; dwelling place
आविष्कार *[āviṣkār]* M invention
आवेदन *[āvedan]* M application, petition
आशंका *[āśaṅkā]* F apprehension
आशय *[āśaya]* M intention, intent; design; purport, import, meaning
आशा *[āśā]* F hope
आशाजनक *[āśājanak]* ADJ hopeful
आशिक़ *[āśiq]* M lover
आशीर्वाद *[āśīrvād]* M blessings, benediction
आश्चर्य *[āścarya]* M wonder; surprise; astonishment
आश्चर्यजनक *[āścaryajanak]* ADJ surprising
आश्रम *[āśram]* M *ashram* (hermitage); one of the four stages of life for Hindus
आश्वस्त *[āśvast]* ADJ assured; convinced; composed
आश्वासन *[āśvāsan]* M

assurance
आषाढ़ *[āṣāṛh]* **M** the fourth month of the Hindiu calendar
आसन *[āsan]* **M** posture; seat
आस-पास *[āspās]* **ADV** nearby, near
आसमान *[āsmān]* **M** sky
आसान *[āsān]* **ADJ** easy, simple; convenient
आसानी *[āsānī]* **F** convenience; easiness
आसानी से *[āsānī se]* **ADV** with ease
आसार *[āsār]* **M** symptom, sign
आस्तीन *[āstīn]* **F** sleeve
आस्था *[āsthā]* **F** faith, belief
आह *[āh]* **INT** ah! **F** a sigh indicating deep agony
आहट *[āhaṭ]* **F** the sound of someone coming; footsteps, noise
आहत *[āhat]* **ADJ** injured, wounded; offended
आहार *[āhār]* **M** food; diet
आहिस्ता *[āhistā]* **ADV** slowly; gently, softly
आहिस्ता-आहिस्ता *[āhistā-āhistā]* **ADV** slowly, gently, gradually
आह्वान *[āhvān]* **M** a call; summons

इ

इंगलिश *[ingliś]* **ADJ** English
इंगलिस्तान *[inglistān]* **M** England
इंग्लैंड *[inglaiṇḍ]* **M** England
इंच *[iñc]* **M** inch
इंजन *[iñjan]* **M** engine
इंजीनियर *[iñjīniyar]* **M** engineer
इंजीनियरी *[iñjīniyarī]* **F** engineering
इंजेक्शन *[iñjekśan]* **M** injection
इंटरनेट *[inṭarneṭ]* **M** Internet
इंटरव्यू *[inṭarvyū]* **M** interview
इंडिया *[inḍiyā]* **M** India
इंतकाल *[intakāl]* **M** death
इंतज़ाम *[intazām]* **M** arrangement, management
इंतज़ार *[intazār]* **M** waiting
इंतहा *[intahā]* **M** limit; extremity
इंतहाई *[intahāī]* **ADJ** extreme
इंतहापसंद *[intahāpasand]* **M** extremist
इंतहापसंदी *[intahāpasandī]* **F** extremism
इंद्र *[indra]* **M** Indra; the king of the gods; the god of rains
इंद्रजाल *[indrajāl]* **M** magic;

trickery; the web of Indra; the Internet
इंद्रधनुष *[indradhanuṣ]* M Indra's bow; rainbow
इंद्रिय *[indriya]* M senses; the organs of sense; the genitals
इंधन *[indhan]* M fuel
इंशाअल्लाह! *[inśā'allāh]* VOC God willing!
इंसान *[insān]* M human being
इंसानियत *[insāniyat]* F humanity; human qualities
इंसाफ़ *[insāf]* M justice, justness, equity
इंसाफ़पसंद *[insāfpasand]* ADJ just and fair, upright
इंसाफ़पसंदी *[insāfpasandī]* F ethicalness
इक- *[ik-]* ADJ one
इकटक *[iktak]* ADJ fixed stare, staring
इकतरफ़ा *[iktarafā]* ADJ one-sided, unbalanced; इकतरफ़ा टिकट *[iktarafā ṭikaṭ]* M one-way ticket
इकलौता *[iklautā]* ADJ only (son); sole
इकट्ठा *[ikaṭṭhā]* ADJ collected, assembled, gathered together
इकतालीस *[iktālīs]* ADJ forty-one
इकत्तीस *[ikattīs]* ADJ thirty-one
इकसठ *[iksaṭh]* ADJ sixty-one
इकसार *[iksār]* ADJ uniform; even
इकहत्तर *[ikhattar]* ADJ seventy-one
इक्का *[ikkā]* M a small one-horse carriage; an ace (in cards)
इक्का-दुक्का *[ikkā-dukkā]* ADJ one or two, a few; rare
इक्कीस *[ikkīs]* ADJ twenty-one
इक्कीसवाँ *[ikkīsvā̃]* ADJ twenty-first
इक्यानवे *[ikyānve]* ADJ ninety-one
इक्यावन *[ikyāvan]* ADJ fifty-one
इक्यासी *[ikyāsī]* ADJ eighty-one
इच्छा *[icchā]* F desire, wish; will
इच्छुक *[icchuk]* ADJ desirous, willing
इज़हार *[izhār]* M expression
इजाज़त *[ijāzat]* F permission
इज़्ज़त *[izzat]* F prestige, respect; honor
इज़्ज़तदार *[izzatdār]* ADJ respectable; honest and decent

इतना *[itnā]* ADJ this much, so much, so
इतने में *[itne mẽ]* ADV in the meantime; meanwhile
इतमीनान *[itmīnān]* M conviction, assurance; trust, confidence
इतमीनान से *[itmīnān se]* ADV with assurance, with confidence
इतवार M Sunday
इतिहास *[itihās]* M history
इतिहासकार *[itihāsār]* M historian
इत्तफ़ाक़ *[ittafāq]* M concurrence, agreement; coincidence; assent, consent
इत्तफ़ाक़ से *[ittafāq se]* ADV by chance
इत्तला *[ittlā]* M information; notice
इत्यादि *[ityādi]* IND etcetera, so on and so forth
इत्र *[itra]* M perfume; scent
इधर *[idhar]* ADV here, this side, over here
इन *[in]* PRO oblique form of ये; इनका *[inkā]* ADJ his/her/their
इनको *[inko]* PRO (to) him/her/them
इनक़लाब *[inqalāb]* M revolution, radical change; इनक़लाब ज़िंदाबाद! *[inqalāb zindābād!]* IND Long live the revolution!
इनकार करना (x से) *[inkār karnā (x se)]* V.T. to refuse, to deny (x)
इनाम *[inām]* M prize, reward, award
इन्हीं *[inhī̃]* PRO इन + ही.
इन्हें/इनको *[inhẽ/inko]* PRO oblique form of ये + को
इन्होंने *[inhõne]* PRO he/she/they/these (oblique form of ये + ने)
इब्तिदा *[ibtidā]* F beginning, commencement
इब्तिदाई *[ibtidāī]* ADJ elementary, introductory, beginning
इमली *[imlī]* F tamarind; इमली की चटनी *[imlī kī caṭnī]* F tamarind sauce
इमाम *[imām]* M religious leader
इमारत *[imārat]* F building
इम्तहान *[imtahān]* M examination
इरादा *[irādā]* M intention
इर्द-गिर्द *[ird-gird]* ADV all around; around, nearby

इल्ज़ाम *[ilzām]* M allegation, accusation, charge

इलाक़ा *[ilāqā]* M area, locality, territory

इलाज *[ilāj]* M remedy, treatment

इलायची *[ilāycī]* F cardamom

इल्म *[ilm]* M knowledge, learning; इल्म-ए-अदब *[ilm-e-adab]* M poetics

इल्मी *[ilmī]* ADJ academic, educational

इशारा *[iśārā]* M indication, sign, signal; hint

इश्क़ *[iśq]* M love; amour

इश्तहार *[iśtahār]* M advertisement; poster

इस *[is]* PRO oblique form of यह; इसका *[iskā]* ADJ his/her/its

इस तरह *[is tarah]* ADV in this way

इस बारे में *[is bāre mẽ]* ADV about this

इस बीच *[is bīc]* ADV meanwhile

इस मामले में *[is māmle mẽ]* ADV about (in) this matter

इसलिये *[isliye]* ADV therefore, for this reason, so

इसलिये कि *[isliye ki]* ADV because, for the reason that

इसने *[isne]* PRO he/she/it/this (oblique form of यह + ने)

इसपात *[ispāt]* M steel

इसलाम *[islām]* M Islam

इसलामी *[islāmī]* M Islamic; pertaining to Islam; a Muslim

इसलाह *[islāh]* F improvement, revision; reform

इसी *[isī]* PRO इस + ही; इसी वजह से *[isī vajah se]* ADV for this very reason

इसी से *[isī se]* ADV for this very reason

इसीलिये *[isīliye]* ADV for this very reason

इसे/इसको *[ise/isko]* PRO oblique form of यह + को

इस्तिरी *[isitrī]* F iron; press

इस्तीफ़ा *[istīfā]* M resignation

इस्तेमाल *[istemāl]* M use, application; vogue

इस्तेमालशुदा *[istemālśudā]* ADJ used; secondhand

इस्म *[ism]* M name; noun (in Urdu grammar)

इस्मे शरीफ़ *[isme śarīf]* M good/noble name

ई

ईंट *[ĩṭ]* F brick
ईंटकारी *[ĩṭkārī]* F brickwork
ईंधन *[īndhan]* M fuel, firewood
ईख *[īkh]* F sugarcane
ईजाद *[ījād]* F invention; Muslim festival Eid; ईदगाह *[īdgāh]* M a place of assembly for offering Eid prayers; ईद-उज़-जुहा *[īd-uz-juhā]* F name of Eid; ईद-उल-अज़हा *[īd-ul-azhā]* F name of Eid
ईमान *[īmān]* M faith, belief, integrity
ईमानदार *[īmāndār]* ADJ honest; faithful; having integrity
ईमानदारी *[īmāndārī]* F honesty, faithfulness, integrity
ईर्ष्या *[īrṣyā]* F jealousy
ईर्ष्यालु *[īrṣyālu]* ADJ jealous
ईश्वर/ईश्वर *[īśvar]* M God
ईश्वरवाद *[īśvarvād]* M theism
ईसवी *[īsvī]* ADJ Christian, pertaining to Christ; ईसवी सन् *[īsvī san]* M Christian era
ईसा *[īsā]* M Jesus Christ
ईसाई *[īsāī]* M Christian

उ

उँगली *[ũglī]* F finger; उँगली उठाना *[ũglī uṭhānā]* V.T. to raise a finger, to reproach
उकड़ू *[ukṛū]* M squatting posture; उकड़ू बैठना *[ukṛū baiṭhnā]* V.I. to squat
उकताना *[uktānā]* V.I. to become bored/tired/sick (of)
उकताहट *[uktāhaṭ]* F boredom, weariness
उकसना *[ukasnā]* V.I. to rise; to come up; to emerge V.T. to raise; to incite; to provoke, to instigate
उक्ति *[ukti]* F saying, statement, dictum
उखड़ना *[ukhaṛnā]* ... uprooted, to be d... to be out of sp... of sorts
उखाड़ना [... to upro... eradi...
उ...
...
wr...

उग्रवाद *[ugravād]* M extremism, radicalism
उग्रवादी *[ugravādī]* ADJ extremist; terrorist; radical
उचटना *[ucaṭnā]* V.I. to withdraw from; to weary of, to feel dejected
उचाट *[ucāṭ]* ADJ lack of enthusiasm; mentally wearied M disinterest, mental fatigue
उचित *[ucit]* ADJ proper, appropriate, right, suitable; reasonable; fair
उच्च *[ucca]* ADJ high, tall; lofty
उच्चता *[uccatā]* F height; loftiness, elevation
उच्चारण *[uccāraṇ]* M pronunciation, articulation, tterance
लना *[uchalnā]* V.I. to hop, , to jump
[uchāl] F jump, leap; nd
[uchālnā] V.T. to toss, up
jarnā] V.I. to become r devastated; to be estroyed
d] ADJ boorish,
J clean, bright; white
उजागर *[ujāgar]* ADJ brilliant; renowned; well-known; manifest
उजाड़ *[ujāṛ]* ADJ deserted, desolate, devastated; barren
उजाड़ना *[ujāṛnā]* V.T. to destroy, to ruin, to devastate
उजाला *[ujālā]* M light, brightness, splendor, bright, shining, luminous
उज्ज्वल *[ujjval]* ADJ bright, splendid, clear; radiant
उठना *[uṭhnā]* V.I. to rise, to get up; to pass away, to expire; उठना-बैठना *[uṭhnā-baiṭhnā]* V.I. to have a close association, an intimate relationship
उठाना *[uṭhānā]* V.T. to get up, to make rise; to raise; to wake up
उड़द *[uṛad]* F black gram; उड़द की दाल *[uṛad kī dāl]* F a type of lentil
उड़ना *[uṛnā]* V.I. to fly
उड़ान *[uṛān]* F flight; sortie
उड़ाना *[uṛānā]* V.T. to make fly; to squander; to steal or kidnap; to explode; to blow away

उड़िया *[uṛiyā]* M the people of Orissa F the language of the state of Orissa

उड़ीसा *[uṛīsā]* M Orissa, the eastern state of the Indian Union

उतना *[utnā]* ADJ that much, to that extent

उतरना *[utarnā]* V.I. to descend, to come down, to alight

उतार *[utār]* M descent; depreciation; fall; ebb-tide; down-gradient; उतार-चढ़ाव *[utār-caṛhāv]* M ups and downs, rise and fall, fluctuation; vicissitude

उतारना *[utārnā]* V.T. to make descend, to bring down, to unload; to take across

उत्तम *[uttam]* ADJ best, superior, excellent

उत्तमता *[uttamtā]* F excellence; उत्तमपुरुष *[uttampuruṣ]* M the best man; the first person (in grammar)

उत्तर *[uttar]* M north; reply, answer; उत्तर भारत *[uttar bhārat]* M north India

उत्तरदायित्व *[uttardāyitva]* M responsibility; obligation; onus; accountability

उत्तरप्रदेश *[uttar pradeś]* M Uttar Pradesh (North Province) the most populous state in the Indian Union, situated in the north of the country

उत्तराखंड *[uttarākhaṇḍ]* M Uttarakhand, a state to the northwest of Uttar Pradesh. This was once a part of U.P.

उत्तराधिकार *[uttarādhikār]* M inheritance; succession; right of succession

उत्तरी *[uttarī]* ADJ northern; उत्तरी ध्रुव *[uttarī dhruv]* the North Pole; the Arctic

उत्तेजक *[uttejak]* ADJ provocative; exciting; stimulating

उत्तेजना *[uttejnā]* F provocation; excitement; stimulation ADJ provoking, exciting; stimulating

उत्तेजित *[uttejit]* ADJ excited; provoked; stimulated

उत्थान *[utthān]* M rising up; the act of rising

उत्पत्ति *[utpatti]* F production, produce; birth; origin

उत्पन्न *[utpanna]* ADJ produced, originated

उत्पादक *[utpādak]* M producer; originater

उत्पादन *[utpādan]* M production, production output

उत्पीड़ित *[utpīṛit]* ADJ oppressed, persecuted; harrassed

उत्सव *[utsav]* M festival; celebration; festivity

उत्साह *[utsāh]* M enthusiasm, zeal

उत्सुक *[utsuk]* ADJ curious; eager, keen

उत्सुकता *[utsuktā]* F curiosity; eagerness

उथल-पुथल *[uthal-puthal]* F upheaval, turmoil

उदय *[uday]* M rising; rise, ascent

उदात्त *[udātt]* ADJ sublime, lofty; acute

उदात्तता *[udāttatā]* F loftiness

उदार *[udār]* ADJ generous, liberal; magnificent

उदारता *[udārtā]* F generosity, magnanimity

उदास *[udās]* ADJ sad, dejected, gloomy

उदासी *[udāsī]* F sadness, dejection, melancholy

उदासीन *[udāsīn]* ADJ indifferent, disinterested, nonchalant

उदासीनता *[udāsīntā]* F indifference; disinterest, nonchalance

उदाहरण *[udaharaṇ]* M example, instance; illustration

उद्घाटन *[udghāṭan]* M inauguration, release; uncovering

उद्दंड *[uddaṇḍ]* ADJ very abusive/humiliating, insolent, impertinent, rude; rebellious

उद्देश्य *[uddeśya]* M object; purpose; motive; subject (in grammar)

उद्धार *[uddhār]* M deliverance; salvation; redemption, riddance; restoration

उद्भव *[udbhav]* M birth; origin; coming into existence

उद्यान *[udyān]* M garden

उद्योग *[udyog]* M industry; labor, effort

उद्योगी *[udyogī]* ADJ industrious

उद्योगीकरण *[udyogīkaraṇ]* M industrialization

उधड़ना *[udharṇā]* V.I. to be unsewn; to be ripped/opened out; to be untwisted; to be unrolled; to be unraveled

उधर *[udhar]* ADV there, over

there; that side, from the other side

उधार *[udhār]* M borrowing; credit, loan; debt

उधेड़ना *[udheṛnā]* V.T. to unsew; to unravel; to open up; to unroll; to untwist; to criticize harshly

उधेड़बुन *[udheṛbun]* F unpicking and weaving; a process of indecision; uneasy constant reflection

उन *[un]* PRO oblique form of वे; those

उनका *[unkā]* ADJ his/her/their

उनचास *[uncās]* ADJ forty-nine

उनतालीस *[untālīs]* ADJ thirty-nine

उनतीस/उनत्तीस *[untīs/unttīs]* ADJ twenty-nine

उनसठ *[unsaṭh]* ADJ fifty-nine

उनहत्तर *[unhattar]* ADJ sixty-nine

उनासी *[unāsī]* ADJ seventy-nine

उन्नति *[unnati]* F progress, rise; promotion, improvement

उन्नति *[unnati]* F development

उन्नीस *[unnīs]* ADJ nineteen

उन्नीसवाँ *[unnīsvā̃]* ADJ nineteenth

उनमाद *[unmād]* M hysteria, insanity; lunacy; mania; intoxication; frenzy

उन्मुक्त *[unmukt]* ADJ liberated; free, unrestrained; open

उन्मुक्तता *[unmuktatā]* F liberation; freedom; lack of restraint

उन्मूलन *[unmūlan]* M uprooting; rooting out; abolition; extermination, extirpation

उन्यासी *[unyāsī]* ADJ seventy-nine

उन्हीं *[unhī̃]* PRO उन + ही

उन्हें/उनको *[unhẽ/unko]* PRO oblique form of वे + को

उन्होंने *[unhõne]* PRO he/she/they/those (oblique form of वे + ने)

उपकरण *[upakaraṇ]* M appliance; equipment

उपकार *[upakār]* M beneficence; benefaction; good

उपकारी *[upakārī]* ADJ beneficial; favorable; helping; obliging M benefactor

उपक्रम *[upakram]* M preparation; a beginning; venture; undertaking

उपग्रह *[upagrah]* M satellite; secondary planet
उपचार *[upacār]* M treatment, remedy; attending (upon)
उपज *[upaj]* F produce, product; crop, harvest, yield
उपजना *[upajnā]* V.I. to be produced; to be born; to grow; to spring up
उपजाऊ *[upajāū]* ADJ fertile, productive
उपजाना *[upajānā]* V.T. to cause to grow; to produce
उपदेश *[upadeś]* M sermon teaching; preaching
उपनिवेश *[upaniveś]* M colony settlement
उपनिवेशवाद *[upaniveśvād]* M colonialism
उपनिषद् *[upaniṣad]* M *Upanishad*, the sacred ancient books of the Hindus
उपन्यास *[upanyās]* M novel
उपन्यासकार *[upanyāskār]* M novelist
उपभोक्ता *[upabhoktā]* M consumer; user
उपमहाद्वीप *[upamahādvīp]* M subcontinent
उपमा *[upamā]* F simile, comparison
उपयुक्त *[upayukt]* ADJ proper, suitable, appropriate; used
उपयुक्तता *[upayukttā]* F propriety; suitability
उपयोग *[upayog]* M use; utilization, utility
उपयोगी *[upayogī]* ADJ useful, helpful; serviceable
उपराष्ट्रपति *[uparāṣṭrapati]* M Vice-President
उपलब्ध *[upalabdh]* ADJ available; acquired
उपलब्धि *[upalabdhi]* F acquisition; achievement; attainment
उपला *[upalā]* M cow-dung cake
उपवन *[upavan]* M garden, park, parkland
उपवास *[upavās]* M a fast (not eating)
उपवासी *[upavāsī]* M one who fasts
उपस्थित *[upasthit]* ADJ present
उपस्थिति *[upasthiti]* F presence; attendance
उपहार *[upahār]* M present, gift
उपाधि *[upādhi]* F degree; qualification; title; attribute
उपाय *[upāy]* M way, measure

device; cure, remedy
उपासना *[upāsnā]* F worship; adoration
उपेक्षा *[upekṣā]* F neglect, disregard
उबरना *[ubarnā]* V.I. to be liberated; to get rid of, to be free; to be salvaged
उबलना *[ubalnā]* V.I. to boil, to simmer
उबाना *[ubānā]* V.T. to be bored, to cause to be fed up
उबालना *[ubālnā]* V.T. to boil; to cause to simmer; to heat until a liquid boils
उभरना *[ubharnā]* V.I. to bulge, to emerge; to protrude or project
उभार *[ubhār]* M bulge, bulging; projection
उभारना *[ubhārnā]* V.T. to incite, to provoke; to instigate; to cause to protrude
उमंग *[umaṅg]* F aspiration; gusto, zeal
उमड़ना *[umaṛnā]* V.I. to surge, to swell, to flood, to gust
उमदा *[umdā]* ADJ fine, excellent
उमर *[umar]* F *see* उम्र
उमस *[umas]* F humidity, sultriness
उमा *[umā]* F the goddess Parvati; Lord Shiva's spouse
उमेठना *[umeṭhnā]* V.T. to twist, to wring; to pull
उम्दा *[umdā]* ADJ *see* उमदा
उम्मीद *[ummīd]* F hope, expectation
उम्मीदवार *[ummīdvār]* M a candidate
उम्र *[umra]* F age; lifetime
उम्रकैद *[umraqaid]* F life imprisonment
उरद *[urad]* F pulse; black gram
उर्दू *[urdū]* F Urdu (language)
उर्दूदाँ *[urdūdā̃]* M a scholar of Urdu
उर्स *[urs]* M celebration to observe the day of a Muslim saint's demise
उलझन *[uljhan]* F complication, entanglement; perplexity
उलझना *[ulajhnā]* V.I. to entangle, to involve; to complicate; to become entangled V.T. to entangle, to involve, to entwine
उलटना *[ulaṭnā]* V.I., V.T. overturned, to overturn, to capsize; to be reversed or to reverse

उलट-फेर *[ulaṭ-pher]* **M** shuffling, upsetting; disarray; reversal; changes; vicissitude
उलटा *[ulṭā]* **ADJ** reverse/reversed, topsy-turvy, opposite; inverted; उलटा-सीधा *[ulṭā-sīdhā]* **ADJ** absurd, irrelevant; hurriedly performed
उलटी *[ulṭī]* **F** vomit, vomitting **ADJ** upside down; topsy-turvy; backwards
उलाँघना *[ulā̃ghnā]* **V.I.** to cross over; to transgress, to disobey
उल्लंघन *[ullaṅghan]* **M** violation, contravention
उल्लास *[ullās]* **M** joy, delight, merriment
उल्लू *[ullū]* **M** owl; idiot, a fool; उल्लू का पट्ठा *[ullū kā paṭṭhā]* **M** an absolute idiot
उल्लेख *[ullekh]* **M** mention; reference; citation; quotation
उस *[us]* **PRO** oblique form of वह
उसका *[uskā]* **ADJ** his/her/its
उसने *[usne]* **PRO** oblique form of वह + ने
उसी *[usī]* **PRO** उस + ही
उसे/उसको *[use/usko]* **PRO** oblique form of वह + को
उसूल *[usūl]* **M** principle
उस्तरा *[ustarā]* **M** razor (blade)
उस्ताद *[ustād]* **M** teacher, master
उस्तादी *[ustādī]* **F** tutorship; teaching; cleverness
उस्तानी *[ustānī]* **F** female teacher

ऊ

ऊँघना *[ū̃ghnā]* **V.I.** to doze; to nap; to be drowsy.
ऊँचा *[ū̃cā]* **ADJ** high; ऊँचा-नीचा *[ū̃cā-nīcā]* **ADJ** uneven; highs and lows; ऊँचा सुनना *[ū̃cā sunnā]* **V.T.** to be hard of hearing
ऊँची जगह *[ū̃cī jagah]* **F** a high position/office
ऊँचाई *[ū̃cāī]* **F** height; altitude, elevation; loftiness
ऊँट *[ū̃ṭ]* **M** camel
ऊखल *[ūkhal]* **M** mortar; *see* ओखली
ऊटपटाँग *[ūṭpaṭā̃g]* **ADJ** slipslop; absurd, ridiculous, incoherent
ऊन *[ūn]* **M** wool
ऊनी *[ūnī]* **ADJ** woolen, woolly
ऊपर *[ūpar]* **ADV** above; on; upon; over; ऊपर की

आमदनी *[ūpar kī āmdanī]* F additional income; extra income; ऊपर का *[ūpar kā]* ADJ superficial
ऊपरवाला *[ūparvālā]* ADJ, M the Almighty
ऊपरी *[ūparī]* ADJ upper; superficial, artificial; showy
ऊब *[ūb]* F boredom, tedium, monotony
ऊबड़-खाबड़ *[ūbaṛ-khābaṛ]* ADJ uneven; rough and rugged
ऊर्जा *[ūrjā]* F energy, vigor and vitality
ऊहा *[ūhā]* F flight of imagination; far-fetched imagination; exaggeration
ऊहापोह *[ūhāpoh]* F reflection on the pros and cons of a problem; indecisive reflection

ऋ

ऋग्वेद *[ṛgved]* M the earliest of the four Vedas.
ऋण *[ṛṇ]* M loan, a debt; minus
ऋणी *[ṛṇī]* M indebted, debtor
ऋतु *[ṛtu]* F season
ऋषि *[ṛṣi]* M sage, seer; preceptor

ए

ए० सी० *[e. sī]* F A.C.
एक *[ek]* ADJ one; एक घंटे बाद *[ek ghanṭe bād]* ADV after an hour; एक तिहाई *[ek tihāī]* ADJ one-third; एक चथाई *[ek cauthāī]* ADJ one-quarter; एक दिन *[ek din]* ADV one day; एक बात करना *[ek bāt karnā]* V.T. to say one thing; एक बार *[ek bār]* ADV once, one time; एक साथ *[ek sāth]* ADV together; एक ही *[ek hī]* ADJ same
एक एक करके *[ek ek kar ke]* one by one
एक से दो भले *[ek se do bhale]* IDIOM two heads are better than one
एकतरफ़ा *[ektarafā]* ADJ one-way, unilateral, one-sided
एकता *[ektā]* F oneness; unity; solidarity
एकत्रित *[ekatrit]* ADJ collected, accumulated, gathered
एकदम *[ek dam]* ADV immediately; suddenly; in one breath; completely ADJ perfect
एकमत *[ekmat]* ADJ having complete accord, unanimous

एकरस *[ekras]* ADJ monotonous
एकरूप *[ekrūp]* ADJ uniform
एकरूपता *[ekrūptā]* F uniformity
एकांत *[ekānt]* ADJ exclusive M solitude, seclusion
एकांतवासी *[ekāntvāsī]* ADJ recluse, one who resides in seclusion
एकाएक *[ekāek]* ADV suddenly; unexpectedly; all at once
एकाकी *[ekākī]* ADJ lonely, solitary; single
एकाग्र *[ekāgra]* ADJ intent, resolute; focused on one point
एकाग्रता *[ekāgratā]* F concentration (of mind); resoluteness
एकाध *[ekādh]* ADJ a few, one or two
एक्स्प्रेस *[ekspres]* ADJ express
एजेंट *[ejenṭ]* M agent
एडिटर *[eḍiṭar]* M editor
एडिशन *[eḍiśan]* M edition
एड़ी *[eṛī]* F heel
एतराज़ *[etrāz]* M objection, exception
एलान *[elān]* M announcement, a declaration
एलार्म *[elārm]* M alarm; एलार्म घड़ी *[elārm ghaṛī]* F alarm clock
एशिया *[eśiyā]* M Asia
एहतियात *[ehtiyāt]* M precaution
एहसान *[ehsān]* M obligation, beneficence
एहसानमंद *[ehsānmand]* ADJ grateful; obliged; एहसानमंद होना *[ehsānmand honā]* V.I. to feel grateful
एहसास *[ehsās]* M feeling, sense

ऐ

ऐंठ *[aĩṭh]* F twist; twine; ply; torque; stiffness; conceit
ऐंठना *[aĩṭhnā]* V.T. to twist; to contort; to fleece; to extort; to be conceited
ऐ *[ai]* VOC O!
ऐक्टर *[aikṭar]* M actor
ऐक्ट्रैस *[aikṭrais]* F actress
ऐतिहासिक *[aitihāisk]* ADJ historical; legendary
ऐतिहासिकता *[aitihāsiktā]* F historicality
ऐन *[ain]* ADJ exact, just; ऐन मौक़े पर *[ain mauqe par]* ADV in the nick of time; at the exact opportunity
ऐनक *[ainak]* F spectacles, glasses

ऐयाश *[aiyāś]* ADJ debauched; lewd F, M one indulging in a lavish lifestyle

ऐयाशी *[aiyāśī]* F debauchery; lewdness; luxury

ऐश *[aiś]* M enjoyment; luxury, sensuous pleasure

ऐश्वर्य *[aiśvarya]* M opulence; prosperity, glory and grandeur

ऐसा *[aisā]* ADJ such, of this type; ऐसा-वैसा *[aisā-vaisā]* ADJ trifling, of no consequence

ऐसे *[aise]* ADV, ADJ in this way, in this manner, thus; ऐसे ही *[aise hī]* ADV no reason, just such

ओ

ओ *[o]* VOC O!

ओखली *[okhlī]* F mortar (to grind grains and spices

ओछा *[ochā]* ADJ mean, petty, low, trifling; small, shallow

ओछापन *[ochāpan]* M meanness, pettiness

ओझल *[ojhal]* ADJ out of sight, evanescent

ओट *[oṭ]* M, F cover, shelter; ओट लेना *[oṭ lenā]* V.T. to take cover, to shelter

ओठ *[oṭh]* M a lip

ओढ़ना *[oṛhnā]* V.T. to cover, to drape; to wrap (one's own body)

ओफ़ *[of]* IND Oh! Ah!; an expression of pain, grief, wonder

ओम् *[om]* M the sacred word prefixed and suffixed to the Veda mantras symbolizing God

ओर *[or]* F direction, side; x की ओर *[x kī or]* ADV in the direction of (x)

ओला *[olā]* M hailstone, hail

ओषधि *[oṣadhi]* F medicinal herb, medicine

ओस *[os]* F dew

ओह *[oh]* VOC oh!

ओहदा *[ohdā]* M post, designation; rank; status

ओहो *[oho]* IND alas! an expression of regret

औ

औंधा *[aũdhā]* ADJ upside down, inverted; with the face downwards

औंधे मुँह *[aũdhe mũh]* ADV with the face down ADJ prostrate

औक़ात *[auqāt]* F status; capacity

औज़ार *[auzār]* M instrument

औद्योगिक *[audyogik]* ADJ industrial

औद्योगिकता *[audyogiktā]* F industralism

औद्योगिक युग *[audyogik jug]* M industrial age

औपचारिक *[aupacārik]* ADJ formal, ceremonial

औपचारिकता *[aupacāriktā]* F formality

और *[aur]* ADJ, AD, CONJ and more

और तो और *[aur to aur]* other things apart, leaving other things

और क्या *[aur kyā]* INT what else, of course!

और नहीं तो क्या! *[aur nahī̃ to kyā]* what else

औरत *[aurat]* F woman; wife

औलाद *[aulād]* F progeny; offspring

औसत *[ausat]* F average; mean ADJ average

औसतन *[ausatan]* ADV average

क

कंकड़ *[kaṅkaṛ]* M gravel, pebble

कंकड़ी *[kaṅkaṛī]* F a small piece of gravel

कंकण *[kaṅkaṇ]* M bracelet

कंकाल *[kaṅkāl]* M skeleton, physical frame

कंगन *[kaṅgan]* M *see* कंकण

कंगाल *[kaṅgāl]* M pauper, poor man ADJ penniless, with little or no money

कंगाली *[kaṅgālī]* F penury, poverty

कंघा *[kaṅghā]* M comb

कंघी *[kaṅghī]* F comb

कंचन *[kañcan]* M gold

कंजूस *[kañjūs]* ADJ miserly F/M miser

कंजूसी *[kañjūsī]* F miserliness, unwillingness to spend money

कँटीला *[kā̃ṭīlā]* ADJ thorny, prickly

कंठ *[kaṇṭh]* M throat; neck; larynx
कंधा *[kandhā]* M shoulder
कंपन *[kampan]* M tremor, quivering, trembling; shivering
कंपनी *[kampanī]* F a company
कंबल *[kambal]* M blanket
कई *[kaī]* ADJ several
ककड़ी *[kakṛī]* F a kind of cucumber
कक्षा *[kakṣā]* F class
कचरा *[kacrā]* M refuse; rubbish; sweepings; debris
कचहरी *[kacahrī]* F court of law
कचौरी *[kacaurī]* F a cake made of flour stuffed with bruised pulse or boiled potato fried in ghee or oil
कच्चा *[kaccā]* ADJ uncooked, unboiled; raw, unripe; green; crude; incomplete, unfinished; rough; imperfect, immature; inauthentic; doubtful; vague; weak
कच्ची उम्र *[kaccī umr]* F immature age
कछुआ *[kachuā]* M turtle, tortoise
कटना *[kaṭnā]* V.I. to be cut, to be wounded; to die in battle; to be destroyed; to pass away; to complete (a journey, punishment, prison sentence, time)
कटहल *[kaṭhal]* M the jack tree or its fruit
कटाक्ष *[kaṭākṣ]* F a side glance; ogling; leer, taunt
कटार *[kaṭār]* F dagger
कटु *[kaṭu]* ADJ bitter; vitriolic; unpleasant
कटुता *[kaṭutā]* F bitterness, vitriol; unpleasantness
कटोरा *[kaṭorā]* M bowl
कटोरी *[kaṭorī]* F a small bowl
कटौती *[kaṭautī]* F rebate, discount, deduction, reduction; cut
कट्टर *[kaṭṭar]* ADJ strict; obdurate, dogmatic; fanatic; rabid
कट्टरपंथी *[kaṭṭarpanthī]* M/F religious zealot; fanatic
कठपुतली *[kaṭhputlī]* F puppet; an underling
कठिन *[kaṭhin]* ADJ difficult
कठोर *[kaṭhor]* ADJ hard; severe; stern; stringent; rough; cruel; rigid; rigorous

कठोरता *[kaṭhortā]* F harshness; severity; cruelty, rigidity; rigor

कड़क *[kaṛak]* F crack; thunder, sudden sharp noise, vigorousness ADJ strong; vigorous

कड़कड़ाना *[kaṛkaṛānā]* V.I. to crack/crackle (as in oil when boiling); to break with a cracking sound

कड़कना *[kaṛaknā]* V.I. to crackle; to thunder; to break with a crack

कड़वा *[kaṛvā]* ADJ bitter, unpleasant; कड़वा तेल *[kaṛvā tel]* M mustard oil

कड़ा *[kaṛā]* ADJ hard; strict; stiff; harsh; cruel; arduous; sharp; rigid; strong

कड़ापन *[kaṛāpan]* M harshness, strictness; rigidity

कड़ाह *[kaṛāh]* M cauldron for boiling; frying pan

कड़ाही *[kaṛāhī]* F a small frying pan

कढ़ाई *[kaṛhāī]* F embroidery; the process of embroidering; a huge cauldron

कढ़ी *[kaṛhī]* F curry; a dish consisting of gram flour seasoned with spices and yoghurt

कतरन *[katran]* F cutting, off-cut; parings

कतरना *[katarnā]* V.T. to clip; to chip; to cut; to pare

क़तरा *[qatrā]* M drop; a cutting

क़तार *[qatār]* F line; row; series

कत्थक *[katthak]* M a particular Hindu group specializing in a kind of classical dance and song

क़त्ल *[qatl]* M murder; slaughter; क़त्ल-ए-आम *[qatl-e-ām]* M mass murder; massacre

कथन *[kathan]* M saying; statement; utterance

कथा *[kathā]* F story

क़द *[qad]* M size, height

क़दम *[qadam]* M step, pace, footstep

क़दर *[qadar]* F extreme; absolute; *see* क़द्र

कद्दू/कद्दू *[kaddū]* M pumpkin

क़द्र *[qadra]* F worth, merit; estimation; appreciation

क़द्रदान *[qadradān]* F/M a connoisseur, a patron, someone who appreciates

कनखी *[kankhī]* F ogle; a sideway glance
कन्या *[kanyā]* F girl; daughter; virgin
कप *[kap]* M cup
कपट *[kapaṭ]* M fraud; ruse; guile; artifice; trickery; hypocrisy; dissimulation
कपटी *[kapaṭī]* ADJ fraudulent, crafty
कपड़ा *[kapṛā]* M cloth
कपड़े *[kapṛe]* M clothes
कपाल *[kapāl]* M skull, head; cranium; destiny; a beggar's bowl
कपास *[kapās]* F cotton; cotton plant
कपि *[kapi]* M monkey
कफ़न *[kafan]* M shroud; pall
कब *[kab]* ADV when; कब से *[kab se]* since when, for how long
कबड्डी *[kabaḍḍī]* F a popular outdoor game played between teams
कबाड़ *[kabāṛ]* M junk, scrap; any disorderly stuff
कबाड़ी *[kabāṛī]* M junk dealer
कबाब *[kabāb]* M roasted meat; roast; meat roasted on a skewer
कबूतर *[kabūtar]* M pigeon
क़बूल *[qabūl]* M agreement, consent; admission; confession
क़ब्ज़ *[qabz]* M constipation
क़ब्ज़ा *[qabzā]* M possession; confiscation
क़ब्र *[qabra]* F a grave
क़ब्रिस्तान *[qabristān]* M graveyard, cemetery
कभी *[kabhī]* ADV ever; sometime; (कब + ही); कभी-कभी *[kabhī-kabhī]* ADV sometimes; कभी नहीं *[kabhī nahī̃]* ADV never
कम *[kam]* ADJ less, too little; कम से कम *[kam se kam]* ADJ at least
कमज़ोर *[kamzor]* ADJ weak, feeble; ineffectual
कमज़ोरी *[kamzorī]* F weakness, feebleness; deficiency
कमबख़्त *[kambakht]* ADJ unfortunate, ill-fated, unlucky
कमर *[kamar]* F waist, loins, girdle; the middle part of something
कमरतोड़ *[kamartoṛ]* ADJ backbreaking; arduous (work)

कमरबंद *[kamarband]* M a girdle
कमरा *[kamrā]* M room
कमल *[kamal]* M lotus
कमाई *[kamāī]* F earnings
कमाना *[kamānā]* V.T. to earn; to merit
कमाल *[kamāl]* M miracle; wonder; excellence
कमी *[kamī]* F shortage, deficiency, paucity; lack
क़मीज़ *[qamīz]* F shirt
कमीना *[kamīnā]* ADJ mean, wicked, vile
कमीनापन *[kamīnāpan]* M meanness; wickness
कर *[kar]* M a hand; a ray; the truck of an elephant; tax, duty, custom SUFFIX agency, doer INVAR absolutive कर (used with the stem of a verb)
करतब *[kartab]* M feat; exploits; skill
करतूत *[kartūt]* F misdeed, evil deed
करना *[karnā]* V.T. to do; to perform; to complete, to act, to execute
क़रार *[qarār]* M agreement; a contract; commitment, undertaking
कराहना *[karāhnā]* V.I. to groan, to moan, to cry in pain
करिश्मा *[kariśmā]* M miracle; magic
करीना *[karīnā]* M orderliness, method; symmetrical technique
क़रीब *[qarīb]* ADV near; close by; about, approximately, almost
क़रीबी *[qarībī]* ADJ near, close
करुणा *[karuṇā]* F pity, compassion, pathos; tenderness of feeling
करेला *[karelā]* M bitter gourd
करोड़ *[karoṛ]* ADJ ten million
कर्ज़ *[karz]* M loan, debt
कर्त्तव्य *[karttavya]* M duty ADJ that which ought to be done
कर्नल *[karnal]* M colonel
कर्म *[karm]* M activity; action; any religious action or rite; fate; object (in grammar)
कर्मचारी *[karmcārī]* M worker; employee; official; a servant
कर्मठ *[karmaṭh]* ADJ diligent; assiduous; active and energetic
कर्मठता *[karmaṭhtā]* F diligence, hard work
कलंक *[kalaṅk]* M blemish;

stigma; slur, disgrace
क़लंदर *[qalandar]* M a kind of Muslim recluse; a carefree type of person
कल *[kal]* M yesterday; tomorrow
क़लम *[qalam]* F pen
कलश *[kalaś]* M pitcher; urn; dome (of a temple)
कलसा *[kalsā]* M a metal pitcher
कला *[kalā]* F art
कलाई *[kalāī]* F wrist
कली *[kalī]* F bud
कलेंडर *[kaleṇḍar]* M calendar
कलेजा *[kalejā]* M liver; heart
कल्पना *[kalpnā]* F imagination; fiction; supposition
कल्पनीय *[kalpnīya]* ADJ worth imagining
कल्याण *[kalyāṇ]* M welfare
कवयित्री *[kavayitrī]* F poetess
कवि *[kavi]* M poet
कविराज *[kavirāj]* M a king of poets
कविता *[kavitā]* F poem
क़व्वाली *[qavvālī]* F *qawwali* (a genre of *sufi* devotional song)
कश *[kaś]* M whip, lash; drawing, pulling; puff; inhalation
कष्ट *[kaṣṭ]* M suffering; pain; hardship; distress
कसना *[kasnā]* V.T. to tighten; to fasten; to bind; to gird up
क़सम *[qasam]* F oath, swearing
कसरत *[kasrat]* F physical exercise; abundance, plenty
कसरती *[kasratī]* ADJ athletic, built up from exercise
क़साई *[qasāī]* M butcher
क़सूर *[kasūr]* M fault; guilt
क़सूरवार *[kasūrvār]* ADJ guilty
कसौटी *[kasauṭī]* F touchstone; test; criterion
क़हक़हा *[qehqahā]* M a burst of laughter
कहना (x से) *[kehnā (x se)]* V.T. say (to x): (x को) (y) कहना *[(x ko)(y) kehnā]* V.T. to call (x) (y)
क़हवा *[qehvā]* M coffee
कहाँ *[kahā̃]* INTER where
कहानी *[kahānī]* F story
कहावत *[kahāvat]* F saying; proverb
कहीं *[kahī̃]* ADV somewhere (कहाँ + ही); कहीं और *[kahī̃ aur]* ADV anywhere/ somewhere else
काँखना *[kā̃khnā]* V.T. to grunt,

to groan

काँच *[kā̃c]* M glass

काँटा *[kā̃ṭā]* M thorn; fork; hook

कांड *[kāṇḍ]* M chapter; division; an untoward/unseemly event or incident

काँपना *[kā̃pnā]* V.I. to tremble; to quiver; to shiver

का *[kā]* PP 's

काई *[kāī]* F moss, algae

काका *[kākā]* M paternal uncle

काकी *[kākī]* M paternal uncle's wife

कागज़ *[kāghaz]* M paper

कागज़ात *[kāghazāt]* M, PL papers

काजल *[kājal]* M collyrium; soot

क़ाज़ी *[qāzī]* M a Muslim judge or magistrate

काजू *[kājū]* M cashew nut

काटना *[kāṭnā]* V.T. to cut; to chop; to bite

काठ *[kāṭh]* M wood, timber; a block

काढ़ना *[kāṛhnā]* V.T. to embroider; to extricate; to comb (hair)

कातना *[kātnā]* V.T. to spin (as in cotton)

कातिक *[kātik]* M the eighth month of the Hindu calendar

क़ातिल *[qātil]* M murderer

कान *[kān]* M ear

क़ानून *[qānūn]* M law, regulation

कापी *[kāpī]* F notebook

क़ाफ़िर *[qāfir]* M unbeliever (in the tenets of Islam) ADJ infidel

काफ़िला *[kāfilā]* M caravan; convey

काफ़ी *[kāfī]* ADJ enough ADV quite F coffee

क़ाबिल *[qābil]* ADJ able; worthy; capable

काम *[kām]* M work; business; performance; passion, lust; desire

कामकाज *[kāmkāj]* M business; work

कामचलाऊ *[kāmcalāū]* ADJ workable; servicable; makeshift

कामचोर *[kāmcor]* ADJ shirker; malingerer

कामदी *[kāmadī]* F comedy

कामना *[kāmnā]* F desire; lust; passion

कामयाब *[kāmyāb]* ADJ successful

कामयाबी *[kāmyābī]* F success

कामुक *[kāmuk]* ADJ amorous; salacious; libidinous; sensual
कामुकता *[kāmuktā]* F sexuality; libidinousness, amorousness
क़ायदा *[qāydā]* M rule; practice; primer; क़ायदा-क़ानून *[qāydā-qānūn]* M rules and regulations
क़ायम *[qāyam]* ADJ firm; established; located
कायर *[kāyar]* ADJ coward, timid
कायरता *[kāyartā]* F cowardice
काया *[kāyā]* F body, person
कारख़ाना *[kārkhānā]* M factory; workshop; mill
कारण *[kāraṇ]* M reason, cause, pretext
कारवाँ *[kārvā̃]* M caravan
कारागार *[kārāgār]* M prison, jail; artisan
कारीगर *[kārīgar]* M craftsman; mechanic
कारीगरी *[kārīgarī]* F craftsmanship; artistry
कारोबार *[kārobār]* M business; occupation
कार्य *[kārya]* M job; task; work; business; ceremony
काल *[kāl]* M time; period; age; era; tense (in grammar); end; death; famine; calamity
कालचक्र *[kālcakra]* M the wheel of time
काला *[kālā]* ADJ black; dark, stained
काली मिर्च *[kālī mirc]* F pepper
काला नमक *[kālā namak]* M rock salt
काला बाज़ार *[kālā bāzār]* M black market
क़ालीन *[qālīn]* M carpet
कॉलेज/कॉलिज *[kālej/kālij]* M college
काव्य *[kāvya]* M poetry
काश *[kāś]* VOC alas!; if only; Had God willed thus!
कि *[ki]* CONJ that, for
कितना *[kitnā]* ADJ how much, many
कितने बजे *[kitne baje]* ADV at what time
किताब *[kitāb]* F book
किधर *[kidhar]* ADV where; at what place
किन *[kin]* PRO oblique plural form of कौन
किनका *[kinkā]* INTER, ADJ whose (oblique form of कौन *[pl]*) M a small particle; granule
किनारा *[kinārā]* M bank;

shore; edge; border
किन्हीं का *[kinhī̃ kā]* ADJ, PL some (people)'s (oblique form of कोई)
किन्हीं को *[kinhī̃ ko]* PRO, PL oblique form of कोई + को
किन्हींने *[kinhī̃ne]* PRO, PL oblique form of कोई + ने
किफ़ायत *[kifāyat]* F economy; thrift; frugality
किफ़ायती *[kifāyatī]* ADJ economical, thrifty
किया *[kiyā]* V.T. did
किरण *[kiraṇ]* F ray, beam
किराया *[kirāya]* M rent
किरायेदार *[kirāyedār]* M renter
क़िला *[qilā]* M fort; castle
किलो *[kilo]* M kilo
किलोग्राम *[kilogrām]* M a kilogram
किलोमीटर *[kilomīṭar]* M a kilometer
किवाड़ *[kivāṛ]* F door leaf; shutter
किशमिश *[kiśmiś]* F raisin
किशोर *[kiśor]* ADJ adolescent; youthful
किस *[kis]* PRO oblique singular form of कौन or क्या; किस समय *[kis samay]* INT at what time
किसका *[kiskā]* INT, ADJ whose
किसके लिये *[kiske liye]* INT, ADV for whom
किसको/किसे *[kisko/kise]* INT, PRO (to) whom (oblique form of कौन + को)
किसने *[kisne]* PRO oblique form of कौन + ने
किसलिये *[kisliye]* INT for what reason, why
किसान *[kisān]* M farmer, peasant
किसी *[kisī]* PRO oblique form of कोई
किसी समय at some time
किसी का *[kisī kā]* ADJ someone's, anyone's
किसी को *[kisī ko]* PRO (to) someone, anyone; oblique form of कोई + को
किसीने *[kisīne]* PRO, SING someone/anyone/some/any (oblique form of कोई + ने)
किसे/किसको *[kise/kisko]* PRO oblique form of कौन + को
क़िस्त *[qist]* F instalment
क़िस्म *[qism]* F type, kind; quality; variety
क़िस्मत *[qismat]* F fate, fortune, lot, luck

की *[kī]* V.T. did (feminine form) PP 's (feminine form); (x) की ओर *[(x) kī or]* (PP) in the direction of (x); (x) की जगह *[(x) kī jagah]* PP in place of (x); (x) की तरह *[(x) kī tarah]* PP like (x); (x) की वजह से *[(x) kī vajah se]* PP on account of (x), because of (x)

कीचड़ *[kīcaṛ]* M mud, slime; sewage; sludge

कीजिये *[kījiye]* please do (honorific form of imperative of करना)

कीटाणु *[kīṭāṇu]* M germ

कीटाणु-नाशक *[kīṭāṇu nāśak]* M insecticide

कीड़ा *[kīṛā]* M insect, worm

क़ीमत *[qīmat]* F price, cost, value

कीर्तन *[kīrtan]* M devotional song

कील *[kīl]* F nail; peg; pin; a gold or silver pin worn by women on one side of the nose

कीलना *[kīlnā]* V.T. to drive a nail in; to spell-bind; to charm

कुंजी *[kuñjī]* F key (for a lock or textbook)

कुंठा *[kuṇṭhā]* F frustration

कुंठित *[kuṇṭhit]* ADJ frustrated; stunted

कुंडली *[kuṇḍalī]* F a coil; horoscope

कुंभ *[kumbh]* M pitcher; pot; Aquarius; a sacred festival for Hindus that falls every twelve years.

कु *[ku]* a Sanskrit prefix meaning "deterioration, depreciation, deficiency, want, guilt, etc."

कुआँ *[kuā̃]* M a (water) well

कुचलना *[kucalnā]* V.I., V.T. to be crushed; to crush; to trample

कुछ *[kuch]* PRO, F/M some; something; कुछ और/और कुछ *[kuch aur/aur kuch]* ADJ some(thing) more, else; कुछ न कुछ *[kuch na kuch]* ADJ something or other; कुछ नहीं *[kuch nahī̃]* PRO nothing; कुछ भी *[kuch bhī]* PRO anything at all

कुछेक *[kuchek]* PRO a few, some, several

कुटुंब *[kuṭumb]* M family, household

कुतूहल *[kutūhal]* M curiosity, inquisitiveness
कुत्ता/कुत्ता *[kuttā]* M dog
कुमार *[kumār]* F/M bachelor
कुमारी *[kumārī]* ADJ an unmarried girl, virgin
कुरता *[kurtā]* M a loose-fitting upper garment, shirt
कुरती *[kurtī]* F a blouse (for women)
क़ुरान *[qurān]* F the Quran; the sacred book of Muslims
कुरूप *[kurūp]* ADJ ugly, unsightly
कुरेदना *[kurednā]* V.T. to rake; to scoop
कुर्ता *[kurtā]* M shirt
क़ुर्बान *[qurbān]* ADJ sacrificed
क़ुर्बानी *[qurbānī]* F sacrifice
कुर्सी/कुरसी *[kursī]* F chair, a position of authority
कुल *[kul]* M total aggregate; lineage, pedigree; family;
कुल मिलाकर *[kul milākar]* ADV in total, overall
क़ुलफ़ी *[qulfī]* F Indian ice-cream frozen in a conical mould
कुल्ला *[kullā]* M gargle, rinsing the mouth; sprout
कुल्हड़ *[kulhaṛ]* M a small earthen cup or bowl often used to serve tea
कुल्हाड़ा *[kulhāṛā]* M a large ax
कुल्हाड़ी *[kulhāṛī]* F a small ax
कुशल *[kuśal]* ADJ skillful, skilled, deft, proficient F well-being, happiness
कुशल-मंगल *[kuśal-maṅgal]* M welfare, well-being
कुशलता *[kuśaltā]* F dexterity, skill, deftness; well-being
कुश्ती *[kuśtī]* F wrestling
कुष्ट *[kuṣt]* M leprosy
कुसुम *[kusum]* M flower
क़ुसूर *[qusūr]* M fault; omission; default
कूच *[kūc]* M march; departure
कूटना *[kuṭnā]* V.T. to pound; to use a pestle; to crush; to beat; to thrash
कूड़ा *[kūṛā]* M rubbish, refuse; sweepings; trash
कूड़ेदान *[kūṛedān]* M trash can
कूद *[kūd]* F leap, jump
कूदना *[kūdnā]* V.I. to leap, to jump; to skip
कृतघ्न *[kṛtaghna]* ADJ ungrateful, thankless
कृतज्ञ *[kṛtajña]* ADJ grateful, indebted
कृति *[kṛti]* F a work (of art or

literature); composition; deed
कृत्रिम *[kṛtrim]* ADJ artificial; synthetic; pseudo; spurious; sham; affected
कृपया *[kṛpayā]* ADV please; kindly
कृपा *[kṛpā]* F mercy; kindness; favor; grace
कृषि *[kṛṣi]* F agriculture, farming; cultivation
कृषिकार *[kṛṣikār]* M farmer
कृष्ण *[kṛṣṇa]* M Lord Krishna (name of a Hindu deity); black; dark
केंद्र *[kendra]* M center
केंद्रीय *[kendrīya]* ADJ central
केतली *[ketlī]* F kettle
केरल *[keral]* M the state of Kerala
केला *[kelā]* M banana
केवल *[keval]* ADV only, merely
केश *[keś]* M hair
केसर *[kesar]* F saffron
कैंची *[qaincī]* F scissors, shears
कैद *[qaid]* F imprisonment; confinement; incarceration
कैदी *[qaidī]* M prisoner
कैमरा *[kaimrā]* M camera
कैसा *[kaisā]* ADJ how; what kind of
कैसे *[kaise]* ADV how; in what manner
को *[ko]* PP a postposition denoting accusative and dative case; "to; for; on the point of"
कोई *[koī]* ADJ, PRO some, any; someone, anyone; कोई और/और कोई *[koī aur/aur koī]* ADJ, PRO some other/more, any other/more; someone else, anyone else; कोई बात नहीं *[koī bāt nahī̃]* no matter; कोई भी *[koī bhī]* PRO anyone at all
कोकीन *[kokīn]* M cocaine
कोट *[koṭ]* M coat
कोटा *[koṭā]* M quota
कोठरी *[koṭhrī]* F cabin; a small room
कोठा *[koṭhā]* M a big room (especially on the upper floor); an extensive chamber; brothel
कोठी *[koṭhī]* F a bungalow, mansion
कोड़ा *[koṛā]* M whip; lash
कोढ़ *[koṛh]* M leprosy
कोढ़ी *[koṛhī]* M leper
कोण *[koṇ]* M corner; angle
कोना *[konā]* M corner
कोमल *[komal]* ADJ soft, tender; delicate; slender

कोयल *[koyal]* F cuckoo
कोयला *[koylā]* M coal
कोरा *[korā]* ADJ blank, unused (as in paper); brand new
कोलाहल *[kolāhal]* M noise; uproar; clamor
कोश/कोष *[koś/koṣ]* M treasure; dictionary; covering; shell
कोसना *[kosnā]* V.T. to curse
कोहनी *[kohnī]* F elbow
कौंधना *[kaũdhnā]* V.I. to flash; to glitter
कौआ *[kauā]* M crow
कौन *[kaun]* PRO who; कौन जाने *[kaun jāne]* who knows; कौन-सा *[kaun-sā]* INTER, PRO which
क़ौम *[qaum]* F nation; community; caste
क़ौमी *[qaumī]* ADJ national; क़ौमी ज़बान *[qaumī zabān]* F national language
कौर *[kaur]* M morsel
कौरव *[kaurav]* M the descendants of the King Kuru in the Indian epic *The Mahabharata*
कौशल *[kauśal]* M skill; dexterity, adroitness
क्या *[kyā]* PRO what (also marks a question); क्या-क्या *[kyā-kyā]* ADV what (the reduplication gives a sense of plurality)
क्यों *[kyõ]* INTER why
क्योंकि *[kyõki]* CONJ because
क्रम *[kram]* M order; system; method; rank; sequence
क्रांति *[krānti]* F revolution
क्रांतिकारी *[krāntikārī]* M revolutionary
क्रिया *[kriyā]* F action; act; verb (in grammar); क्रिया-कर्म *[kriya-karm]* M last rite, funeral rites
क्रूर *[krūr]* ADJ cruel; unkind; merciless, ruthless
क्रूरता *[krūrtā]* F cruelty, ruthlessness
क्रोध *[krodh]* M anger, wrath, fury, rage
क्लास *[klās]* M/F class (as in a Biology class)
क्षण *[kṣaṇ]* M moment, instant
क्षणिक *[kṣaṇik]* ADJ momentary, ephemeral
क्षत्रिय *[kṣatriya]* M the second or the ruling/warrior caste in the traditional Hindu caste-hierarchy
क्षमता *[kṣamtā]* F efficiency, competence, capacity

क्षमा *[kṣamā]* F forgiveness, pardon; क्षमा करना *[kṣamā karnā]* V.T. to forgive
क्षितिज *[kṣitij]* M horizon
क्षुब्ध *[kṣubdh]* ADJ perturbed; agitated; excited
क्षेत्र *[kṣetra]* M area; field; region; domain

ख

खँखारना *[khãkhārnā]* V.T. to expectorate; to hawk
खंजर *[khañjar]* M dagger
खंड *[khaṇḍ]* ADJ whole, complete, undivided
खंडता *[khaṇḍtā]* F completeness, wholeness, integrity
खंडन *[khaṇḍan]* M refutation; rebuttal, repudiation
खंडित *[khaṇḍit]* ADJ broken, divided, impaired
खंडहर *[khaṇḍahar]* M ruins
खंभा *[khambhā]* M pillar; column; post
खचाखच *[khacākhac]* ADJ, ADV overcrowded; absolutely full
ख़च्चर *[khaccar]* M mule
ख़ज़ाना *[khazānā]* M treasure; treasury; repository
खजूर *[khajūr]* F date, date-plum
खटकना *[khaṭaknā]* V.I. to click; to offend; to raise apprehensions or misgivings
खटखटाना *[khaṭkhaṭānā]* V.T. to tap, to knock (on a door)
खटमल *[khaṭmal]* M bedbug
खड़ा *[khaṛā]* ADJ standing
ख़त *[khat]* M letter; line; handwriting
ख़तरनाक *[khatarnāk]* ADJ dangerous; hazardous, risky
ख़तरा *[khatrā]* M danger; hazard
ख़त्म *[khatm]* ADJ ended; completed; concluded
खद्दर *[khaddar]* M handspun coarse cloth.
खनकना *[khanaknā]* V.I. to jingle; to clink
ख़बर *[khabar]* F news
ख़बरदार *[khabardār]* ADJ cautious; watchful
ख़रगोश *[khargoś]* M rabbit, hare
ख़रबूज़ा *[kharbūzā]* M musk melon
खरा *[kharā]* ADJ pure; genuine; straightforward; upright
ख़राब *[kharāb]* ADJ bad (off); broken

ख़राबी *[kharābī]* F badness; wickedness
ख़राश *[kharāś]* M scratch; irritations (in the throat)
ख़रीदना *[kharīdnā]* V.T. to buy
ख़रीदार *[kharīdār]* M buyer, vendor
खरोंच *[kharõc]* F scratch, bruise
खरोंचना *[kharõcnā]* V.T. to scratch, to bruise
ख़र्च *[kharc]* M expenditure, expense
ख़र्चा *[kharcā]* M expenditure, expense, cost
खर्राटा *[kharraṭā]* M snore; खर्राटा भरना *[kharraṭā bharnā]* V.T. to snore
खलना *[khalnā]* V.I. to feel offended/bad
खलबली *[khalbalī]* F agitation, commotion
ख़लास *[khalās]* ADJ discharged; emptied, released
खाँसना *[khā̃snā]* V.I. to cough
खाँसी *[khā̃sī]* F cough
खाई *[khāī]* F ditch, trench, moat
ख़ाक *[khāk]* F ashes, dirt and dust; anything trivial
ख़ाका *[khākā]* M sketch; outline; map
खाट *[khāṭ]* F cot, bedstead
खाड़ी *[khāṛī]* F bay
खाता *[khātā]* M account, ledger
ख़ातिर *[khātir]* F hospitality IND for the sake of, for
ख़ातिरदार *[khātirdār]* ADJ hospitable
ख़ातिरदारी *[khātirdārī]* F hospitality
खादी *[khādī]* see खद्दर.
ख़ानदान *[khāndān]* M family, kinsfolk
खान-पान *[khān-pān]* M (the mode and manner of) eating and drinking; living; social relationship
खाना *[khānā]* M food V.T. to eat
ख़ाना *[khānā]* M shelf, column, compartment
ख़ामी *[khāmī]* F defect, flaw
ख़ामोश *[khāmoś]* ADJ silent
ख़ामोशी *[khāmośī]* F silence
खारा *[khārā]* ADJ brackish, saline, salty
ख़ारिज *[khārij]* ADJ dismissed; rejected
खाल *[khāl]* F skin; hide
ख़ालिस *[khālis]* ADJ pure, uncontaminated
ख़ाली *[khālī]* ADJ empty; free

ख़ास *[khās]* ADJ special
ख़ासा *[khāsā]* ADJ fairly good
ख़ासियत *[khāsiyat]* F quality, special feature
खिंचना *[khĩcnā]* V.I. to pull, to be tightened F the act of pulling or tightening
खिचड़ी *[khicṛī]* F a dish made from lentils and rice boiled together; a mixture; a hotch-potch
खिड़की *[khiṛkī]* F window
ख़िताब *[khitāb]* F title
ख़िदमत *[khidmat]* F service
खिन्न *[khinna]* ADJ gloomy, sad, glum, depressed
खिलखिलाना *[khikhilānā]* V.I. to burst into laughter, to laugh out loud
खिलना *[khilnā]* V.I. to blossom; to bloom; to blow; to be delighted
खिलाड़ी *[khilāṛī]* M player; sportsman
खिलाना *[khilānā]* V.T. to feed; to make blossom; to make play
ख़िलाफ़ *[khilāf]* ADJ against, opposed
खिलौना *[khilaunā]* M toy, plaything
खिसकना *[khisaknā]* V.I. to move slowly; to move farther, to slip away
खींचना *[khĩcnā]* V.T. to pull, to draw
खीर *[khīr]* F rice pudding
खीरा *[khīrā]* M cucumber
खुजली *[khujlī]* F itch, itching sensation
खुजाना *[khujānā]* V.T. to itch; to scratch
खुट्टी *[khuṭṭī]* F severance of friendship (among children)
ख़ुद *[khud]* ADV (by) oneself
ख़ुदा *[khudā]* M God; ख़ुदा हाफ़िज़ *[khudā hāfiz]* May God protect you (used in Urdu when leaving)
ख़ुफ़िया *[khufiyā]* ADJ, M detective; a spy or detective
ख़ुबानी *[khubānī]* F apricot
खुलना *[khulnā]* V.I. to open
ख़ुश *[khuś]* ADJ happy
ख़ुशक़िस्मत *[khuśqismat]* ADJ fortunate; lucky
ख़ुशक़िस्मती *[khuśqismatī]* F good fortune; good luck
ख़ुशख़बरी *[khuśkhabrī]* F good news
ख़ुशनसीब *[khuśnasīb]* ADJ fortunate, lucky

खुशबू *[khuśbū]* F fragrance, aroma; perfume, scent
खुशबूदार *[khuśbūdār]* ADJ fragrant; perfumed; aromatic
खुशमिज़ाज *[khuśmizāj]* ADJ cheerful, happy
खुशहाल *[khuśhāl]* ADJ prosperous, well-to-do, flourishing
खुशामद *[khuśāmad]* F flattery
खुशामदीद *[khuśāmadīd]* IND welcome
खुशी *[khuśī]* F happiness
खूँटा *[khū̃ṭā]* M stake, peg
खूँटी *[khū̃ṭī]* F a small stake; a small peg
खून *[khūn]* M blood
खूनी *[khūnī]* M murderer, assassin ADJ blood-thirsty; ferocious
खूब *[khūb]* ADJ lot; excellent; good; beautiful
खूबसूरत *[khūbsūrat]* ADJ beautiful; pretty; handsome
खूबसूरती *[khūbsūratī]* F beauty, prettiness
खूबी *[khūbī]* F merit; characteristic quality; specialty
खेत *[khet]* M field; farm
खेती *[khetī]* F farming; cultivation; agriculture;
खेती-बाड़ी *[khetī-bāṛī]* F farming; agriculture
खेद *[khed]* M regret, sorrow
खेना *[khenā]* V.T. to row (a boat) M tent, camp
खेल *[khel]* M game; match; sport; show
खेल-कूद *[khel-kūd]* M sports
खेलना *[khelnā]* V.I., V.T. to play; to stage (a play)
ख़ैर *[khair]* F well-being, welfare IND well! All right!
ख़ैरियत *[khairiyat]* F well-being, safety
खोंसना *[khõsnā]* V.T. to tuck in, to stuff in, to thrust in
खोखला *[khokhlā]* ADJ empty, hollow
खोज *[khoj]* F search; quest; investigation; discovery; exploration
खोजना *[khojnā]* V.I to search; to inquire, to seek; to explore
खोटा *[khoṭā]* ADJ defective, faulty; false; counterfeit; spurious
खोदना *[khodnā]* V.T. to dig; to engrave; to excavate
खोना *[khonā]* V.I., V.T. to lose
खोपड़ी *[khopṛī]* F skull
खोया *[khoyā]* M condensed

milk; a milk product made from boiling down milk; masculine singular perfect participle of the verb खोना
खोल *[khol]* M cover; sheath; shell
खोलना *[kholnā]* V.T. to open; to unfold; to untie
ख़ौफ़ *[khauf]* M fear, dread
ख़ौफ़नाक *[khaufnāk]* ADJ fearful, dreadful, terrible
खौलना *[khaulnā]* V.I. to boil (as in blood)
ख्यात *[khyāt]* ADJ reputed, celebrated, famous
ख्याति *[khyāti]* F fame; reputation
ख़्याल/ख़याल *[khyāl/khayāl]* M idea, thought; view, opinion
ख़्वाब *[khvāb]* M dream
ख़्वाहमख़्वाह *[khvāhamkhvāh]* IND uselessly, for no reason; without any purpose
ख़्वाहिश *[khvāhiś]* M desire, wish

ग

गंगा *[gaṅgā]* F Ganges (name of a river in India)
गंजा *[gañjā]* ADJ bald
गंजापन *[gañjāpan]* M baldness
गँठबंधन *[gãṭhbandhan]* M alliance
गंदगी *[gandagī]* F dirt, filth; morbidity
गँदला *[gãdlā]* ADJ muddy (as in water); overcast
गंदा *[gandā]* ADJ dirty, filthy; morbid
गंध *[gandh]* F smell, odor
गंभीर *[gambhīr]* ADJ serious; grave; sober; grim
गंभीरता *[gambhīrtā]* F seriousness, gravity
गँवाना *[gãvānā]* V.T. to waste; to lose; to squander
गँवार *[gãvār]* ADJ uncivilized; rustic; stupid
गँवारू *[gãvārū]* ADJ rustic; rude; vulgar
गगन *[gagan]* M sky; firmament
ग़ज़ब *[ghazab]* F calamity; fury, wrath; tyranny, outrage
ग़ज़ल *[ghazal]* F popular genre of Urdu poetry that may also be sung
गठबंधन *[gaṭhbandhan]* M alliance
गठरी *[gaṭhrī]* F bundle, package

गड़गड़ाना *[gargaṛānā]* V.I. to gurgle; to rumble
गड़ना *[garṇā]* V.I. be buried, to penetrate; to be fixed, to stick into
गड़बड़ *[gaṛbaṛ]* F muddle, mess; confusion, disorder, disquiet
गड़बड़ाना *[gaṛbaṛānā]* V.I. to be confused/confounded; to be spoilt
गड्ढा *[gaḍḍhā]* M pit; ditch; hollow; loss
गढ़ *[gaṛh]* M a fort, castle, citadel
गढ़ना *[gaṛhnā]* V.T. to forge; to mold; to fabricate
गण *[gaṇ]* M a community, union, group; a body
गणतंत्र *[gaṇtantra]* M republic; republic system of government
गणराज्य *[gaṇrājya]* M republic
गणित *[gaṇit]* M mathematics
गणेश *[gaṇeś]* M Ganesh, a popular Hindu deity with the head of an elephant, symbolizing wisdom and auspiciousness
गति *[gati]* F motion, movement
गतिविधि *[gatividhi]* F activity; goings-on
ग़दर *[ghadar]* M rebellion; mutiny
गदा *[gadā]* M club
गद्गद *[gadgad]* ADJ overwhelmed (by emotion); *[gadgad]* ADJ speechless
गद्दा *[gaddā]* M a bed cushion; cushion
ग़द्दार *[ghaddār]* M, ADJ traitor; traitorous
गद्दी *[gaddī]* F a cushion; throne; seat (slang for a car)
गद्य *[gadya]* M prose
गधा *[gadhā]* M ass, donkey; fool, stupid person
ग़नीमत *[ghanīmat]* F redeeming feature; consoling factor; consolation
गन्ना *[ganna]* M sugarcane
गपशप *[gapśap]* F gossip; chit-chat
गप्पी *[gappī]* M gossiper; chatterer ADJ boastful
ग़फ़लत *[ghaflat]* F negligence; carelessness; swoon
ग़बन *[ghaban]* M embezzlement
गबरू *[gabrū]* ADJ youthful; young
ग़म *[gham]* M grief, woe

ग़मगीन *[ghamgīn]* ADJ grief-stricken; full of sorrow
गमला *[gamlā]* M flowerpot
गया *[gayā]* V.I. went, gone; perfect participle of जाना
गरज *[garaj]* F thunder, roar
गरजना *[garajnā]* V.I. to thunder, to roar
गरम/गर्म *[garam/garm]* ADJ hot
गरमी/गर्मी *[garamī/garmī]* F heat; summer; warmth; passion; anger; गर्मी के दिन *[garmī ke din]* M, PL days of heat, summer
गरमागरम *[garmāgarm]* ADJ hot; heated
गरिमा *[garimā]* F dignity; honor; grace
ग़रीब *[gharīb]* ADJ poor
ग़रीबख़ाना *[gharībkhānā]* M a humble dwelling (used to describe one's own home)
ग़रीबनिवाज़ *[gharībnivāz]* ADJ kind to the poor
ग़रीबी *[gharībī]* F poverty; penury
गर्द *[gard]* F dirt; dust
गर्दन *[gardan]* F neck
गर्भ *[garbh]* M the womb; pregnancy; the interior
गर्भवती *[garbhvatī]* ADJ pregnant
गर्म *[garm]* ADJ *see* गरम
गर्मी *[garmī]* F *see* गरमी
गर्व *[garv]* M pride; elation
ग़लत *[ghalat]* ADJ wrong, incorrect; untrue; erroneous
ग़लतफ़हमी *[ghatalfehmī]* F misunderstanding, misgiving
ग़लती *[ghaltī]* F mistake, error, fault
गलना *[galnā]* V.I. to melt; to decay; to rot; to be boiled or cooked till softened
गला *[galā]* M throat
गलियारा *[galiyārā]* M a gallery, corridor
गली *[galī]* F lane, gully; गली-कूचा *[galī-kūcā]* M lanes and bylanes
ग़लीज़ *[ghalīz]* ADJ dirty; filthy
गवर्मेंट *[gavarmeṇṭ]* F government
गवर्नर *[gavarnar]* M governor
गवाँना *[gavā̃nā]* V.T. to lose; to waste; to suffer detriment
गवाह *[gavāh]* M witness
गवाही *[gavāhī]* F evidence; testimony
गश्त *[gaśt]* F patrol; beat
गहन *[gehan]* ADJ deep;

intricate; obscure; mysterious;
गहनता *[gehantā]* F depth; intricacy; obscurity
गहना *[gehnā]* M ornament; jewelry
गहरा *[gehrā]* ADJ deep; profound; intimate
गहराई *[gehrāī]* F depth; profundity
गाँजा *[gā̃jā]* M hemp plant or its leaves
गाँठ *[gā̃ṭh]* F knot; tie; node; knob; bundle; hardened or enlarged gland
गाँठना *[gā̃ṭhnā]* V.T. to cobble; to stitch
गाँड *[gā̃ḍ]* F anus
गांधी *[gāndhī]* M (Mohandas Karamchand) Gandhi; गांधी टोपी *[gāndhī ṭopī]* F a white cloth hat made famous by Gandhi because of the economical use of cloth
गांधीवाद *[gāndhīvād]* M Gandhism
गाँव *[gā̃v]* M village
गाइड *[gāiḍ]* M a guide
गागर *[gāgar]* M an earthen pitcher
गाजर *[gājar]* F carrot
गाड़ना *[gāṛnā]* V.T. to bury; to lay; to implant; to fix; to pitch
गाड़ी *[gāṛī]* F car, vehicle, train
गाढ़ा *[gāṛhā]* ADJ thick, dense; close
गान *[gān]* M song; singing;
गाना *[gānā]* M song V.T. to sing
ग़ाफ़िल *[ghāfil]* ADJ negligent; unaware
गाय *[gāy]* F cow ADJ meek and humble
गायक *[gāyak]* M singer; musician; vocalist
ग़ायब *[ghāyab]* ADJ vanished; disappeared; lost
गाल *[gāl]* M cheek
ग़ालिब *[ghālib]* ADJ predominant; overpowering; overwhelming
गाली *[gālī]* F abuse; invective; abusive songs sung by women at the time of weddings
गाहक *[gāhak]* M customer, purchaser; client
गिड़गिड़ाना *[giṛgiṛānā]* V.I. to entreat; to beseech, to implore humbly
गिड़गिड़ाहट *[giṛgiṛāhaṭ]* F humble; entreaty

गिद्ध *[giddh]* M vulture
गिनती *[gintī]* F counting; calculation; reckoning
गिनना *[ginnā]* V.T. to count; to enumerate
गिने चुने *[gine cune]* ADJ select few
गिरगिट *[girgiṭ]* M chameleon
गिरजा(घर) *[girjā(ghar)]* M church
गिरना *[girnā]* V.I. to fall
गिरफ़्तार *[giraftār]* ADJ arrested
गिरफ़्तारी *[giraftārī]* F arrest, capture
गिरवी *[girvī]* F, ADJ mortgage(d); pawn(ed)
गिरह *[gireh]* F knot; joint
गिराना *[girānā]* V.T. to make (something) fall
गिरावट *[girāvaṭ]* F fall; downfall; degradation; slump
गिरि *[giri]* M mountain; hill
गिरोह *[giroh]* M gang; group
गिर्द *[gird]* IND around, all around
गिलहरी *[gilharī]* F squirrel
गिला *[gilā]* M complaint; reproach
गिलाफ़ *[gilāf]* M cover; pillow cover; case
गिलौरी *[gilaurī]* F a stuffed and folded betel leaf
गिल्ली *[gillī]* F a toggle;
गिल्ली-डंडा *[gillī-ḍaṇḍā]* M a particular Indian game played with a stick and a toggle
गीत *[gīt]* M song, a lyrical poem
गीदड़ *[gīdaṛ]* M a jackel
गीला *[gīlā]* ADJ moist, wet
गीलापन *[gīlāpan]* M moisture
गुंजाइश *[gujāiś]* F scope; capacity
गुंडा *[guṇḍā]* M, ADJ rogue, scoundrel, hoodlum, hooligan
गुंडागीरी *[guṇḍāgīrī]* F hooliganism
गुँथना *[gũthnā]* V.I. to be threaded; to be stitched; to be plaited
गुँधना *[gũdhnā]* V.I. to be kneaded
गुंबद *[gumbad]* M dome; vault
गुच्छा *[gucchā]* M bunch, cluster
गुज़रना *[guzarnā]* V.I. to pass (by); to pass away
गुज़ारना *[guzārnā]* V.T. to pass (time)
गुज़ारा *[guzārā]* M subsistence; livelihood
गुज़ारिश *[guzāriś]* F submission; supplication

गुझिया *[ghujhiyā]* F *gujhiya*, a type of Indian sweetmeat
गुट *[guṭ]* M block; faction; clique; group
गुटिका *[guṭikā]* F a tablet, pill
गुड़ *[guṛ]* F jaggery
गुड़गुड़ *[guṛguṛ]* M a bubbling noise (produced by smoking a *hooqah*)
गुड़िया *[guṛiyā]* F doll
गुण *[guṇ]* M quality
गुणवान *[guṇvān]* ADJ meritorious; possessing good qualities
गुणा *[guṇā]* M multiplication
गुत्थी *[gutthī]* F knot; entanglement; riddle, enigma
गुथना *[guthnā]* V.I. to interweave, to become entwined
गुदगुदा *[gudgudā]* ADJ soft; plump
गुदगुदाना *[gudgudānā]* V.I. to tickle; to titillate
गुदगुदी *[gudgudī]* F tickling sensation
गुदना *[gudnā]* M tattoo V.I. to be tattooed
गुनगुना *[gungunā]* ADJ lukewarm, tepid
गुनगुनाना *[gungunānā]* V.I. to hum; to sing to oneself in subdued tones
गुनाह *[gunāh]* M sin, fault, guilt
गुनाहगार *[gunāhgār]* ADJ guilty
गुप्त *[gupt]* ADJ secret; hidden, latent
गुफा *[guphā]* F cave, cavern
गुफ़्तगू *[guftāgū]* F conversation
ग़ुबार *[g͟hubār]* M dirt; dust; affliction
गुम *[gum]* ADJ lost
गुमराह *[gumrāh]* ADJ misled
गुमशुदा *[gumśudā]* ADJ lost
गुरदा *[gurdā]* M kidney; courage
गुरु *[guru]* M, ADJ teacher; mentor; preceptor; heavy, grave
गुरुत्व *[gurutva]* M gravity
गुरुद्वारा *[gurudvārā]* M Gurdwara (Sikh temple)
गुरुवार *[guruvār]* M Thursday
गुर्राना *[gurrānā]* V.I. to growl; to snarl
गुल *[gul]* M flower; the lighted ash of a cigarette
गुलज़ार *[gulzār]* M a garden
गुलदस्ता *[guldastā]* M a bouquet
गुलदान *[guldān]* M vase

गुलाब *[gulāb]* M rose
गुलाबी *[gulābī]* ADJ rosy
गुलाबजामुन *[gulābjāmun]* M *gulabjamun* (fried sweet dumpling)
ग़ुलाम *[ghulām]* M slave
ग़ुलामी *[ghulāmī]* F slavery; servility
गुलाल *[gulāl]* M colored powder thrown at the time of Holi
गुल्लक *[gullak]* M till; cashbox; a money box
गुल्ली *[gullī]* *see* गिल्ली
ग़ुसलख़ाना *[ghuslkhānā]* M bathroom; bath
गुस्ताख़ी *[gustākhī]* F impertinence; imprudence
ग़ुस्सा *[ghussā]* M anger, rage, fury
गूँगा *[gū̃gā]* ADJ mute, unable to talk
गूँज *[gū̃j]* F an echo
गूँजना *[gū̃jnā]* V.I. to echo, to resound
गूँथना *[gū̃thnā]* V.T. to braid (hair); to plait
गूँधना *[gū̃dhnā]* V.T. to knead
गूढ़ *[gūṛh]* ADJ occult; mysterious, obscure
गृह *[gr̥h]* M a residence
गृहस्थ *[gr̥hasth]* M householder
गृहस्थाश्रम *[gr̥hasthāśram]* M the second stage of the four stages of life or the householder stage
गृहस्थी *[gr̥hasthī]* F household; family
गृहिणी *[gr̥hiṇī]* F wife, housewife
गेंद *[gẽd]* F ball
गेहुँआ *[gehũā]* ADJ wheat-colored; wheatish (complexion)
गेहूँ *[gehū̃]* M wheat
गैंडा *[gaĩḍā]* M rhinoceros
ग़ैर *[ghair]* ADJ, M strange; a stranger; other; (pre) un-, non-, in-; ग़ैर क़ानूनी *[ghair-qānūnī]* ADJ illegal
ग़ैरत *[ghairat]* F sense of honor, self-respect
गैस *[gais]* F gas
ग़ोता *[ghotā]* M dive; dip
गोद *[god]* F lap; गोद लेना *[god lenā]* V.T. to adopt (a child)
गोदना *[godnā]* V.T. to tattoo; to pick; to prick
गोदना *[godnā]* V.T. to puncture
गोदी *[godī]* F lap

गोबर *[gobar]* M cow-dung; dung
गोभी *[gobhī]* F cauliflower
गोरा *[gorā]* ADJ fair-skinned; white M a fair-skinned person
गोल *[gol]* ADJ round, circular; globular; गोल-गप्पा *[gol-gappā]* M a small cake-like Indian preparation eaten with spiced water
गोला *[golā]* M ball; cannon-ball; bomb shell; गोला-बारी *[golā-bārī]* F shelling, bombardment
गोलार्ध *[golārdh]* M hemisphere
गोली *[golī]* F tablet; pill; bullet
गोश्त *[gośt]* M meat, flesh
ग़ौर *[ghaur]* M reflection; deliberation, consideration
गौरव *[gaurav]* M pride, honor
ग्यारह *[gyārah]* ADJ eleven
ग्यारहवाँ *[gyārahvā̃]* ADJ eleventh
ग्रंथ *[granth]* M book, tome
ग्रस्त *[grast]* ADJ caught; possessed by; involved in; तनावग्रस्त *[tanāvgrast]* ADJ anxious, stressed
ग्रह *[greh]* M planet
ग्रहण *[grahaṇ]* M eclipse; taking, catching
ग्राम *[grām]* M village; a gram
ग्रामीण *[grāmīṇ]* ADJ villager; rural
ग्रास *[grās]* M morsel
ग्राहक *[grāhak]* M customer; client
ग्रीक *[grīk]* ADJ Greek
ग्रीष्म *[grīṣm]* M summer; ग्रीष्म ऋतु *[grīṣm ṛtu]* F the summer season
ग्लानि *[glāni]* F langor; fatigue; depression; remorse

घ

घंटा *[ghaṇṭā]* M hour; bell
घंटी *[ghaṇṭī]* F a small bell
घटना *[ghaṭnā]* F incident; event; incidence, occurrence; V.I. to happen; to be subtracted; to decrease, to lessen
घटा *[ghaṭā]* F a dark cloud
घटाना *[ghaṭānā]* V.T. to reduce
घटिया *[ghaṭiyā]* ADJ, INVAR inferior, of low quality
घड़ा *[ghaṛā]* M pitcher, pot
घड़ियाल *[ghaṛiyāl]* M alligator, crocodile
घड़ी *[ghaṛī]* F watch

घन *[ghan]* ADJ dense; solid
घनघोर *[ghanghor]* ADJ very dense; terrible, profound
घनता *[ghantā]* F density, solidity
घना *[ghanā]* ADJ dense, thick; intensive
घनिष्ठ *[ghaniṣṭh]* ADJ close; closest, most intimate
घपला *[ghaplā]* M bungling; mess; confusion; disorder
घबराना/घबड़ाना *[ghabrānā/ ghabṛānā]* V.I. to be nervous; anxious
घबराहट/घबड़ाहट *[ghabrāhaṭ/ ghabṛāhaṭ]* F nervousness; panic
घमंड *[ghamaṇḍ]* M conceit; vanity; arrogance
घमंडी *[ghamaṇḍī]* ADJ conceited, vain; arrogant
घर *[ghar]* M home; घर घर *[ghar ghar]* ADV each and every home
घराना *[gharānā]* M a family, clan
घरेलू *[gharelū]* ADJ domestic; private
घसीटना *[ghasīṭnā]* V.T. to drag; to trail
घाघरा *[ghāghrā]* M petticoat
घाट *[ghāṭ]* M wharf; quay; berth; ferry
घाटा *[ghāṭā]* M loss; deficit
घाटी *[ghāṭī]* F valley; mountain pass
घात *[ghāt]* F ambush; killing; slaughter; stroke
घातक *[ghātak]* ADJ lethal; fatal; ruinous
घाम *[ghām]* M sunshine; heat of the sun
घायल *[ghāyal]* ADJ wounded, injured
घाव *[ghāv]* M wound, injury
घास *[ghās]* F grass; घास काटना/खोदना/छीलना *[ghās kāṭnā/khodnā/chīlnā]* V.T. to idle away one's time
घिघियाना *[ghighiyānā]* V.I. to grovel in the dust; to beg for mercy
घिन *[ghin]* F abhorrence; nausea
घिनौना *[ghinaunā]* ADJ abominable; loathsome; odious
घिरना *[ghirnā]* V.I. to be surrounded
घिसटना *[ghisaṭnā]* V.I. to be dragged
घिसना *[ghisnā]* V.I. rubbed; to be worn; to wear out

घी *[ghī]* M ghee; clarified butter
घुँघरू *[ghũghrū]* M a set of small jingling bells (worn around ankles during a dance performance)
घुटना *[ghuṭnā]* V.I. suffocated; to experience suffocation M knee
घुड़सवार *[ghuṛsavār]* M a horse-rider
घुड़सवारी *[ghuṛsavārī]* F horse-riding
घुड़की *[ghuṛkī]* F hollow threat; rebuff
घुप्प *[ghuppa]* ADJ pitch (as in black); घुप्प अंधेरा *[ghuppa ãdherā]* M pitch black
घुमड़ना *[ghumaṛnā]* V.I. to gather up (as in clouds); to converge
घुमाना *[ghumānā]* V.T. to make revolve; to make wander; to take around
घुलना *[ghulnā]* V.I. dissolved; liquified; to be mixed
घुसना *[ghusnā]* V.I. to enter; to penetrate
घुसपैठ *[ghuspaiṭh]* F intrusion; infiltration
घुसपैठिया *[ghuspaiṭhiyā]* M intruder
घूँघट *[ghũghaṭ]* M veil
घूँट *[ghũṭ]* M draught; sip; a gulp
घूमना *[ghūmnā]* V.I. to revolve; to wander
घूरना *[ghūrnā]* V.T. stare (at); to gloat
घूस *[ghūs]* F bribe, illegal gratification
घृणा *[ghṛṇā]* F hatred; scorn; abhorrence, loathing
घेरना *[ghernā]* V.T. to surround; to beseige; to encircle
घेरा *[gherā]* M seige; enclosure
घोटना *[ghoṭnā]* V.T. to cram; to commit to memory
घोटाला *[ghoṭālā]* M bungling; confusion
घोड़ा *[ghoṛā]* M horse; hammer of a gun
घोर *[ghor]* ADJ awful; formidable; terrible
घोलना *[gholnā]* V.T. to dissolve; to mix
घोषणा *[ghoṣṇā]* F announcement; proclamation
घोषित *[ghoṣit]* ADJ declared; proclaimed

च

चंगा *[caṅgā]* ADJ healed, recovered; good, sound
चंगुल *[caṅgul]* M claw; talon; clutch, grasp
चंचल *[cañcal]* ADJ fickle, unsteady, transient, quivering, shaking, restless, skittish, playful, coquettish, nimble; चंचलता *[cañcaltā]* F unsteadiness; transience; fickleness; restlessness; skittishness
चंड *[caṇḍ]* ADJ fierce, furious; violent; powerful
चंद *[cand]* M moon
चंदन *[candan]* M sandalwood
चंदा *[candā]* M moon; subscription; contribution; donation
चंद्र *[candra]* M moon
चंद्रबिंदु *[candrabindu]* M the nasal symbol represented by a dot and a cresent shape
चंपा *[campā]* M a fragrant light yellow flower and its tree (*michelia champaca*) used in incense
चकला *[caklā]* M brothel; a circular wooden or stone board for rolling dough
चकित *[cakit]* ADJ amazed; surprised; flabbergasted
चक्कर *[cakkar]* M circle; revolution; rotation; odd affair; चक्कर आना *[cakkar ānā]* V.I. to feel giddy
चखना *[cakhnā]* V.T. to taste; to relish
चचा *[cacā]* M paternal uncle (father's younger brother)
चचेरा *[cacerā]* ADJ relating to one's paternal uncle; चचेरा भाई *[cacerā bhāī]* M first cousin (male); चचेरी बहन *[cacerī behan]* F first cousin (female)
चट *[caṭ]* ADV instantly, instantaneously, at once
चटनी *[caṭnī]* F chutney
चटपटा *[caṭpaṭā]* ADJ pungent; spicy
चटपटापन *[caṭpaṭāpan]* M pungency
चटाई *[caṭāī]* F mat
चटाना *[caṭānā]* V.T. to cause to lick; to bribe
चट्टान *[caṭṭān]* F rock; cliff
चड्डी *[caḍḍī]* F underwear (esp for children)
चढ़ना *[caṛhnā]* V.I. to go up; to

ascend; to climb; to rise; to mount; to launch an attack.
चढ़ाई *[caṛhāī]* F ascent, climb; rise; invasion
चढ़ाना *[caṛhānā]* V.T. to cause to go up, to raise; to offer; to place on the fire for cooking
चढ़ाव *[caṛhāv]* M ascent; rise; an ornamental gift for a bride from the bridegroom's side
चतुर *[catur]* ADJ clever; shrewd; skilful
चतुराई *[caturāī]* F cleverness; skill; dexterity
चतुर्थ *[caturth]* ADJ fourth
चद्दर *[caddar]* F *see* चादर
चना *[canā]* M gram; chickpea
चपटी *[capṭī]* F a sexual act between two women
चपत *[capat]* M a slap
चपरासी *[caprāsī]* peon; subordinate
चपल *[capal]* ADJ unsteady; wavering; fickle; restless
चपलता *[capaltā]* F unsteadiness; flippancy
चपाती *[capātī]* F a thin Indian style of bread, cooked most commonly on an iron griddle
चपेट *[capeṭ]* F striking range; stroke (of bad luck etc)
चप्पल *[cappal]* F sandal, slipper
चबाना *[cabānā]* V.T. to chew; to munch; to masticate
चबूतरा *[cabūtrā]* M a raised platform
चमकना *[camaknā]* V.I. to shine; to glitter; to sparkle; to flash
चमकीला *[camkīlā]* ADJ shiny, radiant; brilliant, bright; showy
चमगादड़ *[camgādaṛ]* M bat; vampire
चमचमाना *[camcamānā]* V.I. to shine; to glitter; to sparkle
चमचा *[camcā]* M a large spoon; flunkey; sycophant
चमड़ा *[camṛā]* M leather; hide; skin
चमड़ी *[camṛī]* F skin
चमत्कार *[camatkār]* M miracle, wonder; spectacle
चमन *[caman]* M a small garden; a bed of flowers in a garden
चमार *[camār]* M cobbler, shoe-maker; a scheduled caste among Hindus that traditionally worked with leather

चमेली *[camelī]* F a kind of jasmine (the plant and its flower)
चम्मच *[cammac]* M spoon
चयन *[cayan]* M selection; picking; चयन समिति *[cayan samiti]* F selection committee
चर *[car]* M spy; secret messenger
चरखा *[carkhā]* M a spinning wheel
चरबी *[carbī]* F fat, fats and oils; grease; tallow
चरस *[caras]* M an intoxicating drug prepared from the flowers of hemp
चराना *[carānā]* V.T. to graze; to hoodwink; to fool
चरित्र *[caritra]* M character
चर्चा *[carcā]* F mention; discussion; rumor
चर्चित *[carcit]* ADJ discussed; mentioned
चर्बी *[carbī] see* चरबी
चर्म *[carm]* M leather; skin; hide
चल *[cal]* ADJ unsteady; transient; inconstant
चलता *[caltā]* F movability; unsteadiness ADJ mobile, current
चलन *[calan]* M vogue; usage; custom; conduct
चलना *[calnā]* V.I. to move; to walk; to proceed; to be in vogue; to last; to flow; to blow
चलनी *[calnī]* F a sieve
चलाऊ *[calāū]* ADJ durable; serviceable; lasting; काम चलाऊ *[kām calāū]* ADJ workable; serviceable
चलाना *[calānā]* V.T. to make (something or someone) move; to drive; to operate (a machine)
चवालीस *[cavālīs]* ADJ forty-four
चश्म *[caśm]* M eye
चश्मा *[caśmā]* M spectacles; fountain; spring; धूप का चश्मा *[dhūp kā caśmā]* M sunglasses
चसका *[caskā]* M addiction; proclivity
चहक *[cehak]* F chirping; warbling
चहकना *[cehaknā]* V.I. to chirp; to warble (as in a bird)
चहचहाना *[cehcahānā]* V.I. to chirp; to warble
चहलक़दमी *[cehalqadamī]* F strolling; a leisurely walk

चहल-पहल *[cehal-pehal]* F hustle and bustle; commotion; gaiety
चहेता *[cahetā]* ADJ beloved; favorite
चाँटा *[cā̃ṭā]* M slap
चाँद *[cā̃d]* M moon
चाँदनी *[cā̃dnī]* F moonlight
चाँदी *[cā̃dī]* F silver
चाकर *[cākar]* M servant; menial attendant
नौकर-चाकर *[naukar-cākar]* M, PL servants, retinue
चाकरी *[cākrī]* F service, attendance
चाक़ू *[cāqū]* M knife; चाक़ू घोंपना/भोंकना *[cāqū ghõpnā/bhõknā]* V.T. to stab with a knife
चाखना *[cākhnā]* V.T. to taste, to relish
चाचा *[cācā]* M paternal uncle
चाची *[cācī]* F paternal uncle's wife; aunt
चाट *[cāṭ]* F spicy, fast food
चाटना *[cāṭnā]* V.T. to lick
चादर *[cādar]* F sheet; bedsheet; bed cover
चापलूस *[cāplūs]* ADJ flattering; sycophantic
चापलूसी *[cāplūsī]* F flattery; sycophancy
चाबी *[cābī]* F key
चाबुक *[cābuk]* M whip, flog; lash
चाभी *[cābhī]* F *see* चाबी.
चाय *[cāy]* F tea; चायदानी *[cāydānī]* F teapot
चार *[cār]* ADJ four; चार दिन का मेहमान *[cār din kā mehmān]* M having fleeting existence
चारों *[cārõ]* ADJ all four; चारों तरफ़ *[cārõ taraf]* ADJ in all four directions
चारपाई *[cārpāī]* F bed, cot
चारा *[cārā]* M fodder; feed; bait; lure; remedy; means
चारु *[cāru]* ADJ beautiful, appealing; attractive
चाल *[cāl]* F gait; speed; move; trick; device; custom; चाल चलना *[cāl calnā]* V.T. to play a trick; to make a deft move
चालक *[cālak]* M driver, conductor
चालाक *[cālāk]* ADJ cunning; crafty; clever
चालाकी *[cālākī]* F cunningness, craftiness
चालान *[cālān]* M invoice; traffic; citation

चालीस *[cālīs]* ADJ forty
चालीसवाँ *[cālīsvā̃]* ADJ fortieth
चालू *[cālū]* ADJ current; running; prevalent; cunning; unscrupulous; of easy virtue
चावल *[cāval]* M rice
चाछनी *[cāchnī]* F treacle; syrup
चाह *[cāh]* F liking, love, craving; desire; will
चाहत *[cāhat]* F liking; love; fondness
चाहना *[cāhnā]* V.T. to want
चाहिये/चाहिए *[cāhiye/cahie]* INVAR wanted/needed (subject takes को)
चाहे...चाहे... *[cāhe…cāhe…]* IND either…or…; चाहे जो भी हो *[cāhe jo bhī ho]* whatever may happen
चिंघाड़ना *[ciṅghāṛnā]* V.T. to trumpet (as an elephant); to roar angrily
चिंतन *[cintan]* M thinking; reflection; musing
चिंता *[cintā]* F worry, concern, anxiety
चिंतित *[cintit]* ADJ perturbed; worried; anxious
चिकना *[ciknā]* ADJ smooth; glossy; oily or greasy
चिकनाई *[ciknāī]* F smoothness; greasiness; fat; lubricant
चिकनाहट *[ciknāhaṭ]* F greasiness; fattiness
चिकित्सा *[cikitsā]* F treatment; remedy; medication
चिट *[ciṭ]* F a chit; a small piece of paper for lists etc
चिट्ठी *[ciṭṭhī]* F letter
चिड़िया *[ciṛiyā]* F bird
चिड़ियाघर *[ciṛiyāghar]* M zoo
चिढ़ *[ciṛh]* F irritation; strong aversion
चिढ़ना *[ciṛhnā]* V.I. irritated; teased V.T. to tease; to mock
चित *[cit]* ADJ supine; (lying) on the back M mind, heart
चितवन *[citvan]* F (compelling) glance; look
चिता *[citā]* F funeral pyre
चित्त *[citta]* M mind, heart
चित्र *[citra]* M picture; चित्र-कला *[citra-kalā]* F the art of painting
चित्रण *[citraṇ]* M portrayal, delineation; painting, drawing
चिथड़ा *[cithṛā]* M rag, a shred of clothing, tatter
चिनगारी *[cingārī]* F spark

चिनमय *[cinmay]* ADJ conscious M all consciousness
चिन्ह *[cinha]* M *see* चिह्न
चिपकना *[cipaknā]* V.I. to stick, to adhere, to cling
चिपकाना *[cipkānā]* V.T. to paste; to stick (something); to cause to cling; to embrace
चिपकू *[cipkū]* ADJ, M a hanger-on
चिपटना *[cipaṭnā]* V.I. to cling; to hang on; to embrace
चिमटना *[cimaṭnā]* V.I. to cling; to hang on; to embrace
चिमटा *[cimṭā]* M tongs; pincers
चिमटाना *[cimṭānā]* V.T. to embrace; to stick to
चिमटी *[cimṭī]* F forceps; tweezers; pincers
चिरना *[cirnā]* V.I. torn; to be split
चिराग़ *[cirāgh]* M lamp; a light
चिलम *[cilam]* F an earthen or metallic vessel on the top of a *hookah* that contains tobacco and is lit; pipe
चिल्लाना *[cillānā]* V.I. to scream, to shout
चिह्न/चिह्न *[cihna]* M sign, mark, marking
चींटा *[cĩṭā]* M ant
चींटी *[cĩṭī]* F ant
चींथना *[cĩthnā]* V.T. to tear to pieces
चीख़ *[cīkh]* F scream; shriek; screech
चीख़ना *[cīkhnā]* V.I. to scream
चीज़ *[cīz]* F thing; object; article; item; a commodity
चीड़ *[cīṛ]* M pine tree
चीता *[cītā]* M leopard; panther
चीथड़ा *[cīthṛā]* M, V rag, tatter, rend; to tear to pieces/tatters
चीन *[cīn]* M China
चीनी *[cīnī]* F sugar; ADJ Chinese
चीरना *[cīrnā]* V.T. to saw; to rend; to cleave; to tear; to dissect
चील *[cīl]* F kite (bird)
चुंबक *[cumbak]* M magnet
चुंबन *[cumbam]* M kissing
चुकटी *[cukṭī]* F handful, palmful
चुकना *[cuknā]* V.I. finished; spent, exhausted, completed; paid off
चुकाना *[cukānā]* V.T. to settle; to pay off, to defray
चुगना *[cugnā]* V.T. to peck (food off a plate)

चुग़ल *[cughal]* M back-biter; someone who talks behind another's back
चुग़ली *[cughlī]* F speaking ill of someone, malicious gossip; complaint
चुटकी *[cuṭkī]* F pinch, snapping with the finger
चुटकुला *[cuṭkulā]* M anecdote; joke, pleasantry
चुटिया *[cuṭiya]* F a lock of heir on the top of the head (kept by traditional Hindus)
चुड़ैल *[cuṛail]* F witch; shrew
चुदना *[cudnā]* V.I. to be the subject of sexual intercourse (by a male)
चुदाई *[cudāī]* F the act of copulation (by a male); the performance of a sexual act by a man
चुनना *[cunnā]* V.T. to select, to choose; to pick; to elect
चुनरी *[cunrī]* F a thin cloth with colored specks used to cover the upper body
चुनाँचे *[cunāce]* IND thus, therefore
चुनाव *[cunāv]* M election; selection
चुनिंदा *[cunindā]* ADJ selected, chosen
चुनौती *[cunautī]* F challenge
चुप *[cup]* ADJ silent; quiet
चुपचाप *[cupcāp]* ADV silently; quietly; stealthily
चुप्पी *[cuppī]* F silence
चुभन *[cubhan]* F prickling; pricking sensation
चुभना *[cubhnā]* V.I. pricked; to be pinched; to be punctured; to feel bad
चुभाना *[cubhānā]* V.T. prick; to pinch; to puncture; to pierce slightly
चुम्मा *[cummā]* M kiss
चुराना *[curānā]* V.T. steal
चुल्लू *[cullū]* M the sign of a hollow cup formed by joining two hands together
चुसकी *[cuskī]* F sip, a suck
चुस्त *[cust]* ADJ active; smart; agile
चुस्ती *[custī]* F agility; alertness
चूँकि *[cũki]* CONJ because, as
चूकना *[cūknā]* V.I. to miss; to fail; to err; to make a lapse
चूची *[cūcī]* F nipple, teat
चूड़ा *[cūṛī]* F bangle; ring, pucker
चूड़ी *[cūṛī]* F bangle

चूत *[cūt]* F vagina
चूतिया *[cūtiya]* M dolt, a stupid idiot, blockhead
चूना *[cūnā]* V.I. to leak, to drop; to ooze M lime
चूमना *[cūmnā]* V.T. kiss, to lock lips
चूमा *[cūmā]* M kiss; kissing
चूर *[cūr]* M filings, powder ADJ pulverized; steeped in, as in
चूरा *[cūrā]* M powder; filings; small fragments
चूल्हा *[cūlhā]* F stove; fire-place; hearth
चूसना *[cūsnā]* V.T. to suck, to suck dry; to sip; to exploit
चूहा *[cūhā]* M mouse, rat
चेक *[cek]* M cheque (check)
चेचक *[cecak]* F small pox
चेतना *[cetnā]* F consciousness; awareness; animation
चेतावनी *[cetāvnī]* F warning; an alarm
चेला *[celā]* M pupil; discipline
चेहरा *[cehrā]* M face; countenance; mask
चैत *[cait]* M the first month of the Hindu calendar
चैतन्य *[caitanya]* ADJ conscious; sensitive M consciousness
चैन *[cain]* M peace; rest; tranquility. calm
चोंच *[cõc]* F beak; bill; a dolt
चोट *[coṭ]* F injury, wound, blow, stroke
चोटी *[coṭī]* F apex; crown; braid; a lock of hair (kept by traditional Hindus)
चोदना *[codnā]* V.T. copulate; (for a man) to have sexual intercourse
चोदू *[codū]* M an adept exponent of copulation (with a woman); one who indulges in excessive sexual intercourse
चोर *[cor]* M thief
चोरी *[corī]* F theft
चोला *[colā]* M a long robe, gown; appearance; physical frame, body
चोली *[colī]* F brassiere; bodice
चौंकना *[caũknā]* V.I. startled, alarmed
चौंकाना *[caũkānā]* V.T. to startle, to alarm (someone)
चौंतीस *[caũtīs]* ADJ thirty-four
चौंसठ *[caũsaṭh]* ADJ sixty-four
चौकस *[caukas]* ADJ alert; watchful; cautious

चौकसी *[caukasī]* F watchfulness; vigilance
चौकोना *[caukonā]* ADJ four-sided
चौखट *[caukhaṭ]* F threshold; door frame
चौराहा *[caurāhā]* M crossroads
चौक *[cauk]* M marketplace; crossing; square
चौकी *[caukī]* F checkpost; a low square or rectangular seat
चौकीदार *[caukīdār]* M watchman; guard
चौकीदारी *[caukīdārī]* F watch; guarding; the office or job of a watchman
चौड़ा *[cauṛā]* ADJ broad, wide
चौड़ाई *[cauṛāī]* F width; breadth
चौथा *[cauthā]* ADJ fourth
चौथाई *[cauthāī]* ADJ one-fourth
चौदह *[caudah]* ADJ fourteen
चौदहवाँ *[caudahvā̃]* ADJ fourteenth
चौबीस *[caubīs]* ADJ twenty-four
चौबीसवाँ *[caubīsvā̃]* ADJ twenty-fourth
चौरानबे *[caurānbe]* ADJ ninety-four
चौरासी *[caurāsī]* ADJ eighty-four
चौवन *[cauvan]* ADJ fifty-four
चौवालीस *[cauvālīs]* ADJ forty-four
चौहत्तर *[cauhattar]* ADJ seventy-four

छ

छँटना *[chā̃ṭnā]* V.I. to be sorted; to be thinned
छः *[chaḥ]* ADJ six
छक्का *[chakkā]* M a set of six; sixer (in cricket); six in a pack of cards
छज्जा *[chajjā]* M balcony, terrace
छटपटाना *[chaṭpaṭānā]* V.I. to writhe in pain, to be restless, to toss and turn; to long/yearn impatiently
छठा *[chaṭhā]* ADJ sixth
छड़ी *[chaṛī]* F stick; cane
छत *[chat]* F roof, ceiling
छतरी *[chatrī]* F umbrella; parachute; pavilion
छत्ता *[chattā]* M beehive; archway, corridor
छत्तीस *[chattīs]* ADJ thirty-six
छत्र *[chatra]* M umbrella

छद्म *[chadma]* ADJ a pseudo-, disguised, deceptive
छनकना *[chanaknā]* V.I. to jingle, to tinkle
छपना *[chapnā]* V.I. printed or stamped, to be published
छपाई *[chapāī]* F printing
छप्पन *[chappan]* ADJ fifty-six
छप्पर *[chappar]* M thatch, thatched roof
छबीला *[chabīlā]* ADJ foppish; dandy
छब्बीस *[chabbīs]* ADJ twenty-six
छल *[chal]* M guile; deception; trick; ruse
छलकपट *[chalkapaṭ]* M duplicity and trickery
छलकना *[chalaknā]* V.I. to overflow; to spill over
छलछलाना *[chalchalānā]* V.I. for the eyes to fill with tears
छलना *[chalnā]* V.T. to cheat, to deceive
छलनी *[chalnī]* F sieve, strainer
छलाँग *[chalā̃g]* F leap, bound
छवि *[chavi]* F pretty features, winsomeness; beauty
छह *[cheh]* ADJ six
छाँटना *[chā̃ṭnā]* V.T. to select, to sort out; to cut, to trim
छाँव *[chā̃ya]* F shade; shadow
छाँह *[chā̃h]* F shade; shadow
छाछ *[chāch]* F buttermilk
छाता *[chātā]* M umbrella
छाती *[chātī]* F breast; chest; bosom
छात्र *[chātra]* M student
छात्रावास *[chatrāvās]* M student hostel
छानना *[chānnā]* V.T. to filter; to strain; to percolate
छानबीन *[chānbīn]* F screening, investigation, scrutiny, probe
छाना *[chānā]* V.I. to cover, to thatch; to shadow
छाप *[chāp]* F a print, an imprint; impression
छापना *[chāpnā]* V.T. to print; to publish; to mark
छापा *[chāpā]* M an imprint; a stamp; raid; छापा मारना *[chāpā mārnā]* V.T. to conduct a raid
छापाख़ाना *[chāpākhānā]* M a printing press
छाया *[chāyā]* F shadow; shade; image; reflection; influence; resemblance
छाला *[chālā]* M blister, burn
छावनी *[chāvanī]* F

cantonment
छिछला *[chichlā]* ADJ shallow
छिछलापन *[chichlāpan]* M shallowness
छिटकना *[chiṭaknā]* V.I. scattered; to be spread out
छिड़कना *[chiṛaknā]* V.T. to sprinkle or spray; to water
छिड़काव *[chiṛkāv]* M sprinkling or spraying
छिड़ना *[chiṛnā]* V.I. to be commenced, to begin, to start; to break out (as in war)
छिदना *[chidnā]* V.I. pierced; to be perforated; to be seized; to be snatched
छिनाल *[chināl]* ADJ dissolute; a woman of easy virtue
छिपकली *[chipkalī]* F gecko, a lizard; a hateful creature
छिपना *[chipnā]* V.I. to hide; to lurk; to be covered
छिपाना *[chipānā]* V.T. to hide; to conceal
छियानबे *[chiyānabe]* ADJ ninety-six
छियालीस *[chiyālīs]* ADJ forty-six
छियासी *[chiyāsī]* ADJ eighty-six
छिलका *[chilkā]* M peel; skin; husk
छिलना *[chilnā]* V.I. to be bruised or scratched; to be excoriated; to be peeled
छिहत्तर *[chihattar]* ADJ seventy-six
छींक *[chī̃k]* F sneeze
छींकना *[chī̃knā]* V.I. to sneeze
छींटा *[chī̃ṭā]* M a sprinkle; a splash; bespattering
छी *[chī]* INT tut!; fie!; pish!
छीनना *[chīnnā]* V.T. to snatch, to grab; to seize
छीलना *[chīlnā]* V.T. to scrap; to scratch; to chip; peel
छुआछूत *[chuāchūt]* F untouchability
छुईमुई *[chuīmuī]* F touch-me-not; an overly sensitive person
छुटकारा *[chuṭkārā]* M riddance; acquittal; release, liberation
छुट्टा *[chuṭṭā]* ADJ loose; not tied M small change (money)
छुट्टी *[chuṭṭī]* F holiday
छुड़ाना *[chuṛānā]* V.T. to get (something or someone) released; to cause to set free
छुपना/छिपना *[chupnā/ chipnā]* V.I. to hide, to lurk

छुरा *[churā]* M razor; dagger
छुरी *[churī]* F knife; small dagger
छूट *[chuṭ]* F rebate; discount; allowance; concession; release; riddance; exemption
छूटना *[chūṭnā]* V.I. to depart; to be left behind; to be released
छूत *[chūt]* F contagion
छूना *[chūnā]* V.T. touch, to feel
छेड़ *[cheṛ]* F teasing, offending
छेड़खानी *[cheṛkhānī]* F the act of teasing or provoking; offensive activity
छेड़छाड़ *[cheṛchāṛ]* F provocation; molestation; teasing
छेड़ना *[cheṛnā]* V.T. to tease; to irritate; to meddle (in); to disturb
छेद *[ched]* M hole, bore; perforation; opening
छेदना *[chednā]* V.T. to bore; to make a hole
छै/छह/छः *[chai/chah/chaḥ]* ADJ six
छैला *[chailā]* M dandy, foppish person ADJ dandy
छोकरा *[chokrā]* M a lad; a boy
छोकरी *[chokrī]* F a girl
छोटा *[choṭā]* ADJ small; little; short; younger
छोड़ना *[choṛnā]* V.T. to leave; to abandon; to omit
छोर *[chor]* M end; extremity
छोरा *[chorā]* M a lad
छौंक *[chaũk]* F seasoning with ghee and spices (added to lentils)
छौंकना *[chaũknā]* V.T. to season

ज

जंग *[jaṅg]* F war, battle
ज़ंग *[zaṅg]* M rust
जंगल *[jaṅgal]* M jungle, forest, wood
जंगली *[jaṅgalī]* ADJ savage, wild
जंघा *[jaṅghā]* F thigh
जँचना *[jãcnā]* V.I. to be examined, to be valued to suit
ज़ंजीर *[zañjīr]* F chain, fetters
जकड़ना *[jakaṛnā]* V.T. to grasp, to hold firmly; to tighten
जख़्म *[zakhm]* M wound, cut, injury
जख़्मी *[zakhmī]* ADJ wounded, injured
जग *[jag]* M world, universe; people

जगत *[jagat]* M the world, universe
जगना *[jagnā]* V.I. to wake up, to awaken
जगमगाना *[jagmagānā]* V.I. to be refulgent, to glitter, to shine
जगह *[jagah]* F place; space
जगाना *[jagānā]* V.T. to wake up, to awaken, to rouse
जज *[jaj]* M judge
जज़ीरा *[jazīrā]* M island
जज़्बा *[jazbā]* M emotion, feeling, passion
जटा *[jaṭā]* F matted or tangled hair; fibrous root
जटिल *[jaṭil]* ADJ intricate, complicated; inaccessible
जड़ *[jaṛ]* F root
जड़ना *[jaṛnā]* V.T. to stud, to inlay; to fix, to set, to mount
जड़ी *[jaṛī]* F medicinal root; जड़ी-बूटी *[jaṛī-būṭī]* F roots and herbs used in medicine
जताना *[jatānā]* V.T. to apprise, to make known; to warn
ज़दा *[zadā]* SUFFIX meaning "afflicted by"
जद्दोजहद *[jaddojahad]* F struggle, hard endeavor
जन *[jan]* M people; public; folk, person
जनसंख्या *[jansaṅkhyā]* F population
जनजाति *[janjāti]* F tribe
जनता *[jantā]* M public; people; masses
जनना *[jannā]* V.T. to reproduce, to give birth, to bear
जनवरी *[janvarī]* F January (month)
जनाज़ा *[janāzā]* M corpse wrapped in the coffin-cloth, bier (with the corpse); funeral procession
जनाब *[janāb]* ADJ, M mister; Sir! Your Excellency!
जनेऊ *[janeū]* M the sacred thread worn by Hindus
जन्नत *[jannat]* F paradise, heaven
जन्म *[janma]* M birth
जन्मदिन *[janmadin]* M birthday
जप *[jap]* M adoration by way of repeating passages from scriptures, sacred formulae or a deity's name
जपना *[japnā]* V.T. to murmur or to utter quiet prayers; to repeat reverentially
जब *[jab]* REL ADV when

जब तक *[jab tak]* REL ADV until when
जब भी *[jab bhī]* ADV whenever
जबड़ा *[jabṛā]* M jaw
ज़बर *[zabar]* ADJ strong, huge
ज़बरदस्त *[zabardast]* ADJ strong, powerful, vigorous, violent
ज़बरदस्ती *[zabardastī]* F compulsion; high-handedness; force
ज़बान *[zabān]* F language; tongue
ज़बानी *[zabānī]* ADJ oral; unwritten
ज़ब्त *[zabd]* ADJ forfeited; confiscated, impounded M forbearance, restraint
जमना *[jamnā]* V.I. to freeze, to solidify, to clot
जमा *[jamā]* ADJ collected; deposited M deposit, credit, accumulation
जमात *[jamāt]* F class
ज़मानत *[zamānat]* F bail, surety, security, guarantee
ज़माना *[zamānā]* M age; period
ज़मींदार/ज़मीनदार *[zamĩdār/ zamīndār]* M landowner
ज़मींदारी *[zamĩdārī]* F landlordism; landed estate; cultivation
ज़मीन *[zamīn]* F land
जमुना *[jamunā]* F the river Yamuna
जम्हाई *[jamhāī]* F yawning; जम्हाई लेना *[jamhāī lenā]* V.T. to yawn
जयंती *[jayantī]* F anniversary, jubilee
जय *[jay]* F victory, conquest, triumph
ज़र *[zar]* M wealth, riches, gold
ज़रा *[zarā]* ADJ, INVAR little (also softens a request)
ज़रिया *[zariyā]* M means, medium, instrument
ज़रूर *[zarūr]* ADV certainly
ज़रूरत *[zarūrat]* F necessity
ज़रूरी *[zarūrī]* ADV necessary
ज़र्द *[zard]* ADJ pale yellow
ज़र्दी *[zardī]* F paleness, yellowness
ज़र्रा *[zarrā]* M atom, particle
जल *[jal]* M water, hydro-
जलन *[jalan]* F burning sensation, jealousy
जलना *[jalnā]* V.I. to burn, to be inflamed, to be kindled; to feel jealous
जलपान *[jalpān]* M light

refreshment, breakfast
जलवायु *[jalvāyu]* F climate
जलसा *[jalsā]* M meeting, function, festivity
जलाना *[jalānā]* V.T. to burn, to light, to kindle
जलाल *[jalāl]* M glory, splendor, pre-eminence
ज़लील *[zalīl]* ADJ mean, wretched, contemptible
जलूस *[jalūs]* M procession
जलेबी *[jalebī]* F *jalebi* (a type of Indian sweet)
जल्दी *[jaldī]* ADV quickly
जवान *[javān]* ADJ young, youthful M a youth, soldier
जवानी *[javānī]* F youth, young age, youthfulness
जवाब *[javāb]* M answer
जवाबी *[javābī]* ADJ counter-; (in the nature of or requiring a) reply
जवाहर *[javāhar]* M jewel
जश्न *[jaśna]* M festivity, merriment, festive celebration
जहन्नुम *[jahannum]* M hell
ज़हमत *[zehmat]* F trouble, bother
ज़हर *[zehr]* M poison, venom
ज़हरी *[zehrī]* ADJ poisonous, venomous, full of poison
जहाँ *[jahā̃]* REL ADV where;
जहाँ भी *[jahā̃ bhī]* REL ADV wherever
जहाज़ *[jahāz]* M ship
जहाज़ी *[jahāzī]* ADJ naval, nautical M mariner, sailor
जहान *[jahān]* M the world; the people
ज़हीन *[zahīn]* ADJ sharp; intelligent
जहेज़ *[jahez]* M dowry
जाँघ *[jā̃gh]* F thigh
जाँच *[jā̃c]* F investigation, examination, test
जाँचना *[jā̃cnā]* V.T. to investigate, to verify, to test, to evaluate
जागना *[jāgnā]* V.I. to rise, to wake up, to be alert
जागरण *[jāgaraṇ]* M awakening, wakefulness, vigil
जागरित *[jāgarit]* ADJ awakened, risen, woken up
जागरूक *[jāgrūk]* ADJ alert, vigilant, wakeful
जाट *[jāṭ]* M a Hindu sub-caste mostly inhabiting western Uttar Pradesh, Punjab, Rajasthan and Haryana
जाड़ा *[jāṛā]* M cold, winter

जात *[jāt]* ADJ born, manifest F caste
जाति *[jāti]* F caste, community, sect, genus, type
ज़ाती *[zātī]* ADJ personal, individual
जादू *[jādū]* M magic, charm, spell
जादूगर *[jādūgar]* M magician, sorcerer, conjurer
जान *[jān]* F life, stamina, vitality, energy
जान *[jān]* ADJ dear, beloved.
जानकार *[jānkār]* ADJ knowing, knowledgeable, conversant
जानकारी *[jānkārī]* F knowledge
जानना *[jānnā]* V.T. to know, to perceive
जान-पहचान *[jān-pehcān]* F acquaintance; जान-पहचान का *[jān-pehcān kā]* ADJ known; familiar
जानवर *[jānvar]* M animal
जाना *[jānā]* V.I. to go, to depart, to lose
जापान *[jāpān]* M Japan
जाम *[jām]* ADJ jammed M jam; a peg
जामन *[jāman]* M rennet, curded milk
जामा *[jāmā]* M attire, clothing
जामा मस्जिद *[jāmā masjid]* F Jama Masjid (the main mosque in Delhi)
जामुन *[jāmun]* F *jamun, jambo* (a black plum-like fruit)
ज़ायका *[zāykā]* M taste; relish
जायज़ *[jāyaz]* ADJ suitable, proper, befitting, legitimate
जायदाद *[jāydād]* F property
ज़ाया *[zāyā]* ADJ waste; ruined
जार *[jār]* M adulterer, paramour
जारी *[jārī]* ADJ continued, current, running, issued, in force
जाल *[jāl]* M net, network, mesh, snare; plot
ज़ालिम *[zālim]* ADJ cruel, atrocious, tyrannical
जाली *[jālī]* ADJ, M forged; counterfeit; mesh
जाली *[jālī]* ADJ, M grating; muzzle; hammock
ज़ाहिर *[zāhir]* ADJ apparent, obvious, evident
जाहिल *[jāhil]* ADJ illiterate; uncivil, boorish
ज़िंदगी *[zindagī]* F life
ज़िंदा *[zindā]* ADJ, INVAR alive

ज़िक्र *[zikra]* M mention; reference

जिगर *[jigar]* M liver, heart; courage

जिगरी *[jigrī]* ADJ pertaining to the liver; beloved, dear, very intimate

जिज्ञासा *[jijñāsā]* F curiosity, inquisitiveness, spirit of learning

जिज्ञासु *[jijñāsu]* ADJ curious, inquisitive, willing to learn

जितना *[jitnā]* REL ADJ as many, much

ज़िद/ज़िद्द *[zid/zidd]* F obstinacy, stubbornness, insistence

ज़िद्दी *[ziddī]* ADJ obstinate, stubborn, insistent, inflexible

जिधर *[jidhar]* REL ADV where; जिधर भी *[jidhar bhī]* REL ADV wherever

जिनका *[jinkā]* REL ADJ, PL whose

जिन्न *[jinna]* M genie, a spirit

जिन्हें/जिनको *[jinhẽ/jinko]* REL PRO oblique form of जो + को

जिन्होंने *[jinhõne]* REL PRO जो + ने

ज़िम्मा *[zimmā]* M responsibility, charge, obligation

ज़िम्मादारी *[zimmādārī]* F responsibility, obligation

ज़िला *[zilā]* M district

जिल्द *[jild]* F cover, binding

जिस *[jis]* REL PRO oblique form of जो; जिसका *[jiskā]* REL ADJ whose

जिसने *[jisne]* REL PRO जो + ने

जिसे/जिसको *[jise/jisko]* REL PRO oblique form of जो + को

जिस्म *[jism]* M body, physique

जिहाद *[jihād]* M crusade

जिहादी *[jihādī]* M crusader

जिह्वा *[jihvā]* F tongue

जी *[jī]* M heart; polite suffix; जी नहीं *[jī nahī̃]* ADV no; जी हाँ *[jī hā̃]* ADV yes

जीजा *[jījā]* M elder sister's husband

जीजी *[jījī]* F elder sister

जीत *[jīt]* F victory, success

जीतना *[jītnā]* V.T. to win, to conquer, to prevail upon, to master

जीना *[jīnā]* V.I. to live, to be alive

ज़ीना *[zīnā]* M staircase, ladder

जीभ *[jībh]* F tongue

ज़ीरा *[zīrā]* M cumin seed

जीर्ण *[jīrṇ]* ADJ decrepit; decayed; chronic

जीव *[jīv]* M creature; living being; life; soul
जीवन *[jīvan]* M life
जीवनी *[jīvanī]* F biography
जीव-विज्ञान *[jīv-vijñān]* M biology
जीविका *[jīvikā]* F livelihood, subsistence
जीवित *[jīvit]* ADJ alive, living
जुंबिश *[jumbiś]* F activity, movement
जुआ *[juā]* M gambling, yoke
जुआरी *[juārī]* M gambler
ज़ुकाम *[zukām]* M cold
जुँगनू *[jugnū]* M firefly, glow-worm
जुगल *[jugal]* M pair, couple, duet
जुगाड़ *[jugāṛ]* F way; device, measure, maneuver
जुटना *[juṭnā]* V.I. to be engaged (in a task); to unite; to assemble, to flock; to gather, to procure; to cause to work in full force
जुड़ना *[juṛnā]* V.I. to be attached/added/joined/linked; to be procured or collected
जुड़वाँ *[juṛvā̃]* ADJ, M twin-; twins
जुतना *[jutnā]* V.I. to be tilled/plowed, to be yoked; to be harnessed for work
जुदा *[judā]* ADJ separate, disunited
जुदाई *[judāī]* F separation
जुनून *[junūn]* M craziness; madness; insanity, mania
जुमा *[jumā]* M Friday
जुमेरात *[jumerāt]* F Thursday
जुर्म *[jurm]* M crime, offense
जुर्माना *[jurmānā]* M fine, penalty
जुलाई *[julāī]* F July (month)
जुलाहा *[julāhā]* M weaver
जुलूस *[julūs]* M procession;
ज़ुल्फ़ *[zulf]* M lock of hair, tress
ज़ुल्म *[zulm]* M oppression, tyranny, outrage
ज़ुल्मी *[zulmī]* ADJ tyrannical, oppressive
जूँ *[jū̃]* F louse
जूझना *[jūjhnā]* V.T. to struggle, to combat
जूट *[jūṭ]* M matted hair
जूठन *[jūṭhan]* F leavings (of food, drink, etc.)
जूठा *[jūṭhā]* ADJ defiled by eating, drinking, or otherwise being used
जूता *[jūtā]* M shoe
जूती *[jūtī]* F ladies' footwear
जून *[jūn]* M June (month)

जेठ *[jeṭh]* M third month of the Hindu lunar calendar; husband's elder brother
जेब *[jeb]* F pocket
जेबकतरा *[jebkatrā]* M pick-pocket
जेल *[jel]* F jail, prison
जेलर *[jelar]* M jailor
ज़ेवर *[zevar]* M ornament, piece of, jewelry
ज़ेवरात *[zevrāt]* M ornaments, jewelry
ज़ेहन *[zehn]* F intellect, memory, mind
जैतून *[jaitūn]* M olive (tree and fruit)
जैन *[jain]* M Jain, follower of Jainism
जैसा *[jaisā]* REL ADJ like, resembling, similar to
जैसे *[jaise]* REL ADV as, like, such as, for instance
जोंक *[jõk]* F leech; blood-sucker, parasite
जो *[jo]* REL PRO who
जो भी *[jo bhī]* REL PRO whatever, whichever, whoever
जोखिम *[jokhim]* M risk; danger; enterprise
जोगिन *[jogin]* F female ascetic; mendicant
जोगी *[jogī]* M ascetic; mendicant
जोड़ *[joṛ]* M sum, total, addition; union, joint, match
जोड़ना *[joṛnā]* V.T. to add, to sum up; to link, to unite; to collect, to accumulate
जोड़ा *[joṛā]* M pair, couple; suit
जोड़ी *[joṛī]* F pair, couple; pair of clubs
जोतना *[jotnā]* V.T. to plow, to till a yoke; to harness to work
ज़ोर *[zor]* M strength, force, power; stress, strain; emphasis
जोरू *[jorū]* F wife
जोश *[jоś]* M enthusiasm, excitement, fervor, passion, zeal
जोशीला *[jośīlā]* ADJ spirited, enthusiastic, zealous, vigorous
जौ *[jau]* M barley
ज्ञात *[jñāt]* ADJ known; comprehended
ज्ञान *[jñān]* M knowledge, wisdom
ज्ञानी *[jñānī]* ADJ wise; learned; knowledgeable, well-informed; having attained self-realization
ज़्यादती *[zyādatī]* F excess, highhandedness, injustice

ज़्यादा *[zyādā]* ADJ, INVAR more, much
ज़्यादातर *[zyādātar]* ADJ, ADV mostly
ज्येष्ठ *[jyeṣṭh]* ADJ eldest, senior-most, senior, elder
ज्यों *[jyõ]* IND as, as if
ज्योति *[jyoti]* F light, Jyoti (name)
ज्योत्स्ना *[jyotsnā]* F moonlight
ज्वार *[jvar]* M flood tide
ज्वाला *[jvālā]* F flame, blaze
ज्वालामुखी *[jvālāmukhī]* ADJ, M volcanic; volcano

झ

झंकार *[jhankār]* F tinkling, jingling
झंकारना *[jhankārnā]* V.I. to produce a tinkling/jingling sound; to tinkle/jingle
झंझट *[jhañjhat]* M bother, mess, trouble, imbroglio
झँझोड़ना *[jhãjhoṛnā]* V.T. to jerk violently
झंडा *[jhaṇḍā]* M flag, banner, standard
झंडा फहराना *[jhaṇḍā phehrānā]* V.T. to hoist a flag
झक *[jhak]* F whim, craze
झकझोरना *[jhakjhornā]* V.T. to shake or jerk violently
झकझोरा *[jhakjhorā]* M a violent jerk
झख *[jhakh]* M a blast of air, gust
झगड़ना *[jhagaṛnā]* V.I. to quarrel; to fight
झगड़ा *[jhagṛā]* M quarrel, dispute, altercation
झगड़ालू *[jhagṛālū]* ADJ quarrelsome, disputatious
झट *[jhaṭ]* ADV instantly, at once
झटकना *[jhaṭaknā]* V.T. to jerk off; to twitch; to snatch; to extort; to obtain by fraud
झटका *[jhaṭkā]* M a jerk; jolt; shock; lurch; beheading an animal with one stroke
झटपट *[jhaṭpaṭ]* ADV quickly, promptly
झड़ना *[jhāṛnā]* V.I. to shed; to drop or fall; to be discharged
झपकना *[jhapaknā]* V.T. to blink, to wink; to twinkle
झपकी *[jhapkī]* F nap, short sleep, blink
झपटना *[jhapaṭnā]* V.I. to make a sudden swoop; to pounce, to snatch
झपेट *[jhapeṭ]* F (striking)

range; stroke; swoop
झमेला *[jhamelā]* M mess; imbroglio; trouble
झरना *[jharnā]* M spring, cascade, fall V.I. to spring; to flow forth; to fall
झरोखा *[jharokhā]* M oriel; a small window; a network of airholes/apertures
झलक *[jhalak]* F glimpse; semblance
झलकना *[jhalaknā]* V.I. to show up imperfectly or faintly; to show a glimpse of
झाँकना *[jhā̃knā]* V.T. to peep in or out; to peer
झाग *[jhāg]* M foam; lather; scum; froth
झाड़ *[jhāṛ]* M bush, shrub; small tree
झाड़ना *[jhāṛnā]* V.T. to sweep, to brush, to clean; to chide, to reprimand
झाड़ी *[jhāṛī]* F bush; thicket
झाड़ू *[jhāṛū]* M broom; झाड़ू लगाना *[jhāṛū lagānā]* V.T. to sweep with a broom
झापड़ *[jhāpaṛ]* M slap
झिझक *[jhijhak]* F hesitation; hitch; shyness
झिझकना *[jhijhaknā]* V.I. to hesitate; to feel shy
झिलमिलाना *[jhilmilānā]* V.I. to twinkle; to shimmer; to flicker
झिलमिलाहट *[jhilmilāhaṭ]* F twinkle; flicker
झील *[jhīl]* F lake
झुँझलाना *[jhũjhlānā]* V.I. irritated/petulant/peeved
झुँझलाहट *[jhũjhlāhaṭ]* F irritation, peevishness, petulance, annoyance
झुंड *[jhuṇḍ]* M flock, herd; clump, cluster
झुकना *[jhuknā]* V.I. to bow; to droop; to stoop
झुकना *[jhuknā]* V.I. to bend; to yield; झुकाना *[jhukānā]* V.T. to bend; to cause to stoop, to force to yield
झुकाव *[jhukāv]* M inclination; bent, bias; leaning
झुठलाना *[jhuṭhlānā]* V.T. to belie; to falsify; to give a lie to
झुमका *[jhumkā]* M pendant (of an earring)
झुर्री *[jhurrī]* F wrinkle, crinkle, fold
झुर्रीदार *[jhurrīdār]* ADJ wrinkled

झुलसना *[jhulasnā]* V.I. scorched; singed; to be charred

झुलाना *[jhulānā]* V.T. to swing, to rock; to keep in suspense

झूठ *[jhūṭh]* M lie

झूठ बोलना *[jhūṭh bolnā]* V.I. to lie

झूठा *[jhūṭhā]* ADJ false; fictitious; untrue; sham; mock; feigned

झूमना *[jhūmnā]* V.I. to sway, to swing

झूलना *[jhūlnā]* V.I. to swing; to oscillate; to dangle

झूला *[jhūlā]* M swing; a suspended scaffold; cradle

झेंपना *[jhẽpnā]* V.I. to blush; to feel shy

झेलना *[jhelnā]* V.T. to bear; to endure; to suffer

झोंक *[jhõk]* F impulse; impulsive sway; swing; craze

झोंकना *[jhõknā]* V.T. to throw in; to thrust in; to pour in

झोंका *[jhõkā]* M blast; puff; gust (of wind)

झोंपड़ा *[jhõpṛā]* M shanty, hut

झोंपड़ी *[jhõpṛī]* F hut; a small cottage

झोला *[jholā]* M bag; kit; haversack

झोली *[jholī]* F small bag; begging bag

ट

टंकी *[ṭaṅkī]* F tank; cistern; reservoir

टक *[ṭak]* F stare, gaze; टक बाँधना *[ṭak bā̃dhnā]* V.T. to stare intently

टकटकी *[ṭakṭakī]* F gaze, stare, fixed look

टकराना *[ṭakrānā]* V.I. to clash, to collide; to knock (against).

टक्कर *[ṭakkar]* F collision, clash, crash, impact

टखना *[ṭakhnā]* M ankle; fetlock

टटोलना *[ṭaṭolnā]* V.T. to feel, to grope; to probe; to sound; to reconnoitre

टट्टी *[ṭaṭṭī]* F screen (made of bamboo); latrine, stool; feces

टट्टू *[ṭaṭṭū]* M pony

टपकना *[ṭapaknā]* V.I. to drip; to leak; to drop; to dribble

टमाटर *[ṭamāṭar]* M tomato

टलना *[ṭalnā]* V.I. averted; postponed; to slip or slink away

टहनी *[ṭehnī]* F sprig; twig
टहलना *[ṭahalnā]* V.I. to stroll
टाँकना *[ṭā̃knā]* V.T. to stitch; to stud; to solder; टाँका *[ṭā̃kā]* M a stitch
टाँग *[ṭā̃g]* F leg
टाँगना *[ṭā̃gnā]* V.T. to hang; to suspend
टाइप *[ṭāip]* M type; typing
टाइम *[ṭāim]* M time
टाट *[ṭāṭ]* M sack cloth; floor mat
टापू *[ṭāpū]* M island
टायर *[ṭāyar]* M tire, tyre
टार्च *[ṭārc]* M torch
टालना *[ṭālnā]* V.T. to postpone; to put off; to avert
टिकट *[ṭikaṭ]* M, F ticket
टिकटघर *[ṭikaṭghar]* M booking office
टिकना *[ṭiknā]* V.I. to last, to stay; to tarry; to stand one's ground
टिकाऊ *[ṭikāū]* ADJ durable; lasting; abiding
टिकिया *[ṭikiyā]* F small cake; tablet; patty
टिप्पणी *[ṭippaṇī]* F note; annotation; comment; observation; critical remark
टिमटिमाना *[ṭimṭimānā]* V.I. to twinkle; to glimmer; to flicker
टीका *[ṭīkā]* M vaccination; inoculation; a commentary (on a book)
टीकाकार *[ṭīkākār]* M commentator
टीचर *[ṭīcar]* M, F teacher
टीम *[ṭīm]* F team
टीला *[ṭīlā]* M mount; mound; hillock
टीसना *[ṭīsnā]* V.I. to smart; to throb with pain
टुकड़ा *[ṭukṛā]* M piece; fragment; part; splinter
टुकड़ी *[ṭukṛī]* F detachment of troops, a group
टूटना *[ṭūṭnā]* V.I. to break; broken; fractured
टूटा-फूटा *[ṭūṭā-phuṭā]* ADJ broken; damaged; decrepit; worn out
टेकना *[ṭeknā]* V.T. to lean; to support; to rest; to prop
टेढ़ा *[ṭeṛhā]* ADJ curved; bent; oblique; skew; difficult
टेलीफ़ोन *[ṭelīfon]* M telephone
टेलीविज़न *[ṭelīvizan]* M television
टैंक *[ṭaīk]* M tank
टैक्स *[ṭaiks]* M tax
टैक्सी *[ṭaiksī]* F taxi

टोकना *[ṭoknā]* V.T. to interrupt; to interrogate
टोकरा *[ṭokrā]* M basket
टोकरी *[ṭokrī]* F basket
टोपी *[ṭopī]* F hat, cap
टोल *[ṭol]* M band, batch, group
टोली *[ṭolī]* F team, batch, band, group
टोहना *[ṭohnā]* V.T. to sound; to reconnoitre; to take up the trace of
ट्रक *[ṭrak]* F truck
ट्राम *[ṭrām]* F tram
ट्रेन *[ṭren]* F train

ठ

ठंड *[ṭhanḍ]* F cold
ठंडक *[ṭhanḍak]* F coolness
ठंडा *[ṭhanḍā]* ADJ cool; cold; bleak; dull
ठंडापन *[ṭhanḍāpan]* M coolness; frigidity
ठग *[ṭhag]* M thug; cheat; an imposter
ठगना *[ṭhagnā]* V.T. to cheat; to dupe; to defraud
ठगी *[ṭhagī]* F thuggery, the act of cheating
ठट्ठा *[ṭhaṭṭhā]* M fun, humor, joke
ठनक *[ṭhanak]* F a deep ringing sound like a drum beat
ठनठनाना *[ṭhanṭhanānā]* V.T. to produce a ringing sound
ठप *[ṭhap]* ADV standstill; closed
ठप्पा *[ṭhappā]* M stamp; mould; die; matrix
ठहरना *[ṭheharnā]* V.I. to stop, to halt; to pause; to stay; to wait
ठहराव *[ṭhehrāv]* M stability; settlement
ठहाका *[ṭhahākā]* M peal or explosion of laughter
ठाँसना *[ṭhā̃snā]* V.T. to cram full; to thrust
ठाकुर *[ṭhākur]* M lord; master; God
ठाठ *[ṭhāṭh]* M pomp; splendor, magnificence
ठानना *[ṭhānnā]* V.T. to resolve; to determine
ठाला *[ṭhālā]* ADJ idle; unoccupied
ठिकाना *[ṭhikānā]* M abode; destination; station; place; trust
ठिठकना *[ṭhiṭhaknā]* V.I. to hesitate, to waver, to pause and ponder

ठिठुरना *[ṭhiṭhurnā]* V.I. chilled, to shiver with cold
ठीक *[ṭhīk]* ADJ okay; right; true; proper, appropriate
ठुकराना *[ṭhukrānā]* V.T. to reject contemptuously; to kick off; to knock away
ठुमरी *[ṭhumrī]* F style of classical Indian music
ठूँठ *[ṭhū̃ṭh]* M stump; stub; dead wood
ठूँसना *[ṭhū̃snā]* V.T. to stuff full; to thrust forcibly
ठेंगा *[ṭhẽgā]* M thumb (used to show contempt or defiant refusal)
ठेका *[ṭhekā]* M contract; halting place; rhythmic percussion in music
ठेठ *[ṭheṭh]* ADJ pure, genuine, unadulterated, unsophisticated
ठेला *[ṭhelā]* M trolley; cart; truck; barrow
ठेस *[ṭhes]* F knock to the soul (causing lingering pain); emotional shock
ठोकना *[ṭhoknā]* V.T. to beat; to hammer; to drive into (as a nail)
ठोकर *[ṭhokar]* F kick; stroke; percussion
ठोड़ी *[ṭhoṛī]* F chin
ठोस *[ṭhos]* ADJ solid; sound
ठोर *[ṭhor]* M a place

ड

डंक *[ḍaṅk]* M sting; the tip of a pen
डंका *[ḍaṅkā]* M kettle drum
डंडा *[ḍāṇḍā]* M staff, stick, wand
डंडी *[ḍaṇḍī]* F handle; penis
डँसना *[ḍãsnā]* V.T. to sting; to bite
डकार *[ḍakār]* F belch
डकारना *[ḍakārnā]* V.T. to belch; to swallow; to misappropriate
डकैत *[ḍakait]* M bandit
डकैती *[ḍakaitī]* F banditry
डटना *[ḍaṭnā]* V.I. to stand; to tarry, to take a position
डपट *[ḍapaṭ]* F rebuke
डपटना *[ḍapaṭnā]* V.T. to issue a sharp rebuke
डबडबाना *[ḍabḍabānā]* V.I. tearful; the eyes to fill with tears
डबल *[ḍabal]* ADJ double
डब्बा *[ḍabbā]* M box; chest; a railway; carriage

डर *[ḍar]* M fear; (x से) डरना *[(x se) ḍarnā]* V.I. be afraid (of x)
डरपोक *[ḍarpok]* ADJ coward(ly); timid
डराना *[ḍarānā]* V.T. to scare, to frighten
डरावना *[ḍarāvnā]* ADJ terrible; scary; fierce; fearful
डाँट *[ḍā̃ṭ]* F scolding, reprimand, sharp rebuke
डाँटना *[ḍā̃ṭnā]* V.T. to scold, to rebuke sharply
डाइन *[ḍain]* F witch; hag; sorceress
डाक *[ḍāk]* F post; mail
डाकख़ाना *[ḍākkhānā]* M post office
डाका *[ḍākā]* M banditry
डाकिया *[ḍākiyā]* M postman
डाकू *[ḍākū]* M bandit; dacoit
डॉक्टर *[ḍākṭar]* M doctor
डाट *[ḍāṭ]* F cork; plug; stopper
डाढ़ी *[ḍāṛhī]* F beard
डाल *[ḍāl]* F branch
डालना *[ḍālnā]* V.T. to put, to place
डॉलर *[ḍālar]* M dollar
डाली *[ḍālī]* F branch; basket; a basket full of fruits and sweets given as a present
डिग्री *[ḍigrī]* F degree
डिपो *[ḍipo]* F depot
डिप्टी *[ḍipṭī]* M deputy
डिबिया *[ḍibiyā]* F box
डिब्बा *[ḍibbā]* *see* डब्बा
डींग *[ḍī̃g]* F bragging, boasting
डील *[ḍīl]* M stature, size, physique
डीलडौल *[ḍīlḍaul]* M stature; physique
डुबकी *[ḍubkī]* F dip
डुबाना *[ḍubānā]* V.T. to sink, to immerse, to drown
डुबोना *[ḍubonā]* *see* डुबाना
डूबना *[ḍūbnā]* V.I. to sink; to drown; to plunge down
डेढ़ *[ḍeṛh]* ADJ one and a half
डेरा *[ḍerā]* M camp; encampment; billet
डोलना *[ḍolnā]* V.I. to swing; to oscillate; to wobble
डोला *[ḍolā]* M a kind of sedan (for women); palanquin
ड्योढ़ी *[ḍyoṛhī]* F threshold; vestibule
ड्राइवर *[ḍrāivar]* M driver
ड्रामा *[ḍrāmā]* M drama

ढ

ढंग *[ḍhaṅg]* M manner; method; mode, way

ढँढोरा *[ḍhā̃ḍhorā]* M proclamation by beating a drum

ढकना *[ḍhaknā]* V.I., V.T. to be covered; to cover; to conceal

ढकेलना *[ḍhakelnā]* V.T. to shove, to push

ढक्कन *[ḍhakkan]* M lid; cover

ढब *[ḍhab]* M manner; ways, conduct

ढलना *[ḍhalnā]* V.I. moulded/ cast; poured out; to age; to decline

ढलाई *[ḍhalāī]* F moulding, casting

ढलान *[ḍhalān]* F slope; descent

ढहना *[ḍhehnā]* V.I. to crash down; to fall down

ढाँचा *[ḍhā̃cā]* M frame; framework; skeleton

ढाई *[ḍhāī]* ADJ two and a half

ढाढ़स *[ḍhāṛhās]* M solace; consolation

ढाबा *[ḍhābā]* M small roadside restaurant

ढालना *[ḍhālnā]* V.T. to pour out (as in liquor); to mould; to cast

ढीठ *[ḍhīṭh]* ADJ contumelious; impudent

ढील *[ḍhīl]* F sluggishness; leniency; relaxation

ढीला *[ḍhīlā]* ADJ loose; slack; sluggish; soft

ढीलापन *[ḍhīlāpan]* M slackness

ढूँढना *[ḍhū̃ḍhnā]* V.T. to search; to seek

ढेर *[ḍher]* M heap; pile

ढेला *[ḍhelā]* M a clod; lump of earth

ढोंग *[ḍhõg]* M hypocrisy; fraud

ढोंगी *[ḍhõgī]* ADJ, M fraudulent; hypocritical

ढोना *[ḍhonā]* V.T. to transport; to cart; to haul

ढोलक *[ḍholak]* F drum played on both ends

त

तंग *[taṅg]* ADJ narrow (as in a lane), scarce, troubled, harassed

तंगी *[taṅgī]* F scarcity; poverty; tightness

तंत्र *[tantra]* M arrangement; system, structure, technique, string, a body of mystic formulae or practices (for the attainment of super-human powers); incantation

तंत्र-मंत्र M hocus-pocus, spell and incantation, charms

तंदरुस्त *[tandurust]* ADJ healthy; vigorous, fit

तंदरुस्ती *[tandurusti]* F health; vigor

तंदूर *[tandūr]* M oven

तंदूरी *[tandūrī]* ADJ fired or prepared in a तंदूर

तंबाकू *[tambākū]* M tobacco

तक *[tak]* PP until, to, till, by, up to

तक़रीबन *[taqrīban]* ADV approximately

तक़रीर *[taqrīr]* F speech; lecture

तकलीफ़ *[taklīf]* F trouble, distress; difficulty; hardship

तकल्लुफ़ *[takalluf]* M formality; formality of behavior; etiquette

तक़सीम *[taqsīm]* F division, distribution

तक़ाज़ा *[taqāzā]* M demand; due, request; claim

तकिया *[takiyā]* M pillow; bolster; cushion; prop, support

तख़्त *[takht]* M wooden structure of planks, board, throne, seat

तख़्ता *[takhtā]* M plank, board

तख़्ती *[takhtī]* F small plank, board; a small slate to write on

तगड़ा *[tagṛā]* ADJ strong, powerful, robust

तगा *[tagā]* M thread

तजवीज़ *[tajvīz]* F proposal, suggestion, scheme

तजुरबा/तजुर्बा *[tajurbā]* M experience, experiment

तजुरबेकार *[tajurbekār]* ADJ experienced (person)

तट *[taṭ]* M bank; shore; coast

तटस्थ *[taṭastha]* ADJ neutral, impartial, objective, indifferent

तटस्थता *[taṭasthatā]* F neutrality, objectivity, indifference

तड़कना *[taṛaknā]* V.I. to spit with; to crack; to snap; to burst, to become suddenly angry

तड़का *[taṛkā]* M day-break, dawn, cracking noise, a snap;

seasoning, heated oil or ghee in which spices are fried and added as a relish to pulses

तड़प *[taṛap]* F tossing or rolling about in agony, yearning, smart, restlessness, agitation of feelings, anxiety

तड़प आना *[taṛap ānā]* V.I. to feel pain, to be uneasy

तड़पना *[taṛapnā]* V.I. to toss or roll about restlessly or uneasily; to writhe in pain; to yearn for

तड़पाना *[taṛapānā]* V.T. to make restless, to make uneasy, to be agitated, to cause to stumble

तड़ाका *[taṛākā]* M loud report, crack, snap

ततैया *[tataiyā]* M wasp

तत्काल *[tatkāl]* ADV forthwith, immediately

तत्त्व *[tattva]* M element, essence, principle, substance, factor

तत्पर *[tatpar]* ADJ ready, devoted

तत्परता *[tatpartā]* F readiness, devotedness

तत्र *[tatra]* ADV there, in that place

तथा *[tathā]* IND and, so

तथाकथित *[tathākathit]* ADJ so-called

तथापि *[tathāpi]* IND even so; still, yet, in spite of that

तथ्य *[tathya]* M fact, reality

तदपि *[tadapi]* IND still, even then

तदबीर *[tadbīr]* F effort, means, device, contrivance

तन *[tan]* M body

तनमन से *[tanman se]* ADV wholeheartedly, with all physical and mental resources

तनख़्वाह (also तनख़ार) *[tānkhvāh]* (also *[tankhār]*) F pay, salary

तनना *[tannā]* V.I. to be pulled tight; to be stretched full; to assume an air of affectation

तनहा *[tanhā]* ADJ alone, lonely, solitary

तनहाई *[tanhāī]* F loneliness, solitude

तनाव *[tanāv]* M tension; strain; tautness

तनिक *[tanik]* ADJ little, slight

तन्मय *[tanmay]* fully engrossed/absorbed (in)

तन्मयता *[tanmaytā]* F complete identification; engrossment

तप *[tap]* M devout austerity, asceticism, self-moritfication

तपना *[tapnā]* V.I. heated; to burn with pain or grief; to practice self-mortification

तपस्या *[tapasyā]* F penance, self-mortification; asceticism

तपस्वी *[tapasvī]* M ascetic, devoutly austere (person); *[tapasvinī]* F female ascetic

तफ़रीह *[tafrīh]* F recreation, fun, amusement

तफ़सील *[tafsīl]* F detail, particular

तब *[tab]* ADV then, at that time; तब तक *[tab tak]* ADV until then; तब भी *[tab bhī]* ADV even then

तबक़ा *[tabqā]* M class, status

तबदीली *[tabdīlī]* F change, transformation, alteration

तबला *[tablā]* M tambourine

तबादिला/तबादला *[tabādilā/ tabādlā]* M transfer

तबाह *[tabāh]* ADJ ruined, destroyed

तबाही *[tabāhī]* F ruin, destruction

तबियत/तबीयत *[tabiyat/ tabīyat]* F health, the state of physical and mental wellbeing, disposition, nature

तभी *[tabhī]* ADV right then; at that very time; at that very moment; for this reason (तब + ही)

तम *[tam]* M darkness, gloom; ignorance

-तम *[-tam]* SUFFIX -est (superlative)

तमगा *[tamgā]* M medal

तमतमाना *[tamtamānā]* V.I. (the face) to redden (with rage or heat)

तमन्ना *[tamannā]* F aspiration, longing

तमस *[tamas]* M the third of the three qualities incidental to creation; the quality of darkness or ignorance

तमाचा *[tamācā]* M slap

तमाम *[tamām]* ADJ all, whole, entire

तमाशा *[tamāśā]* M show, spectacle, entertainment

तमिल *[tamil]* F Tamil language

तमीज़ *[tamīz]* F etiquette; decorum; discrimination

तय *[tay]* ADJ decided, settled

तरंग *[taraṅg]* F wave; ripple; whim; caprice

तर *[tar]* ADJ wet, soaked,

damp, dank; fresh; rich (as in food)

-तर *[-tar]* SUFFIX -er (comparative)

तरकारी *[tarkārī]* F vegetable

तरकीब *[tarkīb]* F way; means; tact, contrivance, device

तरक़्क़ी *[taraqqī]* F progress

तर्जुमा *[tarjumā]* M translation

तरतीब *[tartīb]* F order; arrangement

तरना *[tarnā]* V.I. to cross (over); to attain salvation; to fulfil an obligation

तरफ़ *[taraf]* ADV, F towards; side; direction

तरबूज़ *[tarbūz]* M watermelon

तरल *[taral]* ADJ, M fluid; fickle; unsteady; liquid

तरस *[taras]* F compassion, pity

तरसना *[tarasnā]* V.T. to pine for, to crave or long for

तरह *[tarah]* F kind, type, sort, manner; तरह-तरह का *[tarah-tarah kā]* ADJ all manner of

तराई *[tarāī]* F foothill; curing (of concrete, etc.); constant wetting/drenching

तराज़ू *[tarāzū]* F balance, scales

तरीक़ा *[tarīqā]* M method, mode, way, manner, technique

-तरीन *[-tarīn]* SUFFIX -est (superlative)

तरुण *[taruṇ]* ADJ youthful M a youth, young man

तर्क *[tark]* M argument; plea; contention; reason, reasoning, logic; abandonment, relinquishment

तर्जनी *[tarjanī]* F forefinger

तल *[tal]* M bottom; surface; floor

तलक *[talak]* IND to, up to, until; even

तलना *[talnā]* V.T. to fry

तलब *[talab]* F yearning, desire

तलवा *[talvā]* F sole of the foot

तला *[talā]* M bottom, sole (of a shoe), base, floor; keel (of a boat); lower/under side

तलाक़ *[talāq]* M divorce

तलाश *[talāś]* F search, quest

तलाशना *[talāśnā]* V.T. to search, to go in quest (of)

तलाशी *[talāśī]* F search

तली *[talī]* F bottom, sole (of a shoe)

तवा *[tavā]* M griddle; gramophone record; chest shield (used by warriors)

तशरीफ़ *[taśrīf]* F a term signifying honor and respect
तश्तरी *[taśtarī]* F plate, tray
तसवीर *[tasvīr]* F picture, portrait, image
तस्कर *[taskar]* M smuggler
तस्करी *[taskarī]* F the act, process, or practice of smuggling
तस्वीर *[tasvīr]* F picture
तह *[teh]* F layer; fold; bottom
तहज़ीब *[tahzīb]* F culture
तहत *[tehat]* IND under
तहस-नहस *[tehas-nehas]* ADJ ruined, devastated, destroyed
तहसील *[tehsīl]* F *tehsil*, an administrative subdivision of a district
तहाँ *[tahā̃]* ADV there, at that place
ताँगा *[tā̃gā]* M tonga; horse carriage
ताँबा *[tā̃bā]* M copper
ताई *[tāī]* F father's elder brother's wife
ताऊ *[tāū]* M father's elder brother
ताक *[tāk]* F lookout
ताक़त *[tāqat]* F power
ताक़तवर *[tāqatvar]* ADJ powerful, strong, mighty
ताकना *[tāknā]* V.T. to stare, to gaze, to watch intently, to view
ताकि *[tāki]* CONJ so that
तागा *[tāgā]* M thread
ताज *[tāj]* M crown; diadem
ताज़गी *[tāzagī]* F freshness; newness
ताज़ा *[tāzā]* ADJ fresh
ताज्जुब *[tājjub]* M wonder; astonishment
तादाद *[tādād]* F number, count
तानना *[tānnā]* V.T. to stretch, to spread, to tighten, to erect, to brandish
तानपूरा *[tānpūrā]* M *tanpura*, a stringed instrument
ताना *[tānā]* M taunt, sarcasm, gibe
तानाशाह *[tānāśāh]* M dictator
ताप *[tāp]* M heat; temperature; fever, affliction; mental agony
तापना *[tāpnā]* V.T. to heat; to warm
तापमान *[tāpmān]* M temperature
तार *[tār]* ADJ, M high-pitched wire, thread, fiber, chord, string; telegram; series, sequence

तारना *[tārnā]* V.T. to cause to cross over, to deliver, to free from bondage
तारा *[tārā]* M star
तारीख़ *[tārīkh]* F date; history
तारीख़दान *[tārīkhdān]* M historian
तारीफ़ *[tārīf]* F praise; definition; description, introduction
ताल *[tāl]* M pond; pool; tank; rhythm
ताला *[tālā]* M lock
तालाब *[tālāb]* M tank, pool
तालिका *[tālikā]* F list; key; table, schedule
तालिब *[tālib]* ADJ desirous (of) M pupil; student
तालिबे इल्म *[tālibe ilm]* M student
ताली *[tālī]* F key; clapping (of hands)
तालीम *[tālīm]* F education
तालु *[tālu]* M palate
तावीज़ *[tāvīz]* M amulet, talisman
ताश *[tāś]* M, F playing cards
तिकोना *[tikonā]* ADJ triangular, three-cornered
तिजोरी *[tijorī]* F iron safe/ chest
तितर-बितर *[titar-bitar]* ADJ scattered, dispersed, diffused
तितली *[titlī]* F butterfly
तिथि *[tithi]* F date
तिनका *[tinkā]* M straw
तिपाई *[tipāī]* F tripod
तिब्बत *[tibbat]* M Tibet
तिरंगा *[tiraṅgā]* ADJ, M tri-colored; the tri-color flag
तिरछा *[tirchā]* ADJ slanting, oblique, askew
तिरना *[tirnā]* V.I. to float
तिरानबे *[tirānbe]* ADJ ninety-three
तिरासी *[tirāsī]* ADJ eighty-three
तिरसठ/तिरेसठ *[tirsaṭh/ tiresaṭh]* ADJ sixty-three
तिर्यक *[tiryak]* ADJ slanting, oblique, crooked
तिल *[til]* F sesame (plant and seed), mole, pupil (of the eye); small particle
तिलक *[tilak]* M ornamental or religious mark on the forehead; the most eminent member (of a class, clan, dynasty, etc.)
तिलमिलाना *[tilmilānā]* V.I. to be in the grip of impotent anger, to writhe in agitation; to be dazzled

तिलस्म *[tilasm]* M magic, magic spell, talisman
तिलांजलि *[tilāñjali]* F bidding a final goodbye; giving up; abandonment
तिहत्तर *[tihattar]* ADJ, M seventy-three
तिहरा *[tiharā]* ADJ triple, three-fold
तिहाई *[tihāī]* ADJ one-third
तीखा *[tīkhā]* ADJ spicy, sharp (food)
तीतर *[tītar]* M partridge
तीन *[tīn]* ADJ three; तीन चौथाई *[tīn cauthāī]* ADJ three-quarters
तीनों *[tīnõ]* ADJ all three
तीर *[tīr]* M arrow; shaft; bank, shore
तीर्थ *[tīrth]* M place of pilgrimage, sacred place
तीव्र *[tīvra]* ADJ fast; pungent; high, high-pitched; sharp; violent; intense, vehement
तीस *[tīs]* ADJ thirty
तीसरा *[tīsrā]* ADJ third
तुंड *[tuṇḍ]* M trunk (of an elephant), snout
तुंद *[tund]* F belly
तुंदी *[tundī]* F navel
तुक *[tuk]* F rhyme, sense, harmony
तुच्छ *[tucch]* ADJ petty, trivial, trifle, frivolous, contemptible
तुझ *[tujh]* PRO oblique form of तू; तुझी *[tujhī]* PRO तुझ + ही; तुझे/तुझको *[tujhe/tujhko]* oblique form of तू + को
तुड़ाना *[tuṛānā]* V.T. to (cause to) break/pluck; to change (money into smaller denominations); to (be ready to) run away
तुतलाना *[tutlānā]* V.T. to lisp, to babble, to stutter
तुम *[tum]* PRO you (familiar, plural)
तुमने *[tumne]* PRO you (तुम + ने)
तुम्हारा *[tumhārā]* ADJ your
तुम्हीं *[tumhī̃]* PRO you (तुम + ही)
तुम्हें/तुमको *[tumhẽ/ tumko]* PRO oblique form of तुम + को
तुरंत *[turant]* CONJ immediately
तुर्क *[turk]* M Turk
तुर्की *[turkī]* ADJ, F Turkish; the Turkish language
तुलना *[tulnā]* V.I. to be weighed; to be bent on comparison
तुलसी *[tulsī]* F *tulsi*, holy basil

(*Ocimum sanctum*)
तुला *[tulā]* F balance, pair of scales; the sign of Libra
तुष्ट *[tuṣṭ]* ADJ satisfied, gratified, contented
तुष्टि *[tuṣṭi]* F satisfaction, gratification, contentment
तुहिन *[tuhin]* M frost, snow
तू *[tū]* PRO you (intimate, singular)
तूने *[tūne]* PRO you (तू + ने)
तूफ़ान *[tūfān]* M storm, tempest, hurricane, typhoon
तूफ़ानी *[tūfānī]* ADJ stormy, tempestuous, violent and vehement
तूलिका *[tūlikā]* F painter's brush
तृतीय *[tṛtīya]* ADJ third
तृप्त *[tṛpt]* ADJ, F satisfied, fulfilled, gratified
तृप्ति *[tṛpti]* fulfillment, gratification
तृष्णा *[tṛṣṇā]* F thirst, greed, longing, craving
तेंदुआ *[tenduā]* M leopard
तेईस *[teīs]* ADJ twenty-three.
तेईसवाँ *[teīsvā̃]* ADJ twenty-third
तेज़ *[tez]* ADJ sharp, strong, harsh
तेजस्वी *[tejasvī]* ADJ brilliant, luminous, glowing; impressive, imposing
तेज़ाब *[tezāb]* M acid
तेज़ी *[tezī]* F sharpness, acridity, pungency, quickness, swiftness; smartness, intelligence
तेरह *[terah]* ADJ thirteen
तेरहवाँ *[terahvā̃]* ADJ thirteenth
तेरा *[terā]* ADJ your
तेली *[telī]* M oilman, oil maker/seller; the sub-caste of oil makers
तेवर *[tevar]* M eye-brow; frown; stance
तैंतालीस *[taĩtālīs]* ADJ forty-three
तैंतीस *[taĩtīs]* ADJ thirty-three
तैनात *[tainā̄t]* ADJ deployed, posted, appointed
तैयार *[taiyār]* ADJ ready, prepared
तैयारी *[taiyārī]* F preparation
तैरना *[tairnā]* V.I. to swim
तैराकी *[tairākī]* F swimming
तैसा *[taisā]* ADJ like that, similar to that
तोंद *[tõd]* F paunch; potbelly
तो *[to]* CONJ + PART so, then (also emphatic particle)

तोड़ *[toṛ]* M antidote, counter-measure; breach/break; whey; forceful current
तोड़ना *[toṛnā]* V.T. to break; to fracture
तोतला *[totlā]* ADJ, M lisping; one who lisps
तोता *[totā]* M parrot
तोप *[top]* F gun; cannon
तोबा *[tobā]* F vowing to sin no more, vowing never to repeat (an act)
तोलना *[tolnā]* V.T. to weigh, to balance, to assess or to gauge
तोला *[tolā]* M unit of weight, one eightieth of a seer
तोष *[toṣ]* M appeasement, gratification
तोहफ़ा *[tohfā]* M present, gift
तौक़ *[tauq]* M neck-ring; yoke
तौर *[taur]* M mode, method, way; तौर-तरीक़े *[taur-tarīqe]* M methods
तौलिया *[tauliyā]* F, M towel
तौहीन *[tauhīn]* F insult, disrespect, humiliation, contempt
त्याग *[tyāg]* M abandonment, relinquishment
त्यागना *[tyāgnā]* V.T. to abandon, to give up, to relinquish, to renounce, to resign, to abnegate, to forsake, to sacrifice
त्यागी *[tyāgī]* M renouncer, recluse, one who has made sacrifices
त्यौं *[tyaũ]* IND thus, like that, so, in like manner
त्यौरी *[tyaurī]* F wrinkles of the forehead, contracted eyebrows
त्यौहार *[tyauhār]* M festival
त्रसित *[trasit]* ADJ frightened, scared, terrified
त्रस्त *[trast]* ADJ frightened, scared, terrified
त्रासदी *[trāsadī]* F (dramatic) tragedy
त्रि *[tri]* ADJ three
त्रिया *[triyā]* F woman
त्रेता *[tretā]* M the second of the four ages in Hindu mythology, the silver age
त्रेमासिक *[tremāsik]* ADJ quarterly, three-monthly
त्वचा *[tvacā]* F skin

थ

थकना *[thaknā]* V.I. to become tired, fatigued
थकान/थकावट *[thakān/ thakāvaṭ]* F fatigue, tiredness
थन *[than]* M udder
थपथपाना *[thapthapānā]* V.T. to pat lightly
थरथराना *[thartharānā]* V.I. to tremble, to shudder, to quiver
थर्मामीटर *[tharmāmīṭar]* M thermometer
थर्राना *[tharrānā]* V.I. to shudder, to tremble with terror
थल *[thal]* M land, place
था *[thā]* M, SING was
थाना *[thānā]* M police station
थानेदार *[thānedār]* M police sub-inspector
थाप *[thāp]* F pat; tap; palm stroke on a percussion instrument
थापना *[thāpnā]* V.T., M to pat into cakes (cow dung, etc.); installation (of a deity, etc.)
थामना *[thāmnā]* V.T. to hold; to grasp; to prop; to support; to restrain, to resist
थाल *[thāl]* M large, flat metal plate; basin
थाला *[thālā]* M basin (dug around a plant to hold water)
थाली *[thālī]* F small(er) flat metal plate
थाह *[thāh]* F depth; bottom
थिएटर *[thieṭar]* M theater
थिरकना *[thiraknā]* V.I. to make the body parts vibrate rhythmically, to move the feet nimbly in a dance sequence
थीं *[thī̃]* F, PL were
थी *[thī]* F, SING was
थूक *[thūk]* M spit, spittle, saliva
थूकना *[thūknā]* V.T. to spit; to reproach, to treat with contempt
थूथनी *[thūthnī]* F snout, muzzle
थे *[the]* M, PL were
थैला *[thailā]* M bag
थैली *[thailī]* F bag, small bag, pouch
थोक *[thok]* M mass; quantity; wholesale goods
थोड़ा *[thoṛā]* ADJ small, little, some; थोड़ा बहुत *[thoṛā bahut]* ADJ a little bit; थोड़ा सा *[thoṛā sā]* ADJ a little-ish

थोपना *[thopnā]* V.T. to impose, to thrust upon, to implant; to plaster

द

दंग *[daṅg]* ADJ wonder-struck, astonished, flabbergasted

दंगा *[daṅgā]* M riot, disturbance, tumultuous quarrel

दंड *[daṇḍ]* M punishment, penalty, fine; staff, rod, beam, shaft, stalk; measure of time equalling about twenty-four minutes

दंत *[dant]* M tooth

दंत्य *[dantya]* ADJ dental (sound); pertaining to the teeth

दंपति *[dampati]* M married couple, husband and wife

दंश *[danś]* M sting, bite, biting

दक्खिन *[dakkhin]* M the south

दक्ष *[dakṣ]* ADJ efficient, capable

दक्षता *[dakṣtā]* F efficiency; capability

दक्षिण *[dakṣiṇ]* M south

दक्षिणा *[dakṣiṇā]* F honorarium (paid in olden days to a preceptor by his pupil upon the successful conclusion of the latter's course of study), reward, renumeration

दख़लंदाज़ *[dak͟halandāz]* ADJ interfering, intruding, meddling

दख़लंदाज़ी *[dak͟halandāzī]* F interference, intrusion, meddling

दख़ल *[dak͟hal]* M interference, interruption; occupation; authority, authoritative knowledge

दग़ा *[dag͟hā]* F treachery, deception, perfidy

दफ़न *[dafan]* M burial

दफ़नाना *[dafnānā]* V.T. to bury, to entomb

दफ़ा *[dafā]* M time (in counting the number of times); section (of a code of law); warding off, removing

दफ़्तर *[daftar]* M office

दबंग *[dabaṅg]* ADJ over-bearing, strongheaded, dauntless, of commanding presence

दबदबा *[dabdabā]* M awe, sway, overwhelming/commanding influence

दबना *[dabnā]* V.I. pressed,

to yield, to submit; to be subdued; to be repressed; to be covered, to be concealed, to be hushed up; to cool down

दबाना *[dabānā]* **V.T.** to press, to press down, to suppress, to coerce, to subdue; to hush up, to cover; to cool down

दबाव *[dabāv]* **M** pressure; duress; stress/strain; suppression; compression; compulsion, coercion

दम *[dam]* **M** breath; life; stamina; endurance; moment; trick, trickery

दमकना *[damaknā]* **V.I.** to flash, to glimmer, to glitter, to glow

दमकल *[damkal]* **M** fire brigade; fire engine

दमन *[daman]* **M** suppression, repression, subjugation; control

दमा *[damā]* **M** asthma

दमित *[damit]* **ADJ** suppressed, repressed, subjugated

दया *[dayā]* **F** pity, mercy, compassion

दयालु *[dayālu]* **ADJ** kind, kind-hearted, generous

दरकार *[darkār]* **ADJ, F** necessary, needed; necessity, need

दरख़्त *[dara<u>kh</u>t]* **M** tree

दरख़्वास्त *[dar<u>kh</u>vāst]* **F** application; petition; request

दरगाह *[dargāh]* **F** shrine, holy place, tomb (of a saint)

दरबार *[darbār]* **M** royal court

दरबारी *[darbārī]* **ADJ, M** of or pertaining to court; courtier, sycophant

दरमियान *[darmiyān]* **IND, M** during, in between, within, among; the middle

दरवाज़ा *[darvāzā]* **M** door

दरवेश *[darveś]* **M** dervish, Muslim mendicant

दराज़ *[darāz]* **ADJ, F** long, prolonged; drawer (of desk, etc.)

दरार *[darār]* **F** crevice, slit, crack, fissure, breach, rift

दरिद्र *[daridra]* **ADJ, M** poor, shabby, of low quality, wretched; poverty, misery, plight

दरिया *[dariyā]* **M** river

दरियाफ़्त *[dariyāft]* **M** inquiry

दरी *[darī]* **F** cotton carpet; cavern; cave, grotto

दर्ज *[darj]* **ADJ** recorded; entered

दर्ज़न *[darzan]* M dozen
दर्जा *[darjā]* M class; degree, rank, gradation, status, category, quality, order
दर्ज़ी *[darzī]* F tailor
दर्द *[dard]* M pain
दर्पण *[darpaṇ]* M looking glass; mirror
दर्शक *[darśak]* M onlooker, spectator, visitor
दर्शन *[darśan]* M sight, view, appearance, philosophy
दल *[dal]* M party, group, team; swarm, herd; petal, leaf; thickness of layers; used as the second member of compound words to denote multitude
दलदल *[daldal]* M marsh, mire, fen, swamp, bog
दलना *[dalnā]* V.T. to grind coarsely, to mill, to crush; to destroy
दलाल *[dalāl]* M agent, broker, middleman, tout
दलित *[dalit]* ADJ downtrodden, depressed
दलील *[dalīl]* F plea, argument
दवा *[davā]* F medicine
दवाई *[davāī]* F medicine
दवाख़ाना *[davākhānā]* M pharmacy
दवात *[davāt]* F inkpot
दश *[daś]* ADJ ten
दशक *[daśak]* M decade
दशमलव *[daśamlav]* M decimal
दशा *[daśā]* F condition, state, plight
दसवाँ *[dasvā̃]* ADJ tenth
दस्त *[dast]* M loose stool, stool; hand
दस्तक *[dastak]* F knock or rap (with the palm of the hand)
दस्तख़त *[dastakhat]* M signature
दस्ता *[dastā]* M squad, handle, sleeve; bouquet (of flowers); pounder
दस्ताना *[dastānā]* M glove
दस्तावेज़ *[dastāvez]* M document, deed
दस्तूर *[dastūr]* M custom practice; constitution
दहकना *[dehaknā]* V.I. to blaze, to burn with a red hot flame, to be very hot
दहन *[dehan]* M burning; combustion
दहलना *[dehalnā]* V.I. terrorized/terror-stricken, to tremble (with fear), to be

terribly alarmed
दहलीज़ *[dehlīz]* F threshold; entrance
दहशत *[dehśat]* F terror, panic
दहशतगर्द *[dehśatgard]* ADJ, M a terrorist
दहाई *[dahāī]* F the figure ten, the place of tens in numeration
दही *[dahī]* M curd, yogurt
दहेज *[dahej]* M dowry
दाँत *[dā̃t]* M tooth
दाँव *[dā̃v] see* दाव
दाई *[dāī]* ADJ right, right-hand
दाख़िल *[dā<u>kh</u>il]* ADJ entered, admitted
दाख़िला *[dā<u>kh</u>ilā]* M admission, entry
दाग़ *[dā<u>gh</u>]* M speck, stain, scar, mark, blemish
दागना *[dāgnā]* V.T. to burn, to ignite; to cauterize; to brand
दाढ़ी *[dāṛhī]* F beard
दाता *[dātā]* M giver, donor, benefactor
दाद *[dād]* F vocal appreciation; praise; ring worm; shingles
दादा *[dādā]* M paternal grandfather; दादा-दादी *[dādā-dādī]* M paternal grandparents
दादी *[dādī]* F paternal grandmother
दान *[dān]* M donation; charity; alms; suffix used to denote a stand, container, etc.; the fluid that flows from the temples of a rutting elephant
दाना *[dānā]* M grain, parched grain, corn; seed; food, bead; pustule, pimple; piece
दानी *[dānī]* ADJ generous
दाबना *[dābnā]* V.T. to press, to press down, to keep in check
दाम *[dām]* M price
दामन *[dāman]* M skirt of a garment, the extreme end of a sari
दामाद *[dāmād]* M son-in-law
दायर *[dāyar]* ADJ filed (a law suit, etc.)
दायरा *[dāyrā]* M circle, ring, range
दायाँ *[dāyā̃]* ADJ right (as in right hand)
दायित्व *[dāyitva]* F liability, responsibility, obligation, vouchment
दार *[dār]* suffix denoting a person having/owning/possessing something
दारू *[dārū]* F liquor; medical treatment, medicine

दार्शनिक *[dārśanik]* ADJ, M philosophical, philosopher
दाल *[dāl]* F pulse (legume), lentil
दालचीनी *[dālcīnī]* F cinnamon
दालान *[dālān]* M yard, verandah
दाव *[dāv]* M stake, opportunity, chance; trick (in wrestling); strategy; time, turn; forest wood
दावत *[dāvat]* F feast, banquet; invitation
दावा *[dāvā]* M claim, suit
दावेदार *[dāvedār]* M claimant
दावात *[dāvāt]* F inkpot
दास *[dās]* M slave, servant, serf
दासता *[dāstā]* F servility, servile disposition, slavery, bondage, serfdom
दासी *[dāsī]* F maidservant, slave girl
दास्ताँ/दास्तान *[dāstā̃/dāstān]* F tale, narrative, account
दाह *[dāh]* M burning, heat, inflammation; mental agony; cremation
दाहक *[dāhak]* ADJ incendiary, causing burns, inflammatory; agonising
दाहिना *[dāhinā]* ADJ right (hand/side etc)
दिक़ *[diq]* M troubled; harrassed; disturbed
दिक़्क़त *[diqqat]* F difficulty
दिखना *[dikhnā]* V.I. to be visible/seen/sighted/viewed; (x को) दिखना *[(x ko) dikhnā]* V.I. to be visible (to x); (x को) दिखाई देना *[(x ko) dikhāī denā]* V.I. to be visible (to x)
दिखाना *[dikhānā]* V.T. to show
दिखावट *[dikhāvat]* F show; display; ostentation
दिखावा *[dikhāvā]* M show, ostentation, display
दिन *[din]* M day
दिनचर्या *[dincaryā]* F daily routine
दिनांक *[dināṅk]* M date
दिनेश *[dineś]* M sun
दिमाग़ *[dimāgh]* M mind; brain; intellect
दिया *[diyā]* M lamp, earthen lamp
दियासलाई *[diyāsalāī]* F matchstick, matchbox
दिल *[dil]* M heart; courage; spirit

दिलचस्प *[dilcasp]* ADJ interesting
दिलचस्पी *[dilcaspī]* F interest
दिलवाना/दिलाना *[dilvānā/ dilānā]* V.T. to provide, to cause to be given
दिलावर *[dilāvar]* ADJ bold, brave, courageous
दिलासा *[dilāsā]* M consolation, solace, assurance
दिल्लगी *[dillagī]* F jest, joke, fun, humor
दिल्ली *[dillī]* F Delhi
दिवस *[divas]* M day
दिवाना *[divānā]* ADJ mad, crazy, insane
दिवाली/दीपावली *[divālī/ dīpāvalī]* F Diwali (a Hindu festival)
दिव्य *[divya]* ADJ divine, celestial; charming, beautiful, brilliant
दिशा *[diśā]* F direction, line
दिसंबर *[disambar]* M December (month)
दीक्षा *[dīkṣā]* F initiation
दीक्षित *[dīkṣit]* ADJ initiated
दीखना *[dīkhnā]* V.I. visible/seen
दीजिये *[dījiye]* honorific imperative form of the verb देना
दीदी *[dīdī]* F older sister
दीन *[dīn]* ADJ, M poor; miserable; humble; religion
दीप *[dīp]* M earthen lamp; the most eminent person of a family or clan
दीपक *[dīpak]* M lamp
दीपावली *[dīpāvalī]* *see* दिवाली
दीप्ति *[dīpti]* F luster; splendor; luminosity, brilliance
दीबाचा *[dībācā]* M preface
दीमक *[dīmak]* F termite, white ant
दीया *[dīyā]* M lamp
दीर्घ *[dīrgh]* ADJ long, large, wide, tall, huge, deep
दीवान *[dīvān]* M chief minister (in a royal court), a royal court; a couch without back-rest; a collection of poems, anthology
दीवानगी *[dīvāngī]* F craziness, madness
दीवाना *[dīvānā]* ADJ mad, crazy, insane
दीवार *[dīvār]* F wall
दुःख/दुख *[duḥkh/dukh]* M sorrow, sadness
दुःखांत *[duḥkhānt]* ADJ tragic, resulting in grief

दुःखी *[duḥkhī]* ADJ sad, unhappy

दु *[du]* allomorphy of दो used as the first member in compound words

दुआ *[duā]* F prayer

दुकान *[dukān]* F shop

दुकानदार *[dukāndār]* M shopkeeper

दुख *[dukh]* M sorrow, sadness

दुखना *[dukhnā]* V.I. to ache, to suffer pain

दुखिया *[dukhiyā]* ADJ INVAR sad; unfortunate

दुखी *[dukhī]* ADJ sad, unhappy

दुनिया *[duniyā]* F world

दुबला *[dublā]* ADJ lean, thin, weak

दुम *[dum]* F tail, hind-most part (of an animal); hanger-on, constant close follower

दुराग्रह *[durāgrah]* M contumacy, pertinacity, importunity

दुराचरण *[durācaraṇ]* M misconduct, malfeasance, wickedness, immorality, depravity

दुरात्मा *[durātmā]* ADJ wicked, vicious, vile

दुरुपयोग *[durupyog]* M misuse, misusage, misapplication

दुरुस्त *[durust]* ADJ proper; fit; correct, all right

दुर्ग *[durg]* M fort, castle, citadel

दुर्गा *[durgā]* F Durga, spouse of Shiva

दुर्घटना *[durghaṭnā]* F accident, mishap, tragic incident

दुर्दशा *[durdaśā]* F predicament, plight, misery

दुर्बल *[durbal]* ADJ weak, feeble, powerless; emaciated; imbecile

दुर्बलता *[durbaltā]* F weakness, feebleness; emaciation; imbecility

दुर्भाग्य *[durbhāgya]* M misfortune, ill luck, tragedy

दुर्व्यवहार *[durvyavahār]* M misbehavior, misconduct, ill-treatment

दुलहन *[dulhan]* F bride

दुलारा *[dulārā]* ADJ beloved, darling, dear

दुल्हन *[dulhan]* F bride

दुविधा *[duvidhā]* F dilemma

दुश्मन *[duśman]* M enemy

दुश्मनी *[duśmanī]* F enmity

दुष्कर *[duṣkar]* ADJ difficult, hard, arduous

दुष्ट *[duṣṭ]* ADJ, M wicked, vile, bad, malevolent, faulty; scoundrel, rascal

दुहना *[duhnā]* V.T. to milk, to squeeze, to exploit

दुहरा *[duhrā]* ADJ two-fold, double, dual

दुहराना *[duhrānā]* V.T. to repeat; to revise

दूत *[dūt]* M messenger, courier, legate, emissary, envoy

दूतावास *[dūtāvās]* M embassy, high commission

दूध *[dūdh]* M milk

दूर *[dūr]* ADV far

दूरदर्शी *[dūrdarśī]* ADJ far-sighted, wise

दूरदर्शिता *[dūrdarśitā]* F farsightedness, wisdom

दूरी *[dūrī]* F distance, remoteness, range

दूल्हा *[dūlhā]* M bridegroom

दूसरा *[dūsrā]* ADJ second, other, another

दूसरी तरफ़ *[dūsrī taraf]* ADV on the other side

दृग *[dṛg]* M eye

दृढ़ *[dṛṛh]* ADJ firm, solid

दृढ़ता *[dṛṛhtā]* F firmness, resoluteness, toughness, strength; rigidity, tenacity

दृश्य *[dṛśya]* ADJ visible, spectacular M scene, sight; spectacle

दृष्टि *[dṛṭṣi]* F sight, view, vision, glance

देखना *[dekhnā]* V.T. to watch, to see

देखभाल *[dekhbhāl]* F care, maintenance, supervision

देखरेख *[dekhrekh]* F supervision, guidance, care

देन *[den]* F contribution, gift, giving

देना *[denā]* V.T. to give

देर *[der]* F delay; lateness

देरी *[derī]* F delay, lag

देव *[dev]* M god; deity; respectable person; giant, demon

देवता *[devatā]* M god, deity, divine being

देवनागरी *[devanāgarī]* F Hindi script

देवर *[devar]* M husband's younger brother

देवरानी *[devrānī]* F husband's younger brother's wife

देवालय *[devālay]* M temple, seat of a deity

देवी *[devī]* F goddess

देश *[deś]* M country

देशद्रोह *[deśdroh]* M treason, disloyalty to one's country
देशद्रोही *[deśdrohī]* ADJ, M traitor
देशभक्त *[deśbhakt]* ADJ, M patriot
देशभक्ति *[deśbhakti]* F patriotism
देशी *[deśī]* ADJ native; indigenous; local; indigenous; native
देसी *[desī]* ADJ country-made
देह *[deh]* F body; physique; person; soma
देहरी *[dehrī]* F threshold; doorsill; doorstep
देहली *[dehlī]* F *see* देहरी
देहांत *[dehānt]* M death; demise
देहात *[dehāt]* M countryside
दैनिक *[dainik]* ADJ, M daily; daily (newspaper)
दैवी *[daivī]* ADJ divine, ethereal, celestial
दो *[do]* ADJ two
दोना *[donā]* M cup formed by folding up the large leaves of certain trees
दोनों *[donõ]* ADJ both
दोपहर *[dopahar]* F midday; afternoon
दोबारा *[dobārā]* ADV twice, a second time
दोशाला *[dośālā]* M shawl
दोष *[doṣ]* M fault, flaw, defect, demerit, disorder; guilt, blame
दोषी *[doṣī]* ADJ, M guilty; culprit
दोस्त *[dost]* M, F friend
दोस्ती *[dostī]* F friendship
दोहन *[dohan]* M milking, exploitation
दोहरा *[dohrā]* ADJ double; two-fold; equivocal; stoutish
दोहराना *[dohrānā]* V.T. to revise; to recapitulate; to repeat; to reiterate, to make two-fold
दौड़ *[dauṛ]* F race, run, running
दौड़ना *[dauṛnā]* V.I. to run
दौर *[daur]* M phase, stage, round
दौरा *[daurā]* M tour; fit
दौरान *[daurān]* during
दौलत *[daulat]* F wealth
दौलतमंद *[daulatmand]* ADJ wealthy
द्रव *[drav]* M liquid, fluid
द्रविड़ *[draviṛ]* ADJ, M Dravidian; Dravidian country, Dravidian person

द्रोह *[droh]* M malice; rancor, rebellion, hostility

द्रोही *[drohī]* ADJ malicious; rancorous, malignant, rebellious, insubordinate, hostile

द्वंद्व *[dvandva]* M conflict, quarrel, uproar, hubbub, duel; pair, couple; copulative compound (wherein the members if uncompounded would be in the same case and connected by the conjunction "and")

द्वापर *[dvāpar]* M the third of the four ages of Hindu mythology, the age of transition from good to vice

द्वार *[dvār]* M door; doorway

द्वारा *[dvārā]* PP by; through, through the medium of

द्वि *[dvi]* ADJ two

द्वितीय *[dvitīya]* ADJ second

द्वीप *[dvīp]* M island

द्वेष *[dveṣ]* M malice, aversion, repugnance, ill-will, malevolence, dislike, disaffection

द्वैत *[dvait]* M duality; dualism; discrimination

ध

धंधा *[dhandhā]* M vocation; occupation; business; work

धँसना *[dhãsnā]* V.T. to sink; to penetrate into; to enter into

धकेलना *[dhakelnā]* V.T. to shove; to push; to thrust ahead

धक्का *[dhakkā]* M push; shove; shock; setback

धड़ *[dhaṛ]* M torso; trunk

धड़कन *[dhaṛkan]* F throbbing, beating (of the heart)

धड़कना *[dhaṛaknā]* V.I. to beat, to throb

धड़ाका *[dhaṛākā]* M explosion, crash; a loud report

धत् *[dhat]* IND be off!; damn!; धत् तेरे की *[dhat tere kī]* IND damn it!; Gosh!

धन *[dhan]* M wealth, riches, money; धन दौलत *[dhan daulat]* F wealth and affluence

धनिया *[dhaniyā]* M coriander

धनी *[dhanī]* ADJ wealthy, rich, opulent

धनुष *[dhanuṣ]* M bow, arch

धन्य *[dhanya]* ADJ blessed, worthy of felicitation, fortunate IND well done!
धन्यवाद *[dhanyavād]* M thanks; an expression of gratitude IND thank you!
धब्बा *[dhabbā]* M blemish; blot; slur; stain, taint
धमकी *[dhamkī]* F threat, bluster
धरती *[dhartī]* F earth, world
धरना *[dharnā]* V.T. to hold; to place; to put; to arrest
धर्म *[dharm]* M religion; righteousness; action, duty, justice
धर्मांतर *[dharmāntar]* M another religion
धर्मात्मा *[dharmātmā]* ADJ devout, religious
धर्मी *[dharmī]* religious, virtuous, pious
धागा *[dhāgā]* M thread
धातु *[dhātu]* F metal; constituent elements; verbal stem
धाम *[dhām]* M residence; abode; seat of a deity; the four chief pilgrimage centers (for Hindus)
धार *[dhār]* F edge; sharp edge; current; flow; jet
धारण *[dhāraṇ]* M holding; wielding; supporting
धारा *[dhārā]* F current, steam, flow (of water); clause of a bill; धारा-प्रवाह *[dhārā-pravāh]* ADJ fluent, non-stop, incessant
धारावाहिक *[dhārāvāhik]* M serial; serialized
धार्मिक *[dhārmik]* ADJ religious; righteous
धार्मिकता *[dhārmiktā]* F religosity; righteousness
धावा *[dhāvā]* M raid; charge, attack
धिक्कार *[dhikkār]* M censure; curse; opprobrium
धिक्कारना *[dhikkārnā]* V.T. to censure; to curse; to condemn
धीमा *[dhimā]* ADJ slow; dull; mild; low; gentle
धीरज *[dhīraj]* M patience; fortitude; composure
धीरे *[dhīre]* ADV mildly; slowly; gently; धीरे-धीरे *[dhīre-dhīre]* ADV slowly
धुंध *[dhũdh]* F mist; fog; haze
धुँधलका *[dhũdhalkā]* M twilight; darkishness; haziness

धुँधला *[dhũdhlā]* ADJ hazy; dim; misty, foggy; faded; blurred
धुँधलापन *[dhũdhlāpan]* M haziness; fog
धुंधलाना *[dhũdhlānā]* V.I. dimmed; become hazy
धुआँ *[dhuā̃]* M smoke; fume
धुत्त *[dhutt]* ADJ stupified (by alcohol); drunk; besotted (with)
धुन *[dhun]* F assiduity; perseverance; mania; fad; ardor; tune
धुनना *[dhunnā]* V.T. card or comb (cotton)
धुलना *[dhulnā]* V.I. washed
धुलाई *[dhulāī]* F act or process of washing; a wash
धूप *[dhūp]* F sunshine; incense
धूम *[dhūm]* M smoke; fume F fanfare, tumult, bustle, pomp; ado
धूमधाम *[dhūmdhām]* M pomp, fanfare; धूमधाम से *[dhūmdhām se]* ADV with pomp and ceremony
धूमिल *[dhūmil]* ADJ vague; blurred; fumigated
धूम्र *[dhūmra]* M smoke; fume
धूम्रपान *[dhūmrapān]* M smoking
धूर्त *[dhūrt]* ADJ cunning; crooked; rascal
धूल *[dhūl]* F dust; dirt
धूसरित *[dhūsrit]* ADJ filled with dust; turned dusty
धृष्ट *[dhṛṣṭ]* ADJ impudent; insolent; obtrusive; impertinent
धृष्टता *[dhṛṣṭtā]* F impudence; insolence
धैर्य *[dhairya]* M patience; fortitude; endurance
धोखा *[dhokhā]* M deception, fraud, cheating, guile
धोखेबाज़ *[dhokhebāz]* M, ADJ cheat; swindler; deceitful; fraudulent
धोखेबाज़ी *[dhokhebāzī]* F deception; fraud; cheating
धोती *[dhotī]* F loin cloth
धोना *[dhonā]* V.T. to wash, to launder, to cleanse
धोबी *[dhobī]* M washerman; धोबी घाट *[dhobī ghāṭ]* F a washing venue by the side of the river or a tank, often with steps going down to the water and stones to wash clothes
धौंकना *[dhaũknā]* V.T. to blow with bellows; to fan a fire
धौंकनी *[dhaũknī]* F bellows

ध्यान *[dhyān]* M attention; meditation; heed; contemplation
ध्रुपद *[dhrupad]* M a form of classical Indian music
ध्रुव *[dhruv]* M pole; the polar star ADJ fixed, firm, permanent; ध्रुव तारा *[dhruv tārā]* M the polar star
ध्वंस *[dhvans]* M ruin; ruination; destruction, devastation
ध्वज *[dhvaj]* M flag, banner, ensign, colors
ध्वजा *[dhvajā]* F a flag, standard, ensign
ध्वनि *[dhvani]* F sound; suggestion (in poetics); suggested meaning
ध्वस्त *[dhvast]* ADJ ruined; destroyed; devastated

न

न *[na]* ADV no, not, isn't it?
नंगा *[naṅgā]* ADJ naked, nude, bare, uncovered; नंगे पाँव *[naṅge pā̃v]* ADV barefoot
नंबर *[nambar]* M number, marks (in an exam)
नक़द *[naqad]* M cash, ready money
नक़ल *[naqal]* F copy, duplicate, imitation; mimicking, mimicry
नक़लनवीस *[naqalnavīs]* M one who copies
नक़ली *[naqlī]* ADJ couterfeit, false, artificial; fabricated
नक़्शा *[naqśā]* M map, chart, plan
नक़ाब *[naqāb]* F mask, veil; visor
नक़्शा *[naqśā]* M *see* नक़्श
नक्षत्र *[nakṣatra]* M star; constellation
नख़रा *[nakhrā]* M coquetry; flirtatious airs, airs and graces
नगर *[nagar]* M city, town; नगर निगम *[nagar nigam]* M municipal corporation; नगर पालिका *[nagar pālikā]* F municipality; municipal committee
नचाना *[nacānā]* V.T. to cause/make (someone) dance (to one's tune)
नज़दीक *[nazdīk]* ADV close, near
नज़र *[nazar]* F sight, eyesight, vision, look, glance; attention; gift, present;

नज़रबंद *[nazarband]* ADJ in detention, under watch M an internee
नज़राना *[nazrānā]* M present, gift
नज़रिया *[nazariyā]* M point of view; perspective; angle
नज़ाकत *[nazākat]* F delicacy, tenderness, grace
नजात *[najāt]* F salvation; liberation, riddance
नज़ारा *[nazārā]* M scene; view; spectacle, sight
नज़्म *[nazm]* F poem; verse
नटखट *[naṭkhaṭ]* ADJ mischievous, naughty
नतीजा *[natījā]* M result, consequence, conclusion
नथना *[nathnā]* M nostril
नदी *[nadī]* F river
ननद *[nanad]* F sister-in-law; husband's sister
ननदोई *[nandoī]* M brother-in-law, the husband of a woman's ननद
नन्हाँ *[nanhā̃]* ADJ small, tiny, wee (said of children)
नफ़रत *[nafrat]* F hatred, dislike
नफ़ा *[nafā]* M profit, gain; advantage
नफ़ीस *[nafīs]* ADJ nice, fine, excellent, exquisite, dainty
नब्ज़ *[nabz]* F pulse (of the hand)
नब्बे *[nabbe]* ADJ ninety
नम *[nam]* ADJ moist, humid, damp
नमक *[namak]* M salt
नमकीन *[namkīn]* ADJ salty; salted M a salty dish of snacks
नमस्कार *[namaskār]* M hello and goodbye
नमस्ते *[namaste]* M hello and goodbye
नमाज़ *[namāz]* F prayer (by Muslims)
नमी *[namī]* F humidity; dampness, moisture
नमूना *[namūnā]* M sample; specimen; model; design; pattern
नम्र *[namra]* ADJ modest, humble; polite; meek; submissive
नया *[nayā]* ADJ new
नयापन *[nayāpan]* M newness
नर *[nar]* M man; male ADJ male
नरक *[narak]* M hell; inferno; a place of great torture and suffering
नरगिस *[nargis]* F the narcissus plant and its flowers

नरम *[naram]* ADJ soft, gentle, delicate; pliant, flexible

नरमी *[narmī]* F softness, gentleness; delicacy; kindness

नरसों *[narsõ]* ADV two days after tomorrow; two days before yesterday

नर्क *[nark]* M *see* नरक

नर्म *[narm]* ADJ *see* नरम

नल *[nal]* M pipe; tap; hydrant

नली *[nalī]* F tube; a pipe; the barrel of a gun

नवंबर/नवम्बर *[navambar]* M November (month)

नव *[nav]* ADJ new; novel, neo-; young

नवल *[naval]* ADJ new; novel, neo-; fresh

नवाँ *[navā̃]* ADJ ninth

नवासी *[navāsī]* ADJ eighty-nine

नवीन *[navīn]* ADJ new; novel, neo-modern; recent

नवीनता *[navīntā]* F novelty; newness; freshness

नशा *[naśā]* M intoxication; inebriation

नशीला *[naśīlā]* ADJ intoxicating; inebriant

नश्तर *[naśtar]* M lancet; a surgical knife

नष्ट *[naṣṭ]* ADJ destroyed; perished; annihilated; ruined

नस *[nas]* F vein, sinew, nerve

नसल *[nasal]* F breed; pedigree; generation

नसीब *[nasīb]* M fate; fortune; destiny

नस्ल *[nasl]* F *see* नसल

नहर *[nehar]* F canal; channel; waterway

नहलाना *[nahlānā]* V.T. to bathe (someone)

नहाना *[nahānā]* V.I., V.T. to bathe

नहीं *[nahī̃]* ADV no, not; नहीं तो *[nahī̃ to]* ADV certainly not, otherwise

ना *[nā]* ADV no; a word denoting negation

नाइंसाफ़ *[nāinsāf]* ADV unjust

नाइंसाफ़ी *[nāinsāfī]* F injustice

नाउम्मीद *[nāummīd]* ADJ hopeless; disappointed

नाउम्मीदी *[nāummīdī]* F hopelessness; disappointment

नाकाम *[nākām]* ADJ failed; ineffectual; unsuccessful

नाकामी *[nākāmī]* F failure

नाख़ुश *[nākhuś]* ADJ unhappy, displeased

नाख़ुशी *[nākhuśī]* F displeasure, annoyance

नाजायज़ *[nājāyaz]* ADJ improper; undue; illegitimate
नापाक *[nāpāk]* ADJ impure; polluted; unholy; unchaste
नालायक़ *[nālāyaq]* ADJ unworthy, worthless; unfit; incompetent
नाई *[nāī]* M barber; a particular caste in the traditional Hindu social order subsisting on hair-cutting and shaving.
नाक *[nāk]* F nose; (a symbol of) prestige and honor
नाख़ून *[nā<u>kh</u>ūn]* M nail
नाग *[nāg]* M cobra; snake; elephant
नागरिक *[nāgrik]* ADJ civilian; citizen
नागरिकता *[nāgriktā]* F citizenship
नाच *[nāc]* M/F dance
नाचना *[nācnā]* V.I. to dance
नाज़ *[nāz]* M coquetry; airs; feigned air; pride; vanity
नाज़ुक *[nāzuk]* ADJ delicate, frail, tender; critical
नाज़ुक मिज़ाज *[nāzuk mizāj]* ADJ a delicate constitution; touchy; irascible
नाटक *[nāṭak]* M drama
नटकीय *[nāṭkīya]* ADJ dramatic; histrionic
नाटा *[nāṭā]* ADJ short; of short stature; dwarfish
नाड़ी *[nāṛī]* F pulse; vein; artery
नाता *[nātā]* M relation; connection
नाती *[nātī]* M grandson
नाते *[nāte]* M relations; connections; ADV by virtue of; for the sake of; x के नाते *[x ke nāte]* PP by virtue of being x
नातेदार *[nātedār]* M relative, kinsfolk
नाथ *[nāth]* M master, lord; husband
नान *[nān]* F a kind of thick oven-cooked bread made from refined flour
नाना *[nānā]* M maternal grandfather; नाना-नानी *[nānā-nānī]* M maternal grandparents
नानी *[nānī]* F maternal grandmother
नापना *[nāpnā]* V.T. to measure
नाभिक *[nābhik]* M nucleus
नाभिकीय *[nābhikīya]* ADJ nuclear; नाभिकीय परिवार

[nābhikīya parivār] M nuclear family
नाम *[nām]* M name;नामकरण *[nāmkaraṇ]* M baptism; naming
नामक *[nāmak]* ADJ called
नामी *[nāmī]* ADJ famous, reputed, renowned
नायक *[nāyak]* M hero; a leader; chief
नायिका *[nāyikā]* F heroine
नारंगी *[nāraṅgī]* F orange
नारद *[nārad]* M a celestial sage in Indian mythology; one who causes quarrels between people
नारा *[nārā]* M slogan
नाराज़ *[nārāz]* ADJ angry, enraged, displeased
नारियल *[nāriyal]* M coconut
नाला *[nālā]* M rivulet; water course; big drain, gutter
नाली *[nālī]* F drain, drain-pipe, sewer
नाव *[nāv]* F boat; ferry
नावक/नाविक *[nāvak/nāvik]* M sailor, boatman
नाश *[nāś]* M destruction; ruination, devastation; waste
नाशपाती *[nāśpātī]* F pear
नाश्ता *[nāśtā]* M light refreshment; breakfast
नासमझ *[nāsamajh]* ADJ unintelligent; dull; stupid
नास्तिक *[nāstik]* M atheist, unbeliever
निंदा *[nindā]* F censure; condemnation
निकट *[nikaṭ]* ADV, ADJ near, close, proximate
निकटता *[nikaṭta]* F closeness; proximity
निकम्मा *[nikammā]* ADJ inert; idle; indolent; worthless
निकलना *[nikalnā]* V.I. to emerge; to come out, to go out; to proceed; to appear V.T. to take out; to bring out; to expel; to extract
निकास *[nikās]* M outlet, exit, vent; source; origin
निकाह *[nikāh]* M marriage, marriage ceremony
निखरना *[nikharnā]* V.I. to be cleaned/brightened up; to become crystalized
निखार *[nikhār]* M brightness, luster
निगरानी *[nigrānī]* F supervision; guard, watch
निगलना *[nigalnā]* V.I. to swallow; to gulp

निगह *[nigah]* F *see* निगाह
निगाह *[nigāh]* F glance; sight
निचला *[niclā]* ADJ lower; below, beneath
निज़ाम *[nizām]* M management; administration; order
निजी *[nijī]* ADJ one's own; personal; private; unofficial
निठल्ला *[niṭhallā]* ADJ idle; indolent; lazy; unemployed
निठुर *[niṭhur]* ADJ cruel, ruthless
निठुरता *[niṭhurtā]* F cruelty, ruthlessness
निडर *[niḍar]* ADJ fearless; daring; intrepid
नित्य *[nitya]* ADJ excessive; eternal; essential ADV constantly, always, daily
निदान *[nidān]* M diagnosis
निदेश *[nideś]* M direction; directive
निदेशक *[nideśak]* M director
निधन *[nidhan]* M death, passing away
निन्यानबे *[ninyānabe]* ADJ ninety-nine
निपंग *[nipaṅg]* ADJ crippled; invalid; worthless
निपटना *[nipaṭnā]* V.I. to be settled; to be decided; to be finished; to be disposed of
निपुण *[nipuṇ]* ADJ skillful; expert; dexterous; efficient
निबंध *[nibandh]* M essay
निबटना *[nibaṭnā]* V.I. *see* निपटना
निबल *[nibal]* ADJ weak; feeble; invalid
निबाह *[nibāh]* M subsistence; sustenance; maintenance; accommodation; carrying on
निबाहना *[nibāhnā]* V.T. to subsist; to sustain; to accommodate; to maintain; to carry on; to fulfill; to accomplish
निभाना *[nibhānā]* V.T. to carry on; to accommodate; to perform; to maintain
निमंत्रण *[nimantraṇ]* M invitation
नियंत्रण *[niyantraṇ]* M control; restraint
नियम *[niyam]* M rule; canon; law; principle
नियमित *[niyamit]* ADJ regular; regulated
नियुक्त *[niyukt]* ADJ appointed; employed.
नियुक्ति *[niyukti]* F appointment; employment; posting

निरंतर *[nirantar]* ADJ continuous; uninterrupted, incessant

निरक्षर *[nirakṣar]* ADJ illiterate; unlettered

निरक्षरता *[nirakṣartā]* F illiteracy

निरपराध *[niraprādh]* ADJ innocent; guileless

निरपेक्ष *[nirpekṣ]* ADJ absolute; indifferent; without expectation

निरपेक्षता *[nirpekṣtā]* F absoluteness; the state of being unconcerned

निरर्थक *[nirarthak]* ADJ meaningless; vain; useless; fruitless

निरादर *[nirādar]* M disrespect; disgrace; dishonor, insult

निराधार *[nirādhār]* ADJ baseless; groundless; unfounded; without prop or support

निराला *[nirālā]* ADJ unique; peculiar; uncommon; strange

निराश *[nirāś]* ADJ frustrated; disappointed; disheartened; dejected

निराशा *[nirāśā]* F frustration; despair; disappointment; dejection, despondency

निरुपम *[nirupam]* ADJ unequaled; unparalleled; peerless

निरूपण *[nirūpaṇ]* M representation; portrayal; characterization

निरोग *[nirog]* ADJ free from disease; healthy

निरोध *[nirodh]* M restraint, control; obstruction; restriction

निरोधक *[nirodhak]* ADJ, M restrainer; condom

निर्गुण *[nirguṇ]* ADJ without attributes or qualities; an epithet of God who is beyond the three गुण

निर्णय *[nirṇay]* M judgment; decision, conclusion

निर्दय *[nirday]* ADJ ruthless; merciless

निर्दयता *[nirdayatā]* F ruthlessness, mercilessness

निर्देश *[nirdeś]* M specification; mention; reference; direction

निर्देशक *[nirdeśak]* M director

निर्धन *[nirdhan]* ADJ poor; indigent; impoverished

निर्धनता *[nirdhantā]* F poverty

निर्बल *[nirbal]* ADJ weak, feeble, powerless

निर्बलता *[nirbaltā]* F powerlessness, weakness
निर्माण *[nirmāṇ]* M construction; creation; manufacture
निर्माता *[nirmātā]* M constructor, producer
निर्यात *[niryāt]* M export
निर्वाण *[nirvāṇ]* M salvation; liberation (from existence); extinction
निर्वाह *[nirvāh]* M maintenance; subsistence; accomplishment
निवास *[nivās]* M residence; abode; dwelling
निवासी *[nivāsī]* ADJ inhabitant; resident; native
निवृत्त *[nivṛtt]* F resignation; freedom; disencumberance; retirement; absence of occupation
निवेदन *[nivedan]* M supplication; request; application; submission
निवेदनपत्र *[nivedanpatra]* M letter of application
निवेश *[niveś]* M investment; concentration
निशान *[niśān]* M sign; mark; landmark; scar; impression; trace; clue
निशाना *[niśānā]* M target; butt; mark; aim
निशानी *[niśānī]* F momento, keepsake; token; sign
निश्चय *[niścay]* M decision
निश्चल *[niścal]* ADJ steady; unwavering; quiet; stationary
निश्चिंत *[niścint]* ADJ carefree; unconcerned
निश्चित *[niścit]* ADJ definite, certain, sure
निश्चितता *[niścittā]* F free from doubt, state of certainty
निश्छल *[niśchal]* ADJ straightforward; honest; uncanny; without guile
निषेध *[niṣedh]* M taboo; prohibition, ban, negation
निष्कर्ष *[niṣkarṣ]* M conclusion; inference
निष्ठा *[niṣṭhā]* F allegiance; loyalty; faith; fidelity; devotion
निष्ठावान *[niṣṭhāvān]* ADJ faithful; loyal
निष्ठुर *[niṣṭhur]* ADJ ruthless; merciless; brutal; cruel
निष्ठुरता *[niṣṭhurtā]* F ruthlessness
निष्पक्ष *[nispaks]* ADJ objective, neutral, unbiased

निष्पक्षता *[niṣpakṣatā]* F neutrality
निहत्था *[nihatthā]* ADJ unarmed
निहायत *[nihāyat]* ADV extremely, excessively, absolutely, very much
निहारना *[nihārnā]* V.T. to see, to look at, to behold
निहाल *[nihāl]* ADJ fulfilled; gratified; delighted
निहित *[nihit]* ADJ inherent; implied; vested
नींद *[nī̃d]* F sleep; slumber
नींबू *[nī̃bū]* M *see* नीबू
नींव *[nī̃v]* F foundation, base, ground
नीच *[nīc]* ADJ mean, base, vile, inferior
नीचता *[nīcatā]* F meanness, baseness, vileness; inferiority; lowliness
नीचा *[nīcā]* ADJ mean, base, vile; low
नीचे *[nīce]* ADV beneath; below
नीड़ *[nīṛ]* M nest
नीति *[nīti]* F policy; equity
नीबू *[nībū]* M lemon
नीयत *[nīyat]* F motive; intention
नीरस *[nīras]* ADJ sapless; juiceless, dry; flat; insipid
नील *[nīl]* M indigo, the plant and the dye
नीला *[nīlā]* ADJ blue
नीलापन *[nīlāpan]* M blueness
नीलाम *[nīlām]* M auction, public sale
नुकता *[nuktā]* M defect; flaw; fault; deficiency; नुकता-चीनी *[nuktā-cīnī]* F fault-finding, criticism
नुक़्ता *[nuqtā]* M point; dot; blot
नुक़सान *[nuqsān]* M loss; damage; harm; disadvantage
नुकीला *[nukīlā]* ADJ pointed, sharp
नुमाइंदगी *[numāindagī]* F representation; delegacy
नुमाइंदा *[numāindā]* M representative; delegate
नुमाइश *[numāiś]* F exhibition; show; display
नुमाइशी *[numāiśī]* ADJ showy, ostentatious
नुसख़ा *[nuskhā]* M prescription; recipe; formula
नूपुर *[nūpur]* M anklet
नृत्य *[nṛtya]* M dance, dance performance; नृत्य कला *[nṛtya kalā]* F the art of dance

ने *[ne]* PP a postposition denoting the subject case with a transitive verb in the perfective form

नेक *[nek]* ADJ good; virtuous

नेकी *[nekī]* F goodness, virtue, piety

नेता *[netā]* M leader; politician

नेत्र *[netra]* M eye

नेपाल *[nepāl]* M Nepal

नैतिक *[naitik]* ADJ moral; ethical

नैन *[nain]* M eye

नैसर्गिक *[naisargik]* ADJ natural; spontaneous

नोक *[nok]* F point; tip; end; forepart

नोचना *[nocnā]* V.T. to pinch; to scratch

नोट *[noṭ]* M a note; currency note

नोटिस *[noṭis]* M notice

नौ *[nau]* ADJ nine

नौकर *[naukar]* M servant; employee; नौकर-चाकर *[naukar-cākar]* M servants; a retinue of servants

नौकरी *[naukrī]* F employment; work

नौबत *[naubat]* F state of affair; conditions; turn

न्याय *[nyāy]* M justice; fairness

न्यायाधीश *[nyāyādhīś]* M judge

न्यायालय *[nyāyālay]* M a court of law

न्यून *[nyūn]* ADJ less; lacking; deficient

न्यूनतम *[nyūntam]* ADJ minimum, minimal

प

पंकज *[paṅkaj]* M lotus

पंक्ति *[paṅkti]* F line; row, file; rank, queue

पंख *[paṅkh]* M wing; feather, blade

पंखा *[paṅkhā]* M fan; blade

पंगु *[paṅgu]* ADJ lame

पंचायत *[pañcāyat]* F village assembly, village elders

पंछी *[pañchī]* M bird

पंजर *[pañjar]* M skeleton, frame, cage

पंजा *[pañjā]* M claw; paw; an aggregate of five

पंजाब *[pañjāb]* M Panjab, a state in northern India; a region in northwestern India and eastern Pakistan

पंडित *[paṇḍit]* **M** Brahman scholar; learned person
पंथ *[panth]* **M** path; road; creed; sect; religious order
पंथी *[panthī]* **M** traveler; adherent of a sect
पंद्रह *[pandrah]* **ADJ** fifteen
पंद्रहवाँ *[pandrahvā̃]* **ADJ** fifteenth
पकड़ना *[pakaṛnā]* **V.T.** to grab; to catch
पकवान *[pakvān]* **M** rich delicacy (food)
पकाना *[pakānā]* **V.T.** to cook
पकौड़ा *[pakauṛā]* **M** *gram* flour and vegetable fritter
पक्का *[pakkā]* **ADJ** ripe; strong
पक्ष *[pakṣ]* **M** side, party; aspect; fortnight
पक्षपात *[pakṣapāt]* **M** partiality, favoritism
पक्षपाती *[pakṣapātī]* **ADJ** partial, partisan
पक्षी *[pakṣī]* **M** bird
पग *[pag]* **M** foot, step, pace
पगडंडी *[pagḍaṇḍī]* **F** footway; track
पगड़ी *[pagṛī]* **F** turban
पगला *[paglā]* **ADJ** mad, crazy, amuck
पचना *[pacnā]* **V.I.** to be digested, to be assimilated
पचपन *[pacpan]* **ADJ** fifty-five
पचहत्तर *[pachattar]* **ADJ** seventy-five
पचास *[pacās]* **ADJ** fifty
पचासी *[pacāsī]* **ADJ** eighty-five
पचीस *[pacīs]* **ADJ** twenty-five
पच्चीस *[paccīs]* **ADJ** twenty-five
पछताना *[pachtānā]* **V.I.** to repent, to rue, to be penitent
पछतावा *[pachtāvā]* **M** repentance, remorse, penitence
पछत्तर *[pachattar]* **ADJ** seventy-five
पजामा *[pajāmā]* **M** pajamas
पटकना *[paṭaknā]* **V.T.** to throw down, to dash down
पटरी *[paṭrī]* **F** rail; trackway; pavement; ruler, wooden strip
पटाखा *[paṭākhā]* **M** cracker; explosive stuff
पटाना *[paṭānā]* **V.T.** to settle; to conclude; to persuade; to seduce; to repay in full
पट्टा *[paṭṭā]* **M** title deed, lease, lease deed; tenure; dog collar; plank
पट्टी *[paṭṭī]* **F** bandage, band, strip, strap

पट्ठा *[paṭṭhā]* M robust young man, offspring; wrestling apprentice; nerve sinew
पठन *[paṭhan]* M reading, study
पठार *[paṭhār]* ADJ plateau
पड़ताल *[paṛtāl]* F checking up; testing, survey
पड़ना *[paṛnā]* V.I. to fall
पड़ोस *[paṛos]* M neighborhood; vicinity
पड़ोसी *[paṛosī]* M neighbor
पड़ोसिन *[paṛosin]* F neighbor
पढ़ना *[paṛhnā]* V.T. to read; to study
पढ़ाई *[paṛhāī]* F study; studies
पढ़ाना *[paṛhānā]* V.T. to teach, to make read
पतंग *[pataṅg]* F kite M the sun
पतंगा *[pataṅgā]* M moth; insect
पतन *[patan]* M fall; downfall; decline
पतला *[patlā]* ADJ thin; slender, narrow
पता *[patā]* M address; whereabouts
पताका *[patākā]* F flag; banner
पति *[pati]* M husband
पतित *[patit]* ADJ fallen; depraved
पत्ता *[pattā]* M leaf
पत्ती *[pattī]* F small leaf, foliage
पत्थर *[patthar]* M stone
पत्नी *[patnī]* F wife
पत्र *[patra]* M letter
पत्रकार *[patrakār]* M journalist
पत्रिका *[patrikā]* F magazine; journal
पथ *[path]* M path; way; course, route
पथरीला *[pathrīlā]* ADJ stony, littered with stones
पथिक *[pathik]* M traveler; wayfarer
पद *[pad]* M office; status; rank; versified composition; step; expression, term
पदक *[padak]* M medal, medallion, badge
पदवी *[padvī]* F title; status; rank; degree
पद्म *[padma]* M lotus flower, lotus plant
पद्य *[padya]* M verse, poetry
पन *[pan]* suffix added to common and attributive nouns to form abstract nouns
पनपना *[panapnā]* V.I. to be revived/recovered, to thrive, to flourish, to prosper

पनाह *[panāh]* F shelter, refuge
पनीर *[panīr]* M cheese
पन्ना *[pannā]* M page
पपड़ी *[papṛī]* F thin crust, flake, scab; thin cakes of wheat or gram
पपीता *[papītā]* M papaya
परंपरा *[paramparā]* F tradition
परंपरागत *[paramparāgat]* ADJ traditional, orthodox
पर *[par]* PP, CONJ but
परखना *[parakhnā]* V.T. to test, to examine, to judge
परचा *[parcā]* M chit, note, prescription
परचून *[parcūn]* M provisions; grocery
परछाई *[parchāī]* F shadow; reflection
परत *[parat]* F layer; fold, tuck; film, lamination
परदा *[pardā]* M curtain; screen; veil, privacy; ear drum; surface
परदादा *[pardādā]* M paternal great-grandfather
परदेश *[pardeś]* M another country; foreign country
परदेशी *[pardeśī]* M foreigner, alien, stranger
परनाना *[panānā]* M maternal great-grandfather
परपोता *[parpotā]* M great-grandson
परम *[param]* ADJ extreme, ultimate, absolute, supreme, best, utmost
परमाणु *[paramāṇu]* M atom
परमात्मा *[paramātmā]* God, the Supreme Being
परमेश्वर *[parameśvar]* M God, the Almighty
परलोक *[parlok]* M the other world, next world, heavenly paradise
परवाह *[parvāh]* F concern, care, heed
परसों *[parsõ]* ADV the day before yesterday/after tomorrow
परस्पर *[paraspar]* IND mutual; reciprocal
परहेज़ *[parhez]* M abstinence, avoidance, régimen, keeping aloof
पराँठा *[parā̃ṭhā]* M pancake-like preparation of kneaded flour fried in ghee
परात *[parāt]* F large shallow circular metallic vessel
पराधीन *[parādhīn]* ADJ

dependent, subject, subjugated, in bondage
पराधीनता *[parādhīntā]* F dependence
पराया *[parāyā]* ADJ pertaining or belonging to another; alien, foreign
परास्त *[parāst]* ADJ defeated, vanquished, overthrown
परिंदा *[parindā]* M bird
परिक्रमण *[parikramaṇ]* M the act or process of revolving, revolution, going around
परिचय *[paricay]* M introduction, acquaintance, familiarity
परिजन *[parijan]* M body of dependents, kith and kin
परिणाम *[pariṇām]* M result, outcome, consequence, conclusion, effect, magnitude
परिपक्व *[paripakva]* ADJ ripe, mature, fully developed
परिपक्वता *[paripakvatā]* F maturity
परिभाषा *[paribhāṣā]* F definition
परिभाषित *[paribhāṣit]* ADJ defined
परिवर्तन *[parivartan]* M change, alteration, variation; interchange
परिवार *[parivār]* M family
परिवेश *[pariveś]* M environment, enclosure, precinct
परिश्रम *[pariśram]* M labor, industry, hard work, exertion, diligence
परिषद् *[pariṣad]* F council, association
परिसर *[parisar]* M premises, enclave, campus
परिस्थिति *[paristhiti]* F circumstance
परिहास *[parihās]* M joke, humor
परी *[parī]* F fairy, nymph
परीक्षा *[parīkṣā]* F examination
परे *[pare]* IND beyond, across, above, on the other side, afar, afterwards, outside
परेशान *[pareśān]* ADJ troubled; bothered
परेशानी *[pareśānī]* F bother, trouble
परोक्ष *[parokṣ]* ADJ indirect; implicit; invisible, imperceptible; secret
परोपकार *[paropkār]* M beneficence, benevolence; charity, altruism

परोसना *[parosnā]* V.T. to serve food
पर्चा *[parcā]* M piece of paper; question paper, chit; introduction; newspaper; proof; leaflet, handbill
पर्दा *[pardā]* M curtain, screen, veil
पर्यटक *[paryaṭak]* M tourist
पर्यटन *[paryaṭan]* M touring; tourism
पर्याप्त *[paryāpt]* ADJ enough, sufficient, ample, adequate
पर्व *[parva]* M festival, day or occasion for performance of religious rites; chapter
पर्वत *[parvat]* M mountain, hill
पलँग/पलंग *[palãg/palaṅg]* M bed
पल *[pal]* M moment, a measure of time equal to twenty-four seconds
पलक *[palak]* F eyelid
पलटना *[palaṭnā]* V.T., V.I. to turn back; to return; to alter; to overturn; to overthrow; to convert; to upset; to reverse
पलटा *[palṭā]* M turn, change; return, relapse
पलड़ा *[palṛā]* M balance-pan
पलना *[palnā]* V.I., M to be brought up, to be reared, to be nourished; cradle
पल्ला *[pallā]* M hem/border/ extreme end of a garment; side; leaf; flap; facet; scale/ pan of a balance
पवन *[pavan]* M air, breeze, wind
पवित्र *[pavitra]* ADJ sacred
पशु *[paśu]* M animal; beast; cattle; savage brute
पश्चात् *[paścāt]* IND after, afterwards, behind
पश्चाताप *[paścātāp]* M remorse, compunction, repentance
पश्चिम *[paścim]* M west
पसंद *[pasand]* ADJ, F approved, liked, liking, choice, taste, preference
पसली *[paslī]* F rib
पसीना *[pasīnā]* M sweat, perspiration
पहचान *[pehcān]* F identity, acquaintance, familiarity, recognition
पहचानना *[pehcānnā]* V.T. to recognize
पहनना *[pehannā]* V.T. to wear, to put on

पहनाना *[pehnānā]* V.T. to cause to wear, to dress (someone)
पहरा *[pehrā]* M a guard; watch; पहरेदार *[pehredār]* M a guard, sentry
पहरी *[pehrī]* M guard, watchman, sentry
पहल *[pehal]* F initiative
पहलवान *[pehalvān]* M wrestler
पहला *[pehlā]* ADJ first
पहलू *[pehlū]* M side; aspect; facet
पहले *[pehle]* ADV ago, before, previously
पहाड़ *[pahāṛ]* M, ADJ mountain; mountainous; पहाड़ी लोग *[pahāṛī log]* M mountain people
पहिया *[pahiyā]* M wheel
पहुँच *[pahũc]* F reach; access; arrival; receipt
पहुँचना *[pahũcnā]* V.I. to arrive
पहुँचाना *[pahũcānā]* V.T. to cause to reach; to carry; to transmit
पहेली *[pahelī]* F riddle
पाँच *[pā̃c]* ADJ five
पाँचवाँ *[pā̃cvā̃]* ADJ fifth
पांडव *[pāṇḍav]* M the five sons of King Pandu that are the heroes of the epic *Mahabharata*
पांडु *[pāṇḍu]* ADJ, M yellow, yellowish, white, pallid, jaundice; King Pandu, father of the heroes of the epic *Mahabharata*
पांडुलिपि *[pāṇḍulipi]* F manuscript
पाँव *[pā̃v]* M foot, leg
पाँसा *[pā̃sā]* M die, dice
पाक *[pāk]* ADJ, M pure, clean, holy, sacred; cooking, maturation
पाखंड *[pākhaṇḍ]* M hypocrisy, pretense, sham
पाखंडी *[pākhaṇḍī]* ADJ, M hypocritical, pretentious; hypocrite
पाख़ाना *[pāk͟hānā]* M privy, latrine, feces, stool
पागल *[pāgal]* ADJ crazy
पाचन *[pācan]* M digestion
पाठ *[pāṭh]* M lesson, reading
पाठक *[pāṭhak]* M reader
पाठन *[pāṭhan]* M reading, teaching
पाठशाला *[pāṭhśālā]* F school
पाठ्यपुस्तक *[pāṭhyapustak]* F course book

पाताल *[pātāl]* M underworld, the nether-most world

पात्र *[pātra]* M character (in a play); container

पाद *[pād]* M foot, leg; foot of a meter; foul wind, fart; quadrant, one-fourth part

पादना *[pādnā]* V.T. to break wind

पादरी *[pādrī]* M clergy, clergyman, Christian priest/missionary

पान *[pān]* M betel leaf

पाना *[pānā]* V.I., V.T. to find; to obtain; to be able to

पानी *[pānī]* M water

पाप *[pāp]* M sin

पापड़ *[pāpaṛ]* M savory crisp, thin cake

पापड़ी *[pāpṛī]* F type of sweet; small round savory thin and crisp cake

पापा *[pāpā]* M papa, father

पापी *[pāpī]* ADJ, M sinning, sinful, sinner

पाबंद *[pāband]* ADJ bound; obliged; restricted; under control

पाबंदी *[pābandī]* F binding; obligation; restriction, control, ban

पायजामा *[pāyjāmā]* M pajamas; trousers

पायल *[pāyal]* M anklet

पारंपरिक *[pāramparik]* ADJ traditional; hereditary

पार *[pār]* ADJ, ADV, M past, last, next, across, on the other side; the other side/coast/bank; extremity, limit; conclusion

पारदर्शक *[pārdarśak]* ADJ transparent

पारा *[pārā]* M mercury

पारित *[pārit]* ADJ passed

पारी *[pārī]* F shift; turn; innings

पार्क *[pārk]* M park

पार्वती *[pārvatī]* F Parvati, spouse of Shiva, epithet of the Goddess Durga

पाल *[pāl]* F sail; suffix denoting "protector/maintainer/manager/etc."

पालक *[pālak]* M spinach

पालकी *[pālkī]* F palanquin, sedan chair

पालतू *[pāltū]* ADJ tame, tamed, domesticated

पालथी *[pālthī]* F cross-legged sitting posture

पालन *[pālan]* M abiding by observance; upbringing; nourishing; tending, maintenance

पालना *[pālnā]* V.T. to bring up, to rear, to nurture; to tame, to domesticate
पालि *[pāli]* F Pali, a middle Indo-Aryan language used extensively in Buddhist writings
पॉलिश *[pāliś]* F polish
पॉलिसी *[pālisī]* F policy, insurance policy
पाव *[pāv]* ADJ, M one-fourth, quarter; one-fourth of a seer
पावन *[pāvan]* ADJ holy, sacred, immaculate
पावर *[pāvar]* M power
पाशविक *[pāśavik]* ADJ brutal, beastly, savage
पाश्चात्य *[pāścātya]* ADJ western
पास *[pās]* ADJ, ADV, M passed, not failed; nearby; pass
पासपोर्ट *[pāsporṭ]* M passport
पासा *[pāsā]* M dice, die
पिंजड़ा/पिंजरा *[piñjaṛā/ piñjrā]* M cage, trap
पिंजर *[piñjar]* M cage, skeleton, physical frame
पिंड *[piṇḍ]* M body, lump, round mass, ball
पिंडली *[piṇḍalī]* F calf (of a leg)
पिघलना *[pighalnā]* V.I. to melt
पिचक *[picak]* F dent; contraction; deflation
पिचकना *[picaknā]* V.I. to be dented; to be contracted/ deflated
पिचकारी *[pickārī]* F water gun; syringe; water pistol
पिछड़ना *[pichaṛnā]* V.I. to lag, to be left behind, to be defeated
पिछला *[pichlā]* ADJ previous, prior
पिछवाड़ा *[pichvāṛā]* M backyard; rear part, hind part
पिटना *[piṭnā]* V.I. to be beaten; to be thrashed; to flop (as a film)
पिटाई *[piṭāī]* F beating, thrashing; work or wages for thrashing; defeat
पिटारा *[piṭāṛā]* M large basket, big box/chest
पिता *[pitā]* M father
पितामह *[pitāmeh]* M grandfather
पित्ता *[pittā]* M gall bladder
पिय *[piya]* M (darling) husband
पिया *[piyā]* M (darling) husband
पिरोना *[pironā]* V.T. to thread, to string; to use a needle

पिलाना *[pilānā]* V.T. to cause to drink, to serve (a drink)
पिशाच *[piśāc]* M devil, demon, evil spirit
पिसना *[pisnā]* V.I. to be ground/powdered; to be pressed; to labor hard; to be tortured; to be afflicted
पिस्ता *[pistā]* M pistachio
पिस्तौल *[pistaul]* F pistol
पिस्सू *[pissū]* M flea
पीक *[pīk]* F spittle of chewed betel leaf
पीछा *[pīchā]* M back/hind part, pursuit, chase
पीछे *[pīche]* ADV back, behind, after
पीटना *[pīṭnā]* V.T. to beat, to thrash, to punish; to defeat; to finish, to somehow complete
पीठ *[pīṭh]* F, M back, spine; seat; institute
पीड़ा *[pīṛā]* F pain, ache, anguish, agony; suffering
पीड़ित *[pīṛit]* ADJ oppressed, tortured, afflicted
पीढ़ी *[pīṛhī]* F generation
पीतल *[pītal]* M brass
पीना *[pīnā]* V.T. to drink
पीर *[pīr]* M Monday, Muslim saint
पीला *[pīlā]* ADJ yellow
पीसना *[pīsnā]* V.T. to grind, to pound, to powder; to cause to labor hard, to exploit
पुकार *[pukār]* F call
पुकारना *[pukārnā]* V.T. to call (out); to call (someone)
पुख़्ता *[pukhtā]* ADJ strong, lasting, durable, firm, mature
पुजारी *[pujārī]* M worshipper, Hindu priest
पुण्य *[puṇya]* ADJ sacred, holy, virtuous M good virtue, good deed
पुतली *[putlī]* F puppet, doll, marionette, pupil (of the eye)
पुत्र *[putra]* M son
पुत्री *[putrī]* F daughter
पुदीना *[pudīnā]* M mint
पुनः *[punaḥ]* ADV again, once more, anew
पुनर्जन्म *[punarjanma]* M rebirth
पुनर्जीवन *[punarjīvan]* M resurrection, resuscitation, resurgence
पुनर्निर्माण *[punarnirmāṇ]* M reconstruction, recreation, reproduction
पुर *[pur]* M town, city; large leather pot for drawing water;

room, chamber
पुरखा *[purkhā]* M ancestor
पुरज़ा *[purzā]* M chit, piece of paper, bill; part (of a machine)
पुरजोश *[purjoś]* ADJ zealous, enthusiastic
पुरस्कार *[puraskār]* M reward, prize
पुराना *[purānā]* ADJ old (said of things, not people)
पुरुष *[puruṣ]* M man
पुरोहित *[purohit]* M Hindu priest
पुल *[pul]* M bridge
पुलाव *[pulāv]* M pulao, pilaf, rice mixed with vegetables and/or meat and spices
पुलिंदा *[pulindā]* M bundle, sheaf
पुलिस *[pulis]* F police
पुश्तैनी *[puśtainī]* ADJ hereditary, ancestral
पुष्ट *[puṣṭ]* ADJ strong, robust, sturdy; mature; confirmed
पुष्टि *[puṣṭi]* F confirmation; nourishment, strengthening
पुष्प *[puṣpa]* M flower; menses
पुस्तक *[pustak]* F book
पुस्तकालय *[pustakālay]* M library
पूँछ *[pū̃ch]* F tail, rear part; hanger-on
पूँजी *[pū̃jī]* F capital, investment
पूँजीवाद *[pū̃jīvād]* M capitalism
पूँजीवादी *[pū̃jīvādī]* M capitalist
पूछना *[pūchnā]* V.T. to ask
पूजना *[pūjnā]* V.T. to worship; to revere; to respect; to be fulfilled (as in a wish)
पूजा *[pūjā]* F worship; venerable, reverent
पूड़ी *[pūṛī]* F type of fried bread/cake
पूरब *[pūrab]* M east
पूरा *[pūrā]* ADJ complete
पूर्ण *[pūrṇ]* ADJ complete, whole, entire, full, perfect
पूर्णता *[pūrantā]* F perfection, completeness, totality
पूर्णिमा *[pūrṇimā]* F full-moon day
पूर्व *[pūrv]* M east
पूर्वानुमान *[pūrvānumān]* M forecast, estimate
पूर्वी *[pūrvī]* ADJ eastern
पृथक *[pṛthak]* ADJ separate, isolated, distinct, peculiar ADV aloof, apart
पृथ्वी *[pṛthvī]* F earth, world

पृष्ठ *[pṛṣṭh]* M page; back, rear/hind part
पृष्ठभूमि *[pṛṣṭhbhūmi]* F background
पेंशन *[penśan]* F pension
पेंसिल *[pensil]* F pencil
पेच *[pec]* M screw; complication, intricacy trick; artifice
पेचीदगी *[pecīdagī]* F intricacy, complication, complexity
पेचीदा *[pecīdā]* ADJ intricate, complicated, complex
पेट *[peṭ]* M stomach
पेटी *[peṭī]* F casket, small box; belt, girdle
पेडल *[peḍal]* M pedal
पेड़ *[peṛ]* M tree
पेपर *[pepar]* M paper
पेय *[peya]* ADJ, M drinkable, potable; beverage
पेश *[peś]* ADV in front of, before
पेशगी *[peśagī]* F advance, advance payment, deposit
पेशा *[peśā]* M profession, vocation, occupation
पेशेवर *[peśevar]* ADJ professional
पेशाब *[peśāb]* F urine
पेशी *[peśī]* F muscle; presentation, hearing (in a law suit)
पैंट *[paĩṭ]* F pants
पैंतालीस *[paĩṭālīs]* ADJ forty-five
पैंतीस *[paĩṭīs]* ADJ thirty-five
पैंसठ *[paĩsaṭh]* ADJ sixty-five
पैग़म्बर *[paighambar]* M prophet, divine messenger
पैग़ाम *[paighām]* M message
पैदल *[paidal]* ADV on foot
पैदा *[paidā]* ADJ, INVAR born
पैदाइश *[paidāiś]* F birth, creation
पैदावर *[paidāvar]* F product; production, harvest
पैना *[painā]* ADJ sharp, acute
पैमाना *[paimānā]* M scale, meter, measuring device; peg (of liquor)
पैर *[pair]* M foot, leg; footprint
पैरवी *[pairvī]* F advocacy, pleading, championing
पैसा *[paisā]* M paisa; money
पोंछना *[põchnā]* V.T., M to wipe, to clean, to rub, to efface; cloth for wiping/cleaning
पोटली *[poṭlī]* F small bundle
पोतना *[potnā]* V.T to besmear, to whitewash
पोता *[potā]* M grandson; testicle

पोती *[potī]* F granddaughter
पोथा *[pothā]* M big book/ volume
पोथी *[pothī]* F book
पोपला *[poplā]* ADJ toothless; hollow
पोशाक *[pośāk]* F clothes, dress, attire
पोशीदा *[pośīdā]* ADJ privy, secret, concealed
पोषक *[poṣak]* M one who rears/brings up; protector, supporter
पोषण *[poṣaṇ]* M fostering, rearing, bringing up; protection, support
पोसना *[posnā]* V.T. to rear, to bring up, to domesticate
पौ *[pau]* F ray of light, early dawn
पौदा *[paudā]* M plant, sapling
पौन *[paun]* ADJ three-quarters, quarter to one
पौने *[paune]* ADJ quarter to (less a quarter)
पौष *[pauṣ]* M the tenth month of the Hindu calendar
पौष्टिक *[pauṣṭik]* ADJ nutritive, nutritious
प्याज़ *[pyāz]* M onion
प्यादा *[pyādā]* M footman, infantryman; pedestrian; pawn (in chess)
प्यार *[pyār]* M love
प्यारा *[pyārā]* ADJ, M dear, beloved, pleasing, lovely; dear one, beloved
प्याला *[pyālā]* M cup
प्याली *[pyālī]* F cup
प्यास *[pyās]* F thirst
प्यासा *[pyāsā]* ADJ thirsty
प्रकट *[prakaṭ]* ADJ manifest, revealed, apparent
प्रकरण *[prakaraṇ]* M context, section, chapter (in a book)
प्रकार *[prakār]* M type, manner, sort, kind, quality
प्रकाश *[prakāś]* M light; luster; chapter of a book
प्रकाशक *[prakāśak]* M publisher; one who illuminates
प्रकाशन *[prakāśan]* M publication, publishing, release
प्रकाशित *[prakāśit]* ADJ published; brought to light, manifest, obvious; resplendent
प्रकृति *[prakṛti]* F nature, temperament, disposition
प्रकोप *[prakop]* M wrath, rage, fury

प्रक्रिया *[prakriyā]* F process, procedure, technique, method
प्रक्षेप *[prakṣep]* M projection, throw; interpolation
प्रगट *[pragaṭ]* ADJ manifest, revealed, apparent
प्रगति *[pragati]* F progress, development
प्रगाढ़ *[pragāṛh]* ADJ profound, deep, dense; exceeding, abundant
प्रचंड *[pracaṇḍ]* ADJ excessively violent, impetuous, furious; passionate; powerful
प्रचलन *[pracalan]* M currency, prevalence, custom
प्रचलित *[pracalit]* ADJ current, prevalent, in vogue, common, customary
प्रचार *[pracār]* M propaganda, publicity; currency, prevalence
प्रजा *[prajā]* F subjects, public
प्रणाम *[praṇām]* M reverential, salutation; bowing with respect, a term used in greeting elders
प्रणाली *[praṇālī]* F system, method
प्रताप *[pratāp]* M glorious grace, glory, dignity
प्रति *[prati]* F copy, print; Sanskrit prefix imparting the sense of "toward/near/against/again/etc."
प्रतिकूल *[pratikūl]* ADJ adverse, unfavorable, contrary, opposite, hostile
प्रतिक्रिया *[pratikriyā]* F reaction
प्रतिघात *[pratighāt]* M counter-attack, counter-stroke
प्रतिज्ञा *[pratijñā]* F pledge; vow, promise; enunciation
प्रतिदिन *[pratidin]* ADV every day
प्रतिनिधि *[pratinidhi]* M delegate, representative, deputy
प्रतिपक्ष *[pratipakṣ]* M opposition, rival side
प्रतिपक्षी *[pratipakṣī]* M opponent, rival
प्रतिपादन *[pratipādan]* M exposition, treatment; enunciation
प्रतिबंध *[pratibandh]* M restriction, ban; proviso, condition
प्रतिबिंब *[pratibimb]* M reflection, shadow

प्रतिभा *[pratibhā]* F genius, brilliance
प्रतिभाशाली *[pratibhāśālī]* ADJ brilliant
प्रतिमा *[pratimā]* F image, icon, statue
प्रतिरोध *[pratirodh]* M resistance, obstruction, counteraction; contest
प्रतिलिपि *[pratilipi]* F copy, facsimile
प्रतिशत *[pratiśat]* M percent
प्रतिशोध *[pratiśodh]* M revenge, vendetta, reprisal
प्रतिषेध *[pratiṣedh]* M prohibition, forbiddance, taboo
प्रतिस्पर्धा *[pratispardhā]* F rivalry; contest, competition
प्रतीक *[pratīk]* M symbol, fetish
प्रतीकात्मक *[pratīkātmak]* ADJ symbolic; allegorical
प्रतीक्षा *[pratīkṣā]* F waiting (for), expectation
प्रतीक्षालय *[pratīkṣālay]* M waiting room
प्रतीत *[pratīt]* ADJ appeared, known, acquainted
प्रत्यक्ष *[pratyākṣ]* ADJ visible, tangible; direct
प्रत्यय *[pratyaya]* M idea, concept; credit; conviction, assurance; suffix
प्रत्याशित *[pratyāśit]* ADJ expected, anticipated/ anticipatory
प्रत्याशी *[pratyāśī]* M candidate
प्रत्येक *[pratyek]* ADJ each, every one
प्रथम *[pratham]* ADJ first
प्रथा *[prathā]* F custom, practice, usage
प्रदर्शन *[pradarśan]* M show, exhibition, performance, display, demonstration
प्रदर्शनी *[pradarśanī]* F exhibition
प्रदेश *[prades]* M region, zone, state
प्रदेशीय *[pradeśīya]* regional, state-
प्रधान *[pradhān]* ADJ, M chief, principal, main; president, chairman
प्रधान मंत्री *[pradhān mantrī]* M Prime Minister
प्रबंध *[prabandh]* M management, arrangement, administration; dissertation
प्रबंधक *[prabandhak]* M manager, organizer, executive
प्रबल *[prabal]* ADJ strong, mighty, forceful

प्रबोध *[prabodh]* M awakening, consciousness; enlightenment
प्रभा *[prabhā]* F luster, radiance, refulgence
प्रभात *[prabhāt]* M morning, dawn
प्रभाव *[prabhāv]* M influence, effect, impact
प्रभावित *[prabhāvit]* ADJ influenced, impressed
प्रभावशाली *[prabhāvśālī]* ADJ influential; effective; dominant, predominant
प्रभु *[prabhu]* ADJ, M sovereign, hegemonic; sovereign master; Lord
प्रभुता *[prabhutā]* F sovereignty, hegemony, power
प्रमाण *[pramāṇ]* M evidence, proof; testimony
प्रमुख *[pramukh]* ADJ chief, foremost, principal
प्रमोद *[pramod]* M entertainment, joy, delight
प्रयत्न *[prayatna]* M effort, endeavor, attempt; manner of articulation (in phonetics)
प्रयास *[prayās]* M effort, endeavor, attempt
प्रयोग *[prayog]* M use, experiment, employment
प्रयोग *[prayog]* M application
प्रयोगशाला *[prayogśālā]* F laboratory
प्रयोजन *[prayojan]* M purpose, motive, intention
प्रलय *[pralay]* M universal destruction, annihilation; catastrophe
प्रवक्ता *[pravaktā]* M spokesman
प्रवचन *[pravacan]* M discourse; sermon
प्रवर्त्तक *[pravarttak]* M pioneer; innovator; one who persuades; operator
प्रवर्त्तन *[pravarttan]* M pioneering, introducing something new; persuasion; operation
प्रवास *[pravās]* M dwelling abroad, foreign residence; migration
प्रवाह *[pravāh]* M flow, fluency, unbroken sequence
प्रवीण *[pravīṇ]* ADJ proficient, adept, expert
प्रवृत्ति *[pravṛtti]* F mentality, tendency, inclination; instinct; activity
प्रवेश *[praveś]* M entry, admission, access

प्रशंसा *[praśansā]* F praise; admiration; eulogy
प्रशांत *[praśānt]* ADJ tranquil, quiet, calm
प्रशांति *[praśānti]* F peace, tranquillity, quiet
प्रशासक *[praśāsak]* M administrator, ruler
प्रशासन *[praśāsan]* M administration, rule; training
प्रश्न *[praśna]* M question
प्रसंग *[prasaṅg]* M context; occasion; sexual intercourse
प्रसन्न *[prasanna]* ADJ pleased, happy, cheerful
प्रसन्नता *[prasannatā]* F happiness
प्रसव *[prasav]* M delivery (birth), childbirth, labor
प्रसाद *[prasād]* M blessing, boon; offerings made to an idol
प्रसार *[prasār]* M expansion, dispersion, scattering, propagation; circulation
प्रसारण *[prasāraṇ]* M broadcast; the act or process of expanding/dispersing/spreading/etc.
प्रसिद्ध *[prasiddh]* ADJ famous, well-known, renowned
प्रसिद्धि *[prasiddhi]* F fame, repute, renown
प्रस्ताव *[prastāv]* M resolution, motion, proposal
प्रस्तुत *[prastut]* ADJ present(ed), submitted, ready
प्रस्तुति *[prastuti]* F presentation, submission, production
प्रस्थान *[prasthān]* M departure, setting out; march
प्रहर *[prahar]* M measure of time equaling three hours
प्रहसन *[prahasan]* M comedy
प्रहार *[prahār]* M assault
प्रांत *[prānt]* M province, territory, district
प्रांतीय *[prāntīya]* ADJ provincial; territorial
प्राकृतिक *[prākṛtik]* ADJ natural; physical; unsophisticated
प्राक्कथन *[prākkathan]* M foreword
प्राचीन *[prācīn]* ADJ ancient, antique, outdated
प्राण *[prāṇ]* M life, vital breath, vitality
प्राणी *[prāṇī]* M living being, organism, creature
प्राथमिक *[prāthamik]* ADJ primary, elementary

प्राथमिकता *[prāthamiktā]* F priority, precedence
प्राध्यापक *[prādhyāpak]* M lecturer (in a college/ university)
प्राप्त करना *[prapt karnā]* V.T. to obtain
प्राप्ति *[prāpti]* F receipt, acquisition; income, profit
प्रामाणिक *[prāmāṇik]* ADJ authentic, genuine; authoritative
प्रार्थना *[prārthanā]* F prayer
प्राविधान *[prāvidhān]* M provision
प्रासंगिक *[prāsaṅgik]* ADJ relevant; incidental; contextual
प्रिय *[priya]* ADJ dear, beloved, lovely, pleasing, liked M lover, husband
प्रियतम *[priyatam]* ADJ beloved, dearest
प्रीति *[prīti]* F love, affection
प्रेत *[pret]* M ghost, gobblin; frightful person
प्रेम *[prem]* M love
प्रेमिका *[premikā]* F beloved, sweetheart
प्रेमी *[premī]* M lover
प्रेरणा *[prerṇā]* F inspiration, urge, motive
प्रेरित *[prerit]* ADJ inspired, prompted, motivated
प्रेस *[pres]* M printing press; the newspapers (in general)
प्रोत्साहन *[protsāhan]* M encouragement, incentive
प्रोत्साहित *[protsāhit]* ADJ encouraged
प्रौढ़ *[prauṛh]* ADJ mature, full-grown, adult
प्रौढ़ता *[prauṛhtā]* F maturity, adulthood
प्लावन *[plāvan]* M inundation, flood, deluge
प्लेग *[pleg]* M plague
प्लैटफ़ार्म *[plaitfārm]* M platform

फ

फंदा *[phandā]* M trap, noose, snare, loop; trick
फँसना *[phãsnā]* V.I. to be entrapped/ensnared/baited; to be embroiled/implicated/ involved
फँसाना *[phãsānā]* V.T. to trap, to ensnare, to bait, to implicate, to involve
फ़कीर *[fakīr]* M Muslim mendicant, hermit, recluse; beggar, pauper

फ़ज़ूल *[fazūl]* ADJ useless, worthless, futile
फटकना *[phaṭaknā]* V.T. to winnow, to dust, to sift; to shake off; to reach, to go near; to be separated
फटना *[phaṭnā]* V.I. to explode, to break, to burst, to be torn
फड़कना *[phaṛaknā]* V.I. to be thrilled, to throb, to palpitate, to pulsate, to flutter
फड़फड़ाना *[phaṛphaṛānā]* V.T. to flutter, to flap, to throb
फ़तह *[fateh]* F victory, triumph, conquest
फ़न *[fan]* M art, craft, skill, artifice
फफोला *[phapholā]* M blister, eruption
फबना *[phabnā]* V.I. to fit, to befit, to suit, to become
फ़रमाइश *[farmāiś]* F order, imperative, request
फ़रमाना *[farmānā]* V.T. to request
फ़रवरी *[farvarī]* F February (month)
फ़रश *[farś]* M floor, flooring; carpet, mat; pavement
फ़रार *[farār]* ADJ, M at large, absconding; outlaw, fugitive
फ़रियाद *[fariyād]* F petition, complaint
फ़रिश्ता *[fariśtā]* M angel, divine messenger
फ़रेब *[fareb]* M fraud, duplicity, double-dealing
फ़रोख़्त *[farokht]* ADJ, F sold; sale
फ़र्क़ *[farq]* M difference
फ़र्ज़ *[farz]* M duty, obligation
फ़र्श *[farś]* M floor
फल *[phal]* M fruit
फ़लक *[falak]* M sky, heaven
फलना *[phalnā]* V.I. to bear fruit, to be fruitful/useful, to thrive, to prosper
फ़लाँ *[falā̃]* so and so, such and such
फ़व्वारा *[favvārā]* M fountain
फ़सल *[fasal]* F crop, harvest; season, time
फ़साद *[fasād]* M altercation, row, quarrel
फहराना *[phehrānā]* V.T. to hoist, to wave, to flutter in the air, to flap
फाँक *[phā̃k]* F slice (of fruit, etc.); fragment; clove (of garlic); cleft, slit
फाँदना *[phā̃dnā]* V.I. to jump across, to leap over, to skip

फाँसी *[phā̃sī]* F (death by) hanging, execution; noose
फाटक *[phāṭak]* M main gate, gate, entrance
फ़ायदा *[fāydā]* M advantage
फ़ारिग़ *[fārigh]* ADJ free, freed (from work), having fulfilled one's obligation
फ़ालतू *[fāltū]* ADJ spare, extra, surplus, superfluous; useless, worthless
फाल्गुन *[phālgun]* M the last month of the year in the Hindu calendar
फावड़ा *[phāvṛā]* M spade
फ़ासला *[fāslā]* M distance, gap, space, spacing; difference
फ़िक्र *[fikra]* F worry
फ़िक्रमंद *[fikramand]* ADJ worried
फ़ितरत *[fitrat]* F disposition, nature; cunningness, mischievousness
फ़ितरती *[fitratī]* ADJ natural; cunning, mischievous, wily
फ़िदा *[fidā]* ADJ infatuated, charmed, attracted, devoted
फ़िरंग *[firaṅg]* M syphilis; European
फिर *[phir]* CONJ then; again; afterwards; thereafter; in the future; a second time; फिर भी *[phir bhī]* CONJ nevertheless; फिर से *[phir se]* ADV again
फिरना *[phirnā]* V.I. to turn, to return, to wander, to ramble; to be proclaimed/circulated; to undergo a change
फ़िलहाल *[filhāl]* ADV present, for the present, for the time being
फ़िल्म *[film]* F film, movie
फिसलना *[phisalnā]* V.I. to slip, to slide, to skid; to fall for, to be fascinated
फीका *[phīkā]* ADJ tasteless, insipid, vapid; unsweetened; faded, dull, dim
फ़ीता *[fītā]* M lace, ribbon, tape, strap, shoelace
फ़ुज़ूल *[fuzūl]* ADJ useless, worthless, futile
फ़ुरसत *[fursat]* F spare time
फुलाना *[phulānā]* V.T. to puff up, to inflate, to cause to swell; to cause to become proud; to cause to blossom
फुल्का *[phulkā]* M a thin bread
फुव्वारा *[phuvvārā]* M fountain, shower
फुसफुसाना *[phusphusānā]* V.T.

to whisper, to speak in a low or hushed voice

फुसफुसाहट *[phusphusāhaṭ]* F whisper, whispering sound

फूँकना *[phū̃knā]* V.T. to blow, to puff; to burn, to ignite, to set on fire; to waste, to squander away

फूटना *[phūṭnā]* V.I. to break, to be broken, to crack, to split, to burst, to erupt, to explode; to shoot, to sprout; (secret) to be revealed; (eyes) to go blind

फूफा *[phūphā]* M husband of paternal aunt

फूफी *[phūphī]* F paternal aunt

फूल *[phūl]* M flower

फूलना *[phūlnā]* V.I. to flower, to bloom, to blossom, to swell, to inflate; to be joyous; to be puffed up, to assume airs, to feel proud

फेंकना *[phẽknā]* V.T. to throw, to fling, to hurl, to cast, to toss; to waste; to emit

फेंटना *[phẽṭnā]* V.T. to batter, to beat into froth, to mix by trituration; to shuffle

फेन *[phen]* M foam, froth, lather, scum

फेफड़ा *[phephṛā]* M lung

फेरना *[phernā]* V.T. to turn, to return; to invert; to repeat again and again; to change the order, to shuffle; to proclaim, to pronounce

फेरा *[pherā]* M going round, round, circumambulation, circuit; marriage rite in which the bride and groom walk around the sacred fire together

फेरीवाला *[pherīvālā]* ADJ hawker, street vendor

फ़ेल *[fel]* ADJ, M failed, unsuccessful; misdeed, deed, doing, action

फैलना *[phailnā]* V.I. to spread, to be diffused, to expand

फ़ैसला *[faislā]* M decision, judgment, settlement, resolution

फोकट *[phokaṭ]* ADJ free, free of charge, gratis; फोकट में *[phokaṭ mẽ]* ADV for free

फ़ोटो *[foṭo]* M photograph

फोड़ना *[phoṛnā]* V.T. to break, to burst, to split, to cause to defect

फोड़ा *[phoṛā]* M boil, ulcer, tumor

फ़ोन *[fon]* M phone
फ़ौज *[fauj]* F army
फ़ौजी *[faujī]* M soldier; ADJ martial
फ़ौत *[faut]* F death, demise
फ़ौरन *[fauran]* ADV immediately, instantly, at once
फ़्रांस *[frāns]* M France
फ़्रांसीसी *[frānsīsī]* ADJ, F French; the French language
फ़्लैट *[flaiṭ]* M apartment, flat

ब

बंगला *[baṅglā]* F Bengali language M bungalow
बंगाल *[baṅgāl]* M Bengal, a region in the east of the Indian subcontinent that encompasses the Indian state of West Bengal and Bangladesh
बंजर *[bañjar]* ADJ, F barren, unproductive, fallow; fallow/barren land
बँटना *[bā̃ṭnā]* V.I. to be divided/partitioned/distributed
बँटवारा *[bā̃ṭvārā]* M partition, division, distribution
बंद *[band]* ADJ closed, off
बंदगी *[bandagī]* F salutation; prayer, worship
बंदर *[bandar]* M monkey; harbor
बंदरगाह *[bandargāh]* F harbor, port
बंदा *[bandā]* M servant, slave, individual; humble self (used by speaker to express modesty)
बंदी *[bandī]* M captive, prisoner; bard
बंदूक़ *[bandūq]* F gun
बंदोबस्त *[bandobast]* M (land) settlement, management
बंध *[bandh]* M bond. tie, fetter, string, ligature
बंधन *[bandhan]* M bond; tie; the act or process of binding or tying; bondage, restriction
बँधना *[bā̃dhnā]* V.I. to be tied, to be fastened, to be bound
बंधु *[bandhu]* M brother, relative, kinsman
बंब *[bamb]* M bomb
बंबई/बम्बई *[bambaī]* F Bombay
बंसी *[bansī]* F flute; fish hook
बकना *[baknā]* V.T. to babble, to gab, to jabber; to admonish; to rave
बकबक *[bakbak]* F raving, prattle

बक़रईद *[baqarīd]* F name of Eid
बकरा *[bakrā]* M he-goat, goat
बकवास *[bakvās]* F nonsense
बक़ौल *[baqaul]* IND according to, as said by
बखान *[bakhān]* M description, exposition; eulogy, praise
बख़ूबी *[bakhūbī]* IND very well, excellently, thoroughly, amply
बखेरना *[bakhernā]* V.T. to spread, to scatter, to diffuse, to dishevel
बख़ैर *[bakhair]* IND well, safely, safe and sound
बख़ैरियत *[bakhairiyat]* IND well, safely, safe and sound
बख़्श *[bakhś]* adjectival suffix imparting the sense of "causing/giving/bestowing/granting"
बख़्शना *[bakhśnā]* V.T. to bestow, to grant, to give; to pardon, to forgive
बख़्शिश *[bakhśiś]* F gift, grant, tip
बग़ल *[baghal]* F flank, armpit, next to; बग़ल में *[baghal mẽ]* ADV next door
बग़ावत *[baghāvat]* F rebellion, revolt
बग़ीचा *[baghīcā]* M garden
बगुला *[bagulā]* M heron
बग़ैर *[baghair]* IND without, excluding; (x) के बग़ैर *[ke baghair]* PP without (x)
बचकाना *[backānā]* ADJ puerile, childish
बचत *[bacat]* F saving, saving grace; profit, gain
बचना *[bacnā]* V.I. be saved
बचपन *[bacpan]* M childhood
बचाना *[bacānā]* V.T. to save
बचाव *[bacāv]* M safety, protection, defense
बच्चा *[baccā]* M child
बजट *[bajaṭ]* M budget
बजना *[bajnā]* V.I. to be struck, to strike
बज़रिया/बज़रिये *[bazariyā/ bazariye]* IND through, through the agency of
बजाना *[bajānā]* V.T. to strike
बजाय *[bajāy]* IND instead of, in place of, in lieu of; (x) के बजाय *[(x) ke bajāy]* PP instead of (x)
बटुआ *[baṭuā]* M wallet, purse
बटेर *[baṭer]* F quail
बटोरना *[baṭornā]* V.T. to collect, to accumulate, to gather

बट्टा *[baṭṭā]* M discount; brokerage; deficit; division; loss; stone pestle; blemish; looking glass
बड़प्पन *[baṛappan]* M greatness, dignity
बड़बड़ *[baṛbaṛ]* F grumble, grumbling, muttering
बड़बड़ाना *[baṛbaṛānā]* V.T. to grumble, to mutter, to murmur
बड़ा *[baṛā]* ADJ big
बढ़ई *[baṛhaī]* M carpenter
बढ़ती *[baṛhtī]* F increase, rise, growth; progress, prosperity
बढ़ना *[baṛhnā]* V.I. to be increased, to grow
बढ़ाना *[baṛhānā]* V.T. to increase (something), to grow
बढ़ावा *[baṛhāvā]* M encouragement, boosting, incentive
बढ़िया *[baṛhiyā]* ADJ excellent
बढ़ोतरी *[baṛhotrī]* F increase, addition; progress
बतख़ *[batakh]* F a duck
बताना *[batānā]* V.T. to tell
बतियाना *[batiyānā]* V.T. to talk, to converse
बत्ती *[battī]* F wick, taper, light, lamp; traffic light
बत्तीस *[battīs]* ADJ thirty-two
बद *[bad]* ADJ bad, wicked, vile, depraved
बदतर *[badtar]* ADJ worse
बदतरीन *[badtarīn]* ADJ worst
बदन *[badan]* M, F body, physical frame; bet, betting
बदमाश *[badmāś]* ADJ wicked, lewd, mischievous, rowdy
बदमाशी *[badmāśī]* F wickedness, lewdness, mischievousness, rowdiness, hooliganism
बदल *[badal]* F change; alteration; replacement
बदलना *[badalnā]* V.I., V.T. to change
बदला *[badlā]* M revenge, vengeance
बदलाव *[badlāv]* M change, replacement
बदली *[badlī]* F transfer; cloudiness, stray cloud; substitution
बदौलत *[badaulat]* IND through the grace of, by means of, by virtue of, due to
बधाई *[badhāī]* F congratulations, felicitations
बन *[ban]* M forest, wood; bun
बनना *[bannā]* V.I. to be made
बनाना *[banānā]* V.T. to make,

to produce
बनाम *[banām]* IND versus, as against
बनावट *[banāvaṭ]* F composition, structure, make-up; get-up; show, sham, artificiality
बनिया *[baniyā]* M the third of the four major Hindu caste divisions, a trader
बनियाइन *[baniyāin]* F upper under-garment
बयान *[bayān]* M statement, account, deposition
बयार *[bayār]* F breeze
बयालीस *[bayālīs]* ADJ forty-two
बयासी *[bayāsī]* ADJ eighty-two
बर *[bar]* ADJ, IND, M best, foremost; carrying, taking away; on the other hand, on, upon, beyond, above, at; according to, on account of; bridegroom; strength, power
बरतन *[bartan]* M utensil, vessel
बरतना *[baratnā]* V.T. to use; to put to use; to deal with
बरदाश्त *[bardāśt]* F tolerance, endurance, forbearance, patience
बरबाद *[barbād]* ADJ ruined, destroyed, wasted
बरस *[baras]* M year
बरसना *[barasnā]* V.I. to rain, to shower
बरसात *[barsāt]* F rainy season
बरसी *[barsī]* F first death anniversary, rites performed on the first death anniversary
बरात *[barāt]* F marriage party
बराती *[barātī]* M member of a marriage party
बराबर *[barābar]* ADJ, ADV equal, even, level, matching; abreast, constantly, continuously, ever, always
बराबरी *[barābarī]* F equality, parity; rivalry
बरामद *[barāmad]* ADJ exposed, recovered, seized
बरामदा *[barāmdā]* M verandah
बरी *[barī]* ADJ set free, acquitted, absolved
बर्ताव *[bartāv]* M behavior, treatment
बर्फ़ *[barf]* F snow ice
बर्फ़ीला *[barfīlā]* ADJ snowy, icy, glacial
बल *[bal]* M strength, power, potency, force, army;

emphasis, stress; kink, twist, contortion
बलग़म *[balgham]* M phlegm
बलवा *[balvā]* M rebellion, riot, disturbance
बलवान *[balvān]* ADJ strong, powerful
बला *[balā]* F calamity, affliction, misfortune; evil spirit
बलात्कार *[balātkār]* M rape, assault; violence, oppression
बलि *[bali]* F sacrifice, oblation
बलिदान *[balidān]* M sacrifice
बल्कि *[balki]* IND but, rather, on the contrary, on the other hand
बल्ब *[balb]* M bulb
बल्ला *[ballā]* M bat, racket
बवंडर *[bavaṇḍar]* M typhoon, cyclone
बशर्ते *[baśarte]* IND provided that, with the provision that, only if
बसंत *[basant]* M spring
बस *[bas]* INVAR, M okay, enough; power
बस *[bas]* F bus
बसना *[basnā]* V.I. to settle, to inhabit
बसाना *[basānā]* V.T. to colonize, to inhabit, to build (a settlement, town, etc.); to rehabilitate; to become stale, to emit a bad odor
बसेरा *[baserā]* M abode, dwelling; overnight stay, short stay
बस्ता *[bastā]* M (school) bag
बस्ती *[bastī]* F settlement, satellite town, colony; inhabitation; population
बहकना *[behaknā]* V.I. to rave, to talk incoherently; to be intoxicated; to go astray; to be misled; be enticed
बहकाना *[behkānā]* V.T. to lead astray, to mislead; to entice; to instigate
बहत्तर *[behattar]* ADJ seventy-two
बहन *[behan]* F sister
बहना *[behnā]* V.I. to flow
बहनोई *[behnoī]* M (younger) sister's husband
बहरहाल *[beharhāl]* IND at any rate; however; nevertheless
बहलना *[behalnā]* V.I. to be diverted, to be amused, to be entertained
बहलाना *[behlānā]* V.T. to amuse, to entertain; to entice, to allure

बहस *[behas]* F discussion, argument, debate V.T. to debate

बहादुर *[bahādur]* ADJ courageous

बहादुरी *[bahādurī]* F courage

बहाना *[bahānā]* M excuse; to make flow

बहार *[bahār]* F spring (season); bloom, merriment, joviality

बहाल *[bahāl]* ADJ reinstated, restored

बहाव *[bahāv]* M flow, flush, flux

बहिन *[bahin]* F sister

बही *[bahī]* F account book, register

बहु *[bahu]* ADJ many, several

बहुत *[bahut]* ADJ very, a lot, much

बहुतेरे *[bahutere]* ADJ many, numerous

बहुधा *[bahudhā]* IND usually, mostly, generally; in various ways

बहू *[bahū]* F daughter-in-law; wife

बाँका *[bā̃kā]* ADJ dandy, foppish, showy; prankish; chivalrous, gallant

बाँग *[bā̃g]* F prayer call; crowing of a rooster; loud shout

बाँझ *[bā̃jh]* ADJ barren, sterile, infertile

बाँट *[bā̃ṭ]* F division, partition; distribution; deal (in playing cards); share

बाँटना *[bā̃ṭnā]* V.T. to distribute, to allocate, to apportion; to deal (in playing cards); to grind (with a pestle)

बाँध *[bā̃dh]* M dam, weir, dike, barrage, embankment

बाँधना *[bā̃dhnā]* V.T. to tie, to fasten, to bind

बाँसुरी *[bā̃surī]* F flute

बाँह *[bā̃h]* F arm, sleeve

बाइबिल *[bāibil]* F Bible

बाइसिकिल *[bāisikil]* F bicycle

बाईस *[bāīs]* ADJ twenty-two

बाईसवाँ *[bāīsvā̃]* ADJ twenty-second

बाक़ी *[bāqī]* ADJ remaining, rest

बाग *[bāg]* F reins

बाग़ *[bāgh]* M garden, park

बागडोर *[bāgḍaur]* F reins

बाग़ी *[bāghī]* ADJ, M rebel(lious), revolting; rebel, mutineer

बाग़ीचा *[bāghīcā]* M (small) garden

बाघ *[bāgh]* M tiger
बाज़ *[bāz]* ADJ, M desisted; some; hawk, falcon; suffix imparting the sense of "one who indulges/plays with, a performer or monger"
बाजा *[bājā]* M musical instrument; band; बाजा बजाना *[bājā bajānā]* V.T. to play a musical instrument
बाज़ार *[bāzār]* M market
बाज़ारी *[bāzārī]* ADJ of the market place, vulgar, commonplace, cheap
बाज़ारू *[bāzārū]* ADJ vulgar, commonplace
बाज़ी *[bāzī]* F stake, wager, bet; play, performance; turn (as in a game)
बाज़ू *[bāzū]* M arm, side, flank, wing
बाढ़ *[bāṛh]* F flood, inundation; salvo, volley
बात *[bāt]* F matter, talk, thing
बातचीत *[bātcīt]* F talk, conversation, dialogue, negotiations
बातूनी *[bātūnī]* ADJ, M talkative, loquacious, garrulous; chatterbox, excessive talker
बाद *[bād]* IND, ADJ, F after, later, subsequently; subtracted, deducted; air, wind; suffix used imperatively to mean "let it be so"; (x) के बाद *[(x) ke bād]* PP after (x)
बादल *[bādal]* M cloud
बादशाह *[bādśāh]* M king
बादशाहत *[bādśāhat]* F rule, government, sovereignty, kingdom
बादाम *[bādām]* M almond
बाधा *[bādhā]* F hindrance, obstacle, obstruction, impediment; interference, interruption, disturbance; possession (by an evil spirit, etc.), infestation
बाध्य *[bādhya]* ADJ obliged, compelled, forced
बानबे *[bānbe]* ADJ ninety-two
बाना *[bānā]* M style of dress, guise, appearance, deportment; make-up V.T. to open up, to widen
बाप *[bāp]* M father
बापू *[bāpū]* M father
बाबा *[bābā]* M grandfather, an old man, ascetic
बाबू *[bābū]* M educated man, middle-class man, gentleman;

clerk
बायाँ *[bāyā̃]* ADJ left; adverse
बारंबार *[bārambār]* IND, ADV again and again, repeatedly
बार *[bār]* F time; बार-बार *[bār-bār]* ADV time and again
बारह *[bārah]* ADJ twelve
बारहवाँ *[bārahvā̃]* ADJ twelfth
बारात *[bārāt]* F wedding party
बारिश *[bāriś]* F rain
बारी *[bārī]* F turn
बारीक *[bārīk]* ADJ fine, thin, slender, subtle
बारीकी *[bārīkī]* F finesse, subtly
बारूद *[bārūd]* F gunpowder
बारे *[bāre]* IND about, pertaining to, relating to; (x) के बारे में *[(x) ke bāre mẽ]* PP concerning, about (x)
बाल *[bāl]* M, F hair; young one, child, boy; crack (in glass, etc.); ear (of corn)
बालक *[balak]* M boy, child, minor; ignorant person
बालावस्था *[bālāvasthā]* F childhood
बालिका *[bālikā]* F young girl
बालिग़ *[bāligh]* ADJ adult, major
बालू *[bālū]* F sand
बाल्टी *[bālṭī]* F bucket, pail
बावजूद *[bāvajūd]* IND in spite of, despite; (x) के बावजूद *[(x) ke bāvajūd]* PP in spite of (x); despite (x)
बावन *[bāvan]* ADJ fifty-two
बावरची *[bāvarcī]* M cook
बावला *[bāvlā]* ADJ mad, crazy, insane
बावर्ची *[bāvarcī]* M cook
बास *[bās]* F foul smell, disagreeable odor
बासी *[bāsī]* ADJ stale
बाहर *[bāhar]* ADV outside
बाहु *[bāhu]* M arm
बिंदी *[bindī]* F point, dot; zero, cipher
बिंदु *[bindu]* M point, dot; zero, cipher
बिंब *[bimb]* M image, shadow, reflection; disc of the sun or moon; the plant *Momordica monadelpha*
बिकना *[biknā]* V.I. to be sold
बिकाऊ *[bikāū]* ADJ for sale, saleable
बिक्री *[bikrī]* F sale, marketing; circulation; disposal
बिखरना *[bikharnā]* V.I. to be scattered/strewn; to be dispersed, to be diffused; to

be disheveled V.T. to scatter, to strew; to diffuse; to dishevel
बिखेरना *[bikhernā]* v.t. to scatter, to disperse, to diffuse
बिगड़ना *[bigaṛnā]* V.I. to be angry, to lose one's temper; to be spoilt/damaged, to deteriórate; to be wasted; to go astray; to be on bad terms
बिगाड़ना *[bigāṛnā]* V.T. to spoil, to destroy, to ruin, to damage; to cause to go astray
बिगाड़ू *[bigāṛū]* ADJ, M spoiling, destroying, damaging; mischief-maker, saboteur, instigator, one who leads others astray
बिचारा *[bicārā]* ADJ poor, helpless
बिच्छू *[bicchū]* M scorpion; nettle, prickly plant
बिछाना *[bichānā]* V.T. to spread out; to strike down
बिछुड़ना *[bichuṛnā]* V.I. to part company, to separate; to be separated
बिजली *[bijlī]* F electricity, lightning, thunderbolt; ear ornament
बिटिया *[biṭiyā]* F daughter
बिठाना/बैठाना *[biṭhānā/ baiṭānā]* V.T. to seat (someone)
बिताना *[bitānā]* V.T. to spend, to pass (time)
बिदा *[bidā]* F farewell, departure
बिदाई *[bidāī]* F send-off, farewell
बिनती *[bintī]* F entreaty, request, supplication
बिनना *[binnā]* V.T. to knit, to weave; to be picked up
बिना *[binā]* IND without, in the absence of, minus
बिरंग/बिरंगा *[biraṅg/ biraṅgā]* ADJ multicolored; variegated
बिरादरी *[birādrī]* F fraternity, brotherhood, community
बिल *[bil]* M burrow, hole, cavity, bill
बिलकुल *[bilkul]* ADV absolutely
बिलखना *[bilakhnā]* V.T. to wail, to weep bitterly, to lament
बिल्ला *[billā]* M tomcat; badge
बिल्ली *[billī]* F cat
बिसात *[bisāt]* F chess board; capacity, capability, power
बिसारना *[bisārnā]* V.T. to

forget, to force out of the mind
बिस्तर *[bistar]* M bedding, bed
बिस्मिल्ला *[bismillā]* IND, F with the name of God (as said by Muslims at the beginning of a task); beginning, commencement
बिहार *[bihār]* M Bihar, a Hindi-speaking state in eastern India; Buddhist monastery
बिहारी *[bihārī]* ADJ, M from or pertaining to Bihar; Bihari, a person from Bihar
बीच *[bīc]* M middle, center
बीज *[bīj]* M seed; origin, beginning; germ; semen; cause; nucleus
बीड़ी *[bīṛī]* F *bidi*, a type of simple cigarette rolled in a leaf
बीतना *[bītnā]* V.I. to pass, to be spent, to elapse; to expire; to happen/occur/befall
बीनना *[bīnnā]* V.T. to pick up, to pluck; to choose
बीबी *[bībī]* F respected lady
बीमा *[bīmā]* M insurance
बीमार *[bīmār]* ADJ sick, ill
बीमारी *[bīmārī]* F illness, sickness
बीवी *[bīvī]* F wife
बीस *[bīs]* ADJ twenty
बीसवाँ *[bīsvā̃]* ADJ twentieth
बीसियों *[bīsiyõ]* ADJ scores
बीसों *[bīsõ]* ADJ scores, all twenty
बुआ *[buā]* F father's sister, aunt
बुख़ार *[bukhār]* M fever
बुज़ुर्ग *[buzurg]* ADJ, M elderly, old, venerable, respected; forefathers; elderly people
बुझना *[bujhnā]* V.I. to be extinguished/quenched
बुझाना *[bujhānā]* V.T. to extinguish, to put out, to quench, to slake
बुड़बुड़ाना *[buṛbuṛānā]* V.T. to mutter, to murmur, to jabber
बुड्ढा *[buḍḍhā]* ADJ old, aged, senile
बुढ़ापा *[buṛhāpā]* F old age, senility
बुढ़िया *[buṛhiyā]* F old woman
बुत *[but]* ADJ, M dumb and lifeless, motionless; idol, statue, image
बुद्ध *[buddh]* M Buddha
बुद्धि *[buddhi]* F intellect, intelligence, wisdom; mind, sense

बुद्धिमान *[buddhimān]* ADJ intelligent, wise, prudent, sensible; brilliant
बुद्धू *[buddhū]* ADJ stupid, foolish, dullard
बुध *[budh]* ADJ, M wise, intelligent, learned; Wednesday; Mercury
बुधवार *[budhvār (budh)]* M Wednesday
बुनना *[bunnā]* V.T. to weave, to knit, to intertwine
बुनाई *[bunāī]* F the act/process of weaving or knitting or the wages paid for it; texture of cloth
बुनियाद *[buniyād]* F foundation, base, basis
बुरक़ा *[burqā]* M burqa, veil, mantle
बुरा *[burā]* ADJ bad
बुराई *[burāī]* F evil, vice, flaw, fault, defect, badness, wickedness
बुलंद *[buland]* ADJ high, lofty, height
बुलंदी *[bulandī]* F loftiness
बुलबुल *[bulbul]* F nightingale
बुलाना *[bulānā]* V.T. to call, to invite
बुलावा *[bulāvā]* M call, summons; invitation
बूँद *[bū̃d]* F drop
बूँदाबाँदी *[bū̃dābā̃dī]* F drizzle, light shower
बू *[bū]* F disagreeable; odor, foul smell
बूझना *[būjhnā]* V.T. to understand, to make out; to solve; to enquire, to ask
बूट *[būṭ]* M boot, shoe; *gram* pod
बूढ़ा *[būṛhā]* ADJ old, aged, senile
बृहस्पतिवार *[bṛhaspativār]* M Thursday
बेंट *[bẽṭ]* F handle (of an ax, etc.), cane, stick
बे *[be]* Persian prefix imparting the sense of "without"; interjectional particle signifying indignation and disrespect
बेकार *[bekār]* ADJ useless, idle, stupid
बेघर *[beghar]* ADJ homeless
बेचना *[becnā]* V.T. to sell
बेटा *[beṭā]* M son (sometimes used affectionately as a mode of address for a girl)
बेटी *[beṭī]* F daughter
बेधना *[bedhnā]* V.T. to pierce,

to puncture, to bore
बेर *[ber]* M jujube, plum, prune
बेलन *[belan]* M roller, cylinder
बेलना *[belnā]* V.T., M to roll out dough; roller (for rolling dough)
बेला *[belā]* M variety of jasmine (*Jasminum sambac* "Maid of Orleans")
बेवकूफ़ *[bevaqūf]* ADJ, N idiotic, foolish; stupidity
बेवफ़ा *[bevafā]* ADJ unfaithful
बेवा *[bevā]* F widow
बेसन *[besan]* M gram flour
बेहूदा *[behūdā]* ADJ nonsensical, foolish, irrelevant; vulgar
बैंक *[baĩk]* M bank
बैंगन *[baĩgan]* M eggplant, aubergine
बैटरी *[baiṭrī]* F battery, torch, flashlight
बैठक *[baiṭhak]* F sitting room
बैठना *[baiṭhnā]* V.I. to sit
बैठाना *[baiṭānā]* V.T. to be seated, to cause to be seated, to request to take a seat; to press down; to fit in, to install, to readjust; to keep (a woman as a mistress); to see off
बैर *[bair]* M enmity, hostility, animosity
बैरी *[bairī]* ADJ, M hostile, enemy, foe
बैल *[bail]* M ox, bullock; fool
बैलगाड़ी *[bailgāṛī]* F bullock-cart
बैसाख *[baisākh]* M the second month of the Hindu calendar
बैसाखी *[baisākhī]* F festival celebrated on the full moon of the month of
बैसाखा crutch (used for walking)
बोझ *[bojh]* M burden
बोटी *[boṭī]* F piece of slice of flesh
बोतल *[botal]* F bottle
बोध *[bodh]* M perception, sense, knowledge, understanding
बोना *[bonā]* V.T. to sow, to plant
बोर होना *[bor honā]* V.I. to become bored
बोल *[bol]* M speech, utterance; opening words of a song; taunt
बोलबाला *[bolbālā]* M overbearing influence, sway
बोली *[bolī]* F dialect, mode of speaking; bid (in an auction); taunt, sarcastic remark

बोहनी *[bohnī]* F first sale of a day

बौखलाना *[baukhlānā]* V.I. to be furious, to be enraged

बौद्ध *[bauddh]* ADJ, M Buddhist, pertaining to the Buddha or Buddhism; Buddhist; बौद्ध धर्म *[bauddh dharm]* M Buddhism (Buddhist religion)

बौना *[baunā]* ADJ, M dwarf, dwarfish; pygmy

ब्याज *[byāj]* M interest (on money)

ब्याह *[byāh]* M marriage, wedding

ब्याहना *[byāhnā]* V.T. to wed, to marry (off), to get someone married

ब्रह्म *[brahma]* M God, Eternal Spirit; knowledge

ब्रह्मचर्या *[brahmacaryā]* F the first of the four stages of a man's life as prescribed by Hindu scriptures, dedicated to learning and living in celibacy as the disciple of a (religious) teacher until the age of twenty-five

ब्रह्मचारी *[brahmacārī]* M one who is celibate, one who is in the stage of ब्रह्मचर्या

ब्रह्मा *[brahmā]* M the creator; one of the trinity of major Hindu deities, the other being Shiva and Vishnu

ब्राह्मण *[brāhmaṇ]* M Brahmin

ब्रेक *[brek]* M brake

ब्लाउज़ *[blāūz]* M blouse

भ

भंग *[bhaṅg]* M, F dissolution, breach, split, destruction, fracture; drug made from the leaves of hemp (*Cannabis sativa*)

भंगड़ा *[bhaṅgṛā]* M a popular dance form from Punjab

भंडार *[bhaṇḍār]* M storehouse, storage, depository

भइया *[bhaiyā]* M brother

भई *[bhaī]* M brother, friend

भक्त *[bhakt]* M devotee, devotion

भगदड़ *[bhagdaṛ]* F stampede, panic

भगवान् *[bhagvān]* M Lord (God)

भगाना *[bhagānā]* V.T., N to chase away; devotional song, hymn, repetition of the name of god

भजना *[bhajnā]* V.T. to repeat the name of god, to remember god; to be engaged in devotional practices; to enjoy, to derive pleasure

भटकना *[bhaṭaknā]* V.I. to lose one's way, to go astray, to meander; to flare up, to burst forth

भड़काना *[bhaṛkānā]* V.T. to cause to flare up; to set ablaze; to provoke; to excite, to enrage; to startle

भड़कीला *[bhaṛkīlā]* ADJ gaudy, showy, ostentatious, tawdry, flamboyant

भड़ुआ *[bhaṛuā]* M profesional procurer, tout, pimp

भतीजा *[bhatījā]* M nephew

भद्दा *[bhaddā]* ADJ ugly, clumsy, ungainly, unseemly, vulgar, dirty, untoward; asymmetrical

भद्र *[bhadra]* ADJ gentle, noble; good, auspicious

भयंकर *[bhayaṅkar]* ADJ frightful, dreadful, terrible, horrible, dangerous

भय *[bhay]* M fear, fright, horror, scare, danger

भयभीत *[bhaybhīt]* ADJ afraid, frightened, scared, terrified, horrified

भयानक *[bhayānak]* ADJ dreadful, terrible, horrible, frightening, dangerous

भर *[bhar]* ADJ entire, all, whole, full

भरती *[bhartī]* F recruitment, enrolment, admission; packing or filling a void

भरना *[bharnā]* V.I., V.T. to be filled, to fill

भरसक *[bharsak]* IND as far as possible, to the best of one's ability, with all one's might, utmost

भरा *[bharā]* ADJ full, in full strength; rich; flourishing; choked with emotion

भरोसा *[bharosā]* M faith, trust

भला *[bhalā]* ADJ, M gentle, noble, good; well-being, good

भलाई *[bhalāī]* F good, welfare, well-being, goodness, gentleness

भले *[bhale]* IND well!, good!

भवन *[bhavan]* M house, building, mansion; edifice

भविष्य *[bhaviṣya]* M future

भव्य *[bhavya]* ADJ grand, divine; pretty

भस्म *[bhasma]* F ash, cinder
भाँग *[bhā̃g]* F intoxicating; hemp (*Cannabis sativa*)
भाँति *[bhā̃ti]* F kind, type, manner, mode, method
भाँपना *[bhā̃pnā]* V.T. to guess the truth, to make out, to divine
भाई *[bhaī]* M brother; भाई-बहन *[bhāī-behan]* M, PL brothers and sisters; siblings; भाई-साहब *[bhāī-sāhab]* M Sir!
भाग *[bhāg]* M portion, part, fragment, fraction, share, division; luck; भाग-दौड़ *[bhāg-dauṛ]* F running around, strenuous effort
भागना *[bhāgnā]* V.I. to escape, to flee
भाग्य *[bhāgya]* M fortune, fate, luck, destiny
भाग्यवान *[bhāgyavān]* ADJ lucky, fortunate
भाजी *[bhājī]* F vegetable
भाड़ *[bhāṛ]* M parcher's oven
भाड़ा *[bhāṛā]* M fare, rent; freight
भादों *[bhādõ]* M the sixth month of the year in the Hindu calendar
भानजा *[bhānjā]* M sister's son
भाना *[bhānā]* V.I. be liked, be agreeable, to be pleasing/ appealing
भाभी *[bhābhī]* F brother's wife, sister-in-law
भार *[bhār]* M load, weight, burden, encumbrance; onus, obligation, responsibility
भारत *[bhārat]* M India
भारतीय *[bhāratīya]* ADJ Indian
भारी *[bhārī]* ADJ heavy, weighty, massive, grave, burdensome; difficult to digest
भालू *[bhālū]* M bear
भाव *[bhāv]* M cost, price; emotion, sentiment
भावना *[bhāvnā]* F emotion
भावी *[bhāvī]* ADJ, M future-, coming; destiny, future
भावुक *[bhāvuk]* ADJ sentimental, emotional
भावुकता *[bhāvuktā]* F sentimentality
भाषण *[bhāṣaṇ]* M speech
भाषा *[bhāṣā]* F language
भाषी *[bhāṣī]* adjectival suffix that imparts the meaning "one who speaks"
भिंडी *[bhĩḍī]* F okra, lady's finger

भिक्षा *[bhikṣā]* F alms, charity; begging
भिक्षु *[bhikṣu]* M beggar; Buddhist mendicant
भिखारी *[bikhārī]* M beggar
भिगोना *[bhigonā]* V.T. to wet, to drench, to soak, to moisten
भिगौना *[bhigaunā]* M a round household utensil
भिड़ना *[bhiṛnā]* V.I. to collide, to clash; to quarrel
भिनकना *[bhinaknā]* V.I. to hum, to buzz, to swarm; to be extremely shabby or dirty (so as to attract buzzing flies)
भिनभिनाना *[bhinbhinānā]* V.I. to go on buzzing or humming
भिन्न *[bhinna]* ADJ separate, different, distinct; dissimilar; diverse
भिन्नता *[bhinnatā]* F difference, distinction, dissimilarity
भींचना *[bhĩcnā]* V.T. to grasp tightly; to tighten, to hold close together, to squeeze
भी *[bhī]* PART also, even, too
भीगना *[bhīgnā]* V.I. to get wet, to be soaked, to be drenched, to be moistened; to be moved
भीड़ *[bhīṛ]* F crowd
भीतर *[bhītar]* IND inside, within
भीतरी *[bhītarī]* ADJ internal, interior, inner, inward; secret, unexpressed
भीषण *[bhīṣaṇ]* ADJ frightening, scary, awful; tremendous
भीष्म *[bhīṣma]* ADJ terrible, awful, horrible
भुगतना *[bhugatnā]* V.T. to suffer, to undergo, to bear; to be accomplished/concluded
भुगतान *[bhugtān]* M payment; settlement; delivery
भुगताना *[bhugtānā]* V.T. to pay, to settle; to deliver; to conclude, to accomplish
भुजिया *[bhujiyā]* F cooked green vegetable; a typical snack dish
भुट्टा *[bhuṭṭā]* M maize
भुनाना *[bhunānā]* V.T. to get parched; to cash, to change (money into a smaller denomination), to forget
भूँकना *[bhū̃knā]* V.T. to bark; to gabble
भू *[bhū]* F earth, world; ground, soil, land; suffix denoting "born" or "born of"

भूकंप *[bhūkamp]* M earthquake
भूख *[bhūkh]* F hunger
भूखा *[bhūkhā]* ADJ hungry, craving
भूगोल *[bhūgol]* M geography
भूटान *[bhūṭān]* Bhutan
भूत *[bhūt]* ADJ, M past, bygone; ghost, spirit; matter, one of the five elements
भूतिनी *[bhūtinī]* F female ghost or spirit
भूनना *[bhūnnā]* V.T. to parch, to fry, to broil, to roast; to blast, to smash; to reduce to ashes
भूमि *[bhūmi]* F earth, land, soil; zone
भूमिका *[bhūmikā]* F introduction; groundwork; background; role
भूल *[bhūl]* F slip, error, mistake, omission, oversight, fault
भूलना *[bhūlnā]* V.I. to forget
भूषण *[bhūṣaṇ]* M ornament, decoration, embellishment
भूसा *[bhūsā]* M cut straw, chaff
भेंट *[bheṇṭ]* F gift
भेजना *[bhejnā]* V.T. to send, to transmit, to remit
भेजा *[bhejā]* ADJ, M brain
भेड़ *[bheṛ]* F sheep, timid person
भेड़ना *[bheṛnā]* V.T. to close, to shut; to hoodwink someone into losing a bargain
भेड़िया *[bheṛiyā]* M wolf
भेद *[bhed]* M secret; difference, distinction, divergence; schism, split; discrimination; variety, kind, type
भैंस *[bhaīs]* F she-buffalo; an extremely fat woman
भैंसा *[bhaīsā]* M he-buffalo; a stout and sturdy man
भैया *[bhaiyā]* M brother (affectionate term)
भोंकना *[bhõknā]* V.T. to poke, to thrust into, to pierce through, to stab
भोगना *[bhognā]* V.T. to enjoy; to suffer; to undergo, to experience; to derive sexual pleasure
भोज *[bhoj]* M banquet, feast
भोजन *[bhojan]* M food, meals, diet; victuals
भोजनालय *[bhojanālay]* M restaurant, mess
भोर *[bhor]* M dawn, day-break
भौंकना *[bhaũknā]* V.T. to bark, to jabber, to penetrate, to thrust into
भौतिक *[bhautik]* ADJ material,

physical, corporeal, elemental; mundane
भ्रम *[bhram]* M misunderstanding, misconception, illusion, confusion
भ्रमण *[bhramaṇ]* M walk, going round, excursion, travel, roaming
भ्रष्ट *[bhraṣṭ]* ADJ corrupt(ed), spoilt, fallen, ruined, depraved, wanton
भ्रष्टाचार *[bhraṣṭācār]* M corruption, depravity, wantonness
भ्रांति *[bhrā̃ti]* F error, mistake; illusion
भ्रूण *[bhrūṇ]* M fetus, embryo; भ्रूण हत्या *[bhrūṇ hatyā]* F feticide

म

मँगनी *[mãganī]* F betrothal, engagement; loan
मंगल *[maṅgal]* M Mars; Tuesday; auspiciousness; well-being ADJ auspicious
मंगलमय *[maṅgalmay]* ADJ auspicious
मंगलवार *[maṅgalvār]* M Tuesday
मँगवाना *[mãgvānā]* V.T. to have ordered
मँगाना *[mãgānā]* V.T. to cause to bring; to order
मँगेतर *[mãgetar]* M, F fiance or fiancee ADJ betrothed
मंच *[mañc]* M dais, stage; platform
मंज़िल *[manzil]* F floor of a building, story; destination; approved
मंज़ूर *[manzūr]* ADJ sanctioned; granted; accepted
मंज़ूरी *[manzūrī]* F approval; sanction; acceptance
मंडप *[maṇḍap]* M pavilion
मँडराना *[mãḍrānā]* V.I. to hover, to hang around; to gather thick (like clouds)
मंडल *[maṇḍal]* M circle, ring; zone, territory; collection
मंडी *[maṇḍī]* F wholesale market; market; marketplace
मंत्र *[mantra]* M incantation, charm, spell; a vedic hymn
मंत्रालय *[mantrālay]* M ministry; the offices headed by a minister
मंत्रिमंडल *[mantrimaṇḍal]* M cabinet, ministry
मंत्री *[mantrī]* M minister; secretary

मंथन *[manthan]* M churning, stirring, agitation; deep pondering over something
मंद *[mand]* ADJ slow, slow-moving; sluggish
मंदिर *[mandir]* M temple
मई *[maī]* M May (month)
मकड़ा *[makṛā]* M a large spider
मकड़ी *[makṛī]* F spider
मक़बरा *[maqbarā]* M tomb, mausoleum
मक़बूल *[maqbūl]* ADJ accepted, approved, popular
मक़सद *[maqsad]* M aim, object, motive, intention
मकान *[makān]* M house, residence
मकोड़ा *[makoṛā]* M a small insect
मक्का *[makkā]* M maize, corn
मक्खन *[makkhan]* M butter
मक्खी *[makkhī]* F fly
मक्खीचूस *[makkhīcūs]* ADJ stingy, terribly parsimonous
मख़मल *[makhmal]* M velvet, plush
मगर *[magar]* CONJ but M crocodile
मगरमच्छ *[magarmacch]* M crocodile
मग़रिब *[maghrib]* M west, western direction
मग़रिबी *[maghribī]* ADJ western
मग्न *[magna]* ADJ absorbed, engrossed, engaged, busy; immersed; glad
मचना *[macnā]* V.I. to be occasioned, to happen, to be caused, to be raised up
मचली *[maclī]* F nausea
मच्छड़/मच्छर *[macchaṛ/macchar]* M mosquito; gnat
मछली *[machlī]* F fish; Pisces
मज़दूर *[mazdūr]* M laborer, worker
मज़दूरी *[mazdūrī]* F labor charges; act or process of laboring
मज़बूत *[mazbūt]* ADJ strong, sturdy, lasting, durable; firm
मज़बूती *[mazbūtī]* F strength, durability
मजबूर *[majbūr]* ADJ helpless, obliged, compelled
मजबूरन *[majbūran]* ADV under pressure, being compelled/forced
मजबूरी *[majbūrī]* F helplessness, compulsion, obligation
मजलिस *[majlis]* F assembly,

meeting, congregation
मज़हब *[mazhab]* M religion, creed
मज़हबी *[mazhabī]* ADJ religious
मज़ा *[mazā]* M enjoyment, relish
मज़े करना *[maze karnā]* V.T. to enjoy, to have fun
मज़े में *[maze mẽ]* ADV at perfect ease
मज़ेदार *[mazedār]* ADJ tasty; enjoyable
मज़ाक *[mazāk]* M joke; jest; prank
मज़ाकिया *[mazākiyā]* ADJ witty; humorous, waggish, pranky; fun-loving
मज़ार *[mazār]* M tomb, grave
मजाल *[majāl]* F cheek; audacity; strength; power
मटका *[maṭkā]* M a large earthen pitcher/pot
मटकाना *[maṭkānā]* V.T. to move in a coquettish manner
मटमैला *[maṭmailā]* ADJ dusty, dust-colored
मटर *[maṭar]* M pea
मठ *[maṭh]* M monastery
मठा *[maṭhā]* M buttermilk
मत *[mat]* ADV don't, not F/M opinion, view, vote; belief
मतभेद *[matbhed]* M disagreement, difference of opinion
मतलब *[matlab]* M meaning, purpose, concern; aim, motive
मतलबी *[matlabī]* ADJ selfish
मतवाला *[matvālā]* ADJ intoxicated; drunken; wayward; tipsy
मति *[mati]* F intellect, understanding, thought; opinion, view
मत्त *[matt]* ADJ drunken; intoxicated; wayward
मथना *[mathnā]* V.T. to churn; to stir deeply; to batter; to agitate
मद *[mad]* M intoxication; passion; arrogance, pride
मदद *[madad]* F help, assistance; aid; support
मदरसा *[madarsā]* M school
मदहोश *[madhoś]* ADJ dead drunk, rendered senseless
मदिरा *[madirā]* F liquor, wine
मदोन्मत्त *[madonmatt]* ADJ arrogant; intoxicated
मद्धम *[maddham]* ADJ slow; dim; moderate
मधु *[madhu]* M honey; wine, liquor; the spring

मधुमय *[madhumay]* ADJ sweet; attractive, beautiful
मधुर *[madhur]* ADJ sweet, melodious, pleasant; mellifluous
मधुरता *[madhurtā]* F sweetness; melodiousness; softness
मध्य *[madhya]* ADJ middle, central, mid- M middle; center
मध्यकालीन *[madhyakālīn]* ADJ medieval
मध्यवर्ग *[madhyavarg]* M middle class
मध्यम *[madhyam]* ADJ medium; middle; intermediate
मनःस्थिति *[manaḥsthiti]* F mood, state of mind
मन *[man]* M heart, mind
मनचला *[mancalā]* ADJ Don Quixote; frivolous
मनचाहा *[mancāhā]* ADJ favorite, desired, wished or longed for
मनपसंद *[manpasand]* ADJ favorite
मनमुटाव *[manmuṭāv]* M ill-feeling, estrangement, rift; antagonism
मनसूबा *[mansūbā]* M intention; plan; design
मनहूस *[manhūs]* ADJ ominous; inauspicious; ill-fated; gloomy
मना *[manā]* ADJ forbidden, prohibited
मनाना *[manānā]* V.T. to appease, to celebrate, to persuade
मनाही *[manāhī]* F forbiddance, prohibition
मनुष्य *[manuṣya]* M man, human
मनुष्यता *[manuṣyatā]* F humanity, humaneness
मनोबल *[manobal]* M morale, moral strength
मनोरंजन *[manorañjan]* M amusement, entertainment, recreation
मनोरम *[manoram]* ADJ lovely, pretty, charming, attractive
मनोरोग *[manorog]* M psychosis, mental ailment
मनोविज्ञान *[manovijñān]* M psychology
मनोवृत्ति *[manovṛtti]* F mentality; mental disposition
मनोवैज्ञानिक *[manovaijñānik]* ADJ, M psychological; psychologist
मनोहर *[manohar]* ADJ lovely,

comely, charming; alluring
ममता *[mamtā]* F affection, attachment
मयस्सर *[mayassar]* ADJ available
मयूर *[mayūr]* M a peacock
मरकज़ *[markaz]* M center
मरतबा *[martabā]* M rank, order; turn; time
मरना *[marnā]* V.I. to die, to pass away; to wither away; to become ineffective; to vanish
मरमर *[marmar]* M marble
मरम्मत *[marammat]* F repair, mending
मरहम *[marham]* F ointment; salve
मराठा *[marāṭhā]* M Maratha, an inhabitant of Maharashtra
मराठी *[marāṭhī]* F Marathi (spoken in Maharashtra)
मरियल *[mariyal]* ADJ sickly, feeble
मरीज़ *[marīz]* M, ADJ patient; diseased
मरोड़ना *[maroṛnā]* V.T. to twist, to contort; to wring
मर्ज़ *[marz]* M disease, malady, ailment
मर्ज़ी *[marzī]* F desire, will, inclination; pleasure
मर्तबा *[martabā]* M *see* मरतबा
मर्द *[mard]* M, ADJ man; manly; dauntless
मर्दानगी *[mardānagī]* F bravery, valor, masculinity
मर्म *[marm]* M vulnerability, vital part of the body; essence; core; secret
मर्मस्पर्शी *[marmsparśī]* ADJ touching, moving, poignant
मर्यादा *[maryādā]* F dignity, decorum, propriety of conduct; moderation
मल *[mal]* M feces, stool, excrement; sewage; rubbish, filth; dirt
मलना *[malnā]* V.T. to rub; to press hard; to anoint; smear; massage
मलबा *[malbā]* M debris, wreckage
मलाई *[malāī]* F cream
मलिक *[malik]* M king, ruler
मलिन *[malin]* ADJ dirty, filthy, tarnished; shabby; gloomy
मलिनता *[malintā]* F dirtiness, filthiness; shabbiness
मल्लाह *[mallāh]* M sailor, boatman
मशरिक़ *[maśriq]* M east

मशरिक़ी *[maśriqī]* ADJ eastern
मशविरा *[maśvirā]* M advice, counsel
मशहूर *[maśhūr]* ADJ famous, well-known
मशाल *[maśāl]* F torch
मशीन *[maśīn]* F machine
मसका *[maskā]* M butter
मसजिद *[masjid]* F mosque
मसरूफ़ *[masrūf]* ADJ busy, occupied
मसलन *[masalan]* ADV for example, for instance
मसलना *[masalnā]* V.T. to rub; to press hard, to crush
मसला *[maslā]* M issue, question, problem
मसहरी *[masharī]* F mosquito net/curtain
मसाला *[masālā]* M spices; condiments
मसालेदार *[masāledār]* ADJ pungent
मसीह *[masīh]* M Jesus Christ
मसीहा *[masīhā]* M messiah; one endowed with powers to revive the dead
मसूड़ा *[masūṛā]* M gum (in the mouth)
मसौदा *[masaudā]* M draft
मस्जिद *[masjid]* F mosque
मस्त *[mast]* ADJ intoxicated; carefree; wanton; sexually excited; radiant with joy
मस्तिष्क *[mastiṣk]* M brain, mind
मस्ती *[mastī]* F the state of being intoxicated; passion; sexual excitement; joyous radiance
महँगा *[mahãgā]* ADJ expensive, dear, costly
महँगाई *[mahãgāī]* F expensiveness, costliness
महक *[mehak]* F fragrance, aroma, perfume, scent
महकना *[mehaknā]* V.I. to emit a perfume/fragrance
महज़ *[mehaz]* ADV merely, only; absolutely
महत्त्व *[mahattva]* M importance, significance; greatness
महत्त्वपूर्ण *[mahttvapūrṇ]* ADJ important, significant
महत्त्वाकांक्षा *[mahattvākāṅkṣā]* F ambition
महत्त्वाकांक्षी *[mahattvākāṅkṣī]* ADJ ambitious
महफ़िल *[mehfil]* F party; a private congregation
महफ़ूज़ *[mehfūz]* ADJ safe, secure, protected

महबूब *[mehbūb]* ADJ beloved, dear
महल *[mehal]* M palace
महसूस *[mehsūs]* ADJ felt, perceived, experienced
महा *[mahā]* PREFIX great
महात्मा *[mahātmā]* ADJ, M saint, sage, saintly person
महाद्वीप *[mahādvīp]* M continent
महान *[mahān]* ADJ great; big, eminent
महानता *[mahāntā]* F greatness
महामारी *[mahāmārī]* F epidemic
महाराज *[mahārāj]* M king; cook
महारानी *[mahārānī]* F queen
महाराष्ट्र *[mahārāṣtra]* M Mahrashtra (a state in India)
महासभा *[mahāsabhā]* F congress
महिला *[mahilā]* F woman, lady
महीना *[mahīnā]* M month; menses
महेश *[maheś]* M Lord Shiva
महोदय *[mahoday]* ADJ Sir; an honorific used as a form of address
माँ *[mā̃]* F mother; माँ-बाप *[mā̃-bāp]* M, PL parents
माँग *[mā̃g]* F demand; requirement; requisition
माँगना *[mā̃gnā]* V.T. to demand; to ask for (something); to solicit
माँजना *[mā̃jnā]* V.T. to cleanse; to scour; to polish
मांस *[mā̃s]* M meat, flesh
मांसपेशी *[mā̃speśī]* F muscle
मांसाहारी *[mā̃sāhārī]* ADJ non-vegetarian
माखनचोर *[mākhancor]* M an epithet for Lord Krishna
माघ *[māgh]* M the name of the eleventh month of the Hindu calendar
माजरा *[mājrā]* M matter; affair; incident
मातम *[mātam]* M mourning, bereavement; grief
माता *[mātā]* F mother, small pox; माता-पिता *[mātā-pitā]* M, PL parents; mother and father
मात्र *[mātra]* IND only, merely, barely; mere
मात्रा *[mātrā]* F degree, quantity; scale, dose; a vowel mark in the Devanagari script
माथा *[māthā]* M forehead; forepart

मादक *[mādak]* ADJ intoxicating; bewitching, fascinating
मादर *[mādar]* F mother
मादरी ज़बान *[mādarī zabān]* F mother tongue
माधव *[mādhav]* M an epithet of Lord Krishna; the spring
माधुरी *[mādhurī]* F sweetness, pleasantness
माध्यमिक *[mādhyamik]* ADJ secondary; middle; intermediary
मान *[mān]* M esteem, respect, prestige, dignity; value; measure; conceit
मानचित्र *[māncitra]* M map
मानक *[mānak]* ADJ, M standard
मानना *[mānnā]* V.I., V.T. to accept; to regard; to respect; to confess; to suppose
माननीय *[mānnīya]* ADJ honorable; revered; respectable; INT respectable
मानव *[mānav]* M man, human being, mankind; मानव जाति *[mānav jāti]* F the human race
मानवता *[mānavtā]* F humanity; humaneness; mankind
मानस *[mānas]* M psyche; mind; heart; a famous lake in the Himalayas
मानसिकता *[mānsiktā]* F mentality
मानसून *[mānsūn]* M the monsoon
मानी *[mānī]* M meaning, purport, import
माने *[māne]* M meaning, purport, import
मानो *[māno]* IND as if, as though; supposing
माप *[māp]* M measurement/ measure; size; dimension
मापना *[māpnā]* V.T. to measure, to scale
माफ़ *[māf]* ADJ excused; forgiven, pardoned
माफ़ी *[māfī]* F forgiveness, pardon; exemption
मामला *[māmlā]* M issue, matter, cause, business
मामा *[māmā]* M maternal uncle
मामी *[māmī]* F maternal aunt
मामूली *[māmūlī]* ADJ ordinary, so-so, common; commonplace
माया *[māyā]* F illusion, delusion, unreality; trick
मायाजाल *[māyājāl]* M the web of worldy illusion

मायूस *[māyūs]* ADJ frustrated, dejected; disappointed
मायूसी *[māyūsī]* F frustration, dejection
मार *[mār]* M beating, thrashing, belaboring
मारना *[mārnā]* V.T. to beat, to strike, to kill
मारे *[māre]* IND due to, because of; on account of; for
मार्ग *[mārg]* M way, path, route, course; road; track; passage
मार्च *[mārc]* M March (month)
मार्जन *[mārjan]* M cleansing, cleaning
मार्जित *[mārjit]* ADJ cleansed, cleaned; refined
माल *[māl]* M goods, commodity, things; articles; effects; stuff; merchandise
मालगाड़ी *[mālgāṛī]* F goods train
माला *[mālā]* F garland, wreath, rosary, a string of beads; series
मालामाल *[mālāmāl]* ADJ wealthy, opulent; immensely rich
मालकिन *[mālkin]* F owner; mistress
मालिक *[mālik]* M owner, master, employer
मालिश *[māliś]* F massage
माली *[mālī]* M gardener ADJ economic
मालूम *[mālūm]* ADJ known
माशाअल्लाह *[māśā allāh]* IND Good God! Excellent! Wonderful!
माशूक *[māśūq]* M beloved
मास *[mās]* M month
मासिक *[māsik]* ADJ monthly; M menstruation; monthly magazine; मासिकधर्म *[māsik dharm]* M menstruation
मासूम *[masūm]* ADJ innocent; harmless; guileless
मासूमियत *[masūmiyat]* F innocence
माह *[māh]* M month
माहवारी *[māhvārī]* F menstruation
माहिर *[māhir]* M, ADJ expert, specialist; adept
माहौल *[māhaul]* M atmosphere
मिज़ाज *[mizāj]* M mood, temperament, nature; temper
मिटना *[miṭnā]* V.I. be effaced/ erased
मिट्टी *[miṭṭī]* F soil, earth, clay; dirt
मिठाई *[miṭhāī]* F sweetmeat

मिठास *[miṭhās]* F sweetness
मितव्ययी *[mitvyayī]* ADJ thrifty, frugal
मित्र *[mitra]* M friend, ally
मित्रता *[mitratā]* F friendship
मिथ्या *[mithyā]* ADJ untrue, false M untruth, falsehood; myth
मिनट *[minaṭ]* M minute
मिन्नत *[minnat]* F entreaty, request; supplication
मियाँ *[miyā̃]* M husband; मियाँ-बीवी *[miyā̃-bīvī]* M husband and wife
मिरगी *[mirgī]* F epilepsy
मिर्च *[mirc]* F chilies; pepper
मिलन *[milan]* M meeting; union; contact
मिलनसार *[milansār]* ADJ sociable; affable
मिलना *[milnā]* V.I. to meet, to encounter, to be mixed, to be united, to mingle
मिलाना *[milānā]* V.T. to mix, to unite, to compare, to blend, to cause to meet, to bring together
मिलाप *[milāp]* M meeting, reconciliation; union
मिलावट *[milāvaṭ]* F adulteration; mixing; alloy
मिश्रण *[miśraṇ]* M mixture, blend; combination
मिसाल *[misāl]* F precedent, example
मींचना *[mĩcnā]* V.T. to shut, to close (eyes)
मीठा *[mīṭhā]* ADJ sweet
मीन *[mīn]* F fish; Pisces—the twelfth sign of the zodiac
मीनार *[mīnār]* F minaret; tower
मील *[mīl]* F mile
मुंड़ना *[mũṛnā]* V.I. to have the head shaved; to be fleeced
मुंड़ाना *[mũṛānā]* V.T. to get shaved; to cause to be fleeced
मुँदना *[mũdnā]* V.I. to be closed/shut
मुंबई *[mumbaī]* F Mumbai
मुँह *[mũh]* M face; mouth, opening
मुक़दमा *[muqadmā]* M case, suit, law suit
मुकम्मल *[mukammal]* ADJ complete, completed; finished; perfected
मुक़ाबला *[muqāblā]* M encounter, opposition, comparison
मुक़ाम *[muqām]* M place, site, halting place

मुक्त *[mukt]* ADJ free/freed; independent; released; unfettered

मुक्ति *[mukti]* F salvation; emancipation, deliverance; liberation; release; freedom

मुख *[mukh]* M mouth; face; front; brim

मुख़ातिब *[mukhātib]* address

मुख्य *[mukhya]* ADJ principal; chief; main; salient; leading; मुख्य पात्र *[mukhya pātra]* M principal character; मुख्य मंत्री *[mukhya mantrī]* M chief minister

मुग़ल *[mughal]* M Mughal

मुग्ध *[mugdh]* ADJ infatuated, charmed, under a spell; attracted

मुजरिम *[mujrim]* M criminal

मुझ *[mujh]* PRO me (oblique form of मैं); मुझी *[mujhī]* PRO me (मुझ + ही)

मुझे/मुझको *[mujhe/mujhko]* PRO (to) me (oblique form of मैं + को)

मुट्ठी *[muṭṭhī]* F fist; grip; clutch

मुठभेड़ *[muṭhbheṛ]* F encounter; confrontation

मुड़ना *[muṛnā]* V.I. to turn; to be twisted; to bend

मुद्दा *[muddā]* M issue; theme, intention

मुद्रा *[mudrā]* F seal, stamp; money; countenance; pose, posture

मुनाफ़ा *[munāfā]* M profit, gain

मुनासिब *[munāsib]* ADJ reasonable, proper, fit, appropriate

मुफ़ीद *[mufīd]* ADJ useful, beneficial

मुफ़्त *[muft]* ADJ free of charge, gratis; मुफ़्त में *[muft mẽ]* ADV gratis, for free

मुबारक *[mubārak]* ADJ auspicious, blessed, fortunate; (x) मुबारक हो! *[(x) mubārak ho!]* may (x) be auspicious!

मुमकिन *[mumkin]* ADJ possible, feasible

मुरझाना *[murjhānā]* V.I. to wither, to fade; to lose luster

मुरदा *[murdā]* M, ADJ corpse, dead body, dead; lifeless

मुर्ग़ी *[murghī]* F chicken

मुलाक़ात *[mulāqāt]* F meeting

मुलायम *[mulāyam]* AD soft, tender, gentle

मुल्क *[mulk]* M country

मुशायरा *[muśāyrā]* M poetry symposium
मुश्किल *[muśkil]* ADJ difficult F difficulty
मुसलमान *[musalmān]* M Muslim
मुसाफ़िर *[musāfir]* M traveler, wayfarer
मुसीबत *[musībat]* F difficulty, disaster, affliction; misfortune
मुस्कराना/मुस्कुराना *[muskarānā/muskurānā]* V.I. to smile
मुहब्बत *[muhabbat]* F love, affection
मुहर *[muhar]* F seal, stamp
मुहर्रम *[muharram]* M Muharram, the month of Imam Hussain's martyrdom which is held sacred and celebrated by Shia Muslims
मुहल्ला *[muhallā]* M locality, neighborhood
मुहावरा *[muhāvrā]* M idiom, expression; practice, habit
मुहिम *[muhim]* F expedition, campaign; an arduous task
मुहूर्त्त *[muhūrtt]* M an auspicious moment (to commence a task)
मूँग *[mū̃g]* F green lentil
मूँगफली *[mū̃gphalī]* F peanut
मूँछ *[mū̃ch]* F mustache
मूँड़ना *[mū̃ṛnā]* V.T. to shave the hair on the head
मूँदना *[mū̃dnā]* V.T. to close/ shut (the eyes etc.)
मूक *[mūk]* ADJ dumb, mute; speechless
मूतना *[mūtnā]* V.T. to urinate; to piss
मूर्ख *[mūrkh]* ADJ foolish, stupid
मूर्खता *[mūrkhtā]* F foolishness, stupidity
मूर्च्छित *[mūrcchit]* ADJ fainted, swooned
मूर्ति *[mūrti]* F idol, statue; image
मूल *[mūl]* M root, origin, source; मूल रूप से *[mūl rūp se]* ADV originally
मूली *[mūlī]* F radish
मूल्य *[mūlya]* M cost, price, worth; value
मूल्यवान *[mūlyavān]* ADJ valuable
मूसलाधार *[mūslādhār]* ADJ heavy rain, torrential downpour
मूसली *[mūslī]* F a small pestle
मूसीकी *[mūsīqī]* F music
मृग *[mṛg]* M deer

मृत्यु *[mṛtyu]* F death, demise
मृत्युदंड *[mṛtyudaṇḍ]* M death penalty
मृदु *[mṛdu]* ADJ soft, sweet, tender; gentle
में *[mẽ]* PP in; में से *[mẽ se]* PP from amongst
मेंढक *[mẽḍhak]* M frog, toad
मेंहदी *[mẽhdī]* F myrtle (the leaves of this plant are powdered and the powder is soaked in water and then applied to the hands and the feet)
मेघ *[megh]* M cloud
मेघा *[meghā]* F cloud
मेज़ *[mez]* F table
मेज़बान *[mezbān]* M host
मेथी *[methī]* F fenugreek
मेमना *[memnā]* M lamb
मेरा *[merā]* ADJ my
मेल *[mel]* M concord; agreement; match; mixture
मेला *[melā]* M fair
मेवा *[mevā]* M dry fruit
मेहनत *[mehnat]* F hard work
मेहनती *[mehnatī]* ADJ hardworking, industrious
मेहमान *[mehmān]* M guest
मेहमाननवाज़ी *[mehmānnavāzī]* F hospitality
मेहर *[mehar]* F kindness, favor
मेहरबानी *[meharbānī]* F kindness, favor
मेहराब *[mehrāb]* F arch; vault
मैं *[maĩ]* PRO I
मैंने *[maĩne]* PRO I (मैं + ने)
मैच *[maic]* M a match
मैदा *[maidā]* M flour
मैदान *[maidān]* M field, battlefield, plains
मैना *[mainā]* F Indian black bird
मैल *[mail]* F dirt, filth, scum
मैलख़ोर *[mailkhor]* ADJ a material that absorbs dirt and doesn't show it
मोक्ष *[mokṣ]* M salvation, deliverance
मोच *[moc]* F sprain, twist
मोची *[mocī]* M cobbler
मोज़ा *[mozā]* M sock; stocking
मोटरसाइकिल *[moṭarsāikil]* F motorcycle
मोटा *[moṭā]* ADJ fat, plump, corpulent
मोटापा *[moṭāpā]* M plumpness, fatness, corpulence
मोड़ *[moṛ]* M turn, turning point, bend
मोड़ना *[moṛnā]* V.T. to turn; to turn in another direction

मोती *[motī]* M pearl
मोम *[mom]* F wax
मोमबत्ती *[mombattī]* F candle
मोर *[mor]* M peacock
मोल *[mol]* M cost, price
मोलतोल *[moltol]* M haggling, bargaining
मोह *[moh]* M illusion, ignorance; affection; fascination
मोहक *[mohak]* ADJ charming, fascinating
मोहन *[mohan]* ADJ charming, attractive M enchantment; charm; an epithet of Lord Krishna
मोहर *[mohar]* F stamp, seal
मोहल्ला *[mohallā]* *see* मुहल्ला
मोहित *[mohit]* ADJ charmed, attracted
मौक़ा *[mauqā]* M opportunity
मौखिक *[maukhik]* ADJ oral, verbal
मौज *[mauj]* F whim; caprice; delight; luxury; wave
मौजूद *[maujūd]* ADJ present; existing
मौजूदगी *[maujūdagī]* F presence; existence
मौत *[maut]* F death; demise; mortality
मौन *[maun]* ADJ silent, speechless, mute
मौनी *[maunī]* ADJ someone who has pledged to remain silence
मौलवी *[maulvī]* M scholar of Islamic law, Arabic and Persian
मौला *[maulā]* M Master, a typical carefree man with no encumbrances
मौलाना *[maulānā]* M title given to a Muslim scholar
मौलिक *[maulik]* ADJ original, fundamental, essential; radical
मौसंबी *[mausambī]* F big sweet variety of the citrus family
मौसम *[mausam]* M weather, season
मौसा *[mausā]* M husband of one's mother's sister
मौसी *[mausī]* F aunt
म्यान *[myān]* F sheath
म्लेच्छ *[mlecch]* M alien, non-Aryan; lowly; unclean, shabby; un-Indian (in a contemptuous sense)

य

यंत्र *[yantra]* M machine; instrument; amulet, talisman, mystical diagram
यक़ीन *[yaqīn]* M trust, faith, confidence, certainty, assurance
यज्ञ *[yajña]* M sacrifice, ancient Hindu ritual of sacrifice and oblation
यदि *[yadi]* CONJ if
यद्यपि *[yadyapi]* IND though, although, even though
यमुना *[yamunā]* F Yamuna (river)
यश *[yaś]* M fame, reputation, glory
यह *[yeh]* PRO he/she/this/it (close to the speaker)
यहाँ *[yahā̃]* ADV here
यहीं *[yahī̃]* ADV right here (यहाँ + ही)
यही *[yahī]* this very (person, thing) (यह + ही)
यहूदी *[yahūdī]* M Jew
या *[yā]* CONJ or
याचना *[yācnā]* F begging, entreaty, asking for something
यातना *[yātnā]* F torture, torment
यात्रा *[yātrā]* F journey, travel, trip, tour, pilgrimage
यात्री *[yātrī]* M traveler, passenger, pilgrim
याद *[yād]* F memory
यादगार *[yādgār]* F monument, memorial, memento
यार *[yār]* M friend; mate; lover
यारी *[yārī]* F friendship, alliance; romantic intimacy, illicit relationship
यीशु *[yīśu]* M Jesus
युग *[yug]* M age, epoch, era; one of the four ages of Hindu cosmogony; pair, couple
युद्ध *[yuddh]* M war, battle, fighting, combat, hostilities
युरोप *[yurop]* M Europe
युरोपीय *[yuropīya]* ADJ European
युवक *[yuvak]* M youth, young man
युवती *[yuvatī]* F young woman
युवराज *[yuvrāj]* M prince
युवा *[yuvā]* ADJ, M youthful; youth
यूँ *[yū̃]* ADJ thus
यूनानी *[yūnānī]* ADJ Greek
यूनिवर्सिटी *[yūnivarsiṭī]* F university
ये *[ye]* PL, PRO these/he/she/they

यों *[yõ]* ADV like this, in this manner, thus
योग *[yog]* M total, sum; recipe; combination, addition, joining together; conjugation; contribution, yoga
योगदान *[yogdān]* M contribution
योगासन *[yogāsan]* M posture adopted in contemplative meditation, yoga
योगी *[yogī]* M one who practices yoga, ascetic
योग्य *[yogya]* ADJ worthy, qualified, able
योजना *[yojnā]* F plan, planning, scheme
योद्धा *[yoddhā]* M warrior, fighter, combatant
योनि *[yoni]* F vagina; for of existence or station fixed at birth
यौवन *[yauvan]* M youth, youthfulness

र

रंग *[raṅg]* M color
रंगत *[rãgat]* F color; complexion; plight, condition; relish, delight
रँगना *[rãgnā]* V.T. to color, to dye, to paint
रंगीन *[raṅgīn]* ADJ colored, colorful, lively; luxury-loving; jovial
रँगीला *[raṅgīlā]* ADJ colorful, sportive, mirthful
रंडी *[raṇḍī]* F prostitute, sex worker
रईस *[raīs]* M noble, aristocratic
रईसी *[raīsī]* F nobility; wealthiness, richness; grandiosity
रक़म *[raqam]* F sum
रक्त *[rakt]* ADJ, M amount; crafty, cunning (person); red; saffron; attached; blood
रक्षक *[rakṣak]* ADJ, M protecting, defending; protector, defender, savior, guard, keeper, custodian
रक्षा *[rakṣā]* F protection
रखना *[rakhnā]* V.T. to put, to place, to keep
रखवाली *[rakhvālī]* F guarding, watching, safe-keeping
रग *[rag]* F vein, fiber
रगड़ना *[ragaṛnā]* V.T. to rub, to scrub, to grate; to bruise; to cause harassment; to toil without progress
रचना *[racnā]* V.T., F to create,

to compose, to construct; composition, artistic creation; structure

रचयिता *[racyitā]* M composer, creator, author

रज *[raj]* F, M menstruation, dust; the second of the three qualities characterizing human nature

रजत *[rajat]* ADJ, M silvery, white, bright; silver; will

रज़ा *[razā]* F wish, consent, permission; quilt

रज़ाई *[razāī]* F quilt

रज़ामंद *[razāmand]* ADJ willing, consenting, agreeing

रज़ामंदी *[razāmandī]* F willingness

रटना *[raṭnā]* V.T. to repeat/ reiterate constantly; to commit to memory, to memorize

रण *[raṇ]* V.T. to cram M war F battle, fighting

रत्न *[ratna]* M gem, precious stone; the most outstanding individual of a class or group

रद्द *[radd]* ADJ rejected, cancelled, annulled

रद्दी *[raddī]* ADJ, F worthless, inferior, rough; waste paper; spoilage

रफ़्तार *[raftār]* F speed, pace

रफ़्ता-रफ़्ता *[raftā-raftā]* ADV slowly, gradually, by degrees

रब *[rab]* M God

रबड़ *[rabaṛ]* F rubber; eraser

रबड़ी *[rabṛī]* F a sweet dish made from milk and sugar

रमज़ान *[ramazān]* M Ramadan, the holy ninth month of the Islamic calendar during which one is supposed to fast from sunrise to sunset

रमना *[ramnā]* V.T. to enjoy, to make merry; to roam, to rove, to wander about

रमा *[ramā]* F Lakshmi, the goddess of wealth

रमेश *[rameś]* M Vishnu

रवानगी *[ravānagī]* F departure, setting-out

रवाना *[ravānā]* ADJ departed, set out, despatched

रवानी *[ravānī]* F flow; fluency

रवि *[ravi]* M sun

रविवार *[ravivār]* M Sunday

रवैया *[ravaiyā]* M attitude, behavior, practice

रस *[ras]* M juice, essence; aesthetic relish, sentiment, pleasure

रसद *[rasad]* F supply, provision(s)
रसवान *[rasvān]* ADJ filled with or possessing रस
रसायन *[rasāyan]* ADJ, M chemical, chemistry
रसिक *[rasik]* ADJ, M having aesthetic sense, appreciating beauty or excellence; one who has aesthetic sense or appreciates beauty or excellence; dilettante
रसीद *[rasīd]* F receipt
रसूल *[rasūl]* M prophet, divine messenger
रसोई *[rasoī]* F cooked food; kitchen
रस्सा *[rassā]* M stout, thick rope
रस्सी *[rassī]* F rope
रह *[reh]* allomorph of राह used in some compound words; रहन-सहन *[rehan-sehan]* M living, ways
रहना *[rehnā]* V.I. to live, to remain, to stay
रहम *[reham]* M pity, mercy, compassion
रहस्य *[rahasya]* M secret, mystery; secrecy
रहित *[rahit]* ADJ without, devoid of, bereft of
राँड़ *[rā̃ṛ]* F widow; term of abuse
राई *[rāī]* F mustard, black mustard
राकेश *[rākeś]* M moon
राक्षस *[rākṣas]* ADJ, M ruthless, demonic; demon, monster
राख *[rākh]* F ash(es)
राखी *[rākhī]* F sacred thread tied by girls on the wrist of a brother or a male friend considered to be like a brother as a sign of affection and as an enjoinder to protect her
राग *[rāg]* M melodic mode, melody, tune; attraction, attachment; passion, emotion, love
राज *[rāj]* M kingdom, realm; state; reign; allomorph of राज; used as a prefix or suffix to impart the sense of "king, state, or excellence/supremacy"; builder, mason
राज़ *[rāz]* M secret
राजधानी *[rājdhānī]* F capital
राजनीति *[rājnīti]* F politics
राजनीतिज्ञ *[rājnītijña]* M politician
राजभवन *[rājbhavan]* M governor's house, palace

राजभाषा *[rājbhāṣā]* F official language
राजस्थान *[rājasthān]* M Rajasthan, a Hindi-speaking state in northwestern India
राजा *[rājā]* M king
राज़ी *[rāzī]* ADJ willing, approving
राजीव *[rājīv]* M lotus flower
राज्य *[rājya]* M kingdom, state, policy, rule
रात *[rāt]* F night
रात्रि *[rātri]* F night
राधा *[rādhā]* F Radha, the favorite beloved of Krishna
रान *[rān]* F thigh
रानी *[rānī]* F queen
राम *[rām]* M Ram, the ancient Indian king of the solar dynasty who is the hero of the epic *Ramayana*, often deified as an incarnation of Vishnu; राम राम *[rām rām]* Ram Ram (an orthodox Hindu greeting)
राय *[rāy]* F, M opinion, view, advice; king
रायता *[rāytā]* M dish made of minced vegetables and yogurt
रावण *[rāvaṇ]* M Ravana, the demonic villain of the epic *Ramayana* who kidnaps Sita and is later vanquished by Ram
राशन *[rāśan]* M ration, rationing
राशि *[rāśi]* F sum, amount, quantity; sign of the zodiac
राष्ट्र *[rāṣṭra]* M nation
राष्ट्रभाषा *[rāṣṭrabhāṣā]* F national language
राष्ट्रीय *[rāṣṭrīya]* ADJ national
राष्ट्रीयता *[rāṣṭrīyatā]* F nationality; nationalism
रास्ता *[rāstā]* M way, path, route, course; passage; approach
रास्ती *[rāstī]* F patience; straightforwardness; uprightness
राह *[rāh]* F way, path
राहत *[rāhat]* F comfort, relief
राही *[rāhī]* M traveler, wayfarer, pedestrian
रिआयत *[riāyat]* F concession, favor
रिकशा *[rikśā]* M rickshaw
रिकार्ड *[rikārḍ]* M record, gramophone record
रिक्त *[rikt]* ADJ empty, void; evacuated
रिक्तता *[riktatā]* F vacancy; vacuum, void, emptiness

रिक्शा *[rikśā]* M rickshaw
रिटायर *[riṭāyar]* ADJ retired
रिपोर्ट *[riport]* F report
रिमझिम *[rimjhim]* F drizzling (as in rain)
रियाज़ *[riyāz]* M practice, exercise
रियायत *[riyāyat]* F concession; favor
रियासत *[riyāsat]* F state, princely state; estate
रिवाज *[rivāj]* M custom practice, vogue
रिश्ता *[riśtā]* M relation, relationship; affinity, connection
रिश्तेदार *[riśtedār]* M relative
रिश्वत *[riśvat]* F bribe, illegal gratification
रिसना *[risnā]* V.I. to leak, to ooze; to percolate
रिहा *[rihā]* ADJ released, set free, discharged
रिहाई *[rihāī]* F release, setting free
रीछ *[rīch]* M bear
रीझना *[rījhnā]* V.I. to be fascinated/charmed/ infatuated/attracted
रीढ़ *[rīṛh]* F backbone, spine
रीति *[rīti]* F method, manner, style, mode; custom, tradition
रुई *[ruī]* F cotton
रुकना *[ruknā]* V.I. to stop, to wait, to tarry
रुकावट *[rukāvaṭ]* F hurdle, obstacle, hindrance, barricade, blockade; resistance
रुख़ *[rukh]* ADJ, M in the direction, attitude, direction; trend; aspect; forepart, face, favorable eye; castle (in chess)
रुख़सत *[rukhsat]* F permission, departure; leave, leisure
रुचि *[ruci]* F interest, liking, taste
रुचिकर *[rucikar]* ADJ interesting
रुझान *[rujhān]* M inclination, aptitude, proclivity; trend; bias
रुतबा *[rutbā]* M status, rank, position; overwhelming influence
रुद्र *[rudra]* M Rudra, epithet of Shiva and inferior manifestations of the divine
रुपया *[rupayā]* M rupee (the Indian currency), money
रुलाई *[rulāī]* F a feeling like crying; crying, weeping, wailing

रुलाना *[rulānā]* V.T. to cause to cry/weep/lament; to harass, to trouble
रुष्ट *[ruṣṭ]* ADJ displeased, angry
रूँधना *[rū̃dhnā]* V.T. to obstruct, to block, to surround
रूखा *[rūkhā]* ADJ dry, rough; harsh; blunt, unsympathetic; without ghee; रूखा-सूखा *[rūkhā-sūkhā]* ADJ dry and unpalatable; tasteless
रूठना *[rūṭhnā]* V.T. to sulk, to be displeased
रूढ़ि *[rūṛhi]* F convention, usage
रूढ़िवाद *[rūṛhivād]* M conventionality, conservatism
रूढ़िवादी *[rūṛhivādī]* ADJ conventional, conservative
रूप *[rūp]* M form, shape, appearance; beauty; aspect; image; mould; type
रूपक *[rūpak]* M metaphor, allegory; play, feature
रूपरेखा *[rūprekhā]* M outline, synopsis, blueprint
रूमाल *[rūmāl]* M handkerchief
रूसी *[rūsī]* ADJ, F Russian; the Russian language
रूह *[rūh]* F soul, spirit, essence
रूहानी *[rūhānī]* ADJ spiritual
रेंगना *[rẽgnā]* V.I. to creep, to crawl
रे *[re]* IND, M vocative particle expressing indifference, contempt, or disrespect; second note of the Indian musical scale
रेखा *[rekhā]* F line, mark, furrow
रेखांकित *[rekhāṅkit]* ADJ underlined
रेगिस्तान *[registān]* M desert
रेट *[reṭ]* F rate
रेडियो *[reḍiyo]* M radio
रेत *[ret]* F sand
रेतीला *[retīlā]* ADJ sandy, gritty
रेल *[rel]* F railways, rail
रेलगाड़ी *[relgāṛī]* F train
रेलवे *[relve]* F railway
रेवड़ी *[revṛī]* F type of crisp, sweetmeat
रेशम *[reśam]* M silk
रेशमी *[reśmī]* ADJ silky, silken, soft
रोआँ *[roā̃]* M body hair
रोक *[rok]* F ban, restriction; check, prevention; hindrance, barrier
रोकना *[roknā]* V.T. to stop; to detain; to prevent, to ban, to repress, to curb

रोग *[rog]* M disease, illness, ailment
रोगी *[rogī]* M diseased person; patient
रोचक *[rocak]* ADJ interesting, pleasing, entertaining
रोज़ *[roz]* ADV, M daily, day
रोज़मर्रा *[rozmarrā]* ADJ everyday, daily
रोज़गार *[rozgār]* M business, trade, employment, profession, occupation
रोज़ा *[rozā]* M fast (as observed by Muslims during Ramadan); रोज़ा रखना *[rozā rakhnā]* V.T. to observe a fast
रोज़ी *[rozī]* F livelihood, living; रोज़ी रोटी *[rozī roṭī]* F daily bread; livelihood
रोटी *[roṭī]* F roti, chapatti, Indian bread
रोना *[ronā]* V.I. to cry
रोपना *[ropnā]* V.T. to plant, to transplant, to sow; to establish firmly
रोब *[rob]* M overbearing influence, sway, commanding or imposing quality
रोम *[rom]* M hair
रोमानी *[romānī]* ADJ romantic
रोयाँ *[royā̃]* M hair
रोशन *[rośan]* ADJ lighted, lit; shining, bright; famous; manifest
रोशनी *[rośnī]* F light, illumination; eyesight
रोष *[roṣ]* M anger, rage; resentment
रोहन *[rohan]* M climbing, ascending, mounting
रौनक़ *[raunaq]* F color, gaiety, vibrancy

ल

लँगड़ा *[lãgṛā]* ADJ lame, limp M a lame person
लंगर *[laṅgar]* M anchor; public kitchen, alms house; pendulum
लंगूर *[laṅgūr]* M monkey with a stiff long tail
लंड *[laṇḍ]* M penis
लंबा/लम्बा *[lambā]* ADJ tall
लंबाई *[lambāī]* F height, length; लंबाई-चौड़ाई *[lambāī-cauṛāī]* F length and breadth/width
लकड़ी *[lakṛī]* F wood, fuel, firewood; timber
लक़वा *[laqvā]* M paralysis, palsy

लकीर *[lakīr]* F line; trail; streak; track

लक्षण *[lakṣaṇ]* M symptom; indication; mark; trait; characteristic feature

लक्ष्मण *[lakṣmaṇ]* M Laxman, the younger brother of Lord Rama in the epic *Ramayana*

लक्ष्मी *[lakṣmī]* F Laxmi, the goddess of wealth, and the spouse of Lord Vishnu; fortune

लक्ष्य *[lakṣya]* M aim, intention, objective

लखपती *[lakhpatī]* M millionaire; a very wealth person

लगना *[lagnā]* V.I. to attach; to seem; to appear; to be engaged in; to be employed; to be united

लगभग *[lagbagh]* ADV approximately

लगातार *[lagātār]* ADV, ADJ continuously, incessantly, constantly; continuous, continual

लगाना *[lagānā]* V.T. to attach; to engage; to employ; to join

लगाम *[lagām]* F reins, bridle

लगाव *[lagāv]* M attachment; love, affection

लघु *[laghu]* ADJ tiny, small, little, short; light; acute

लघुकथा *[laghukathā]* F short story

लजाना *[lajānā]* V.I. be embarrassed, to blush

लज़ीज़ *[lazīz]* ADJ tasty, delicious

लज़्ज़त *[lazzat]* F taste, relish; deliciousness

लज्जा *[lajjā]* F shame; modesty, shyness, bashfulness

लज्जित *[lajjit]* ADJ ashamed, blushed

लट *[laṭ]* F tress; lock of hair

लटकना *[laṭaknā]* V.I. to hang, to overhang; to be suspended

लटकाना *[laṭkānā]* V.T. to hang, to suspend; to keep waiting

लटपटाना *[laṭpaṭānā]* V.I. to stumble, to stagger; to falter

लट्टू *[laṭṭū]* M spinning top; bulb knob

लड़कपन *[laṛakpan]* M childhood; childishness

लड़का *[laṛkā]* M boy

लड़की *[laṛkī]* F girl

लड़खड़ाना *[laṛkhaṛānā]* V.I. to stagger, to falter, to stumble; to wobble

लड़ना *[laṛnā]* V.I., V.T. to fight, to quarrel; to collide, to clash; to contend

लड़ाई *[laṛāī]* F fight, war, battle; quarrel; encounter, clash

लड़ाकू *[laṛākū]* ADJ quarrelsome; pugnacious; warlike

लड्डू *[laḍḍū]* M *laddu*, an Indian sweet

लत *[lat]* F an addiction, a bad habit

लता *[latā]* F creeper, vine

लतिका *[latikā]* F creeper, vine

लतीफ़ा *[latīfā]* M anecdote, witticism

लथपथ *[lathpath]* ADJ soaked, drenched, besmeared

लदना *[ladnā]* V.I. be loaded, to be laden, to be burdened

लपकना *[lapaknā]* V.I. to catch; to rush forth; to pounce

लपट *[lapaṭ]* F flame, blaze; heatwave

लपेट *[lapeṭ]* F fold, twist, turn; ambiguity, embroilment

लपेटना *[lapeṭnā]* V.T. to fold; to roll up; to cover; to entangle

लफ़ंगा *[lafaṅgā]* M, ADJ loafer, rogue; roguish

लफ़्ज़ *[lafz]* M word

लब *[lab]* M lip; brim; rim; edge; bank (of a river)

लबालब *[labālab]* ADV, ADJ full to the brim; brimful

लमहा *[lamhā]* M moment

लय *[lay]* F rhythm, concord, cadence, melody, tune; fusion; merging; disappearance

लरजना *[larajnā]* V.I. to vibrate, to quiver

ललकना *[lalaknā]* V.T. to crave, to have a longing

ललकार *[lalkār]* F challenge; gage

ललकारना *[lalkārnā]* V.T. to challenge; to throw down the gauntlet

ललचना *[lalacnā]* V.I. to be tempted; to be allured, to tempt

ललचाना *[lalcānā]* V.T. to allure; to entice

ललित *[lalit]* ADJ pretty, comely; sweet; elegant

लवण *[lavaṇ]* M salt

लवणीय *[lavaṇīya]* ADJ saline

लशकर/लश्कर *[laśkar]* M cantonment; encampment (of an army)

लस्सी *[lassī]* F *lassi*, a yogurt drink served cold with ice and sugar

लहँगा *[lahãgā]* M a long loose skirt worn around the loins down to the ankles
लहर *[lehar]* F wave, ripple, surge; undulation; whim
लहराना *[lehrānā]* V.I. to undulate, to wave; to fluctuate
लहू *[lahū]* M blood
लाँघना *[lā̃ghnā]* V.T. to cross, to jump over, to transgress
लांछन *[lā̃chan]* M stigma, blemish; slander
लाइन *[lāin]* F line
लाइलाज *[lāilāj]* ADJ incurable
लाख *[lākh]* M one hundred thousand F lac; sealing lac
लागत *[lāgat]* F cost, cost price, expenditure
लागू *[lāgū]* ADJ applicable; enforceable; in force
लाचार *[lācār]* ADJ helpless, obliged, constrained
लाचारी *[lācārī]* F helplessness; compulsion
लाज *[lāj]* F shame; shyness, bashfulness, modesty; honor
लाज़मी *[lāzmī]* ADJ essential, inevitable; obligatory, compulsory
लाजवाब *[lājavāb]* ADJ unique, matchless; peerless; unable to respond
लाठी *[lāṭhī]* F stick; लाठी-चार्ज *[lāṭhī-cārj]* F a lathi charge (by police)
लाड़ *[lāṛ]* M affection, fondness, endearment
लाड़ला *[lāṛlā]* ADJ dear, darling
लात *[lāt]* F leg; kick
लादना *[lādnā]* V.T. to load, to burden, to encumber
लानत *[lānat]* F condemnation, reproach; reproof; rebuke
लाना *[lānā]* V.I. to bring
लापता *[lapatā]* ADJ missing, disappeared
लापरवाह *[lāparvāh]* ADJ careless, negligent; heedless
लापरवाही *[lāparvāhī]* F carelessness, inattention
लाभ *[lābh]* M profit, gain, advantage
लायक़ *[lāyaq]* ADJ worthy, capable, able
लार *[lār]* F drivel, saliva
लाल *[lāl]* ADJ red, ruddy; angry
लालच *[lālac]* M greed, avarice, allurement
लालची *[lālcī]* ADJ greedy, avaricious

लालटेन *[lālṭen]* F lantern
लाली *[lālī]* F redness; lipstick; rouge
लावारिस *[lāvāris]* ADJ unclaimed, unowned, heirless (used for both things and people)
लाश *[lāś]* F corpse, dead body
लिंग *[liṅg]* M penis; the male genital organ; phallus representing Lord Shiva; gender (in grammar)
लिए *[lie]* ADV for, with a view to, for the sake of, on account of; taking, carrying
लिखना *[likhnā]* V.T. to write, to note down, to record
लिखाई-पढ़ाई *[likhāī-paṛhāī]* F reading and writing, study
लिखित *[likhit]* ADJ written, recorded
लिटाना *[liṭānā]* V.T. to make someone lie down
लिपटना *[lipaṭnā]* V.I. to embrace; to cling; to coil around
लिपि *[lipi]* F script, writing system
लिफ़ाफ़ा *[lifāfā]* M envelope
लिबास *[libās]* M dress, attire
लिहाज़ *[lihāz]* M consideration, deference, respect; point of view
लिहाज़ा *[lihāzā]* IND thus, therefore; on this account
लिहाफ़ *[lihāf]* M quilt
लीक *[līk]* F track; rut; trace
लीजिये *[lījiye]* please take
लीन *[līn]* ADJ absorbed, engrossed; merged, vanished, disappeared
लीपना *[līpnā]* V.T. to plaster, to coat, to smear
लीला *[līlā]* F sport, play amorous sport; fun and frolic
लुंगी *[luṅgī]* F *sarong*, a strip of cloth worn around the waist
लुगाई *[lugāī]* F woman
लुटना *[luṭnā]* V.I. to be plundered, be robbed
लुटाना *[luṭānā]* V.T. to squander; to blow the expense
लुटेरा *[luṭerā]* M robber, bandit
लुढ़कना *[luṛhaknā]* V.I. to roll down, to be toppled, to tumble down
लुत्फ़ *[lutf]* M fun, pleasure, enjoyment
लुप्त *[lupt]* ADJ disappeared, vanished
लुभाना *[lubhānā]* V.T. to lure, to charm, to attract; to entice

लू *[lū]* F warm air; heatwave; sunstroke
लूट *[lūṭ]* F plunder, booty; spoil
लूटपाट *[lūṭpāṭ]* F plundering and killing
लूटना *[lūṭnā]* V.T. to loot, to plunder
लेकिन *[lekin]* CONJ but
लेख *[lekh]* M article; paper; writing; handwriting
लेखक *[lekhak]* M author, writer
लेखन *[lekhan]* M writing, scribing, writing work
लेखिका *[lekhikā]* F female author
लेटना *[leṭnā]* V.I. to lie (down), to repose, to recline
लेन *[len]* M taking, receiving
लेन-देन *[len-den]* M transaction; exchange; dealings
लेना *[lenā]* V.T. to take, to accept, to borrow, to buy
लेपना *[lepnā]* V.T. to anoint; to coat; to smear
लैस *[lais]* ADJ equipped, fitted (with); ready
लो *[lo]* IND term expressing surprise
लोक *[lok]* M world; one of the three worlds
लोकतंत्र *[loktantra]* M democracy
लोकप्रिय *[lokpriya]* ADJ popular
लोकसभा *[loksabhā]* F the lower house of Indian Parliament (the house of the people)
लोकल *[lokal]* ADJ local
लोग *[log]* M, PL people
लोचन *[locan]* M eye
लोटना *[loṭnā]* V.I. to roll, to wallow, to welter; to toss
लोटा *[loṭa]* M a small round metal utensil for the household
लोप *[lop]* M disappearance; elision
लोभ *[lobh]* M greed, avarice; temptation; lure
लोभी *[lobhī]* ADJ greedy, covetous
लोमड़ी *[lomṛī]* F fox, vixen
लोहा *[lohā]* M, ADJ iron; very hard; very strong
लोहार *[lohār]* M blacksmith; forgeman
लौंग *[laũg]* F clove; nose-stud
लौंडा *[laũḍā]* M boy, lad
लौंडी *[laũḍī]* F girl, servant girl
लौ *[lau]* F flame; glow; deep concentration

लौकी *[laukī]* F bottle gourd
लौटना *[lauṭnā]* V.I. to return; to go back
लौटाना *[lauṭānā]* V.T. to return (something), to give back; to send back

व

वंचित *[vañcit]* ADJ deprived; cheated, deceived
वंदना *[vandnā]* F deferential salutaion, obseisance, worship
वंश *[vanś]* M lineage; family; clan; stock; dynasty
व *[va]* CONJ and
वकील *[vakīl]* M lawyer, advocate
वक़्त *[vaqt]* M time
वक्ता *[vaktā]* M talker, spokesman, speaker
वग़ैरह *[vaghairah]* etcetera
वचन *[vacan]* M promise, utterance; speech; talk; a quotation or treatise
वज़न *[vazan]* M weight; importance, value
वज़नी *[vazanī]* ADJ heavy, weighty
वजह *[vajah]* F cause, reason; (x की) वजह से *[(x kī) vajah se]* PP on account (of x)
वज़ीफ़ा *[vazīfā]* M scholarship; stipend
वज़ीर *[vazīr]* M minister, the queen (in chess); वज़ीरे आज़म *[vazīre āzam]* M Prime Minister
वजूद *[vajūd]* M existence, presence
वज्र *[vajra]* M thunderbolt, lightning; a fatal weapon
वतन *[vatan]* M homeland, native country
वध *[vadh]* M killing, murder
वधू *[vadhū]* F bride, wife
वन *[van]* M forest
वनस्पति *[vanaspati]* F vegetation; vegetable; hydrogenated oil from groundnut
वफ़ा *[vafā]* F fidelity, loyalty
वफ़ादार *[vafādār]* ADJ faithful, loyal
वयोवृद्ध *[vayovṛddh]* ADJ aged, old; veteran
वर *[var]* M bridegroom; boon; Persian suffix meaning "having, possessing"
वरक़ *[varaq]* M thin and fine leaves of silver or gold; pages of a book

वरदी *[vardī]* F uniform
वरना *[varnā]* V.T. to select or choose IND otherwise CONJ otherwise, or else
वरिष्ठ *[variṣṭh]* ADJ senior; best
वरिष्ठता *[variṣṭhtā]* F seniority
वर्ग *[varg]* M class, category, group; group of letters produced in the same part of the mouth
वर्जन *[varjan]* M inhibition, taboo, prohibition
वर्जित *[varjit]* ADJ inhibited; prohibited
वर्ण *[varṇ]* M caste; color; dye
वर्णमाला *[varṇmālā]* F alphabet; syllabary
वर्णव्यवस्था *[varṇvyavasthā]* F caste system
वर्णन *[varṇan]* M description; narration
वर्तनी *[vartanī]* F spelling
वर्तमान *[vartamān]* ADJ present; existing; the present
वर्दी *[vardī]* see वरदी
वर्ष *[varṣ]* M year
वर्षा *[varṣā]* F rain, rainfall
वश *[vaś]* M power control
वशीभूत *[vaśībhūt]* ADJ overpowered; tamed; brought under control
वसंत *[vasant]* M spring (season)
वसंती *[vasantī]* ADJ pertaining to spring
वसा *[vasā]* F fat; fats and oils
वसीयत *[vasīyat]* F will; testament; legacy
वसूल *[vasūl]* ADJ realized; collected
वसूली *[vasūlī]* F realization (of dues); recovery
वस्तु *[vastu]* F thing; article; object; substance, material
वस्त्र *[vastra]* M clothing; textile
वह *[voh]* PRO he/she/that/it (far from the speaker); वह तो है। *[voh to hai]* That's true.
वहन *[vahan]* M conveying, carrying
वहम *[vaham]* M doubt, suspicion; false notion
वहमी *[vehmī]* ADJ suspicious; superstitious
वहशत *[vehśat]* F savagery; embarrassment; madness
वहशी *[vehśī]* ADJ savage; barbarous; mad
वहाँ *[vahā̃]* ADV there

वहीं *[vahī̃]* ADV right (over) there, only there
वही *[vahī]* PRO only he/she, that very (person/thing) (वह + ही)
वाँ *[vā̃]* ADJ a suffix added to most cardinal numbers to create ordinals
वा *[vā]* CONJ or, or else; IND Oh!
वाक़ई *[vāqaī]* IND actually
वाक़िफ़ *[vāqif]* ADJ acquainted
वाक़िया *[vāqiyā]* M incident; event; happening
वाक्य *[vākya]* M sentence
वाटिका *[vāṭikā]* F a small garden
वाणिज्य *[vāṇijya]* M commerce; trade
वाणी *[vāṇī]* F speech, voice
वातानुकूलित *[vātānukūlit]* ADJ airconditioned
वातावरण *[vātāvaraṇ]* M atmosphere
वात्सल्य *[vātsalya]* M affection, affectionate love
वादक *[vādak]* M an instrumentalist; one who plays a musical instrument
वाद्य *[vādya]* M musical instrument
वानप्रस्थ *[vānprasth]* M the third of four stages of life
वापस *[vāpas]* ADJ returned; given back
वापसी *[vāpasī]* F return; coming back
वाम *[vām]* ADJ left; reverse; contrary; adverse
वामपंथी *[vāmpanthī]* F left wing (politics)
वायदा *[vāydā]* M promise, commitment
वायु *[vāyu]* F air; wind; windy humor
वार *[vār]* M assault; stroke, blow; a day of the week
वारदात *[vārdāt]* F mishap; unfortunate/untoward event
वारिस *[vāris]* M heir, successor
वार्ता *[vārtā]* F talk; negotiation
वार्तालाप *[vārtālāp]* M conversation, talks; negotiation
वार्षिक *[vārṣik]* ADJ annual, yearly
वाला *[vālā]* ADJ a suffix denoting agent, doer, owner, possessor, keeper or inhabitant
वालिद *[vālid]* ADJ father
वालिदा *[vālidā]* F mother
वालिदैन *[validain]* M parents
वालैकुम अस्सलाम *[vālaikum assalām]* And peace be upon

you! (a return greeting, *see* अस्सलाम अलैकुम)
वासना *[vāsnā]* F passion, intense sexual desire; knowledge derived from memory
वासी *[vāsī]* M dweller; inhabitant
वास्तव *[vāstav]* M real, actual, factual; genuine
वास्ता *[vāstā]* M concern; connection; relation
वास्तु *[vāstu]* M building
वास्तुकला *[vāstukalā]* F architecture
वास्ते *[vāste]* IND for, for the sake of; in the name of
वाह *[vāh]* IND an exclamatory word denoting admiration, appreciation
वाहन *[vāhan]* M vehicle; converyance
वाहियात *[vāhiyāt]* ADJ nonsensical; useless; ridiculous
वि *[vi]* a prefix to express division, distinction, distribution, arrangement
विकट *[vikaṭ]* ADJ horrible, dreadful, frightful.
विकल *[vikal]* ADJ restless, agitated; dismembered, mutilated
विकल्प *[vikalp]* M alternative option
विकसित *[vikasit]* ADJ developed, grown; opened
विकार *[vikār]* M deformation; defilement; change or variation
विकास *[vikās]* M evolution; development; growth
विकासशील *[vikāsśīl]* developing; evolving
विकृत *[vikṛt]* ADJ deformed; defiled; mutilated; perverted
विक्रय *[vikray]* M sale, selling
विक्रेता *[vikretā]* M seller, vendor
विख्यात *[vikhyāt]* ADJ renowned, well-known, famous
विख्याति *[vikhyāti]* F fame, name, renown, repute
विगति *[vigati]* F past; sad plight
विघटन *[vighaṭan]* M disintegration; disorganization; disruption
विघ्न *[vighna]* M interruption; interference, meddling
विचल *[vical]* ADJ moving about, unsteady

विचलित *[vicalit]* ADJ restless, nervous; fickle, unsteady
विचार *[vicār]* M thought, idea
विचारधारा *[vicārdhārā]* F ideology
विचारना *[vicārnā]* V.T. to think, to deliberate
विचित्र *[vicitra]* ADJ strange; wonderful; amazing; curious
विच्छेद *[vicched]* M dissection, division; difference; disintegration
विजय *[vijay]* F victory, conquest, triumph
विजेता *[vijetā]* M conqueror
विज्ञान *[vijñān]* M science
विज्ञापन *[vijñāpan]* M advertisement; announcement; poster
विडंबना *[viḍambanā]* F anomaly; mockery
वितरण *[vitaraṇ]* M distribution; disbursement; delivery
वित्त *[vitta]* M finance; wealth
वित्तमंत्री *[vittamantrī]* M Finance Minister
विदा *[vidā]* F taking leave, farewell, adieu; a woman's departure from her mother's or from her in-law's house
विदाई *[vidāī]* F farewell, sending off; departure
विदुषी *[viduṣī]* F learned/wise woman
विदेश *[videś]* M foreign country
विदेशी *[videśī]* ADJ foreign, alien; exotic; M foreigner
विद्या *[vidyā]* F knowledge, learning, education, science
विद्यार्थी *[vidyārthī]* M student; scholar
विद्यालय *[vidyālay]* M school
विद्युत *[vidyut]* M electricity, power; lightning
विद्रोह *[vidroh]* M uprising, revolt, rebellion, mutiny
विद्रोही *[vidrohī]* ADJ revolting, rebel/mutineer
विद्वान *[vidvān]* ADJ, M scholar
विधवा *[vidhvā]* F widow
विधा *[vidhā]* F genre; form; type
विधाता *[vidhātā]* M creator; Brahma; Destiny personified
विधान *[vidhān]* M legislation, rule, regulation; disposition; manner; method
विधायक *[vidhāyak]* ADJ, M legislative; creative; legislator
विधि *[vidhi]* F law; method; manner; system; direction;

rule; prescribed act or rite
विधुर *[vidhur]* M widower
विनती *[vinati]* F request, entreaty
विनम्र *[vinamra]* ADJ humble, meek, submissive; respectful
विनय *[vinay]* F modesty, politeness, humbleness, humility
विनाश *[vināś]* M destruction, devastation, disaster, ruin, wreck
विनाशी *[vināśī]* ADJ destructive
विनोद *[vinod]* M wit, humor; amusement, recreation
विपक्ष *[vipakṣ]* M opposition (party)
विपक्षी *[vipakṣī]* ADJ opposition, hostile, rival N opponent, rival
विपत्ति *[vipatti]* F distress; affliction; calamity; hardship
विपरीत *[viparīt]* ADJ opposite/ opposed, contrary, reverse
विफल *[viphal]* ADJ failed, unsuccessful; vain
विफलता *[viphaltā]* F failure, lack of success; futility
विभाग *[vibhāg]* M department; division; portion
विभाजन *[vibhājan]* M division, partition
विभाजित *[vibhājit]* ADJ divided, partitioned
विभिन्न *[vibhinna]* ADJ different, various, diverse
विभिन्नता *[vibhinnatā]* F difference, variety; diversity
विभूति *[vibhūti]* F ash; majesty, magnificence
विमर्श *[vimarś]* M consultation, consideration, examination, reflection
विमान *[vimān]* M airplane, airliner
वियोग *[viyog]* M separation, disunion
विरह *[vireh]* M separation (from loved one)
विराग *[virāg]* M renunciation, detachment; aversion, dislike
विराजमान *[virājmān]* ADJ (graciously) seated; sitting; gracing with one's presence
विराट *[virāṭ]* ADJ colossal, gigantic, enormous, huge
विराम *[virām]* M pause; pause at the end of a sentence, period
विरासत *[virāsat]* F legacy, inheritance

विरुद्ध *[viruddh]* ADJ against; opposed; opposite
विरोध *[virodh]* M opposition; antagonism; hostility, resistance, objection
विरोधाभास *[virodhābhās]* M paradox
विरोधी *[virodhī]* ADJ, M adversary; rival; opponent; objector; hostile
विलंब *[vilamb]* M delay, procrastination; lag
विलाप *[vilāp]* M lamentation, crying, weeping, wailing
विलायत *[vilāyat]* F foreign land/country; Europe; England
विलायती *[vilāyatī]* ADJ foreign
विलास *[vilās]* M enjoyment; luxury; amorous playfulness
विलासिता *[vilāsitā]* F debauchery, wantonness, luxuriousness
विलीन *[vilīn]* ADJ disappeared, vanished; merged; absorbed; engrossed
विवरण *[vivaraṇ]* M account, description; commentary; particulars
विवश *[vivaś]* ADJ compelled, helpless
विवशता *[vivaśatā]* F helplessness; compulsion
विवाद *[vivād]* M dispute, altercation, quarrel; discussion; controversy
विवादास्पद *[vivādāspad]* ADJ controversial
विवाह *[vivāh]* M marriage, wedding
विवाहित *[vivāhit]* ADJ married, wedded
विविध *[vividh]* ADJ different, diverse, various, miscellaneous
विवेक *[vivek]* M reason; discretion; judgment
विवेचन *[vivecan]* M critical appreciation; evaluation; investigation
विशाल *[viśāl]* ADJ huge; large, big, spacious, grand, extensive, vast
विशेष *[viśeṣ]* ADJ special; specific; particular
विशेषता *[viśeṣtā]* F specialty, peculiarity, singularity
विशेषण *[viśeṣaṇ]* M adjective; attribute
विश्लेषण *[viśleṣaṇ]* M analysis
विश्व *[viśva]* M world, universe
विश्वकोश *[viśvakoś]* M

encylopaedia
विश्वविजयी *[viśvavijayī]* ADJ, M world conqueror
विश्वशांति *[viśvaśānti]* F world peace
विश्वविद्यालय *[viśvavidyālay]* M university
विश्वसनीय *[viśvasnīya]* ADJ reliable, dependable, trustworthy
विश्वसनीयता *[viśvasnīyatā]* F reliability, dependability
विश्वास *[viśvās]* M belief, confidence, trust, faith, reliance
विश्वासघात *[viśvāsghāt]* M betrayal, treachery; infidelity
विष *[viṣ]* M poison, venom
विषम *[viṣam]* ADJ odd, incongruous, uneven, rough; adverse, dissimilar
विषमता *[viṣamtā]* F contrast; dissimilarity; inequity; oddity
विषय *[viṣay]* M subject, topic; matter; sexual pleasure; affair
विषाणु *[viṣāṇu]* F virus
विषाद *[viṣād]* M gloom, somberness, melancholy
विषैला *[viṣailā]* ADJ poisonous, venomous, toxic
विष्णु *[viṣṇu]* M Vishnu, one of the Hindu mythological divine trinity
विसंगत *[visaṅgat]* ADJ irrelevant, illogical, incoherent
विसंगति *[visaṅgati]* F illogicality
विसर्जन *[visarjan]* M dispersal; abandonment
विसर्जित *[visarjit]* ADJ dispersed; abandoned
विस्तार *[vistār]* M expanse, span, spread; elaboration
विस्फोट *[visphoṭ]* M explosion, blast
विस्फोटक *[visphoṭak]* ADJ explosive
विस्मय *[vismay]* M surprise, wonder; astonishment, amazement
वीकेंड *[vīkeṇḍ]* M weekend
वीर *[vīr]* ADJ heroic, brave, galant M hero
वीरता *[vīrtā]* F heroism, bravery, valor, daring, gallantry
वीरान *[vīrān]* ADJ, M deserted, devastated, desolate
वीर्य *[vīrya]* M semen, potency, manly valor, virility; heroism, valor

वुज़ू *[vuzū]* M act of washing the face, hands and feet by a Muslim before prayers
वुजूद *[vujūd]* M existence, being
वृक्ष *[vṛkṣ]* M tree
वृत्तांत *[vṛttānt]* M news; report, narrative, account
वृद्ध *[vṛddh]* ADJ elderly, old, aged
वृद्धावस्था *[vṛddhāvasthā]* F old age, senility
वृद्धि *[vṛddhi]* F increase/increment, rise, growth; progress
वे *[vo]* PRO they/those/he/she; वे लोग *[vo log]* PRO those people
वेग *[veg]* M speed, velocity
वेणी *[veṇī]* F a braid of hair, or braided hair
वेतन *[vetan]* M salary, pay; wages
वेद *[ved]* M the most ancient and sacred scriptures of the Hindus
वेदना *[vednā]* F ache, pain, agony
वेश *[veś]* M guise; external appearance; dress, costume
वेशभूषा *[veśbhūṣā]* F apparel; get-up
वेश्या *[veśyā]* F sex worker, prostitute
वैज्ञानिक *[vaijñānik]* M, ADJ scientist; scientific
वैध *[vaidh]* ADJ legal, valid, legitimate
वैभव *[vaibhav]* M grandeur, glory, magnificence; wealth, prosperity, riches
वैर *[vair]* M enmity, animosity; hostility
वैरागी *[vairāgī]* ADJ, M detached; recluse
वैराग्य *[vairāgya]* M the attitude of renunciation, detachment
वैवाहिक *[vaivāhik]* ADJ married; marital
वैशाख *[vaiśākh]* M the second month of the Hindu calendar
वैश्य *[vaiśya]* M the third class of the traditional caste set-up in Hinduism, with trade as the main profession
वैसा *[vaisā]* ADJ of that kind/nature, such as that, like that
वैसे *[vaise]* ADV that way, in that manner, in the same manner
वो *[vo]* PRO variant of वह
वोट *[voṭ]* M vote

वोटर *[voṭar]* M voter
व्यंग्य *[vyañgya]* M suggestions; irony, sarcasm, innuendo
व्यंजन *[vyañjan]* M consonant; a cooked dish
व्यक्ति *[vyakti]* M individual
व्यक्तिवाद *[vyaktivād]* M individualism
व्यक्तित्व *[vyaktitva]* M personality, individuality
व्यग्र *[vyagra]* ADJ restless, perturbed
व्यग्रता *[vyagratā]* F restlessness, anxiety
व्यथा *[vyathā]* F pain, agony, anguish
व्यय *[vyay]* M expense, expenditure; cost, outlay
व्यर्थ *[vyarth]* ADJ useless, fruitless, futile; ineffective
व्यवस्था *[vyavasthā]* F order, system, management, arrangement
व्यवहार *[vyavahār]* M behavior, dealings, treatment, transaction
व्यसन *[vyasan]* M addiction
व्यस्त *[vyast]* ADJ busy, occupied, engaged
व्यस्तता *[vyasttā]* F the state of being busy
व्याकरण *[vyākaraṇ]* M grammar
व्याकुल *[vyākul]* ADJ perturbed, upset, restless, impatient
व्याकुलता *[vyākultā]* F restlessness, impatience
व्याख्या *[vyākhyā]* F interpretation; explanation, elaboration; commentary
व्यापक *[vyāpak]* ADJ comprehensive, extensive; pervasive
व्यापार *[vyāpār]* M business, trade
व्यापारी *[vyāpārī]* M businessman, trader, merchant
व्यायाम *[vyāyām]* M physical exercise; gymnastics
व्यावहारिक *[vyāvahārik]* ADJ practical, customary
व्रत *[vrat]* M fast; vow; pledge

श

शंकर *[śaṅkar]* M Shankar (name of Shiva)
शंका *[śaṅkā]* F doubt, suspicion, mistrust
शंख *[śaṅkh]* M conch shell; a number equal to a thousand billion

शक *[śak]* M doubt, suspicion
शक्कर/शकर *[śakkar/śakar]* M sugar
शक्ति *[śakti]* F power, strength, potency, energy; name of the goddess personifying divine power
शक्तिशाली *[śaktiśālī]* ADJ powerful
शक्ल *[śakla]* F countenance, face, shape, form, appearance
शख़्स *[śakhs]* M person; a human being, individual
शग़ल *[śaghal]* M pastime, recreation; hobby
शत *[śat]* M one hundred
शतक *[śatak]* M century, one hundred
शतरंज *[śatrañj]* F chess; a chess-board
शताब्दी *[śatābdī]* F century
शत्रु *[śatru]* M enemy
शत्रुता *[śatrutā]* F enmity, animosity, hostility
शनि *[śani]* M Saturn; Saturday;
शनिवार/शनिश्चर *[śanivār/ śaniścar]* M Saturday
शपथ *[śapath]* F oath, swearing
शब *[śab]* F night
शबनम *[śabnam]* F dew; a very fine quality of muslin
शबाख़ैर *[śabākhair]* IND Good night!
शब्द *[śabd]* M word
शब्दकोष *[śabdkoṣ]* M dictionary
शब्दावली *[śabdāvalī]* F glossary; vocabulary
शरण *[śaraṇ]* F shelter, refuge; recourse; protection
शरणार्थी *[śarṇārthī]* M refugee
शरद *[śarad]* F autumn
शरबत *[śarbat]* M a sweet beverage, sherbet
शरम *[śaram]* *see* शर्म
शरमाना *[śarmānā]* *see* शर्माना
शरमिंदगी *[śarmindagī]* *see* शर्मिंदगी
शरमिंदा *[śarmindā]* *see* शर्मिंदा
शरमीला *[śarmīlā]* *see* शर्मीला
शराब *[śarāb]* F alcohol, wine
शराबी *[śarābī]* ADJ, N alcoholic; drunkard
शरारत *[śarārat]* F mischief; wickedness
शरारती *[śarāratī]* ADJ naughty; playful; mischievous
शरीक *[śarīk]* ADJ participating, associating; partnering, playful
शरीफ़ *[śarīf]* ADJ noble; virtuous

शरीफ़ा *[śarīfā]* M custard apple
शरीर *[śarīr]* M, ADJ body, physique; mischievous
शर्त *[śart]* F condition; pre-condition, term; provision
शर्त *[śart]* F bet, wager
शर्बत/शरबत *[śarbat/śarabat]* M sherbet
शर्म *[śarm]* F shame
शर्मनाक *[śarmnāk]* ADJ shameful
शर्मिंदगी *[śarmindagī]* F embarrassment, shame
शर्मिंदा *[śarmindā]* ADJ embarrassed, ashamed
शर्माना *[śarmānā]* V.I. be embarrassed, to be ashamed
शर्मीला *[śarmīlā]* ADJ coy, shy, bashful
शव *[śav]* M corpse, dead body
शहंशाह *[śahanśāh]* M emperor, a king of kings
शह *[śeh]* F instigation; check (in chess)
शहद *[śehad]* M honey
शहनाई *[śehnāī]* F a clarinet; the *shenai*
शहर *[śehar]* M city
शहीद *[śahīd]* ADJ, M martyr
शांत *[śānt]* ADJ peaceful; tranquil
शांति *[śānti]* F peace, calmness, quiet, tranquillity
शांतिप्रिय *[śāntipriya]* ADJ peace-loving
शाक *[śāk]* M vegetable
शाकाहारी *[śākāhārī]* M vegetarian
शाखा *[śākhā]* F branch; offshoot; sect
शागिर्द *[śāgird]* M pupil, disciple, apprentice
शादी *[śādī]* F wedding, marriage
शान *[śān]* F magnificence, splendor, grandeur; pomp
शानदार *[śāndār]* ADJ grand, glorious
शाप *[śāp]* M curse
शाबाश *[śābāś]* INT Bravo!, Well done!; Excellent!
शाबाशी *[śābāśī]* F applause; praise
शाम *[śām]* F evening, dusk
शामत *[śamat]* F misfortune; ill-luck; affliction
शामियाना *[śāmiyānā]* M canopy, large tent
शामिल *[śāmil]* ADJ included, associated, connected; annexed
शायद *[śāyad]* CONJ perhaps; probably

शायर *[śāyar]* M poet
शायरी *[śāyrī]* F poetry
शारीकि *[śārīrik]* ADJ physical, bodily, corporeal
शाल *[śāl]* M shawl
शाला *[śālā]* F house; residence; used as a suffix to denote a place dedicated to a particular function; पाठशाला *[pāṭhśālā]* F school
शासक *[śāsak]* M ruler; king; mater
शासन *[śāsan]* M government, administration; rule
शास्त्र *[śāstra]* M scripture(s), a religious or scientific treatise; a discipline; literature or knowledge
शास्त्री *[śāstrī]* M scholar of or authority in the scriptures
शाहंशाह *[śāhanśāh]* M emperor, monarch
शाह *[śāh]* M king; the king (in chess or cards)
शाही *[śāhī]* ADJ royal, regal, majestic; a suffix to denote a system; नौकरशाही *[naukarśāhī]* F royal, regal, majestic; the bureaucracy; the administration
शिकवा *[śikavā]* M complaint, grudge; grievance
शिकस्ता *[śikastā]* ADJ broken; defeated; devastated
शिकायत *[śikāyat]* F complaint; grievance; accusation
शिकार *[śikār]* M victim; prey
शिकारी *[śikārī]* ADJ, M hunting; hunter
शिक्षक *[śikṣak]* M teacher
शिक्षा *[śikṣā]* F education, instruction, teaching; शिक्षा प्रणाली *[śikṣā praṇālī]* F education system
शिक्षिका *[śikṣikā]* F teacher
शिक्षित *[śikṣit]* ADJ educated
शिखर *[śikhar]* M peak, summit; top; pinnacle
शिथिल *[śithil]* ADJ loose, lax; slow; tardy; languid; weary
शिथिलता *[śithiltā]* F looseness; tardiness
शिद्दत *[śiddat]* F difficulty, severity, intensity; vehemence
शिल्प *[śilp]* M craft; architecture
शिव *[śiv]* M Lord Shiva, one of the divine trio in Hinduism; the good; auspicious
शिवरात्रि *[śivrātri]* F a Hindu festival observed on the fourteenth day of the dark

half of the month of Magh
शिविर *[śivir]* M camp, tent
शिशिर *[śiśir]* M winter
शिशु *[śiśu]* M infant, baby; child
शिष्य *[śiṣya]* M disciple; female disciple
शीघ्र *[śīghra]* ADV immediately, soon; urgently; promptly
शीत *[śīt]* ADJ cold, frigid, chilly
शीतल *[śītal]* ADJ cool, cold; frigid
शीर्षक *[śīrṣak]* M title, heading
शीशा *[śīśā]* M glass; mirror; a large glass bottle
शीशी *[śīśī]* F glass bottle
शुक्र *[śukra]* M semen; the planet Venus; thanks
शुक्र *[śukra]* M Friday
शुक्रवार *[śukravār]* M Friday
शुक्रिया *[śukriyā]* M thank you!
शुदा *[śudā]* ADJ a suffix giving the sense of that which has been performed or is accompanied by; शादीशुदा *[śādīśudā]* ADJ married
शुद्ध *[śuddh]* ADJ pure, unadulterated
शुद्धि *[śuddhi]* F purity, correction, purification
शुभ *[śubh]* ADJ, M auspicious, good; well-being
शुभकामना *[śubhkāmnā]* F auspicious wish
शुभकामनाएँ *[śubhkāmnāẽ]* F good wishes
शुमार *[śumār]* M number; accounting; calculation
शुमाल *[śumāl]* M north
शुमाली *[śumālī]* ADJ northern
शुरुआत *[śuruāt]* F beginning, commencement
शुरू *[śurū]* M beginning, commencement
शूद्र *[śūdra]* M Shudra, a member of the fourth of the four original castes in the caste system.
शून्य *[śūnya]* ADJ, M empty, void, vacant; zero; void
शून्यता *[śūnyatā]* F emptiness; a void; nothingness; non-existence
शूर *[śūr]* ADJ, M valient, brave, heroic
शूरता *[śūrtā]* F bravery
शृंखला *[śṛṅkhlā]* F chain; series; order; range; connection
शृंगार *[śṛṅgār]* M beautification, adornment, love, the erotic sentiment

शेर *[śer]* M lion; tiger; couplet
शेरवानी *[śervānī]* F a typical long, tight coat
शेष *[śeṣ]* ADJ, M rest, remaining, residue, balance
शैतान *[śaitān]* M Satan, devil; naughty, mischievous person; naughtiness
शैतानी *[śaitānī]* F wickedness
शैव *[śaiv]* ADJ pertaining to or belonging to Lord Shiva
शोक *[śok]* M sorrow, grief
शोध *[śodh]* M research, refinement; purification
शोधकार्य *[śodhkārya]* M research
शोधना *[śodhnā]* V.T. to purify, to refine
शोबा *[śobā]* M branch, part; a division
शोभा *[śobhā]* F grace, elegance, beauty, luster
शोभित *[śobhit]* ADJ splendid, radiant, beautiful; adorned
शोर *[śor]* M noise, tumult, din, hue and cry
शोरगुल *[śorgul]* M din; hue and cry; noise
शोला *[śolā]* M flame of fire
शोषण *[śoṣaṇ]* M exploitation; soaking
शोहरत *[śohrat]* F fame, renown
शौक़ *[śauq]* M interest, hobby
शौक़ीन *[śauqīn]* ADJ fashionable; fond of fine things; foppish
शौच *[śauc]* M ablution; evacuation of excrement; toilet
शौचालय *[śaucālaya]* M toilet
शौहर *[śauhar]* M husband.
श्मशान *[śmaśān]* M cremation ground
श्याम *[śyām]* ADJ black, dark-colored; Lord Krishna
श्रद्धांजलि *[śraddhāñjali]* F tribute, offering
श्रद्धा *[śraddhā]* F faith; veneration; reverence
श्रद्धालु *[śraddhālu]* ADJ having faith, trustful
श्रम *[śram]* M labor, toil, exertion
श्रमिक *[śramik]* ADJ, M laborer; labor
श्रावण *[śrāvaṇ]* M the fifth month of the Hindu calendar (one of the rainy months)
श्री *[śrī]* ADJ an honorific adjective prefixed to male names—Mr. F Lakshmi (the goddess of wealth)
श्रुति *[śruti]* F Vedas; ear

श्रेष्ठ *[śreṣṭh]* ADJ best; good, excellent, superior
श्रेष्ठता *[śreṣṭhtā]* F excellence; superiority
श्रोता *[śrotā]* M listener, audience
श्लोक *[ślok]* M Sanskrit couplet; praise
श्वास *[śvās]* M breath, respiration
श्वेत *[śvet]* ADJ white, bright, spotless, fair-complexioned

ष

षंड *[ṣaṇḍ]* M a bull; bullock
षट *[ṣaṭ]* M six
षड्यंत्र *[ṣaḍyantra]* M conspiracy, plot, intrigue
षष्टि *[ṣaṣṭi]* M sixty

स

संकट *[saṅkaṭ]* M crisis, emergency, danger
सँकड़ा *[sãkaṛā]* ADJ narrow strait
संकलित *[saṅkalit]* ADJ compiled, collected, assembled
संकल्प *[saṅkalp]* M determination; resolve; resolution
संकल्पना *[saṅkalpnā]* V.T., F to make a resolve of; to conceive; concept
संकीर्ण *[saṅkīrṇ]* ADJ parochial, narrow
संकुचित *[saṅkucit]* ADJ parochial, narrow, contracted
संकेत *[saṅket]* M sign, signal, indication; rendezvous
संक्रामक *[saṅkrāmak]* ADJ infectious, contagious
संक्षिप्त *[saṅkṣipt]* ADJ brief, short, abridged
संक्षेप *[saṅkṣep]* M compendium, summary, brief, abridgment
संख्या *[saṅkhyā]* F number, numeral, figure
संग *[saṅg]* M company, association, contact, stone
संगत *[saṅgat]* ADJ, F relevant; logical; compatible; company, accompaniment
संगति *[saṅgati]* M company, association; consistence, coherence; rationality; compatibility; relevance
संगी *[saṅgī]* M companion; associate

संगीत *[saṅgīt]* M music
संग्रह *[saṅgrah]* M collection, compilation, compendium; depository, storage, reserve
संग्रहालय *[saṅgrahālay]* M museum
संग्राम *[saṅgrām]* M war, battle, combat
संघ *[saṅgh]* M federation, union, league, association, organization
संघटन *[saṅghaṭan]* M organization, formation, composition
संघर्ष *[saṅghars̩]* M struggle, conflict, friction
संचार *[sañcār]* M communication; transmission; movement
संचारण *[sañcāraṇ]* M communication/transmission; movement
संचालन *[sañcālan]* M direction; conduction (as of an event)
संजीदगी *[sañjīdagī]* F solemnity; gravity; seriousness
संजीदा *[sañjīdā]* ADJ solemn; serious; grave
संत *[sant]* M saint
संतरा *[santarā]* M mandarin orange
संतान *[santān]* F offspring; progeny
संतुलन *[santulan]* M balance, equilibrium, equipoise
संतुलित *[santulit]* ADJ balanced, in equilibrium
संतोष *[santoṣ]* M satisfaction, gratification, contentment
संदर्भ *[sandarbh]* M context; reference, allusion
संदिग्ध *[sandigdh]* ADJ doubtful; uncertain; ambiguous
संदक़ *[sandūq]* M box
संदेश *[sandeś]* M message
संदेह *[sandeh]* M doubt, suspicion
संधि *[sandhi]* F treaty; junction, union
संध्या *[sandhyā]* F evening, twilight
संन्यास *[sannyās]* M renunciation, asceticism; the fourth life stage in Hindu tradition
संन्यासी *[sannyāsī]* M ascetic, renouncer
संपत्ति *[sampatti]* F property; estate; wealth; prosperity
संपन्न *[sampanna]* ADJ prosperous, rich, completed, accomplished

संपन्नता *[sampannatā]* F prosperity
संपर्क *[sampark]* M contact, liaison
संपादक *[sampādak]* M editor
संपादन *[sampādan]* M editing; accomplishment
संपूर्ण *[sampūrṇ]* ADJ whole, entire, perfect
संपूर्णता *[sampūrṇatā]* F entirety, completeness, perfection
सँपेरा *[sãperā]* M snake-charmer
संप्रदाय *[sampradāy]* M community, sect
संप्रेषण *[sampreṣaṇ]* M communication; despatch
संबंध *[sambandh]* M relation, association, connection, relationship
संबंधित *[sambandhit]* ADJ related; connected, affiliated
संबद्ध *[sambaddh]* ADJ joined, connected, attached to, bound; relevant
संबोधन *[sambodhan]* M address
संबोधित *[sambodhit]* ADJ addressed
सँभलना *[sãbhalnā]* V.I. to be alert, to be supported, to be cautious
संभव *[sambhav]* ADJ possible
संभालना *[sambhālnā]* V.T. to be steady; to maintain; to take care of
संभावना *[sambhāvnā]* F possibility, probability, likelihood
संभोग *[sambhog]* M sexual intercourse; delight, pleasure
संयम *[sanyam]* M restraint; moderation; sobriety
संयुक्त *[sanyukt]* ADJ united; joint; blended
संयोग *[sanyog]* M coincidence, chance, accident; mixture, combination, contact, union; conjunct
संरक्षा *[sanrakṣā]* F protection, safety
सँवरना *[sãvarnā]* V.I. to be mended, to be put in order; to be arranged
संवाद *[samvād]* M dialogue, conversation; news; information, message
संवाददाता *[samvāddātā]* M correspondent
संवारना *[samvārnā]* V.T. to mend, to arrange, to make up, to decorate

संविधान *[saṃvidhān]* M constitution
संवेदन *[saṃvedan]* M sensation, feeling; (the act or process of) experiencing
संवेदना *[saṃvednā]* F sensitivity, sensibility, feeling
संशय *[sanśay]* M suspicion, doubt, uncertainty
संशोधन *[sanśodhan]* M amendment, correction, revision
संसद *[sansad]* F/M parliament
संसार *[sansār]* M world
संस्कार *[sanskār]* M mental impression(s) (that constitute the mind); sacrament rite ceremony; purification, refinement
संस्कृत *[sanskṛt]* F, ADJ Sanskrit language; refined
संस्कृति *[sanskṛti]* F culture
संस्था *[sansthā]* F institution, organization
संस्थापक *[sansthāpak]* M founder
संस्थापन *[sansthāpan]* M founding, establishment
संस्थापित *[sansthāpit]* ADJ founded
संहार *[sanhār]* M annihilation, massacre
संहिता *[sanhitā]* F code
सकना *[saknā]* V.I. to be able to
सकपकाना *[sakpakānā]* V.I. be startled; be confounded, to be awed
सकल *[sakal]* ADJ whole, all, entire, total
सकारना *[sakārnā]* V.T. to accept
सकारात्मक *[sakārātmak]* ADJ positive, affirmative
सकुचना *[sakucnā]* V.I. to hesitate, to be abashed, to wither, to shrink
सक्रिय *[sakriya]* ADJ active
सक्रियता *[sakriyatā]* F the state of being active
सख़्त *[sa<u>kh</u>t]* ADJ hard; harsh; strong, stiff, rigorous
सख़्ती *[sa<u>kh</u>tī]* F hardness, harshness; stiffness, rigorousness
सगा *[sagā]* ADJ born of the same parents; kin; सगा-भाई *[sagā-bhāī]* M blood-brother
सगाई *[sagāī]* F betrothal, engagement
सच *[sac]* ADJ true
सचमुच *[sacmuc]* ADV really
सचाई *[sacāī]* F truth, truthfulness, reality

सचिव *[saciv]* M secretary
सचेत *[sacet]* ADJ conscious, careful; alert, attentive
सच्चा *[saccā]* ADJ true; truthful; genuine
सच्चाई *[saccāī]* F truth
सजग *[sajag]* ADJ alert; cautious; vigilant
सजना *[sajnā]* V.I to be adorned/decorated/beautified
सज़ा *[sazā]* F punishment
सजाना *[sajānā]* V.T. to adorn/decorate/beautify; to furnish; to arrange
सजावट *[sajāvaṭ]* F decoration, ornamentation, make-up
सजीव *[sajīv]* ADJ living, alive, vivacious
सज्जन *[sajjan]* ADJ, M noble, gentle; gentleman
सटकना *[saṭaknā]* V.I. to slip away
सटना *[saṭnā]* V.I. to be in close proximity, to stick, to adhere
सटाना *[saṭānā]* V.T. to bring together, to stick together
सट्टा *[saṭṭā]* M speculation; सट्टा बाज़ार *[saṭṭā bāzār]* M stock market
सठियाना *[saṭhiyānā]* V.I. senile decay, to be decrepit
सड़क *[saṛak]* F street
सड़ना *[saṛnā]* V.I. to decay, to decompose, to rot
सतर्क *[satark]* ADJ, ADV cautious, vigilant, alert
सतह *[sateh]* F surface, level
सतहत्तर *[sathattar]* ADJ seventy-seven
सतही *[satahī]* ADJ superficial
सताना *[satānā]* V.T. to harass, to torment, to torture, to trouble
सती *[satī]* ADJ, F chaste, virtuous; a virtuous loyal wife; a woman who burns herself on her husband's funeral pyre
सत्तर *[sattar]* ADJ seventy
सत्ता *[sattā]* F being, existence, power, sway, authority
सत्ताईस *[sattāīs]* ADJ twenty-seven
सत्तानवे *[sattanve]* ADJ ninety-seven
सत्तावन *[sattāvan]* ADJ fifty-seven
सत्तासी *[sattāsī]* ADJ eighty-seven
सत्त्व *[sattva]* M being, existence, entity, reality, quintessence; strength, vitality

सत्य *[satya]* ADJ, M true; veracity; truth, verity
सत्र *[satra]* M session, semester
सत्रह *[satrah]* ADJ seventeen
सत्रहवाँ *[satrahvā̃]* ADJ seventeenth
सदन *[sadan]* M house, house/ chamber of legislature
सदमा *[sadmā]* M shock, blow
सदर *[sadar]* ADJ, M head, main, chief; chairman, president
सदस्य *[sadasya]* M member
सदा *[sadā]* ADV always, ever
सदी *[sadī]* F century
सदृश *[sadṛś]* ADJ like, similar, resembling
सदृशता *[sadṛśatā]* F similarity, resemblance
सन् *[san]* M year (of the Christian calendar)
सनक *[sanak]* F whim, caprice, eccentricity; mania, frenzy
सनकना *[sanaknā]* V.I. to go crazy, to be in a frenzy
सनकी *[sankī]* ADJ eccentric, capricious, crazy
सनद *[sanad]* F certificate, testimonial; deed
सनना *[sannā]* V.I. to be kneaded; to be besmeared/ soiled/stained; to be drowned
सनसनाना *[sansanānā]* V.I. to produce a whizzing sound; to experience a thrilling sensation
सनसनाहट *[sansanāhaṭ]* F whizzing sound, thrilling sensation
सनसनी *[sansanī]* F thrilling sensation, excitement
सनसनीख़ेज़ *[sansanīkhez]* ADJ sensational
सनातन *[sanātan]* ADJ eternal, orthodox, time-honored
सनीचर *[sanīcar]* M Saturn; Saturday; ominous person
सन्न *[sanna]* ADJ, M stunned, dumbfounded, flabbergasted; hotheadedness, arrogance, hubris
सन्नाटा *[sannāṭā]* M silence, quiet
सपना *[sapnā]* M dream
सपाट *[sapāṭ]* ADJ flat, plain, smooth; unfeeling
सप्त *[sapt]* ADJ seven
सप्तक *[saptak]* M group of seven, heptad; octave
सप्ताह *[saptāh]* M seven days, a week
सप्लाई *[saplāī]* F supply
सफ़र *[safar]* M travel, journey

सफल *[saphal]* ADJ successful
सफलता *[saphaltā]* F success
सफ़ाई *[safāī]* F cleanliness, purity; defense (in a law suit); clarification
सफ़ाया *[safāyā]* M clean sweep; ruination, destruction
सफ़ेद *[safed]* ADJ white, clean, blank
सब *[sab]* ADJ all; सब कुछ *[sab kuch]* PRO everything; सब लोग *[sab log]* M all people
सबक़ *[sabaq]* M lesson; moral
सबल *[sabal]* ADJ strong, forceful, powerful; valid
सबलता *[sabaltā]* F strength, forcefulness
सबूत *[sabūt]* M proof, evidence
सब्ज़ *[sabz]* ADJ green
सब्ज़ी *[sabzī]* F vegetable
सब्र *[sabra]* M patience
सभा *[sabhā]* F assembly, meeting, association, society
सभी *[sabhī]* ADJ all (सब + ही)
सभ्य *[sabhya]* ADJ civilized
सभ्यता *[sabhyatā]* F civilization
समंदर *[samandar]* M ocean
सम *[sam]* ADJ even, equal, same
समकालीन *[samkālīn]* ADJ contemporary, contemporaneous
समग्र *[samagra]* ADJ total, whole, entire
समग्रता *[samagratā]* F totality
समझ *[samajh]* F understanding, comprehension; intellect
समझना *[samajhnā]* V.I., V.T. to regard; to consider; to understand; to explain
समझाना *[samjhānā]* V.T. to explain
समझौता *[samjhautā]* M compromise, agreement, settlement
समता *[samtā]* F equality, parity
समय *[samay]* M time
समयोन *[samyon]* ADJ lesbian
समर *[samar]* M war, battle; fruit
समराट् *[samrāṭ]* M emperor
समर्थ *[samarth]* ADJ capable, competent
समर्थन *[samarthan]* M support, corroboration, vindication
समर्पण *[samarpaṇ]* M dedication, surrender
समर्पित *[samarpit]* ADJ dedicated, surrendered

समलैंगिक *[samlaiṅgik]* ADJ, M homosexual, gay; homosexual man
समलैंगिकता *[samlaiṅgiktā]* F homosexuality
समस्त *[samast]* ADJ all, whole, complete, entire; compounded
समस्या *[samasyā]* F problem
समांतर *[samāntar]* ADJ parallel
समाचार *[samācār]* M news, information
समाज *[samāj]* M society
समाधान *[samādhān]* M solution (to a problem)
समाधि *[samādhi]* F trance, intense meditation; place of cremation or burial
समान *[samān]* ADJ equal, equivalent, alike, identical, tantamount
समानता *[samāntā]* F equality, equivalence, parity
समाना *[samānā]* V.I. to be contained (in), to fit; to enter; to permeate
समाप्त *[samāpt]* ADJ finished, ended
समाप्ति *[samāpti]* F end, conclusion, termination
समारोह *[samāroh]* M celebration, festivity, function
समालोचक *[samālocak]* M critic
समावेश *[samāveś]* M inclusion, entry, incorporation
समीकरण *[samīkaraṇ]* M equation
समीक्षा *[samīkṣā]* F review, criticism, commentary
समीप *[samīp]* ADJ near, proximate, at hand
समीपता *[samīptā]* F nearness, closeness
समीर *[samīr]* M air, breeze
समुंदर *[samundar]* M ocean
समुदाय *[samudāy]* M community; aggregate, collection
समुद्र *[samudra]* M ocean
समूचा *[samūcā]* ADJ all, whole, entire
समूह *[samūh]* M group, collection, aggregate, assemblage
समृद्ध *[samṛddh]* ADJ prosperous, flourishing, affluent
समृद्धि *[samṛddhi]* F prosperity, affluence, richness
समेटना *[sameṭnā]* V.T. to wrap up, to roll up, to wind; to gather, to collect, to rally

समोसा *[samosā]* M samosa, pastry filled with vegetables or meat

सम्मत *[sammat]* ADJ supported; approved, authenticated

सम्मति *[sammati]* F opinion, advice; consent

सम्मान *[sammān]* M respect, honor, prestige

सम्मानित *[sammānit]* ADJ honored, respected

सम्मिलित *[sammilit]* ADJ united, mixed; included

सम्मेलन *[sammelan]* M conference, meeting, assembly

सम्मोह *[sammoh]* M hypnosis, fascination, stupefaction

सम्मोहन *[sammohan]* ADJ, M hypnotizing, fascinating, stupefying; hypnosis

सम्मोहित *[sammohit]* ADJ hypnotized, fascinated, stupefied

सम्राट् *[samrāṭ]* M emperor

सम्हलना *[samhalnā]* V.I. to recover, to pick oneself up; to be supported

सयाना *[sayānā]* ADJ grown-up; clever, cunning

सर *[sar]* ADJ, M head; pond; pool; arrow

सरकना *[saraknā]* V.I. to slip, to slide, to creep

सरकाना *[sarkānā]* V.T. to move aside, to pass; to relegate, to postpone

सरकार *[sarkār]* F government

सरकारी *[sarkārī]* ADJ governmental, public, official

सरदर्द *[sardard]* M headache

सरदार *[sardār]* M leader, head, chief; honorific title used for Sikh men

सरदारनी *[sardārnī]* F leader's wife; wife of a Sikh; Sikh woman

सरदारी *[sardārī]* F leadership; rank or position of a सरदार

सरमाया *[sarmāyā]* M capital

सरमायादार *[sarmāyādār]* M capitalist

सरमायादारी *[sarmāyādārī]* F capitalism

सरल *[saral]* ADJ easy, simple, straightforward

सरलता *[saraltā]* F easiness, simplicity, straightforwardness

सरस *[saras]* ADJ juicy, sweet, delicious

सरसता *[sarastā]* F juiciness, freshness
सरसठ *[sarsaṭh]* ADJ sixty-seven
सरसरी *[sarasarī]* ADJ cursory, casual, perfunctory
सरसों *[sarsõ]* F mustard (seed and plant)
सरस्वती *[sarasvatī]* F Sarasvati, name of a deity, river
सरहद *[sarhad]* F boundary, frontier
सराहना *[sarāhnā]* V.T. to praise, to approve, to admire
सरोकार *[sarokār]* M concern, business
सरोद *[sarod]* F *sarod*, a stringed musical instrument
सरोवर *[sarovar]* M pond, pool
सर्द *[sard]* ADJ cold; cool; lifeless
सर्दी *[sardī]* F cold, cold winter
सर्व *[sarv]* ADJ whole, entire
सलवार क़मीज़ *[salvār qamīz]* F *shalwar kameez* (a loose-fitting trouser and shirt)
सलाद *[salād]* M salad
सलाम *[salām]* M salutation, greeting; goodbye
सलामत *[salāmat]* ADJ safe, sound, secure
सलामती *[salāmatī]* F safety, well-being, welfare
सलामी *[salāmī]* F salutation, salute; guard of honor
सलाह *[salāh]* F advice, counsel; reconciliation
सलूक *[salūk]* M treatment, behavior
सवा *[savā]* ADJ, INVAR one-and-a-quarter
सवार *[savār]* ADJ, M riding, mounted; rider
सवारी *[savārī]* F conveyance, vehicle, passenger; procession
सवाल *[savāl]* M question
सवेरा *[saverā]* M morning
ससुर *[sasur]* M father-in-law
ससुराल *[sasurāl]* F in-laws' house
सस्ता *[sastā]* ADJ cheap
सहकार *[sehkār]* M cooperation, collaboration; colleague, collaborator
सहकारी *[sehkārī]* ADJ cooperative, collaborative
सहज *[sehaj]* ADJ easy, simple, spontaneous
सहन *[sehan]* M patience, endurance, forbearance;

tolerance; courtyard
सहना *[sehnā]* V.T. to endure, to tolerate
सहपाठी *[sehpāṭhī]* M fellow student
सहम *[seham]* M fear
सहमत *[sehmat]* ADJ agreed, consented
सहमना *[sehamnā]* V.I. panicked, to be nervous
सहयोग *[sehyog]* M cooperation, collaboration
सहरा *[sehrā]* M desert
सहलाना *[sehlānā]* V.I. to rub gently, to tickle, to titillate, to caress
सहसा *[sehsā]* ADV suddenly, rashly, hastily
सहस्र *[sahasra]* ADJ thousand
सहाना *[sahānā]* V.T. to cause to bear/endure
सहायक *[sahāyak]* ADJ, M assistant, helper
सहायता *[sahāytā]* F help, support, assistance
सहारा *[sahārā]* M support, backing, aid
सहित *[sahit]* IND with, together with, accompanied by
सहिष्णु *[sahiṣṇu]* ADJ enduring, tolerant
सहिष्णुता *[sahiṣṇutā]* F tolerance, endurance
सही *[sahī]* ADJ correct, right, true
सहूलियत *[sahūliyat]* F convenience, facility
सहेली *[sahelī]* F female friend of a female
साँकरी *[sā̃krī]* F small chain
साँकल *[sā̃kal]* F chain
साँझ *[sā̃jh]* F evening, dusk
साँड़ *[sā̃ṛ]* M bull
सांत्वना *[sāntvanā]* F consolation, solace
साँप *[sā̃p]* M snake, serpent
सांप्रदायिक *[sāmpradāyik]* ADJ communal, sectarian
सांप्रदायिकता *[sāmpradāyiktā]* F communalism, sectarianism
साँवला *[sā̃vlā]* ADJ dark-complexioned
साँस *[sā̃s]* F breath/breathing
सा *[sā]* ADJ "ish," like, similar to, resembling (a suffix)
साइकिल *[sāikil]* F bicycle
साइत *[sāit]* F moment, hour, auspicious point in time
साकार *[sākār]* ADJ formal; concrete
साक्षर *[sākṣar]* ADJ literate
साक्षरता *[sākṣartā]* F literacy

साग *[sāg]* M vegetable, greens
सागर *[sāgar]* M ocean
साज़ *[sāz]* M musical instrument; implement; equipment; suffix denoting one who makes or mends something
साजन *[sājan]* M lover, husband
साज़िश *[sāziś]* F conspiracy, plot, intrigue
साझी *[sājhī]* M partner
साठ *[sāṭh]* ADJ sixty
साड़ी *[sāṛī]* F sari
साढ़े *[sāṛhe]* ADJ plus one half (from three and one half onwards)
सात *[sāt]* ADJ seven
सातवाँ *[sātvā̃]* ADJ seventh
साथ *[sāth]* ADV with, together, along with; साथ साथ *[sāth sāth]* ADV together
साथिन *[sāthin]* F female companion
साथी *[sāthī]* M companion, fellow
सादगी *[sādagī]* F simplicity, plainness
सादा *[sādā]* ADJ simple, plain, flat
साधन *[sādhan]* M medium; means; equipment, device; processing, solution; resources; realization
साधना *[sādhnā]* V.T., F to tame; to train; devotion, mental practice, spiritual endeavor
साधारण *[sādhāraṇ]* ADJ ordinary, simple, common
साधु *[sādhu]* M sadhu
साफ़ *[sāf]* ADJ clear, clean
साफ़ा *[sāfā]* M turban, a head covering by Sikh men
साबित *[sābit]* ADJ entire; complete; steady; proved
साबुत *[sābut]* ADJ entire, complete, unbroken
साबुन *[sābun]* M soap
सामंजस्य *[sāmañjasya]* M harmony, consistence, consistency
सामग्री *[sāmagrī]* F matter, material, stuff; data
सामना *[sāmnā]* M confrontation, encounter, meeting
सामने *[sāmne]* ADV in front
सामाजिक *[sāmajik]* ADJ, M social; member, viewer, reader
सामान *[sāmān]* M goods, luggage, stuff

सामान्य *[sāmānya]* ADJ general, common, normal
सामान्यता *[sāmānyatā]* F generality, normality, commonness
साम्राज्य *[sāmrājya]* M empire
साया *[sāyā]* M shade, shadow; influence; shelter; petticoat
सार *[sār]* M substance, gist, purport; iron
सारस *[sāras]* M heron, crane
सारा *[sārā]* ADJ entire
सार्थक *[sārthāk]* ADJ articulate; meaningful, significant; effective, useful
सार्थकता *[sārthaktā]* F articulation; significance; usefulness
सार्वजनिक *[sārvajanik]* ADJ universal, common, public
साल *[sāl]* M year
सालन *[sālan]* M curry (dish)
साला *[sālā]* M brother-in-law; term of abuse
सालाना *[sālānā]* ADJ yearly, annual
साली *[sālī]* F wife's sister, sister-in-law; term of abuse
सावधान *[sāvdhān]* ADJ vigilant, careful, alert, attentive
सावधानी *[sāvdhānī]* F precaution, carefulness, attention
सावन *[sāvan]* M the fifth month of the Hindu calendar
साहब *[sāhab]* M sir, sahib
साहबा *[sāhabā]* F lady, dame
साहस *[sāhas]* M courage, nerve, boldness
साहसी *[sāhsī]* ADJ courageous, enterprising, adventurous
साहित्य *[sāhitya]* M literature
साहिबा *[sāhibā]* F lady, dame
साहिल *[sāhil]* M shore, bank
साहू *[sāhū]* M banking, money-lending
साहूकार *[sāhūkār]* M money-lender, private banker; rich man
सिंकना *[sĩknā]* V.I. to be roasted, to be heated, to be fomented
सिंघ *[singh]* M lion
सिंचना *[sĩcnā]* V.I. to be watered, to be irrigated
सिंचाई *[sĩcāī]* F irrigation, wages paid for irrigation
सिंचाना *[sĩcānā]* V.T. to cause to be watered/irrigated
सिंचित *[sĩcit]* ADJ irrigated; drenched

सिंदूर *[sindūr]* M vermillion; symbol of a married woman's status
सिंध *[sindh]* M Sindh, a region in southern Pakistan
सिंधी *[sindhī]* ADJ, F pertaining to or from Sindh; the Sindhi language
सिंह *[sinh]* M lion; Leo
सिकड़ना *[sikaṛnā]*/सिकुड़ना *[sikuṛnā]* V.I. to shrink, to shrivel, to contract; to cower
सिकोड़ना *[sikoṛnā]* V.T. to contract, to cause to shrink, to draw together
सिक्का *[sikkā]* M coin; coinage; lead
सिक्ख *[sikkh]* M Sikh
सिखनी *[sikhnī]* F female Sikh
सिखाना *[sikhānā]* V.T. to teach
सिगरेट *[sigreṭ]* F cigarette
सितंबर *[sitambar]* M September
सितम *[sitam]* M tyranny; oppression
सितमगर *[sitamgar]* ADJ, M tyrannical; tyrant
सितार *[sitār]* M sitar (musical instrument)
सितारा *[sitārā]* M star; planet; fate; small sparkling metal or mica pieces worked onto fabric
सिद्ध *[siddh]* ADJ, M proved; accomplished; perfected; saint, one who has supernatural powers
सिद्धि *[siddhi]* F acquisition; proof; accomplishment
सिधारना *[sidhārnā]* V.T. to go, to depart, to expire; to pass away
सिनेमाहाल *[sinemāhāl]* M theater
सिपाही *[sipāhī]* M soldier; constable, policeman
सिफ़त *[sifat]* F characteristic, attribute; objective
सिफ़र *[sifar]* M cipher; zero; blank
सिफ़ारिश *[sifāriś]* F recommendation
सिफ़ारिशी *[sifāriśī]* ADJ recommendatory; सिफ़ारिशी ख़त *[sifāriśī khat]* M letter of recommendation
सिमटना *[simaṭnā]* V.I. to contract, to shrink; to be concentrated
सियार *[siyār]* M jackal; cunning person
सियासत *[siyāsat]* F politics

सियासी *[siyāsī]* ADJ political
सियाह *[siyāh]* ADJ black
सिर *[sir]* M head
सिरका *[sirkā]* M vinegar
सिरजना *[sirajnā]* V.T. to create, to give birth to, to make
सिरहाना *[sirhānā]* M bedhead; head of a bed, head of a tomb
सिरा *[sirā]* M extremity, end, edge
सिराज *[sirāj]* M lamp; candle; sun
सिर्फ़ *[sirf]* ADV only, just
सिलना *[silnā]* V.T., V.I. to sew, to stitch; to be sewn, to be stitched
सिलवाना *[silvānā]* V.T. to cause to be stitched, to have sewn
सिलसिला *[silsilā]* M chain, series, line
सिलाई *[silāī]* F sewing/stitching
सिलाना *[silānā]* V.T. to cause to be stitched, to have made
सिवा *[sivā]* IND except for, but
सिवैयाँ *[sivaiyā̃]* F vermicelli
सिसकना *[sisaknā]* V.I. to sob
सिसकारना *[siskārnā]* V.I. to hiss, to sob
सिसकी *[siskī]* F sobs, sobbing
सिहरन *[sihran]* F thrill, shiver
सिहरना *[siharnā]* V.I. to be thrilled; to shiver
सींग *[sī̃g]* M horn
सींच *[sī̃c]* F watering; irrigation
सींचना *[sī̃cnā]* V.T. to irrigate; to water
सीख *[sīkh]* F teaching, advice
सीखना *[sīkhnā]* V.T. to learn
सीटी *[sīṭī]* F whistle
सीढ़ी *[sīṛhī]* F ladder; stairs, staircase
सीतल *[sītal]* ADJ cool
सीताफल *[sītāphal]* M custard apple
सीधा *[sīdhā]* ADJ straight, simple; right, erect
सीना *[sīnā]* V.T., M to sew, to stitch; chest, breast
सीप *[sīp]* F oyster shell, mother-of-pearl
सीमा *[sīmā]* F border, limit, extent
सीमित *[sīmit]* ADJ restricted, limited, bound
सीलन *[sīlan]* F dampness, moisture
सीलना *[sīlnā]* V.I. to become damp
सुंदर *[sundar]* ADJ beautiful, handsome, pretty
सुंदरता *[sundartā]* F beauty

सु *[su]* PREFIX denoting "good, beautiful, pleasant, etc."
सुअवसर *[suavsar]* M opportunity, good chance
सुई *[suī]* F needle; hand of a watch
सुकुमार *[sukumār]* ADJ delicate, tender
सुकुमारता *[sukumārtā]* F delicacy, tenderness
सुकून *[sukūn]* M peace, comfort, consolation
सुख *[sukh]* M happiness, pleasure, comfort
सुखमय *[sukhmay]* ADJ full of happiness
सुखाना *[sukhānā]* V.T. to dry, to desiccate
सुखी *[sukhī]* ADJ happy, contented
सुगंध *[sugandh]* F scent, fragrance, perfume
सुगति *[sugati]* F salvation, beatitude
सुचारु *[sucāru]* ADJ lovely; delightful; satisfactory
सुझाना *[sujhānā]* V.T. to suggest, to propose, to indicate
सुझाव *[sujhāv]* M suggestion, proposal
सुडौल *[suḍaul]* ADJ shapely; well-built; having a good physique
सुत *[sut]* M son
सुथरा *[suthrā]* ADJ clean, neat and tidy; साफ़-सुथरा *[sāf-suthrā]* ADJ neat and clean
सुदर्शन *[sudarśan]* ADJ good-looking, winsome
सुध *[sudh]* F memory, consciousness, senses
सुधरना *[sudharnā]* V.I. to be reformed; be improved; to be amended
सुधा *[sudhā]* F nector
सुधार *[sudhār]* M reform; uplift; repair
सुधारना *[sudhārnā]* V.T. to reform; to repair; to improve
सुधि *[sudhi]* F *see* सुध
सुनना *[sunnā]* V.T. to hear, to listen
सुनवाही *[sunvāhī]* F hearing
सुनसान *[sunsān]* ADJ desolate, empty
सुनहरा *[sunharā]* ADJ golden
सुनाना *[sunānā]* V.T. to tell, to relate (a story, news, etc.)
सुनार *[sunār]* M goldsmith
सुन्दर *[sundar]* ADJ beautiful
सुन्न *[sunna]* ADJ still(ed); insensitive; benumbed;

stupefied
सुन्नत *[sunnat]* F circumcision
सुन्नी *[sunnī]* M Sunni, one of the two major sects of Islam (the other being शिया)
सुपारी *[supārī]* F betel-nut
सुपुर्द *[supurd]* ADJ entrusted; committed; charged with
सुप्रभात *[suprabhāt]* M good morning
सुबह *[subah]* F morning, dawn
सुबोध *[subodh]* ADJ intelligible, easy
सुभानअल्ला *[subhānallā]* INT Thou art great! What a wonder! How wonderful!
सुयोग *[suyog]* M a happy chance; a happy coincidence
सुरंग *[suraṅg]* F tunnel; mine
सुर *[sur]* M tone; note in music; vowel; god
सुरक्षा *[surakṣā]* F protection, security
सुरभि *[surabhi]* F fragrance, aroma, perfume, scent
सुरमा *[surmā]* M collyrium
सुराग़ *[surāgh]* M clue, trace
सुरीला *[surīlā]* ADJ sweet, melodious
सुरीलापन *[surīlāpan]* M sweetness; melodiousness
सुरूर *[surūr]* M mild intoxication; the pleasant after-effects of intoxication
सुर्ख़ *[surkh]* ADJ red, ruddy
सुर्ख़ी *[surkhī]* F redness, ruddiness; headline (in a newspaper); lipstick
सुलगना *[sulagnā]* V.I. to smoulder, to burn, be ignited, to kindle
सुलगाना *[sulgānā]* V.T. to ignite; to cause to burn
सुलझना *[sulajhnā]* V.I. to be disentangled; to become unravelled; be solved
सुलझाना *[suljhānā]* V.T. to untangle, to unravel, to solve
सुलझाव *[suljhāv]* M solution, disentanglement
सुलतान *[sultān]* M Sultan
सुलाना *[sulānā]* V.T. to cause to sleep; to lull to sleep
सुलूक *[sulūk]* M treatment; behavior
सुविधा *[suvidhā]* F facility, convenience
सुविधाजनक *[suvidhājanak]* ADJ convenient
सुव्यवस्था *[suvyavasthā]* F order, good arrangement; a good system

सुशील *[suśīl]* ADJ courteous; suave; modest
सुशीलता *[suśīltā]* F modesty; courteousness
सुस्त *[sust]* ADJ slow, languid; indolent; lazy, idle; depressed
सुस्ताना *[sustānā]* V.I. to relax, to rest; to have a rest
सुस्ती *[sustī]* F languor; indolence; laziness, idleness; depression
सुहबत *[suhbat]* F company, association; cohabitation
सुहाग *[suhāg]* M the happy state of a woman whose husband is alive; good fortune
सुहाना *[suhānā]* ADJ pleasing; charming; likable
सुहावना *[suhāvnā]* ADJ charming; pleasing; likable
सूँघना *[sū̃ghnā]* V.T. to smell, to scent, to sniff
सूँड़ *[sū̃ṛ]* F trunk of an elephant
सूँस *[sū̃s]* F porpoise
सूअर *[sūar]* M boar, pig, swine
सूई *[sūī]* F needle; hand of a watch/clock
सूक्ष्म *[sūkṣma]* ADJ subtle; fine, minute
सूक्ष्मता *[sūkṣmatā]* F subtly; finesse; precision
सूखना *[sūkhnā]* V.I. to dry up; to wither; to dwindle
सूखा *[sukhā]* ADJ dry; lifeless; blunt
सूचना *[sūcnā]* F information, notice, notification
सूचित *[sūcit]* ADJ informed; intimated
सूची *[sūcī]* F list, catalog
सूजन *[sūjan]* F swelling, inflammation
सूजना *[sūjnā]* V.I. to swell
सूझ *[sūjh]* F insight, vision, perception
सूझना *[sūjhnā]* V.I. to occur (to one); to appear (to)
सूती *[sūtī]* ADJ made of cotton
सूत्र *[sūtra]* M thread, yarn, fiber; source; aphorism
सूद *[sūd]* M interest (money)
सूना *[sūnā]* ADJ desolate, empty
सूनापन *[sūnāpan]* M desolation; emptiness
सूफ़ी *[sūfī]* M Sufi, a sect of Muslim saints
सूर *[sūr]* ADJ brave; blind
सूर *[sūr]* M sun
सूरज *[sūraj]* M sun; सूरज निकलना *[sūraj nikalnā]* V.I.

the sun to rise; सूरज ढलना *[sūraj ḍhalnā]* V.I. the sun to set

सूरत *[sūrat]* F countenance, face, appearance, looks; form; condition

सूरते हाल *[sūrate hāl]* F present condition

सूरमा *[sūrmā]* ADJ, M brave, hero

सूराख़ *[sūrā<u>kh</u>]* M hole; aperture

सूर्य *[sūrya]* M sun

सूर्यास्त *[sūryāst]* M sunset

सूर्योदय *[sūryoday]* M sunrise

सूली *[sūlī]* M gallows

सृजन *[sṛjan]* M creation

सृष्टि *[sṛṣṭi]* F creation; world

सेंकना *[sẽkna]* V.T. to foment; to bake; to roast

से *[se]* PP from, since, by, with; (x) से लेकर (y) तक *[(x) se lekar (y) tak]* from (x) until (y); (x) से पहले *[(x) se pahle]* PP before (x)

सेकंड *[sekaṇd]* M second

सेज *[sej]* F bed

सेठ *[seṭh]* M wealthy merchant; wealthy person

सेतु *[setu]* M bridge, causeway

सेना *[senā]* F army

सेनापति *[senāpati]* M commander of the army

सेब *[seb]* M apple

सेर *[ser]* M a seer; a weight equivalent to just over two pounds

सेवक *[sevak]* M servant, attendant

सेवन *[sevan]* M taking, consuming (as in medicine); using

सेवा *[sevā]* F service; attendance

सेशन *[seśan]* M session

सेहत *[sehat]* F health

सेहतमंद *[sehatmand]* ADJ healthy

सैंतालीस *[saĩtālīs]* ADJ forty-seven

सैंतीस *[saĩtīs]* ADJ thirty-seven

सैकड़ा *[saikṛā]* ADJ hundred

सैकड़ों *[saikṛõ]* ADJ hundreds

सैनिक *[sainik]* M soldier ADJ military; pertaining to the military

सैयद *[saiyad]* M Sayyad, a particular subdivision of the Muslim religion

सैर *[sair]* F walking, wandering, excursion

सैलानी *[sailānī]* M tourist; wanderer; holiday-maker

सैलाब *[sailāb]* M flood
सोखना *[sokhnā]* V.T. to absorb
सोच *[soc]* F anxiety, brooding, musing; consideration
सोचना *[socnā]* V.T. to think
सोना *[sonā]* V.I., M to sleep; gold
सोफ़ा *[sofā]* M sofa
सोम *[som]* M moon; Monday
सोमवार *[somvār]* M Monday
सोलह *[solah]* ADJ sixteen
सोलहवाँ *[solahvā̃]* ADJ sixteenth
सोहबत *[sohbat]* F company, association
सौंदर्य *[saũdarya]* M beauty
सौंपना *[saũpnā]* V.T. to hand over, to entrust, to surrender
सौंफ़ *[saũf]* F anise, aniseed, fennel
सौ *[sau]* ADJ one hundred
सौगंध *[saugandh]* F oath, swearing
सौजन्य *[saujanya]* M goodness; courtesy
सौत *[saut]* F a co-wife
सौतेला *[sautelā]* ADJ pertaining or related with, or born of a co-wife; half-blood
सौदा *[saudā]* M bargain, transaction, negotiation; goods
सौदागर *[saudāgar]* M trader
सौभाग्य *[saubhāgya]* M good luck, good fortune
सौरभ *[saurabh]* M fragrance, aroma
स्कूल *[skūl]* M school
स्टेशन *[sṭeśan]* M station
स्टोर *[sṭor]* M store
स्टोव *[sṭov]* M stove
स्तन *[stan]* M breast; udder; स्तन चचुक *[stan cacuk]* M nipple
स्तब्ध *[stabdh]* ADJ stupefied; stilled; stunned
स्तर *[star]* M standard , level; layer; fold; stratum
स्त्री *[strī]* F woman
स्थगित *[sthagit]* ADJ postponed, adjourned
स्थल *[sthal]* M land, place, site; location
स्थान *[sthān]* M place, position
स्थानीय *[sthānīya]* ADJ local; colloquial
स्थापक *[sthāpak]* M founder
स्थापन *[sthāpan]* M foundation, erection, establishment
स्थापना *[sthāpnā]* F founding, establishing; installing
स्थापित *[sthāpit]* ADJ established, installed; founded

स्थायी *[sthāyī]* ADJ permanent; stable; lasting, durable; regular
स्थित *[sthit]* ADJ situated, located
स्थिति *[sthiti]* F situation, state
स्थिर *[sthir]* ADJ stable, firm, steady
स्नान *[snān]* M bath, bathing, ablution
स्नेह *[sneh]* M affection; oil, oily substance
स्पर्धा *[spardhā]* F rivalry; envy
स्पर्श *[spārś]* M touch, contact; feel
स्पष्ट *[spaṣṭ]* ADJ clear, vivid, lucid, evident, apparent; obvious
स्फीति *[sphīti]* F inflation; swelling; मुद्रा स्फीति *[mudrā sphīti]* F (monetary) inflation
स्फूर्ति *[sphūrti]* F agility, smartness
स्फोट *[sphoṭ]* M explosion, burst
स्मरण *[smaraṇ]* M memory, remembrance, recollection
स्मारक *[smārak]* M monument, memorial
स्मृति *[smṛti]* F memory; remembrance; the traditional books of Hindu laws
स्यार *[syār]* M jackal
स्याह *[syāh]* ADJ black, dark
स्याही *[syāhī]* F ink; darkness, blackness
स्रोत *[srot]* M source; resource
स्व *[sva]* PRO one's own, personal
स्वतंत्र *[svatantra]* ADJ independent
स्वतंत्रता *[svatantratā]* F independence
स्वदेश *[svadeś]* M motherland
स्वदेशी *[svadeśī]* ADJ native; indigenous
स्वप्न *[svapna]* M dream
स्वभाव *[svabhāv]* M nature, temperament, disposition
स्वयं *[svayaṃ]* ADV oneself
स्वर *[svar]* M vowel, sound, voice; tone
स्वरूप *[svarūp]* M shape, form; appearance; character; nature
स्वर्ग *[svarg]* M heaven, paradise
स्वर्गीय *[svargīya]* ADJ deceased; late; dead
स्वर्ण *[svarṇ]* M gold; स्वर्ण मंदिर *[svarṇ mandir]* M golden temple (Amritsar)

स्वस्तिक *[svastik]* **M** swastika, a benedictory or auspicious mark for Hindus
स्वस्थ *[svasth]* **ADJ** healthy, robust
स्वाँग *[svā̃g]* **M** mimicry; farce
स्वागत *[svāgat]* **M** welcome, reception
स्वागतम् *[svāgatam]* **PHR** Welcome!
स्वाद *[svād]* **M** taste, flavor
स्वाधीन *[svādhīn]* **ADJ** free, independent
स्वाभाविक *[svābhāvik]* **ADJ** natural, innate, inherent, inborn
स्वामी *[svāmī]* **M** master, lord; proprietor, owner
स्वार्थ *[svārth]* **M** selfishness, self-interest
स्वार्थी *[svārthī]* **ADJ** selfish
स्वास्थ्य *[svāsthya]* **M** health
स्वीकार *[svīkār]* **ADJ** accepted **M** acceptance
स्वीकृत *[svīkṛt]* **ADJ** accepted, approved
स्वीकृति *[svīkṛti]* **F** acceptance
स्वेच्छा *[svecchā]* **F** own's own will, free will
स्वेद *[sved]* **M** sweat, perspiration

ह

हंगामा *[haṅgāmā]* **M** uproar, tumult, upheaval
हंडा *[haṇḍā]* **M** large brass pot; cauldron; big gas lantern
हंस *[hans]* **M** swan, goose; noble/liberated soul; sun
हँसना *[hā̃snā]* **V.I.** to laugh
हँसमुख *[hā̃smukh]* **ADJ** cheerful, jovial, having a smiling face
हँसाना *[hā̃sānā]* **V.T.** to cause to laugh, amuse
हँसिया *[hā̃siyā]* **M** sickle
हँसी *[hā̃sī]* **F** laughter, joke, derision, ridicule
हक़ *[haq]* **M** right, entitlement, due, return; truth, reality
हकलाना *[haklānā]* **V.T.** to stammer
हक़ारत *[haqārat]* **F** contempt
हक़ीक़त *[haqīqat]* **F** reality, fact, truth
हगना *[hagnā]* **V.T.** to discharge feces
हज *[haj]* **M** Hajj; the pilgrimage to Mecca
हज़म *[hazam]* **ADJ** digested; usurped
हज़रत *[hazrat]* **ADJ, M** mis-

chievous, cunning; vocative term of honor, title for eminent men; the Prophet Muhammad
हजामत *[hajāmat]* F shaving, hair-cutting
हज़ार *[hazār]* ADJ thousand
हज़ारों *[hazārõ]* ADJ thousands
हजूम *[hajūm]* M crowd, multitude
हटना *[haṭnā]* V.I. to move, to go away, to recede, to withdraw
हट्टा-कट्टा *[haṭṭā-kaṭṭā]* ADJ strong and sturdy, well-built
हठ *[haṭh]* M obstinacy, stubbornness
हठी *[haṭhī]* ADJ obstinate, stubborn
हड़ताल *[haṛtāl]* F strike
हड़पना *[haṛapnā]* V.T. to swallow; to gulp down; to purloin; to usurp
हड़बड़ाना *[haṛbaṛānā]* V.I. be impetuous, to act hastily; be confused
हड़बड़ी *[haṛbaṛī]* F impetuousness, hastiness, rashness
हड्डी *[haḍḍī]* F bone
हत *[hat]* ADJ killed, struck
हतक *[hatak]* F insult, defamation
हताश *[hatāś]* ADJ despondent, hopeless
हत्या *[hatyā]* F murder, assassination
हत्यारा *[hatyārā]* M murderer, assassin
हथकड़ी *[hathkaṛī]* F handcuffs
हथियाना *[hathiyānā]* V.T. to usurp, to grab, to seize, to acquire by force
हथियार *[hathiyār]* M weapon, arms
हथेली *[hathelī]* F palm of the hand
हथौड़ा *[hathauṛā]* M hammer, mallet
हद *[had]* F limit, limitation, boundary, extent
हफ़्ता *[haftā]* M week/ Saturday
हम *[ham]* PRO we
हमने *[hamne]* PRO we (हम + ने)
हमल *[hamal]* M conception, pregnancy
हमला *[hamlā]* M attack, assault
हमारा *[hamāra]* ADJ our

हमीं *[hamī̃]* PRO we (emphatic), only we (हम + ही)
हमें/हमको *[hamẽ/hamko]* PRO oblique form of हम + को
हमेशा *[hameśā]* ADV always; हमेशा से *[hameśā se]* ADV always
हया *[hayā]* F shame; sense of shame; modesty
हयात *[hayāt]* F life
हर *[har]* ADJ all, every
हरकत *[harkat]* F movement, activity, mischief
हरगिज़ *[hargiz]* IND ever, under any circumstances
हरज *[haraj]* M harm, loss, damage
हरण *[haraṇ]* M kidnapping, abduction, seizing; as a suffix imparts the meaning of "the one or that which carries away, seizes, kidnaps, etc."
हरना *[harnā]* V.T. to kidnap, to abduct, to carry away by force, to seize
हरम *[haram]* M harem, women's apartment
हरा *[harā]* ADJ green; verdant; fresh; delighted, jovial
हराना *[harānā]* V.T. to defeat, to vanquish
हराम *[harām]* ADJ unlawful, forbidden, improper
हरामी *[harāmī]* ADJ, M illegitimate; unscrupulous; utterly indolent; bastard, rascal, scoundrel
हरि *[hari]* M Vishnu/Krishna
हरिजन *[harijan]* M untouchable
हरियाली *[hariyālī]* F greenery, vegetation
हरे *[hare]* INT O God!
हरेक *[harek]* ADJ each
हर्ज *[harj]* M harm, loss, damage
हर्फ़ *[harf]* M letter (of the alphabet)
हर्ष *[harṣ]* M joy, jubilation, mirth, delight, happiness
हर्षित *[harṣit]* ADJ joyous, delighted, cheerful
हल *[hal]* M plow; solution (to a problem)
हलक़ *[halaq]* M throat, windpipe
हलका *[halkā]* ADJ, M light, thin; faint; cheap; circle, area
हलचल *[halcal]* F commotion, hustle, agitation, movement
हल्दी *[haldī]* F tumeric (spice)

हलवा *[halvā]* M pudding-like Indian sweetmeat
हलवाई *[halvāī]* M sweetmeat manufacturer or seller, confectioner
हलाक *[halāk]* ADJ slaughtered, slain
हलाल *[halāl]* ADJ, M legitimate; hard-earned, well-begotten; animal slaughtered according to Islamic religious prescription
हल्का *[halkā]* ADJ light (not heavy); weak
हल्दी *[haldī]* F turmeric
हवा *[havā]* F wind, air
हवाई अड्डा *[havāī aḍḍā]* M airport
हवाई जहाज़ *[havāī jahāz]* M airplane
हवाला *[havālā]* M reference; trust, custody
हवालात *[havālāt]* F lock-up, police custody
हवेली *[havelī]* F mansion
हशीश *[haśīś]* F hashish, drug made from hemp (*Cannabis sativa*)
हसरत *[hasrat]* F wistfulness, longing, craving, (unfulfilled) desire
हसीन *[hasīn]* ADJ beautiful, pretty, charming
हस्त *[hast]* M hand; trunk of an elephant
हस्तक्षेप *[hastakṣép]* M interference
हस्ताक्षर *[hastākṣar]* M signature, handwriting
हस्ती *[hastī]* F, M existence, being, worth, personage; elephant
हाँ *[hā̃]* ADJ yes
हाँकना *[hā̃knā]* V.T. to drive (an animal or animal-driven vehicle)
हाँड़ी *[hā̃ṛī]* F small earthen pot
हाँफना *[hā̃phnā]* V.T. to pant, to breathe heavily
हाकिम *[hākim]* M ruler, boss
हाज़िर *[hāzir]* ADJ present; ready
हाट *[hāṭ]* F temporary and periodic market, improvised market-place
हाथ *[hāth]* M hand, arm
हाथापाई *[hāthāpāī]* F scuffle, skirmish, tussle
हाथी *[hāthī]* M elephant
हानि *[hāni]* F loss, damage, detriment, harm
हाफ़िज़ *[hāfiz]* M protector;

one who has memorized the Quran

हामी *[hāmī]* F, M assent; acceptance; supporter, champion

हाय *[hāy]* M hi! (a greeting)

हार *[hār]* F defeat, loss; garland; necklace; suffix denoting a doer or the one or that which carries away by force or usurps

हारना *[hārnā]* V.I. to be defeated, to lose; to be wearied

हार्दिक *[hārdik]* ADJ cordial, hearty

हाल *[hāl]* M condition, state

हालचाल *[hālcāl]* M state and condition

हालत *[hālat]* F state, condition

हालाँकि *[hālā̃ki]* IND though, although

हावी *[hāvī]* ADJ dominant

हाशिया *[hāśiyā]* M margin, border, fringe

हासिल *[hāsil]* ADJ acquired, obtained

हास्यास्पद *[hāsyāspad]* ADJ ludicrous, ridiculous, funny

हिंद *[hind]* M India

हिंदवी *[hindavī]* F medieval name for early forms of the Hindi language

हिंदी/हिन्दी *[hindī]* F Hindi language

हिन्दुत्व *[hindutva]* M Hinduism; the state of being a Hindu; the ideology of Hindu nationalism

हिंदुस्तान/हिन्दुस्तान *[hindustān]* M India

हिंदुस्तानी/हिन्दुस्तानी *[hindustānī]* ADJ Indian

हिंदू *[hindū]* ADJ, M Hindu

हिंसक *[hinsak]* ADJ, M violent, ferocious, fierce; murderer, killer

हिंसा *[hinsā]* F violence

हिक़ारत *[hiqārat]* F contempt

हिचक *[hicak]* F hitch; hesitation

हिचकना *[hicaknā]* V.I. to hesitate

हिचकिचाना *[hickicānā]* V.I. to hesitate

हिचकी *[hickī]* F hiccup

हिजड़ा *[hijṛā]* ADJ, M impotent; eunuch, male-to-female transgender person

हिजरी *[hijrī]* F Islamic era or calendar

हित *[hit]* M welfare, well-

being; interest, gain, benefit
हिदायत *[hidāyat]* F instruction
हिनहिनाना *[hinhinānā]* V.T. to neigh
हिफ़ाज़त *[hifāzat]* F protection, security, safety
हिम *[him]* M snow, ice, frost
हिमालय *[himālaya]* M Himalayas
हिम्मत *[himmat]* F courage; हिम्मत जुटाना *[himmat juṭānā]* V.T. to summon courage
हिरण *[hiraṇ]* M deer, antelope
हिरन *[hiran]* M deer, antelope
हिरासत *[hirāsat]* F custody
हिलना *[hilnā]* V.I. to move, to shake, to swing; to get very familiar
हिलाना *[hilānā]* V.T. to shake; to wave
हिलोर *[hilor]* F surge; billow
हिसाब *[hisāb]* M account, calculation; rate; manner; custom
हिस्सा *[hissā]* M part, portion
हिस्सेदार *[hissedār]* M sharer
हींग *[hĩg]* F asafetida
ही *[hī]* INVAR only, just; emphatic particle
हीरा *[hīrā]* M diamond
हुकूमत *[hukūmat]* F government, rule, jurisdiction
हुक़्क़ा *[huqqā]* M *hookah*, hubble-bubble, water pipe
हुक्म *[hukm]* M order, command; spade (in a deck of cards)
हुजूम *[hujūm]* M crowd, multitude
हुज़ूर *[huzūr]* INT, M Your Honor, Your Majesty; Sir; gracious presence
हुनर *[hunar]* F art craft, skill
हुसन *[husan]* M beauty, prettiness
हूँ *[hū̃]* V.I. am (verb to be)
हूबहू *[hūbahū]* ADJ exactly alike, similar in all respects
हूर *[hūr]* F fairy, a very beautiful woman
हृदय *[hṛday]* M heart
हृष्ट *[hṛṣṭ]* ADJ glad, delighted, pleased
हे *[he]* VOC Hey!
हेकड़ी *[hekṛī]* F hubris, arrogance, stubbornness; exercise of coercion, show of force
हेतु *[hetu]* M reason, cause, motive
हेमंत *[hemant]* M winter

हेराफेरी *[herāpherī]* F manipulation, unscrupulous activity
हैं *[haĩ]* V.I. is/are (plural)
है *[hai]* V.I. is/are (singular)
हैज़ा *[haizā]* M cholera
हैरत *[hairat]* F amazement, astonishment
हैरान *[hairān]* ADJ tired, wearied, perplexed, confounded, amazed, astonished
हैरानी *[hairānī]* F surprise, amazement; trouble; weariness; harassment
हैसियत *[haisiyat]* F status; capacity
हों *[hõ]* V.I. may be (plural)
होंठ *[hõṭh]* M lip
हो *[ho]* V.I. are (plural) may be (singular/plural)
होटल *[hoṭal]* M hotel
होड़ *[hoṛ]* F competition, race; bet
होनहार *[honhār]* ADJ, M promising; the inevitable, destiny
होना *[honā]* V.I. to be, to become, to occur, to happen, to take place, to exist
होलिका *[holikā]* F festival of Holi
होली *[holī]* F Holi (the Indian festival of colors); होली खेलना *[holī khelnā]* V.T. to play (celebrate) Holi
होश *[hoś]* M sense, consciousness
होशियार *[hośiyār]* ADJ clever, sharp, intelligent, shrewd
हौज़ *[hauz]* M tank; reservoir; sink
हौले-हौले *[haule-haule]* ADV slowly, gently, quietly
हौसला *[hauslā]* M courage; morale
ह्रास *[hrās]* M decay, fall, downfall
ह्विस्की *[hviskī]* F whisky

English–Hindi

A

a ADJ एक *[ek]*
abandon; omit V.T. छोड़ना *[chorṇā]*
abduct; kidnap V.T. अपहरण करना *[apaharaṇ karnā]*
abduction M अपहरण *[apaharaṇ]*
ability F योग्यता *[yogyatā]*
able ADJ क़ाबिल *[qābil]*
abode M निवास *[nivās]*
abominable ADJ घिनौना *[ghinaunā]*
aboriginal; first settler ADJ आदिवासी *[ādivāsī]*
abortion M गर्भपात *[garbhpāt]*
about (x) PP (x) के बारे में *[(x) ke bāre mẽ]*
above (x) PP (x) के ऊपर *[(x) ke ūpar]*
above; on; upon ADV ऊपर *[ūpar]*
abridgment M संक्षेप *[saṅkṣep]*
abroad (foreign land) M परदेश *[pardeś]*
absconding; outlaw ADJ, M फ़रार *[farār]*
absence, want, dearth, deficiency M अभाव *[abhāv]*
absent ADJ अनुपस्थित *[anupasthit]*
absolute (complete, entire) ADJ संपूर्ण *[sampūrṇ]*
absolutely (completely) ADV एकदम *[ekdam]*; बिल्कुल *[bilkul]*
absorb V.T. सोखना *[sokhnā]*
absorbed ADJ मग्न *[magna]*
abstinence M परहेज़ *[parhez]*
absurd ADJ अटपटा *[aṭpaṭā]*
abuse F गाली *[gālī]*
abuse V.T. गाली देना *[gālī denā]*
academic (intellectual) ADJ, M बुद्धिजीवी *[buddhijīvī]*
accelerate V.T. गति बढ़ाना *[gati baṛhānā]*
accent M उच्चारण *[uccāraṇ]*
accept V.T. मानना *[mānnā]*
accept V.T. स्वीकार करना *[svīkār karnā]*

access (entry) M प्रवेश *[praveś]*
accident F दुर्घटना *[durghaṭnā]*
accompany (x) V.T. (x) का साथ देना *[(x) kā sāth denā]*
accomplish (complete) V.T. पूरा करना *[pūrā karnā]*
accomplishment F उपलब्धि *[uplabdhi]*
according to x PP के अनुसार *[ke anusār]*
account M खाता *[khātā]*; हिसाब *[hisāb]*
account, deposition M बयान *[bayān]*
accountability (responsibility) F ज़िम्मेदारी *[zimmedārī]*
accumulate, gather V.T. बटोरना *[baṭornā]*
accurate ADJ ठीक *[ṭhīk]*
accusation (allegation) M आरोप *[ārop]*
accuse V.T. आरोप लगाना *[ārop lagānā]*
accustomed ADJ आदी *[ādī]*
ache F पीड़ा *[pīṛā]*
achieve (obtain) V.T. प्राप्त करना *[prāpt karnā]*
achievement F प्राप्ति *[prāpti]*
acid M तेज़ाब *[tezāb]*
acquaintance F जान-पहचान *[jān-pehcān]*
acquaintance, familiarity M परिचय *[paricaya]* F पहचान *[pehcān]*
acquit V.T. बरी करना *[barī karnā]*
across, on the other side ADJ, ADV, M पार *[pār]*
acting; performing (on stage or in films) M अभिनय *[abhinay]*
action F क्रिया *[kriyā]*
active ADJ सक्रिय *[sakriya]*
activity F हरकत *[harkat]*
actor M अभिनेता *[abhinetā]*
actress F अभिनेत्री *[abhinetrī]*
actual, factual; genuine ADJ वास्तविक *[vāstavik]*
adapt (change) V.I. बदलना *[badalnā]*
add V.T. जोड़ना *[joṛnā]*
addiction, bad habit F लत *[lat]*
addition M जोड़ *[joṛ]*: addition to (x) PP (x) के अलावा *[(x) ke alāvā]*
additional (extra) ADJ अतिरिक्त *[atirikt]*
address M पता *[patā]*
adequate (enough) ADJ काफ़ी *[kāfī]*

adjective; attribute M विशेषण *[viśeṣaṇ]*
adjust (to correct) V.T. ठीक करना *[ṭhīk karnā]*
administration; rule M शासन *[śāsan]*
admission; packing or filling a void F भरती *[bhartī]*
adolescent ADJ किशोर *[kiśor]*
adopt (a child) V.T. गोद लेना *[god lenā]*
adoption (acceptance) F स्वीकृति *[svīkṛti]*
adorn/decorate/beautify V.T. सजाना *[sajānā]*
adult ADJ वयस्क *[vayask]*
adulteration F मिलावट *[milāvaṭ]*
advance, advance payment F पेशगी *[peśagī]*
advantage M फ़ायदा *[fāydā]*; लाभ *[lābh]*
adversary ADJ, M विरोधी *[virodhī]*
adverse ADJ प्रतिकूल *[pratikūl]*
advertisement; announcement; poster M विज्ञापन *[vijñāpan]*
advice F सलाह *[salāh]*
advise V.T. सलाह देना *[salāh denā]*
advisor M सलाहकार *[salāhkār]*
aesthetic relish, sentiment, pleasure M रस *[ras]*
affable ADJ मिलनसार *[milansār]*
affair M विषय *[viṣay]*: an affair to go on V.I. चक्कर चलना *[cakkar calnā]*; an affair to happen V.I. चक्कर होना *[cakkar honā]*
affection M स्नेह *[sneh]*; लगाव *[lagāv]* F मुहब्बत *[muhabbat]*
affirmative ADJ सकारात्मक *[sakārātmak]*
afraid ADJ भयभीत *[bhaybhīt]*
afraid (of x) V.I. (x से) डरना *[(x se) ḍarnā]*
afresh ADV नये सिरे से *[naye sire se]*
after (x) PP (x) के बाद *[(x) ke bād]*
afternoon F दोपहर *[dopahar]*
afterwards; thereafter; in the future; a second time CONJ फिर *[phir]*
again CONJ फिर *[phir]*
against ADJ ख़िलाफ़ *[khilāf]*: **against (x)** PP (x) के ख़िलाफ़ *[(x) ke khilāf]*
age M ज़माना *[zamānā]*

age; lifetime F उम्र *[umra]*
aged ADJ वृद्ध *[vṛddh]*
aged, senile ADJ बुड्ढा *[buḍḍhā]*
agent M दलाल *[dalāl]*
aggression (attack) M आक्रमण *[ākramaṇ]*
aggressive ADJ आक्रमक *[ākramak]*
agitation M क्षोभ *[kṣobh]* F ख़लबली *[khalbalī]*
ago, before ADV पहले *[pehle]*
agree (with x) V.I. (x से) सहमत होना *[(x se) sehmat honā]*
agree, consent; confess V.T. क़बूल करना *[qabūl karnā]*
agreement, settlement M समझौता *[samjhautā]*
agriculture F कृषि *[kṛṣi]*
ah F आह *[āh]*
ahead, in ADV आगे *[āge]*
aid; support F मदद *[madad]*
aide (assistant) ADJ, M सहायक *[sahāyak]*
ailment M रोग *[rog]*
aim M मक़सद *[maqsad]*; लक्ष्य *[lakṣya]*
aim V.T. निशाना बाँधना *[niśānā bā̃dhnā]*
air F हवा *[havā]*
air force F वायु सेना *[vāyu senā]*
airplane M हवाई जहाज़ *[havāī jahāz]*
airport M हवाई अड्डा *[havāī aḍḍā]*
alarm (warning) F चेतावनी *[cetāvanī]*
alcohol F शराब *[śarāb]*
alcoholic ADJ शराबी *[śarābī]*
alert, attentive ADJ सावधान *[sāvdhān]*
alien; exotic; foreigner ADJ विदेशी *[videśī]*
alight V.I. उतरना *[utarnā]*
alike ADJ समान *[samān]*
alive, living ADJ जीवित *[jīvit]*
alive ADJ, INVAR ज़िंदा *[zindā]*
all ADJ सब *[sab]*; हर *[har]*
all manner of ADJ तरह-तरह का *[tarah-tarah kā]*
Allah, God M अल्लाह *[allāh]*
allegation M आरोप *[ārop]*
alley F गली *[galī]*
allocate, apportion V.T. बाँटना *[bā̃ṭnā]*
allow (permit) V.T. अनुमति देना *[anumati denā]*
all-rounder M हरफ़न मौला *[harfan maulā]*
ally (friend) M दोस्त *[dost]*, मित्र *[mitra]*

almond M बादाम *[bādām]*
almost ADV लगभग *[lagbhag]*, तक़रीबन *[taqrīban]*
alone ADJ अकेला *[akelā]*
along ADV साथ साथ *[sāth sāth]*
already (previously) ADV पहले से *[pehle se]*
alter (change) V.I., V.T. बदलना *[badalnā]*
also PART भी *[bhī]*
altercation M फ़साद *[fasād]*; विवाद *[vivād]*
alternative M विकल्प *[vikalp]*
although IND हालाँकि *[hālā̃ki]*
altogether ADV साथ मिलकर *[sāth milkar]*
always ADV हमेशा *[hameśā]*
am (verb to be) V.I. हूँ *[hū̃]*
AM (morning) F सुबह *[subah]*
amazed ADJ चकित *[cakit]*
amazement F हैरानी *[hairānī]*
amazing ADJ आश्चर्यजनक *[āścaryajanak]*
ambassador M राजदूत *[rājdūt]*
ambition F महत्त्वाकांक्षा *[mahattvākāṅkṣā]*
amendment M संशोधन *[sanśodhan]*
America M अमरीका *[amrīkā]* ADJ अमरीकी *[amrīkī]*
amongst (x) PP (x) के बीच में *[(x) ke bīc mẽ]*
amount (total) M कुल *[kul]*
amuse V.T. बहलाना *[behlānā]*; हँसाना *[hãsānā]*
amusement M अनुरंजन *[anurañjan]*; मनोरंजन *[manorañjan]*
analysis M विश्लेषण *[viśleṣaṇ]*
anarchy; chaos F अराजकता *[arājaktā]*
ancestor M पूर्वज *[pūrvaj]*
ancient, antique, outdated ADJ प्राचीन *[prācīn]*
and ADJ, AD, CONJ और *[aur]*
anecdote M चुटकुला *[cuṭkulā]*
angel M फ़रिश्ता *[fariśtā]*
anger M गुस्सा *[ghussā]*
angle M कोण *[koṇ]*
angry ADJ क्रोधित *[krodhit]*:
(x) to become angry V.I. (x को) गुस्सा आना *[(x ko) ghussā ānā]*
anguish, agony F पीड़ा *[pīṛā]*
animal M जानवर *[jānvar]*
animosity; hostility M वैर *[vair]*
aniseed F सौंफ़ *[saũf]*
ankle M टखना *[ṭakhnā]*
annihilation M संहार *[sanhār]*
anniversary F जयंती *[jayantī]*

announce V.T. घोषित करना *[ghoṣit karnā]*
announcement F घोषणा *[ghoṣṇā]*
annoyance F नाख़ुशी *[nākhuśī]*
annual ADJ सालाना *[sālānā]*
annually (every year) ADV हर साल *[har sāl]*
anonymous ADJ अनाम *[anām]*
another (other) ADJ दूसरा *[dūsrā]*
answer M जवाब *[javāb]* V.T. जवाब देना *[javāb denā]*
ant F चींटी *[cīṭī]*
anxiety F चिंता *[cintā]*
anxious, stressed ADJ तनावग्रस्त *[tanāvgrast]*
anxious V.I. घबराना/घबड़ाना *[ghabrānā/ghabṛānā]*
any (some) ADJ कोई, कुछ *[koī, kuch]*
anybody PRO कोई *[koī]*
anymore (now) ADJ अब *[ab]*
anyone PRO कोई *[koī]*
anything (something) PRO कुछ *[kuch]*
anyway (somehow) ADV किसी तरह *[kisī tarah]*
anywhere ADV कहीं *[kahī̃]*
apart (separate) ADJ अलग *[alag]*
apartment, flat M फ़्लैट *[flaiṭ]*
apologize V.T. माफ़ी माँगना *[māfī mā̃gnā]*
apology (forgiveness) F माफ़ी *[māfī]*
apparent (obvious) ADJ ज़ाहिर *[zāhir]*
appeal F अपील *[apīl]*
appear (to) V.I. सूझना *[sūjhnā]*
appear; be engaged in; be employed; be united V.I. लगना *[lagnā]*
appearance M रूप *[rūp]*
appearance, looks; form; condition F सूरत *[sūrat]*
appease V.T. मनाना *[manānā]*
applaud V.T. दाद देना *[dād denā]*; तालियाँ बजाना *[tāliyā̃ bajānā]*
apple M सेब *[seb]*
appliance; equipment M उपकरण *[upakaraṇ]*
applicable; enforceable; in force ADJ लागू *[lāgū]*
application F अर्ज़ी *[arzī]* M प्रयोग *[prayog]*
application letter M आवेदन-पत्र *[āvedan-patra]*
application; vogue M इस्तेमाल *[istemāl]*

apply V.T. लागू करना *[lāgū karnā]*; अर्ज़ी देना *[arzī denā]*
appointed ADJ नियुक्त *[niyukt]*
appointment F नियुक्ति *[niyukti]*
apprentice M शागिर्द *[śāgird]*
apprise, make known; warn V.T. जताना *[jatānā]*
approach (come near) V.I. पास आना *[pās ānā]*
approach (method) M तरीक़ा *[tarīqā]*
appropriate, right ADJ उचित *[ucit]*
appropriateness, validity M औचित्य *[aucitya]*
approve, admire V.T. सराहना *[sarāhnā]*
approve, sanction V.T. मंज़ूरी देना *[manzūrī denā]*
approved ADJ, F पसंद *[pasand]*
approximately ADJ लगभग *[lagbagh]*
apricot F ख़ुबानी *[khubānī]*
April M अप्रैल *[aprail]*
Arab ADJ, M अरब *[arab]*
Arabic F अरबी *[arabī]*
architect M वास्तुकार *[vāstukār]*
architecture F वास्तुकला *[vāstukalā]*
area M इलाक़ा *[ilāqā]*
arena (field) M मैदान *[maidān]*
argue V.T. बहस करना *[behas karnā]*
argument M तर्क *[tark]*
argument, debate F बहस *[behas]*
arise (be born) V.I. उत्पन्न होना *[utpanna honā]*
arm M बाहु *[bāhu]*
arm, sleeve F बाँह *[bā̃h]*
armed ADJ सशस्त्र *[saśastra]*
armpit, next to F बग़ल *[baghal]*
arms M हथियार *[hathiyār]*
army F फ़ौज *[fauj]*; सेना *[senā]*
aroma F सुरभि *[surabhi]* M सौरभ *[saurabh]*
aroma, perfume, scent F महक *[mehak]*
around, nearly (x) PP (x) के आसपास *[(x) ke āspās]*
arrange V.T. सजाना *[sajānā]*
arrange/organize x V.T. x का इंतज़ाम करना *[x kā intazām karnā]*
arrange, make up, decorate V.T. संवारना *[samvārnā]*
arrangement, management M इंतज़ाम *[intazām]*

arrest V.T. गिरफ़्तार करना *[giraftār karnā]*
arrive V.I. पहुँचना *[pahũcnā]*
arrogance M घमंड *[ghamaṇḍ]*
art F कला *[kalā]*
article M लेख *[lekh]*
article; item; commodity F चीज़ *[cīz]*
articulation, utterance M उच्चारण *[uccāraṇ]*
artifact (thing) F वस्तु *[vastu]*
artificial; fabricated ADJ नक़ली *[naqlī]*
artisan M कारीगर *[kārīgar]*
artist M कलाकार *[kalākār]*
as, like, such as, for instance REL ADV जैसे *[jaise]*
ascend V.I. चढ़ना *[caṛhnā]*
ascetic M संन्यासी *[sannyāsī]*
asceticism; the fourth life stage in Hindu tradition M संन्यास *[sannyās]*
ashamed ADJ शर्मिंदा *[śarmindā]*
ash(es) F राख *[rākh]*; ख़ाक *[khāk]*
ask V.T. पूछना *[pūchnā]*
ask for (something); solicit V.T. माँगना *[mā̃gnā]*
ask a question V.T. सवाल पूछना *[savāl pūchnā]*
aspect M पहलू *[pehlū]*
aspirant ADJ आकांक्षी *[ākāṅkṣī]*
aspiration F आकांक्षा *[ākāṅkṣā]*
aspiration, longing M अरमान *[armān]*
ass M गधा *[gadhā]*
assassin M हत्यारा *[hatyārā]*
assault M हमला *[hamlā]*
assault (rape); violence, oppression M बलात्कार *[balātkār]*
assemble, flock V.I. जुटना *[juṭnā]*
assembled, gathered together ADJ इकट्ठा *[ikaṭṭhā]*
assembly F सभा *[sabhā]*
assent V.T. हामी करना *[hāmī karnā]*
assent; approval; leave F अनुमति *[anumati]*
assess (test) V.T. जाँचना *[jā̃cnā]*
assessment (testing) F जाँच *[jā̃c]*
asset (wealth) F संपत्ति *[sampatti]*
assign (attach) V.T. लगाना *[lagānā]*
assignment (task) M काम *[kām]*

assimilate V.T. आत्मसात् करना *[ātmasāt karnā]*
assist V.T. मदद करना *[madad karnā]*
assistance F मदद *[madad]*
assistant ADJ, M सहायक *[sahāyak]*
association, society F सभा *[sabhā]*
assume (accept) V.T. मानना *[mānnā]*
assumption (estimate) M अनुमान *[anumān]*
assurance M आश्वासन *[āśvāsan]*
assure V.T. आश्वस्त करना *[āśvast karnā]*
asthma M दमा *[damā]*
astonishment M ताज्जुब *[tājjub]*; विस्मय *[vismay]*
at (on) PP पर *[par]*
atheist, unbeliever M नास्तिक *[nāstik]*
athlete (player) खिलाड़ी *[khilāṛī]*
atmosphere M माहौल *[māhaul]*
atom; minute particle M अणु *[aṇu]*
atop (above) ADV ऊपर *[ūpar]*
attach V.I. लगना *[lagnā]* V.T. लगाना *[lagānā]*
attached/added/joined/linked; be procured or collected V.I. जुड़ना *[juṛnā]*
attack M हमला *[hamlā]*
attempt (endeavor) F कोशिश *[kośiś]*
attempt (try) V.T. कोशिश करना *[kośiś karnā]*
attend V.I. शरीक होना *[śarīk honā]*
attendance (presence) F उपस्थिति *[upasthiti]*
attention M ध्यान *[dhyān]*
attire F पोशाक *[pośāk]*
attitude M रवैया *[ravaiyā]*
attorney M वकील *[vakīl]*
attraction, charm, allurement M आकर्षण *[ākarṣaṇ]*
attractive ADJ आकर्षक *[ākarṣak]*
attribute (quality) M गुण *[guṇ]*
auction M नीलाम *[nīlām]*
audience M दर्शक *[darśak]*
auspicious ADJ, M शुभ *[śubh]*: **auspicious wish** F शुभकामना *[śubhkāmnā]*
author M लेखक *[lekhak]*
authority M अधिकार *[adhikār]*

autobiography F आत्मकथा *[ātmakathā]*
automatic ADJ स्वचलित *[svacalit]*
automobile F गाड़ी *[gāṛī]*
autonomy (independence) F स्वाधीनता *[svādhīntā]*
availability F उपलब्धि *[upalabdhi]*
available; acquired ADJ उपलब्ध *[uplabdh]*
avarice M लालच *[lālac]*
avaricious ADJ लालची *[lālacī]*
average ADJ औसत *[ausat]*
avert V.T. टालना *[ṭālnā]*
averted V.I. टलना *[ṭalnā]*
avoid V.T. परहेज़ करना *[parhez karnā]*
avoidance, régimen, keeping aloof M परहेज़ *[parhez]*
awake ADJ जागा हुआ *[jāgā huā]*
awakening M जागरण *[jāgaraṇ]*
award M इनाम *[ināṃ]*
aware (vigilant) ADJ सावधान *[sāvdhān]*
awareness (vigilance) F सावधानी *[sāvdhānī]*
away (outside) ADV बाहर *[bāhar]*
ax: a large ax M कुल्हाड़ा *[kulhāṛā]*: **a small ax** F कुल्हाड़ी *[kulhāṛī]*

B

baby; child M शिशु *[śiśu]*
back F, M पीठ *[pīṭh]*
back (returned) ADJ वापस *[vāpas]*
back, behind, after ADV पीछे *[pīche]*
back/hind part M पीछा *[pīchā]*
backbone F रीढ़ *[rīṛh]*
bad ADJ बुरा *[burā]*
bad (off) ADJ ख़राब *[kharāb]*
badly ADV बुरी तरह *[burī tarah]*
badness, wickedness F बुराई *[burāī]*
bag M झोला *[jholā]*
bake; roast V.T. सेंकना *[sẽknā]*
balance M संतुलन *[santulan]*
balanced, in equilibrium ADJ संतुलित *[santulit]*
bald ADJ गंजा *[gañjā]*
ball F गेंद *[gẽd]*
balloon (bubble) M बुलबुला *[bulbulā]*; गुब्बारा *[gubbārā]*

ban V.T. प्रतिबंध लगाना *[pratibandh lagānā]*
ban; proviso, condition M प्रतिबंध *[pratibandh]*
banana M केला *[kelā]*
band M बैंड *[baiḍ]*
bandage F पट्टी *[paṭṭī]*
bandit M डाकू *[ḍākū]*
bangle F चूड़ी *[cūṛī]*
bank M किनारा *[kinārā]*; बैंक *[baiṇk]*
banner, standard M झंडा *[jhaṇḍā]*
banquet M दावत *[dāvat]*
bar M बार *[bār]*
barber; a particular caste in the traditional Hindu social order subsisting on hair-cutting and shaving M नाई *[nāī]*
bare, uncovered ADJ नंगा *[naṅgā]*
barefoot ADJ, ADV नंगे पाँव *[naṅge pā̃v]*
bargain V.T. मोलतोल करना *[moltol karnā]*
bargaining M मोलतोल *[moltol]*
bark, jabber V.T. बौंकना *[baũknā]*
barrier (obstacle) F रुकावट *[rukāvaṭ]*
base M अड्डा *[aḍḍā]*
base, basis F बुनियाद *[buniyād]*
basement F तहख़ाना *[tehkhānā]*
bashful ADJ शर्मीला *[śarmīlā]*
basic (simple) ADJ आसान *[āsān]*
basket F टोकरी *[ṭokrī]*
bat, racket M बल्ला *[ballā]*
bath M स्नान *[snān]*
bathe V.T. स्नान करना *[snān karnā]* V.I., V.T. नहाना *[nahānā]*
bathroom M ग़ुसलख़ाना *[ghusalkhānā]*
battery F बैटरी *[baiṭrī]*
battle; quarrel: encounter, clash F लड़ाई *[laṛāī]*
bay F खाड़ी *[khāṛī]*
be V.I. होना *[honā]*
be able to V.I. सकना *[saknā]*
be adorned/decorated/ beautified V.I. सजना *[sajnā]*
be agreeable, be pleasing/ appealing V.I. भाना *[bhānā]*
be alert, be supported V.I. सँभलना *[sãbhalnā]*
be amused, be entertained V.I. बहलना *[behalnā]*
be beaten V.T. पिटना *[piṭnā]*

be born v.i. पैदा होना *[paidā honā]*
be broken v.i. टूटना *[ṭūṭnā]*; फूटना *[phūṭnā]*
be brought up v.i., M पलना *[palnā]*
be cautious v.i. सँभलना *[sãbhalnā]*
be closed, be turned off v.i. बंद होना *[band honā]*
be collected, gathered, amassed v.i. इकट्ठा होना *[ikaṭṭhā honā]*
be commenced v.i. छिड़ना *[chiṛnā]*
be completed v.i. पूरा होना *[pūrā honā]*
be concentrated v.i. सिमटना *[simaṭnā]*
be confused v.i. हड़बड़ाना *[haṛbaṛānā]*
be confused/confounded; to be spoilt v.i. बिगड़ना *[bigaṛnā]*
be crushed v.i., v.t. कुचलना *[kucalnā]*
be deceived v.t. धोखा खाना *[dhokhā khānā]*
be decrepit v.i. सठियाना *[saṭhiyānā]*
be deep in thought v.i. सोच में पड़ना *[soc mẽ paṛnā]*
be defeated v.i. हारना *[hārnā]*
be deployed v.i. तैनात होना *[taināt honā]*
be destroyed v.i. तबाह होना
be disentangled; become unraveled v.i. सुलझना *[sulajhnā]*
be disgraced, to be stigmatized v.i. कालिख लगना *[kālikh lagnā]*
be disgraced, to lose one's honor v.t. इज़्ज़त खोना/ गँवाना *[izzat khonā/ gãvānā]*
be distracted; to be repelled v.i. मन हटना *[man haṭnā]*
be divided/partitioned/ distributed v.i. बँटना *[bãṭnā]*
be dragged v.i. घिसटना *[ghisaṭnā]*
be drenched v.i. भीगना *[bhīgnā]*
be effaced v.i. मिटना *[miṭnā]*
be embarrassed, be ashamed v.i. शर्माना *[śarmānā]*
be examined, be valued v.i. जँचना *[jãcnā]*
be exposed v.i. पोल खुलना *[pol khulnā]*

be fascinated/charmed/ infatuated/attracted V.I. रीझना *[rījhnā]*
be fed up, be tired, be distressed V.I. तंग आना *[taṅg ānā]*
be filled V.I., V.T. भरना *[bharnā]*
be finished V.I. ख़त्म होना *[khatm honā]*
be fixed, be okay, appropriate V.I. ठीक होना *[ṭhīk honā]*
be improved; be amended V.I. सुधरना *[sudharnā]*
be in the grip of impotent anger V.I. तिलमिलाना *[tilmilānā]*
be increased V.I. बढ़ना *[baṛhnā]*
be infatuated (with x) V.I. (x पर) फ़िदा होना *[(x par) fidā honā]*
be jealous V.I. जलन होना *[jalan honā]*
be kicked V.T. लात खाना *[lāt khānā]*
be lucky; have a turn of good fortune V.I. क़िस्मत खुलना *[qismat khulnā]*
be made V.I. बनना *[bannā]*
be obliged to x; grateful V.I. (x का) आभारी होना *[(x kā) ābhārī honā]*
be of service; be of use V.I. काम आना *[kām ānā]*
be overwhelmed (by emotion); become speechless V.I. गद्गद होना *[gadgad honā]*
be packed full V.I. खचाखच भरा होना *[khacākhac bharā honā]*
be passed V.I. पारित होना *[pārit honā]*
be present, attend V.I. उपस्थित होना *[upasthit honā]*
be produced V.I. पैदा होना *[paidā honā]*
be produced; be born; grow; spring up V.I. उपजना *[upajnā]*
be reared, be nourished; cradle V.I., M पलना *[palnā]*
be refulgent; glitter, shine V.I. जगमगाना *[jagmagānā]*
be saved V.I. बचना *[bacnā]*
be separated V.I. जुदा होना *[judā honā]*
be shamed; be dishonored; have one's name

tarnished V.I. नाक कटना *[nāk kaṭnā]*
be seized; be snatched V.I. छिनना *[chinnā]*
be silent V.I. चुप होना *[cup honā]*
be slaughtered, slain V.I. हलाक होना *[halāk honā]*
be soaked V.I. भीगना *[bhīgnā]*
be sold V.I. बिकना *[biknā]*
be sorted; be thinned V.I. छँटना *[chãṭnā]*
be sprained V.I. मोच आना *[moc ānā]*
be stiff V.I. अकड़ना *[akaṛnā]*
be struck; strike V.I. बजना *[bajnā]*
be surprised/astonished; be confounded V.I. अचकचाना *[ackacānā]*
be stubborn; insist V.T. ज़िद्द करना *[zidd karnā]*
be (the) subject of sexual intercourse (by a male) V.I. चुदना *[cudnā]*
be tied V.I. बँधना *[bãdhnā]*
be tired, be astonished V.I. हैरान होना *[hairān honā]*
be unsewn V.I. उधड़ना *[udhaṛnā]*
be visible (to x) V.I. (x को) दिखना *[(x ko) dikhnā]*, (x को) दिखाई देना *[(x ko) dikhāī denā]*
be watered, be irrigated V.I. सिंचना *[sĩcnā]*
be willing, approve V.I. राज़ी होना *[rāzī honā]*
be worried V.I. परेशान होना *[pareśān honā]*
be wounded/injured V.T. घाव खाना *[ghāv khānā]*
bear V.T. झेलना *[jhelnā]* M भालू *[bhālū]*
beard F दाढ़ी *[dāṛhī]*
beast (animal) M जानवर *[jānvar]*
beat V.I. धड़कना *[dhaṛaknā]* V.T. मारना *[mārnā]*
beating M मार *[mār]*
beautiful ADJ सुंदर *[sundar]*
beauty F सुंदरता *[sundartā]*
because CONJ क्योंकि *[kyõki]*
become V.I. होना *[honā]*
become bored V.I. बोर होना *[bor honā]*, उकताना *[uktānā]*
become crazy V.I. पागल होना *[pāgal honā]*
become damp V.I. सीलना *[sīlnā]*
become developed V.I.

विकसित होना *[vikasit honā]*
become lost V.I. खो जाना *[kho jānā]*, गुम होना *[gum honā]*
become manifest V.I. प्रकट होना *[prakaṭ honā]*
become marginalized V.I. किनारे होना *[kināre honā]*
become separated V.I. अलग होना *[alag honā]*
become tired V.I. थक जाना *[thak jānā]*
bed M पलँग/पलंग *[palãg/ palaṅg]*
bedroom M सोने का कमरा *[sone kā kamrā]*
bedsheet; bed cover F चादर *[cādar]*
bee M मधुमक्खी *[madhumakkhī]*
beef M गाय का मांस *[gāy kā māns]*
beer F बियर *[biyar]*
before (x) PP (x) से पहले *[(x) se pehle]*
beg (ask for alms) V.T. भीख माँगना *[bhīkh mā̃gnā]*
begin V.T. शुरू करना *[śurū karnā]* V.I. शुरू होना *[śurū honā]*
beginning F शुरुआत *[śuruāt]* M शुरू *[śurū]*
behalf (on) PP की तरफ़ *[kī taraf]*
behave with formality, stand on ceremony V.T. तकल्लुफ़ करना *[takalluf karnā]*
behavior M व्यवहार *[vyavahār]*; सलूक *[salūk]*
behavior, attitude M रवैया *[ravaiyā]*
behind ADV पीछे *[pīche]* ADJ पिछड़ा *[pīchṛā]*
being (existence) M अस्तित्व *[astitva]*
belief M विश्वास *[viśvās]*
belief to occur, trust to occur V.I. विश्वास होना *[viśvās honā]*
believe V.T. विश्वास करना *[viśvās karnā]*
bell M घंटा *[ghaṇṭā]*: a small bell F घंटी *[ghaṇṭī]*
belly M पेट *[peṭ]*
beloved ADJ, M प्यारा *[pyārā]*
below ADV नीचे *[nīce]*
below, beneath (low) ADJ निचला *[niclā]*
belt F पेटी *[peṭī]*
bench M बेंच *[beñc]*

bend; yield V.I. झुकना *[jhuknā]*
bend M मोड़ *[moṛ]*
beneath ADV नीचे *[nīce]*:
beneath (x) PP (x) के नीचे *[(x) ke nīce]*
beneficial ADJ मुफ़ीद *[mufīd]*
benefit M लाभ *[lābh]*
bent ADJ टेढ़ा *[ṭeṛhā]*
beseige; to encircle V.T. घेरना *[ghernā]*
beside ADV बग़ल में *[baghal mẽ]*
besides PP X के अलावा *[x ke alāvā]*
best ADJ सब से अच्छा *[sab se acchā]*
bet F शर्त *[śart]* V.T. शर्त लगाना *[śart lagānā]* V.I. बाज़ी लगाना *[bāzī lagānā]*
bet F बाज़ी *[bāzī]*
betel-nut F सुपारी *[supārī]*
between ADV बीच में *[bīc mẽ]*
beyond (x) ADV (x) से परे *[(x) se pare]*
bias M पूर्वग्रह *[pūrvagrah]*
bicycle, bike F साइकिल *[sāikil]*
bid V.T. बोली लगाना *[bolī lagānā]*
bid (contract) M ठेका *[ṭhekā]*
big ADJ बड़ा *[baṛā]*
bill M बिल *[bil]*
billion ADJ अरब *[arab]*
bind (bond) M बंधन *[bandhan]*
biography F जीवनी *[jīvanī]*
biology M जीवविज्ञान *[jīvvijñān]*
bird F चिड़िया *[ciṛiyā]*
birth M जन्म *[janma]* F पैदाइश *[paidāiś]*
birthday M जन्मदिन *[janam-din]*
bit (piece) M टुकड़ा *[ṭukṛā]*
bite V.T. काटना *[kāṭnā]*; डँसना *[ḍãsnā]*
bitter ADJ कड़वा *[kaṛvā]*
black ADJ काला *[kālā]*
blade M पंखा *[paṅkhā]*
blame V.T. दोष देना *[doṣ denā]*
blank, unused (as in paper); brand new ADJ कोरा *[korā]*
blanket M कंबल *[kambal]*
blast M विस्फोट *[visphoṭ]*
blaze F ज्वाला *[jvālā]*
blend V.T. मिलाना *[milānā]*
blessed, fortunate ADJ भाग्यवान *[bhāgyavān]*
blessings M आशीर्वाद *[āśīrvād]*

blind, irrational ADJ अंधा *[andhā]*
blink V.I. पलक झपकना *[palak jhapaknā]*
bliss M आनंद *[ānand]*
blister, burn M छाला *[chālā]*
block M ब्लॉक *[blāk]*
block (stop) V.T. रोकना *[roknā]*
blood M खून *[khūn]*
bloody ADJ खूनी *[khūnī]*
bloom; be delighted V.I. खिलना *[khilnā]*
blossom V.I. खिलना *[khilnā]*; फूलना *[phūlnā]*
blouse M ब्लाउज़ *[blāūz]*
blow (shock) F ठेस *[ṭhes]*
blow V.T. फूँकना *[phūknā]*
blow money V.T. पैसे उड़ाना *[paise uṛānā]*
blue ADJ नीला *[nīlā]*
board M तख़्त *[takht]*
boast V.T. डींग मारना *[ḍīg mārnā]*
boat F नाव *[nāv]*
body M शरीर *[śarīr]*
body, part M अंग *[aṅg]*
body, physical frame M/F बदन *[badan]*
boil M फोड़ा *[phoṛā]*
boil; cause to simmer V.T. उबालना *[ubālnā]*
bold (brave) ADJ साहसी *[sāhasī]*
bolt F चटकनी *[caṭkanī]*
bomb V.T. बॅमबारी करना *[bambārī karnā]*
bond M बंधन *[bandhan]*
bone F हड्डी *[haḍḍī]*
book F किताब *[kitāb]*
boom (explosion) M धड़ाका *[dhaṛākā]*
boot, shoe; gram pod M बूट *[būṭ]*
booth M बूथ *[būth]*
border M किनारा *[kinārā]*
boring (insipid) ADJ नीरस *[nīras]*
born ADJ, INVAR पैदा *[paidā]*
borrowing; credit M उधार *[udhār]*
boss M मालिक *[mālik]*
both ADJ दोनों *[donõ]*
bother F परेशानी *[pareśānī]*
bother/harass; distress V.T. तंग करना *[taṅg karnā]*
bother/take trouble तकलीफ़ करना *[taklīf karnā]*
bothered ADJ परेशान *[pareśān]*
bottle F बोतल *[botal]*
bottom (sole) M तला *[talā]*
boundary, extent F हद *[had]*
bow V.I. झुकना *[jhuknā]*

bowl M कटोरा *[kaṭorā]*: a small bowl F कटोरी *[kaṭorī]*
box M डब्बा *[ḍabbā]*
boy M लड़का *[laṛkā]*
bracelet M कंकण *[kaṅkaṇ]*
brag, boast V.T. डींग मारना *[ḍīg mārnā]*
braid (hair) V.T. गूँथना *[gū̃thnā]*
brain (mind) M दिमाग़ *[dimāgh]*
brake M ब्रेक *[brek]*
branch F डाल *[ḍāl]*
brassiere; bodice F चोली *[colī]*
brave ADJ, M बहादुर *[bahādur]*
bread F रोटी *[roṭī]*: **thin Indian style of bread, cooked most commonly on an iron griddle** F चपाती *[capātī]*
break V.I. टूटना *[ṭūṭnā]* V.T. तोड़ना *[toṛnā]*
break an oath V.T. क़सम तोड़ना *[qasam toṛnā]*
break wind V.T. पादना *[pādnā]*
breakfast M नाश्ता *[nāśtā]*
breast F छाती *[chātī]*
breath M दम *[dam]*; श्वास *[śvās]*
breathe V.T. साँस लेना *[sā̃s lenā]*
breeze M अनिल *[anil]*
bribe, illegal gratification F घूस *[ghūs]*
brick F ईंट *[ī̃ṭ]*
bride F दुल्हन *[dulhan]*
bridegroom M दूल्हा *[dūlhā]*
bridge M पुल *[pul]*
briefly ADV संक्षेप में *[saṅkṣep mẽ]*
bright ADJ उज्ज्वल *[ujjval]*
bright, shining, luminous ADJ उजाला *[ujālā]*
brilliance F प्रतिभा *[pratibhā]*
bring V.T. लाना *[lānā]*
bring out; expel; extract V.T. निकालना *[nikālnā]*
bring together, stick together V.T. सटाना *[saṭānā]*
bring up V.T. पालना *[pālnā]*
British ADJ अंग्रेज़ *[eṅgrez]*
broad ADJ चौड़ा *[cauṛā]*
broadcast M प्रसारण *[prasāraṇ]*
broken ADJ ख़राब *[kharāb]*
broker M दलाल *[dalāl]*
broom M झाड़ू *[jhāṛū]*
brother M भाई *[bhaī]*
brotherhood, community F बिरादरी *[birādrī]*
brothers and sisters M PL भाई-बहन *[bhāī-behan]*
brown ADJ भूरा *[bhūrā]*
brush V.T. ब्रश करना *[braś karnā]*

brutal (violent) ADJ हिंसक *[hinsak]*
bubble M बुलबुला *[bulbulā]*
bucket F बाल्टी *[bālṭī]*
bud F कली *[kalī]*
budget M बजट *[bajaṭ]*
bug (insect) M कीड़ा *[kīṛā]*
build (make) V.T. बनाना *[banānā]*
builder ADJ बनानेवाला *[banānevālā]*
building F इमारत *[imārat]*
bulb M बल्ब *[balb]*
bulge V.I. उभरना *[ubharnā]*
bulk M थोक *[thok]*
bullet F गोली *[golī]*
bunch, cluster M गुच्छा *[gucchā]*
bundle F गठरी *[gaṭhrī]*
bungalow M बंगला *[baṅglā]*
burden M बोझ *[bojh]* V.T. लादना *[lādnā]*
burial M दफ़न *[dafan]*
buried V.I. गड़ना *[gaṛnā]*
burn V.T. जलाना *[jalānā]*
burn, be inflamed, be kindled; feel jealous V.I. जलना *[jalnā]*
burning sensation F जलन *[jalan]*
burqa, veil, mantle M बुरक़ा *[burqā]*
burst V.I. फटना *[phaṭnā]*
burst into laughter V.I. खिलखिलाना *[khilkhilānā]* V.T. क़हक़हा लगाना *[qehqahā lagānā]*
bury V.T. गाड़ना *[gāṛnā]*
bury, entomb V.T. दफ़नाना *[dafnānā]*
bus INVAR, M बस *[bas]*
business M व्यापार *[vyāpār]*
businessman M व्यापारी *[vyāpārī]*
busy ADJ व्यस्त *[vyast]*
but CONJ लेकिन *[lekin]*
butcher M क़साई *[qasāī]*
butt (anus) M गाँड *[gā̃ḍ]*
butter M मक्खन *[makkhan]*
butter up; flatter V.T. मसका लगाना *[maskā lagānā]*
butterfly F तितली *[titlī]*
button M बटन *[baṭan]*
buy V.T. ख़रीदना *[kharīdnā]*
buyer ADJ, M ख़रीदार *[kharīdār]*
by PP से *[se]*
by, up to PP तक *[tak]*
by chance ADV इत्तफ़ाक़ से *[ittafāq se]*
(by) oneself ADV अपने-आप *[apne āp]*

C

cabin; small room F कोठरी *[koṭhrī]*
cabinet (government) M मंत्रिमंडल *[mantrimaṇḍal]*
cabbage F बंदगोभी *[bandgobhī]*
cage M पिंजरा *[piñjrā]*
calamity F बला *[balā]*
calculate V.T. हिसाब लगाना *[hisāb lagānā]*
calendar M कलेंडर *[kaleṇḍar]*, पंचांग *[pañcāṅg]*
call V.T. बुलाना *[bulānā]*: call (x) (y) V.T. (x को) (y) कहना *[(x ko)(y) kehnā]*
call (out); call (someone) V.T. पुकारना *[pukārnā]*
calm V.T. शांत करना *[śānt karnā]*
calm ADJ शांत *[śānt]*
calmness, quiet F शांति *[śānti]*
camel M ऊँट *[ū̃ṭ]*
camera M कैमरा *[kaimrā]*
camp M शिविर *[śivir]*
campaign F मुहिम *[muhim]*
campus M परिसर *[parisar]*
cancel V.T. रद्द करना *[radd karna]*
candidate M उम्मीदवार *[ummīdvār]*
candle F मोमबत्ती *[mombattī]*
cane F छड़ी *[chaṛī]*
cap F टोपी *[ṭopī]*
capable ADJ क़ाबिल *[qābil]*
capable, able ADJ लायक़ *[lāyaq]*
capacity F हैसियत *[haisiyat]*
capital F राजधानी *[rājdhānī]*
capital, investment F पूँजी *[pū̃jī]*
capitalism M पूँजीवाद *[pū̃jīvād]*
capitalist M पूँजीवादी *[pū̃jīvādī]*
capsize; be reversed; reverse V.I., V.T. उलटना *[ulaṭnā]*
captain M कप्तान *[kaptān]*
capture (grab) V.T. पकड़ना *[pakaṛnā]*
car F गाड़ी *[gāṛī]*
caravan M कारवाँ *[kārvā̃]*
cardamom F इलायची *[ilāycī]*
care, heed F परवाह *[parvāh]*: care (for x) V.T. (x की) परवाह करना *[(x kī) parvāh karnā]*
career (profession) M पेशा *[peśā]*

careful ADJ सावधान *[sāvdhān]*
carefully ADV सावधानी से *[sāvdhānī se]*
carefulness, attention F सावधानी *[sāvdhānī]*
careless ADJ लापरवाह *[lāparvāh]*
carelessness, inattention F लापरवाही *[lāparvāhī]*
cargo M कारगो *[kārgo]*
carpet M क़ालीन *[qālīn]*
carrot F गाजर *[gājar]*
carry (transport) V.T. ढोना *[ḍhonā]*
cart M ठेला *[ṭhelā]*
cart; haul V.T. ढोना *[ḍhonā]*
case M केस *[kes]*
cash, ready money M नक़द *[naqad]*
cashew nut M काजू *[kājū]*
casket, small box F पेटी *[peṭī]*
cast V.T. ढालना *[ḍhālnā]*
cast (throw) V.T. फेंकना *[phĕknā]*
caste F जाति *[jāti]*
caste system F वर्णव्यवस्था *[varṇvyavasthā]*
casual (informal) ADJ अनोपचारिक *[anopcārik]*
casualty (wounded) ADJ घायल *[ghāyal]*
cat F बिल्ली *[billī]*
catalog F सूची *[sūcī]*
catch V.T. पकड़ना *[pakaṛnā]*
category M वर्ग *[varg]*
cattle M ढोर *[ḍhor]*
cauliflower F गोभी *[gobhī]*
cause M कारण *[kāraṇ]*
cause someone to accept/ agree to V.T. मनवाना *[manvānā]*
cause to be built V.T. बनवाना *[banvānā]*
cause to be created, create V.T. सिरजाना *[sirjānā]*
cause to be stitched, have made V.T. सिलाना *[silānā]*
cause to bring; order V.T. मँगाना *[mãgānā]*
cause to cry/weep/lament; harass, trouble V.T. रुलाना *[rulānā]*
cause to drink, serve (a drink) V.T. पिलाना *[pilānā]*
cause to go up, raise; offer; place on the fire for cooking V.T. चढ़ाना *[caṛhānā]*
cause to grow; produce V.T. उपजाना *[upjānā]*

cause to sleep; lull to sleep V.T. सुलाना *[sulānā]*
cause to wear V.T. पहनाना *[pehnānā]*
cause trouble, distress (to, को) तकलीफ़ पहुँचाना *[taklīf pahũcnā]*
cause/make (someone) dance (to one's tune) V.T. नचाना *[nacānā]*
cause to reach V.T. पहुँचाना *[pahũcānā]*
cave F गुफा *[guphā]*
cease V.I. रुकना *[ruknā]*
ceiling F छत *[chat]*
celebrate, persuade V.T. मनाना *[manānā]*
celebrate a festival V.T. त्यौहार मनाना *[tyauhār manānā]*
celebrate a holiday V.T. छुट्टी मनाना *[chuṭṭī manānā]*
celebration M जश्न *[jaśn]*
celebrity (fame) M यश *[yaś]*
cemetery M क़ब्रिस्तान *[qabristān]*
center M केंद्र *[kendra]*
central ADJ केंद्रीय *[kendrīya]*
century F शताब्दी *[śatābdī]*
ceremony M समारोह *[samāroh]*
certain ADJ निश्चित *[niścit]*
certainly ADV ज़रूर *[zarūr]*
certificate F सनद *[sanad]*
chain M सिलसिला *[silsilā]*
chain, fetters F ज़ंजीर *[zañjīr]*
chair F कुर्सी/कुरसी *[kursī]*
chairman M सभापति *[sabhāpati]*
challenge F चुनौती *[cunautī]*
chamber (room) M कमरा *[kamrā]*
champion (conqueror) M विजेता *[vijetā]*
championship (competition) F प्रतियोगिता *[pratiyogitā]*
chance (coincidence) M संयोग *[sanyog]*: a happy chance; a happy coincidence M सुयोग *[suyog]*
chance (opportunity) M मौक़ा *[mauqā]*
change M परिवर्तन *[parivartan]* V.I., V.T. बदलना *[badalnā]*
chapter M अध्याय *[adhyāya]*
character (in a play); container M पात्र *[pātra]*
characteristic (virtue) M गुण *[guṇ]*
charge; imputation; imposition M आरोप *[ārop]*

charity M दान *[dān]*
charmed, under a spell; attracted ADJ मुग्ध *[mugdh]*
charming ADJ सुहावना *[suhāvnā]*
chart, plan M नक़्शा *[naqśā]*
chase (follow) V.T. पीछा करना *[pīchā karnā]*
cheap ADJ सस्ता *[sastā]*
cheat V.T. धोखा देना *[dhokhā denā]*
check (evaluate) V.T. जाँचना *[jā̃cnā]*
check (bill) M बिल *[bil]*
check (cheque) M चेक *[cek]*
cheek M गाल *[gāl]*
cheer (applaud) V.T. दाद देना *[dād denā]*
cheerful ADJ हँसमुख *[hãsmukh]*
cheese M पनीर *[panīr]*
chemistry (subject) M रसायन शास्त्र *[rasāyan śāstra]*
chest M सीना *[sīnā]*
chew V.T. चबाना *[cabānā]*
chicken F मुर्ग़ी *[murghī]*
chief (main), foremost ADJ प्रमुख *[pramukh]*
chief minister M मुख्य मंत्री *[mukhya mantrī]*
child M बच्चा *[baccā]*
childhood M बचपन *[bacpan]*
chilies; pepper F मिर्च *[mirc]*
chill (shiver) M कंपन *[kampan]*
chin F ठोड़ी *[ṭhoṛī]*
Chinese ADJ चीनी *[cīnī]*
chip; cut; pare V.T. कतरना *[katarnā]*
chocolate F चॉकलेट *[cākleṭ]*
choice F पसंद *[pasand]*
choose; pick; elect V.T. चुनना *[cunnā]*
chop V.T. काटना *[kāṭnā]*
Christian ADJ ईसाई *[īsāī]*
Christianity M ईसाई धर्म *[īsāī dharm]*
Christmas M बड़ा दिन *[baṛā din]*
chunk (piece) M टुकड़ा *[ṭukṛā]*
church M गिरजाघर *[girjāghar]*
chutney F चटनी *[caṭnī]*
cigarette F सिगरेट *[sigreṭ]*
circle M चक्कर *[cakkar]*
circular; globular ADJ गोल *[gol]*
circumstance F परिस्थिति *[paristhiti]*
citizen ADJ नागरिक *[nāgrik]*
citizenship F नागरिकता *[nāgriktā]*

city M शहर *[śehar]*
civilization F सभ्यता *[sabhyatā]*
civilized ADJ सभ्य *[sabhya]*
claim V.T. दावा करना *[dāvā karnā]*
clapping (of hands) F ताली *[tālī]*
clash V.I. टकराना *[ṭakrānā]* F टक्कर *[ṭakkar]*
class M दर्जा *[darjā]*; वर्ग *[varg]*
class (as in a Biology class) M, F क्लास *[klās]*
classroom F कक्षा *[kakṣā]*
classic ADJ क्लासिक *[klāsik]*
classical ADJ क्लासिकी *[klāsikī]*
claw M चंगुल *[caṅgul]*
clay; dirt F मिट्टी *[miṭṭī]*
clean V.T. सफ़ाई करना *[safāī karnā]* ADJ साफ़ *[sāf]*
cleanse V.T. धोना *[dhonā]*
clear ADJ साफ़ *[sāf]*
clerk M क्लर्क *[klark]*
clever ADJ होशियार *[hośiyār]*
client M ग्राहक *[grāhak]*
cliff F चट्टान *[caṭṭān]*
climate F जलवायु *[jalvāyu]*
climb V.I. चढ़ना *[caṛhnā]*
cling V.I. चिपकना *[cipaknā]*
clock (timepiece) F घड़ी *[ghaṛī]*
close ADV नज़दीक *[nazdīk]*
close to (x) PP (x) के क़रीब *[(x) ke qarīb]*
close; turn off V.T. बंद करना *[band karnā]*
closed ADJ बंद *[band]*
closet (almirah) F अलमारी *[almārī]*
cloth M कपड़ा *[kapṛā]*
clothes M कपड़े *[kapṛe]*
cloud M बादल *[bādal]*
clove; nose-stud F लौंग *[laũg]*
club M क्लब *[klab]*
clue M सुराग़ *[surāgh]*
cluster (group) M झुंड *[jhuṇḍ]*
coal M कोयला *[koylā]*
coast M तट *[taṭ]*
coat; smear V.T. लेपना *[lepnā]*
coat M कोट *[koṭ]*
cocaine F कोकीन *[kokīn]*
coffee F कॉफ़ी *[kāfī]*
coin M सिक्का *[sikkā]*
cold M जाड़ा *[jāṛā]*; ज़ुकाम *[zukām]* F सर्दी *[sardī]*; ठंड *[ṭhaṇḍ]*: a cold to occur (to x) V.I. (x को) ज़ुकाम होना *[(x ko) zukām honā]*; (x) to feel cold V.I. (x को) ठंड लगना *[(x ko) ṭhaṇḍ lagnā]*

collaboration (cooperation) M सहयोग *[sehyog]*
collapse (destruction) M नाश *[nāś]*
collar M कॉलर *[kālar]*
colleague, supporter M सहयोगी *[sehyogī]*
collect V.T. बटोरना *[baṭornā]*
collect, amass, gather V.T. इकट्ठा करना *[ikaṭṭhā karnā]*
collected ADJ इकट्ठा *[ikaṭṭhā]*
collection M संकलन *[sañkalan]*
collective (group) M समूह *[samūh]*
college M कॉलेज/कॉलिज *[kālej/kālij]*
collide; knock (against) V.I. टकराना *[ṭakrānā]*
collision F टक्कर *[ṭakkar]*
colony M उपनिवेश *[upniveś]*
color M रंग *[raṅg]*
color V.T. रंग लगाना *[raṅg lagānā]*
colorful, gay; luxury-loving ADJ रंगीन *[raṅgīn]*
column M स्तंभ *[stambh]*
comb F कंघी *[kaṅghī]*
come V.I. आना *[ānā]*
come out, go out; proceed; appear V.I. निकलना *[nikalnā]*
combat (fighting) F लड़ाई *[laṛāī]*
combination (agreement, concord) M मेल *[mel]*
combine V.T. मिलाना *[milānā]*
comedy F कामदी *[kāmadī]*
comely ADJ मनोहर *[manohar]*
comfort F राहत *[rāhat]*
comfortably ADV आराम से *[ārām se]*
coming (advent) M आगमन *[āgaman]*
command (order) V.T. आज्ञा देना *[ājñā denā]*
commander M कमाण्डर *[kamāṇḍar]*
commencement F शुरुआत *[śuruāt]* M शुरू *[śurū]*
commercial ADJ वाणिज्यिक *[vāṇijyik]*
commission M आयोग *[āyog]*
commissioner M आयुक्त *[āyukt]*
commit suicide V.T. आत्म-हत्या करना *[ātma-hatyā karnā]*
commitment (promise) M वचन *[vacan]*
committee F समिति *[samiti]*
common; commonplace ADJ मामूली *[māmūlī]*

common sense F अक़्ल *[aql]*
commonly (generally) ADV आम तौर पर *[ām taur par]*
communicate V.T. संप्रेषण करना *[sampreṣaṇ karnā]*
community M संप्रदाय *[sampradāy]*
companion, fellow M साथी *[sāthī]*
company F सोहबत *[sohbat]*, कंपनी *[kampanī]*
compare V.T. तुलना करना *[tulnā karnā]*
compassion F करुणा *[karuṇā]*
compel V.T. विवश करना *[vivaś karnā]*
compelled ADJ विवश *[vivaś]*
compensation (remuneration) M मुआवज़ा *[muāvzā]*
competition F प्रतिस्पर्धा *[pratispardhā]*
competitor M प्रतिस्पर्धी *[pratispardhī]*
complain V.T. शिकायत करना *[śikāyat karnā]*
complain about; speak ill of V.T. चुग़ली करना *[cughlī karnā]*
complaint F शिकायत *[śikāyat]*
complete ADJ पूरा *[pūrā]* V.T. पूरा करना *[pūrā karnā]*
complete, act, execute V.T. करना *[karnā]*
completed; concluded ADJ ख़त्म *[khatm]*
completely ADV पूर्ण रूप से *[pūrṇ rūp se]*
complex ADJ पेचीदा *[pecīdā]*
complexity F पेचीदगी *[pecīdagī]*
complication F उलझन *[uljhan]*
comply V.T. पालन करना *[pālan karnā]*
component (limb, member) M अंग *[aṅg]*
compose V.T., F रचना *[racnā]*
composition, artistic creation; structure F रचना *[racnā]*
comprehension; intellect F समझ *[samajh]*
compromise M समझौता *[samjhautā]*
compromise V.T. समझौता करना *[samjhautā karnā]*
computer M कम्प्यूटर *[kampyūṭar]*
conceal V.T. छिपाना *[chipānā]*
concede (accept) V.T., V.I. मानना *[mānnā]*

conceit M घमंड *[ghamaṇḍ]*
conceited, vain; arrogant ADJ घमंडी *[ghamaṇḍī]*
concentrate (on x) V.T. (x पर) ध्यान देना *[(x par) dhyān denā]*
concentration (attention) M ध्यान *[dhyān]*
concept V.T., F संकल्पना *[saṅkalpnā]*
concern F चिंता *[cintā]*; परवाह *[parvāh]*
concern; aim, motive M मतलब *[matlab]*
concerned (worried) ADJ चिंतित *[cintit]*
concerning (about) PP के बारे में *[ke bāre mẽ]*
conclude (end) V.I. समाप्त होना *[samāpt honā]*
conclusion M निष्कर्ष *[niṣkarṣ]*
condemn V.T. निंदा करना *[nindā karnā]*
condition F दशा *[daśā]*; हालत *[hālat]* M हाल *[hāl]*
condition; term F नौबत *[naubat]*, शर्त *[śart]*
conduct (behavior) M आचरण *[ācaraṇ]*
conference M सम्मेलन *[sammelan]*
confess (accept) V.T. स्वीकार करना *[svīkār karnā]*
confession F स्वीकारोक्ति *[svīkārokti]*
confidence, certainty, assurance M यक़ीन *[yaqīn]*
confident (assured) ADJ विश्वस्त *[viśvast]*
confirm V.T. पुष्ट करना *[puṣṭ karnā]*
confiscate; impound V.T. ज़ब्त करना *[zabt kanrā]*
conflict (war) M युद्ध *[yuddh]*
confounded, amazed, astonished ADJ हैरान *[hairān]*
confront (x) M (x का) सामना करना *[(x kā) sāmnā karnā]*
confrontation; coming face-to-face M आमना-सामना *[āmnā-sāmnā]*
confusion, disorder, disquiet F गड़बड़ *[gaṛbaṛ]*
congratulate V.T. बधाई देना *[badhāī denā]*
congratulations, felicitations F बधाई *[badhāī]*
connect (join) V.T. जोड़ना *[joṛnā]*
connection M संबंध *[sambandh]*

conquer, prevail upon, master V.T. जीतना *[jītnā]*
conquest, triumph F विजय *[vijay]*
conscience M अंतःकरण *[antaḥkaraṇ]*
conscious ADJ सचेत *[sacet]*
consciousness M होश *[hoś]*
consciousness; awareness; animation F चेतना *[cetnā]*
consecutive (continuous) ADJ निरंतर *[nirantar]*
consensus F सहमति *[sehmati]*
consequence M नतीजा *[natījā]*
conservative ADJ रूढ़िवादी *[rūṛhivādī]*
consider V.I., V.T. समझना *[samajhnā]*
considerable (much) ADJ बहुत *[bahut]*
consideration (thinking) F सोच *[soc]*
console, assure V.T. दिलासा देना *[dilāsā denā]*
conspiracy F साज़िश *[sāziś]*
constant (continuous) ADJ निरंतर *[nirantar]*
constantly, continuous, continual ADV, ADJ लगातार *[lagātār]*
constitution M संविधान *[samvidhān]*
constraint F रोक *[rok]*
construct V.T. निर्माण करना *[nirmaṇ karnā]*
construction M निर्माण *[nirmāṇ]*
consult (ask for advice) V.T. सलाह माँगना *[salāh mā̃gnā]*
consultant M सलाहकार *[salāhkār]*
consume (eat) V.T. खाना *[khānā]*
consumer; user M उपभोक्ता *[upbhoktā]*
consumption M उपभोक्तावाद *[upabhoktāvād]*
contact V.T. संपर्क करना *[sampark karnā]*
contain (restrain) V.T. रोकना *[roknā]*
container M डिब्बा *[ḍibbā]*
contemplate (think) V.T. सोचना *[socnā]*
contemplation M ध्यान *[dhyān]*
contemporary ADJ समकालीन *[samkālīn]*
content (satisfied) ADJ संतुष्ट *[santuṣṭ]*

contented (happy) ADJ सुखी *[sukhī]*
contest F प्रतियोगिता *[pratiyogitā]*
context M संदर्भ *[sandarbh]*
continent M महाद्वीप *[mahādvīp]*
continue, maintain V.T. जारी रखना *[jārī rakhnā]*
continued ADJ जारी *[jārī]*
continuously ADV लगातार *[lagātār]*
contract M अनुबंध *[anubandh]*
contract, cause to shrink, draw together V.T. सिकोड़ना *[sikoṛnā]*
contract; cower V.I. सिकुड़ना *[sikuṛnā]*
contractor M ठेकेदार *[ṭhekedār]*
contribution M योगदान *[yogdān]*
control M नियंत्रण *[niyantraṇ]*, वश *[vaś]*
controversial ADJ विवादास्पद *[vivādāspad]*
controversy (dispute) M विवाद *[vivād]*
convention M रिवाज *[rivāj]*
conventional (traditional) ADJ परंपरागत *[paramparāgat]*
conversation F बातचीत *[bātcīt]*
converse (to/with x) V.T. (x से) बात करना *[(x se) bāt karnā]*
conversion (transformation) M रूपांतरण *[rūpāntaraṇ]*
convert (change) V.T. बदलना *[badalnā]*
convict (prisoner) M क़ैदी *[qaidī]*
conviction (belief) M विश्वास *[viśvās]*
convince (make believe) V.T. विश्वास दिलाना *[viśvās dilānā]*
convinced (assured) ADJ आश्वस्त *[āśvast]*
cook M रसोइया *[rasoiyā]*, बावरची *[bāvarcī]*
cook V.T. पकाना *[pakānā]*
cool; cold ADJ ठंडा *[ṭhaṇḍā]*
cooperate V.T. सहयोग देना *[sehyog denā]*
cope (steady oneself) V.I. संभलना *[sambhalnā]*
copy F नक़ल *[naqal]*
copy V.T. नक़ल करना *[naqal karnā]*
cord F डोरी *[ḍorī]*

coriander M धनिया *[dhaniyā]*
corn F मक्का *[makkā]*
corner M कोना *[konā]*
corpse F लाश *[lāś]*
corpulent ADJ मोटा *[moṭā]*
correct V.T. ठीक करना *[ṭhīk karnā]*
correct ADJ ठीक *[ṭhīk]*
correctly ADV ठीक ढंग से *[ṭhīk ḍhaṅg se]*
corruption M भ्रष्टाचार *[bhraṣṭācār]*
cost F क़ीमत *[qīmat]*
costly ADJ महँगा *[mahãgā]*
costume (clothing) वस्त्र *[vastra]*
cot F चारपाई *[cārpāī]*
cottage F कुटी *[kuṭī]*
cotton carpet F दरी *[darī]*
cough V.I. खाँसना *[khãsnā]* F खाँसी *[khãsī]*
council F परिषद् *[pariṣad]*
counsel; reconciliation F सलाह *[salāh]*
counselor (advisor) M सलाहकार *[selāhkār]*
count V.T. गिनना *[ginnā]*; गिनती करना *[gintī karnā]*
countenance; mask M चेहरा *[cehrā]*
counting F गिनती *[gintī]*
country M देश *[deś]*
countryside M देहात *[dehāt]*
couple F जोड़ी *[joṛī]*
courage F हिम्मत *[himmat]*
courageous ADJ बहादुर *[bahādur]*
course M कोर्स *[kors]*
course (path) M मार्ग *[mārg]*
court of law F अदालत *[adālat]*
courtyard M आँगन *[ãgan]*
cousin M चचेरा/ममेरा भाई *[cacerā/mamerā bhaī]* F चचेरी/ममेरी बहन *[cacerī/ mamerī behn]*
cover V.T. ओढ़ना *[oṛhnā]*
cover M ढक्कन *[ḍhakkan]*
cover, thatch; shadow V.I. छाना *[chānā]*
covered V.I., V.T. ढकना *[ḍhaknā]*
cow F गाय *[gāy]*, गो *[go]*
coward(ly) ADJ डरपोक *[ḍarpok]*
crack V.I. फूटना *[phūṭnā]*
crack, snap M तड़ाका *[taṛākā]*
crack/crackle (as in oil when boiling); break with a cracking sound V.I. कड़कड़ाना *[kaṛkaṛānā]*

crackle V.I. कड़कना *[karaknā]*
craft M फ़न *[fan]*
cram; commit to memory V.T. घोटना *[ghoṭnā]*
cram full V.T. ठाँसना *[ṭhā̃snā]*
crash, impact F टक्कर *[ṭakkar]*
crash V.I. टकराना *[ṭakrānā]*
crawl V.I. रेंगना *[rẽgnā]*
crazy ADJ पागल *[pāgal]*; सनकी *[sankī]*
cream F मलाई *[malāī]*
create V.T., F रचना *[racnā]*
creative ADJ रचनात्मक *[racnātmak]*
creator, author M रचयिता *[racyitā]*
crew (gang) M गिरोह *[giroh]*
crime; offense; fault M अपराध *[aprādh]*
criminal; guilty; offending ADJ, M अपराधी *[aprādhī]*
cripple ADJ अपंग *[apaṅg]*
crisis M संकट *[saṅkaṭ]*
criterion (principle) M सिद्धांत *[siddhānt]*
critic M आलोचक *[ālocak]*
criticism F आलोचना *[ālocnā]*
crop F फ़सल *[fasal]*
cross F सूली *[sūlī]*
crossroads M चौराहा *[caurāhā]*
crowd F भीड़ *[bhīr]*
crucial ADJ निर्णायक *[nirṇāyak]*
cruel ADJ निष्ठुर *[nisṭhur]*
crush; trample V.I., V.T. कुचलना *[kucalnā]*
cry V.I. रोना *[ronā]*
cucumber M खीरा *[khīrā]*: a kind of cucumber F ककड़ी *[kakṛī]*
cultural ADJ सांस्कृतिक *[sānskṛtik]*
culture F संस्कृति *[sanskṛti]*
cup M प्याला *[pyālā]*
cupboard F अलमारी *[almārī]*
curd M दही *[dahī]*
cure (treatment) M इलाज *[ilāj]*
curiosity F जिज्ञासा *[jijñāsā]*
curious ADJ उत्सुक *[utsuk]*
currency F मुद्रा *[mudrā]*
current ADJ चालू *[cālū]*
currently (these days) ADV आजकल *[ājkal]*
curriculum M पाठ्यक्रम *[pāṭhyakram]*
curtain M परदा *[pardā]*
curved ADJ टेढ़ा *[ṭeṛhā]*
cushion; prop, support M तकिया *[takiyā]*
custody F हिरासत *[hirāsat]*

custom M रिवाज *[rivāj]*
customer M ग्राहक *[grāhak]*
cut V.I. कटना *[kaṭnā]* V.T. काटना *[kāṭnā]*
cycle M चक्र *[cakra]*

D

dad M पिता *[pitā]*
dagger M छुरा *[churā]*
daily ADV, M रोज़ *[roz]*
dam M बांध *[bāndh]*
damage; harm M नुक़सान *[nuqsān]*
damage V.T. नुक़सान पहुँचाना *[nuqsān pahũcānā]*
dance M, F नाच *[nāc]* V.I. नाचना *[nācnā]*
dancer M नाचनेवाला *[nācnevālā]*
danger M ख़तरा *[khatrā]*
dangerous ADJ ख़तरनाक *[khatarnāk]*
dare (challenge) V.T. ललकारना *[lalkārnā]*
dare (risk) V.T. जोखिम उठाना *[jokhim uṭhānā]*
dark ADJ अंधेरा *[andherā]*
dark (black) ADJ काला *[kālā]*
darkness ADJ, M अंधेरा *[andherā]*
date F तारीख़ *[tārīkh]*
date (meeting) M मिलन *[milan]*
daughter F बेटी *[beṭī]*
dawn M प्रभात *[prabhāt]*
day M दिन *[din]*
days of heat, summer M, PL गर्मी के दिन *[garmī ke din]*
dead ADJ मरा हुआ *[marā huā]*
deadly ADJ जानलेवा *[jānlevā]*
deal M सौदा *[saudā]*
deal (in playing cards); V.T. बाँटना *[bā̃ṭnā]*
dealer M सौदागर *[saudāgar]*
dear ADJ, M प्यारा *[pyārā]*
dear ADJ, M प्रिय *[priya]*
death M देहांत *[dehānt]* F मौत *[maut]*
debate F बहस *[behas]*
debate (dispute) M विवाद *[vivād]*
debris M मलबा *[malbā]*
debt M कर्ज़ *[karz]*
decade M दशक *[daśak]*
decay V.I. सड़ना *[saṛnā]*
decay; rot; be boiled or cooked till softened V.I. गलना *[galnā]*
deceive V.T. धोखा देना

[dhokhā denā]; छलना *[chalnā]*
December (month) M दिसंबर *[disambar]*
decent ADJ भला *[bhalā]*
decide V.T. तय करना *[tay karnā]*
decision M फ़ैसला *[faislā]*
declaration M एलान *[elān]*
declare; proclaim V.T. घोषित करना *[ghoṣit karnā]*
decline (fall) V.I. पतन होना *[patan honā]*
decompose, rot V.I. सड़ना *[saṛnā]*
decorate V.I. सजाना *[sajānā]*
decrease V.I. कम होना *[kam honā]*
dedicate V.T. समर्पित करना *[samarpit karnā]*
deep ADJ गहरा *[gehrā]*
deer M हिरण *[hiraṇ]*
defeat F हार *[hār]*
defeat V.T. हराना *[harānā]*
defeated ADJ पराजित *[parājit]*
defect, demerit, disorder; guilt, blame M दोष *[doṣ]*
defraud, beguile V.T. कपट करना *[kapaṭ karnā]*
defend V.T. रक्षा करना *[rakṣā karnā]*
defendant (accused) M अभियुक्त *[ābhiyukt]*
defender (protector) M रक्षक *[rakṣak]*
defense (protection) F रक्षा *[rakṣā]*
deficit M घाटा *[ghāṭā]*
definite ADJ निश्चित *[niścit]*
definitely ADV अवश्य *[avaśya]*
definition F परिभाषा *[paribhāṣā]*
degree F डिग्री *[ḍigrī]*
deity; respectable person; giant, demon M देव *[dev]*
dejected, gloomy ADJ उदास *[udās]*
dejection F उदासी *[udāsī]*
delay F देर *[der]*
delay V.T. देर करना *[der karnā]*
Delhi F दिल्ली *[dillī]*
deliberately ADV जानबूझकर *[jānbūjhkār]*
delicate ADJ नाज़ुक *[nāzuk]*
delicious ADJ लज़ीज़ *[lazīz]*
delight M हर्ष *[harṣ]*
deliver V.T. पहुँचाना *[pahũcānā]*
delivery (birth) M प्रसव *[prasav]*
demand F माँग *[mā̃g]* V.T. माँगना *[mā̃gnā]*

democracy M लोकतंत्र *[loktantra]*
demonstration M प्रदर्शन *[pradarśan]*
denial M खंडन *[khaṇḍan]*
dense; close ADJ गाढ़ा *[gāṛhā]*
density F घनता *[ghanatā]*
deny V.T. खंडन करना *[khaṇḍan karnā]*
depart, set out V.I. रवाना होना *[ravānā honā]*
depart, expire V.T. सिधारना *[sidhārnā]*
depart; be left behind; be released V.I. छूटना *[chūṭnā]*
department M विभाग *[vibhāg]*
departure M प्रस्थान *[prasthān]*
depend(ent) (on x) V.I. (x पर) निर्भर होना *[(x) par nirbhar honā]*
dependent ADJ अधीन *[adhīn]*
depict (describe) V.T. वर्णन करना *[varṇan karnā]*
deployed, posted, appointed ADJ तैनात *[taināt]*
deposit F पेशगी *[peśagī]*
depressed ADJ निराश *[nirāś]*
depression F निराशा *[nirāśā]*
depth F गहराई *[gehrāī]*
descend, come down V.I. उतरना *[utarnā]*
describe V.T. वर्णन करना *[varṇan karnā]*
description M वर्णन *[varṇan]*
desert M रेगिस्तान *[registān]*
deserted ADJ, M वीरान *[vīrān]*
design M नमूना *[namūnā]*
desire F इच्छा *[icchā]*
desolate ADJ सुनसान *[sunsān]*
despair F निराशा *[nirāśā]*
desperate ADJ निराश *[nirāś]*
despite (x) PP (x) के बावजूद *[(x) ke bāvajūd]*
dessert ADJ, M मीठा *[mīṭhā]*
destination F मंज़िल *[manzil]*
destiny M भाग्य *[bhāgya]*
destroy V.T. नष्ट करना *[naṣṭ karnā]*
destruction M विनाश *[vināś]*
detail M ब्योरा *[byorā]*
detain V.T. रोकना *[roknā]*
detect (find out) V.T. पता करना *[patā karnā]*
determination F दृढ़ता *[dṛṛhtā]*
determine (decide) V.T. निश्चय करना *[niścay karnā]*
develop V.T. विकसित करना *[vikasit karnā]*

developed ADJ विकसित *[vikasit]*
developing; evolving विकासशील *[vikāsśīl]*
development; growth M विकास *[vikās]*
devote (dedicate) V.T. समर्पित करना *[samarpit karnā]*
device; cure M उपाय *[upāy]*
devil M शैतान *[śaitān]*
dew F ओस *[os]*
diabetes F मधुमेह की बीमारी *[madhumeh kī bīmārī]*
diagnosis M निदान *[nidān]*
dialect, mode of speaking; bid (in an auction); taunt, sarcastic remark F बोली *[bolī]*
diamond M हीरा *[hīrā]*
diary F डायरी *[ḍāyrī]*
dictionary M शब्दकोश *[śabdkoś]*
die, take one's final breath अंतिम साँस लेना *[antim sā̃s lenā]*
diet (food) M आहार *[āhār]*
differ (separate) V.I. अलग होना *[alag honā]*
difference M फ़र्क़ *[farq]*
different ADJ अलग *[alag]*
differently ADV अलग ढंग से *[alag ḍhaṅg se]*
difficult ADJ मुश्किल *[muśkil]*
difficulty F मुश्किल *[muśkil]*
dig V.T. खोदना *[khodnā]*
dignity (honor) F इज़्ज़त *[izzat]*
dilemma F दुविधा *[duvidhā]*
dimension (aspect) M पहलू *[pehlū]*
diminish V.I. कम होना *[kam honā]*
dining (eat food) V.T. खाना खाना *[khānā khānā]*
dinner M रात का खाना *[rāt kā khānā]*
dip (swim) V.T. ग़ोता लगाना *[ghotā lagānā]*
diplomat ADJ राजदूत *[rājdūt]*
direct (straight) ADJ सीधा *[sīdhā]*
direction M निर्देशन *[nirdeśan]*
direction ADV, F तरफ़ *[taraf]*
directly ADV सीधे *[sīdhe]*
director M निर्देशक *[nirdeśak]*
dirt F गंदगी *[gandagī]*
dirty ADJ गंदा *[gandā]*
disabled; crippled ADJ अपंग *[apaṅg]*
disadvantage M नुक़सान *[nuqsān]*
disagree V.I. असहमत होना *[asehmat honā]*

disappear V.I. गायब होना *[ghāyab honā]*
disappeared; lost ADJ गायब *[ghāyab]*
disappointed ADJ निराश *[nirāś]*
disappointment F निराशा *[nirāśā]*
disaster (calamity) M विपत्ति *[vipatti]*
discipline M अनुशासन *[anuśāsan]*
discount F कटौती *[kaṭautī]*
discourse (conversation) F बातचीत *[bātcīt]*
discover (search) V.T. खोजना *[khojnā]*
discovery; exploration F खोज *[khoj]*
discrimination M भेदभाव *[bhedbhāv]*
discuss (talk) V.T. बात करना *[bāt karnā]*
discuss (x) V.T. (x की) चर्चा करना *[(x kī) carcā karnā]*
discussion F बातचीत *[bātcīt]*
disease M रोग *[rog]*, मर्ज़ *[marz]*
disgrace; affront M अपमान *[apamān]*
dish (food) M व्यंजन *[vyañjan]*
dishonor V.T. नाक काटना *[nāk kāṭnā]*
dismiss V.T. ख़ारिज करना *[khārij karnā]*
dismiss (reject) V.T. ठुकराना *[ṭhukrānā]*
disorder; disarray; chaos F अव्यवस्था *[avyvasthā]*
dispel, get rid of V.T. दूर करना *[dūr karnā]*
display (exhibition) F प्रदर्शनी *[pradarśanī]*
displeased ADJ नाख़ुश *[nākhuś]*
disposition, nature F तबियत/तबीयत *[tabiyat/tabīyat]*
dispute, altercation M झगड़ा *[jhagṛā]*
dissolve V.T. घोलना *[gholnā]*
distance F दूरी *[dūrī]*
distant ADJ दूर (का) *[dūr (kā)]*
distinct (separate) ADJ अलग *[alag]*
distinction (trait) M विशिष्टता *[viśiṣṭtā]*
distract V.T. बहलाना *[behlānā]*
distress F तकलीफ़ *[taklīf]*
distribute V.T. बाँटना *[bā̃ṭnā]*
distribution M वितरण *[vitaraṇ]*

district M ज़िला *[zilā]*
disturb (bother) V.T. परेशान करना *[pareśān karnā]*
ditch F खाई *[khāī]*
diverse ADJ विविध *[vividh]*
diversity F विविधता *[vividhtā]*
divide V.T. बाँटना *[bā̃ṭnā]*
divine ADJ दिव्य *[divya]*
division M विभाजन *[vibhājan]*
divorce M तलाक़ *[talāq]*
divorce V.T. तलाक़ देना *[talāq denā]*
divorced ADJ तलाक़शुदा *[talāqśudā]*
do V.T. करना *[karnā]*
do business V.T. कारोबार करना *[kārobār karnā]*
doctor M डॉक्टर *[ḍākṭar]*
doctrine (principle) M सिद्धांत *[siddhānt]*
document M दस्तावेज़ *[dastāvez]*
document (write) V.T. लिखना *[likhnā]*
documentary M वृत्तचित्र *[vṛttcitra]*
dog M कुत्ता/कुत्ता *[kuttā]*
doll F गुड़िया *[guṛiyā]*
domain (area) M क्षेत्र *[kṣetra]*
domestic ADJ घरेलू *[gharelū]*
dominant (imposing) ADJ रोबदार *[robdār]*
dominate (suppress) V.T. दबाना *[dabānā]*
donation (charity) M दान *[dān]*
don't ADV मत *[mat]*
donkey M गधा *[gadhā]*
donor M, ADJ दान देनेवाला *[dān denevālā]*
door M दरवाज़ा *[darvāzā]*
doorway F देहरी *[dehrī]*
dot; blot M नुक़्ता *[nuqtā]*
dot; zero, cipher F बिंदी *[bindī]*
double ADJ दोहरा *[dohrā]*
double ADJ दोगुना *[dugunā]*
doubt M शक *[śak]*
down (below) ADV नीचे *[nīce]*
dowry M दहेज *[dahej]*
doze; nap; be drowsy V.I. ऊँघना *[ū̃ghnā]*
dozen M दर्ज़न *[darzan]*
draft M मसौदा *[masaudā]*
draft (wind) F हवा *[havā]*
drag; trail V.T. घसीटना *[ghasīṭnā]*
drain F नाली *[nālī]*
drama M नाटक *[nāṭak]*
drape V.T. ओढ़ना *[oṛhnā]*

Dravidian; Dravidian country, Dravidian person ADJ, M द्रविड़ *[dravir]*
draw V.T. खींचना *[khĩcnā]*
drawer (of a table) F दराज़ *[darāz]*
drawing (sketch) M ख़ाका *[khākā]*
dreadful ADJ भयंकर *[bhayaṇkar]*
dream M सपना *[sapnā]*
dream V.T. सपना देखना *[sapnā dekhnā]*
dress F पोशाक *[pośāk]*
dress (someone) V.T. पहनाना *[pahnānā]*
dried ADJ सूखा *[sūkhā]*
drift (float) V.I. बहना *[behnā]*
drink V.T. पीना *[pīnā]*
drive (a car/vehicle) V.T. गाड़ी चलाना *[gāṛī calānā]*
drive; operate (a machine) V.T. चलाना *[calānā]*
driver M ड्राइवर *[ḍrāivar]*
drop F बूँद *[bū̃d]*
drop; dribble V.I. टपकना *[ṭapaknā]*
drum played on both ends F ढोलक *[ḍholak]*
drunk V.I. नशे में होना *[naśe mẽ honā]*
dry ADJ सूखा *[sukhā]*
dry up V.I. सूखना *[sūkhnā]*
duck F बतख़ *[batakh]*
dumb (idiot) ADJ बेवकूफ़ *[bevaqūf]*
dump (throw) V.T. फेंकना *[phẽknā]*
durable ADJ टिकाऊ *[ṭikāū]*
duration M अरसा *[arsā]*
during x x के दौरान *[x ke daurān]*
dust F धूल *[dhūl]*
duty, justice M धर्म *[dharm]*
duty, that which ought to be done M कर्त्तव्य *[kart-tavya]*
dweller; inhabitant M वासी *[vāsī]*
dye, paint V.T. रँगना *[rãgnā]*

E

each (every) ADJ हरेक *[harek]*
each other, one another PRO आपस *[āpas]*
eager, keen ADJ उत्सुक *[utsuk]*
ear M कान *[kān]*
early ADV जल्दी *[jaldī]*
earn; merit V.T. कमाना *[kamānā]*

earnings F कमाई *[kamāī]*
earring ADJ, F बाली *[bālī]*
earth F धरती *[dhartī]*; मिट्टी *[miṭṭī]*
earthquake M भूकम्प *[bhūkamp]*
ease F आसानी *[āsānī]*
easily ADV आसानी से *[āsānī se]*
east M पूर्व *[pūrv]*
eastern ADJ पूर्वी *[pūrvī]*
easy ADJ आसान *[āsān]*
eat V.T. खाना *[khānā]*
eat breakfast V.T. नाश्ता करना *[nāśtā karnā]*
echo, resound V.I. गूँजना *[gū̃jnā]*
echo F गूँज *[gū̃j]*
economical, thrifty ADJ किफ़ायती *[kifāyatī]*
economics M अर्थ-शास्त्र *[arth-śāstra]*
economist ADJ अर्थ-शास्त्री *[arth-śāstrī]*
economy; economic system F अर्थव्यवस्था *[arthvyavasthā]*
edge M किनारा *[kinārā]*
edition M संस्करण *[sanskaraṇ]*
editor M संपादक *[sampādak]*
educate V.T. शिक्षा देना *[śikṣā denā]*
educated ADJ शिक्षित *[śikṣit]*
education F शिक्षा *[śikṣā]*
educator (teacher) M शिक्षक *[śikṣak]*
effect M प्रभाव *[prabhāv]*
efficiency, competence, capacity F क्षमता *[kṣamtā]*
effort M प्रयास *[prayās]*
egg M अंडा *[aṇḍā]*
ego M अहंकार *[ahankār]*
Eid F ईद *[īd]*
eight ADJ आठ *[āṭh]*
eighteen ADJ अट्ठारह/अठारह *[aṭṭhārah/aṭhārah]*
eighteenth ADJ अट्ठारहवाँ *[aṭṭhāhvā̃]*
eighth ADJ आठवाँ *[āṭhvā̃]*
eighty ADJ अस्सी *[assī]*
eighty-eight ADJ अट्ठासी *[aṭṭhāsī]*
eighty-five ADJ पचासी *[pacāsī]*
eighty-four ADJ चौरासी *[caurāsī]*
eighty-nine ADJ नवासी *[navāsī]*
eighty-one ADJ इक्यासी *[ikyāsī]*
eighty-seven ADJ सत्तासी *[sattāsī]*
eighty-six ADJ छियासी *[chiyāsī]*

eighty-three ADJ तिरासी *[tirāsī]*
eighty-two ADJ बयासी *[bayāsī]*
elapse; expire; happen/ occur/befall V.I. बीतना *[bītnā]*
elbow F कोहनी *[kohnī]*
elder ADJ बुज़ुर्ग़ *[buzurgh]*
election M चुनाव *[cunāv]*
electric ADJ बिजली का *[bijlī kā]*
electricity F बिजली *[bijlī]*
elegance F शोभा *[śobhā]*
element M तत्त्व *[tattva]*
elementary ADJ प्राथमिक *[prāthamik]*
elephant M हाथी *[hāthī]*
elevator M लिफ़्ट *[lift]*
eleven ADJ ग्यारह *[gyārah]*
eligible (deserving) ADJ योग्य *[yogya]*
else ADJ अन्य *[anya]*
elsewhere ADV कहीं और *[kahī̃ aur]*
embarrassed ADJ शर्मिंदा *[śarmindā]*
embarrassment F शर्मिंदगी *[śarmindagī]*
embezzle V.T. ग़बन करना *[ghaban karnā]*
embrace M आलिंगन *[āliṅgan]*
embrace V.T. गले लगाना *[gale lagānā]* V.I. लिपटना *[lipaṭnā]*, गले मिलना *[gale milnā]*
embrace (x) V.T. (x का) आलिंगन करना *[(x kā) āliṅgan karnā]*
emerge V.I. निकलना *[nikalnā]*
emerge; protrude, project V.I. उभरना *[ubharnā]*
emergency M संकट *[saṅkaṭ]*
emotion F भावना *[bhāvnā]*
emotional ADJ भावुक *[bhāvuk]*
emperor, monarch M शाहंशाह *[śāhanśāh]*
emphasis M ज़ोर *[zor]*
emphasize V.T. ज़ोर देना *[zor denā]*
empire M साम्राज्य *[sāmrājya]*
employee M कर्मचारी *[karmcārī]*
employer (boss) M मालिक *[mālik]*
employment F नौकरी *[naukrī]*
empty ADJ ख़ाली *[khālī]*
enact (bring into effect) V.T. लागू करना *[lāgū karnā]*
encounter; be mixed, be united; mingle V.I. मिलना *[milnā]*

encourage V.T. बढ़ावा देना *[baṛhāvā denā]*
end M अंत *[ant]*
end V.T. ख़त्म करना *[khatm karnā]*
endeavor, attempt M प्रयास *[prayās]*
endeavor (to x), try (to x) (used with oblique infinitives) V.T. (x की) कोशिश करना *[(x kī) kośiś karnā]*
ended ADJ ख़त्म *[khatm]*
endless ADJ अनंत *[anant]*
endorse (support) V.T. समर्थन करना *[samarthan karnā]*
endure V.T. सहना *[sehnā]*
enemy M दुश्मन *[duśman]*
energy F ऊर्जा *[ūrjā]*
enforce; implement V.T. लागू करना *[lāgū karnā]*
engage; employ; join V.T. लगाना *[lagānā]*
engaged (in a task); unite V.I. जुटना *[juṭnā]*
engagement; loan F मंगनी *[mãgnī]*
engine M इंजन *[injan]*
engineer M इंजीनियर *[iñjīniyar]*
engineering F इंजीनियरी *[iñjīniyarī]*
English language F अंगरेज़ी *[aṅgrezī]*
English person M अंगरेज़ *[aṅgrez]*
enjoy, have fun V.T. मज़े करना *[maze karnā]*: (x) to enjoy V.I. (x को) मज़ा आना *[(x ko) mazā ānā]*; (x) to enjoy (one/first time) V.I. (x को) पसंद आना *[(x ko) pasand ānā]*; (x) to enjoy, like V.I. (x को) पसंद होना *[(x ko) pasand honā]*
enjoyable ADJ मज़ेदार *[mazedār]*
enjoyment, relish M मज़ा *[mazā]*
enmity F दुश्मनी *[duśmanī]*
enormous (expansive) ADJ विशाल *[viśāl]*
enough ADJ काफ़ी *[kāfī]*
enough; power INVAR, M बस *[bas]*
enquire V.T. दरियाफ़्त करना *[dariyāft karnā]*
enraged, displeased ADJ नाराज़ *[nārāz]*
enroll V.T. भरती कराना *[bhartī karānā]*
ensnare, bait, implicate, involve V.T. फँसाना *[phãsānā]*

entangle V.T. उलझाना *[uljhānā]*
entangled V.I. उलझना *[ulajhnā]*
entanglement F उलझन *[uljhan]*
enter V.I. घुसना *[ghusnā]*
entered ADJ दाख़िल *[dākhil]*
enterprise M उद्यम *[udyam]*
entertain; entice, allure V.T. बहलाना *[behlānā]*
entertainment M मनोरंजन *[manorañjan]*
enthusiasm M उत्साह *[utsāh]*
entire ADJ भर *[bhar]*; सारा *[sārā]*
entirely ADV पूरी तरह *[pūrī tarah]*
entity F वस्तु *[vastu]*
entrapped/ensnared/ baited; be embroiled/ implicated/involved V.I. फँसना *[phãsnā]*
entrust V.T. सौंपना *[saũpnā]*
entry M प्रवेश *[praveś]*
enumerate V.T. गिनना *[ginnā]*
envelope M लिफ़ाफ़ा *[lifāfā]*
environment M परिवेश *[pariveś]*
envision (imagine) V.T. कल्पना करना *[kalpanā karnā]*
epidemic F महामारी *[mahāmārī]*
episode M प्रकरण *[prakaraṇ]*
equal ADJ, ADV बराबर *[barābar]*
equality F बराबरी *[barābarī]*
equation M समीकरण *[samīkaraṇ]*
equipment (goods) M सामान *[sāmān]*
equivalent ADJ समान *[samān]*
era; one of the four ages of Hindu cosmogony; pair, couple M युग *[yug]*
erase V.I. मिटना *[miṭnā]*
err; make a lapse V.I. चूकना *[cūknā]*
error F ग़लती *[ghaltī]*
escape V.I. भागना *[bhāgnā]*
especially ADV विशेष रूप से *[viśeṣ rūp se]*
essay M निबंध *[nibandh]*
essence M सार *[sār]*
essential ADJ लाज़मी *[lāzmī]*
establish V.T. स्थापित करना *[sthāpit karnā]*
establish one's authority/ influence V.T. रोब जमाना *[rob jamānā]*
establishment F स्थापना *[sthāpnā]*

estate (property) F जायदाद *[jāyadād]*
esteem M आदर *[ādar]*
estimate M अंदाज़ा *[andāzā]*
estimate V.T. अंदाज़ा लगाना *[andāzā lagānā]*
etcetera वग़ैरह *[vaghairah]*
ethical (moral) ADJ नैतिक *[naitik]*
ethics F नैतिकता *[naitiktā]*
etiquette F तमीज़ *[tamīz]*
evaluate V.T. जाँचना *[jā̃cnā]*
even PART भी *[bhī]*
even now ADV अभी भी *[abhī bhī]*
evening F शाम *[śām]*
event F घटना *[ghaṭnā]*
eventually ADV अंत में *[ant mẽ]*
ever ADV कभी *[kabhī]*
every ADJ हर *[har]*
everybody PRO सब लोग *[sab log]*
everyday ADV रोज़ *[roz]*
everything PRO सब कुछ *[sab kuch]*
everywhere ADV सर्वत्र *[sar-vatra]*
evidence M प्रमाण *[pramāṇ]*
evil F बुराई *[burāī]*
evolution M विकास *[vikās]*
exact (correct) ADJ ठीक *[ṭhīk]*
examination F परीक्षा *[parīkṣā]*
examine, judge V.T. परखना *[parakhnā]*
example M उदाहरण *[udāharaṇ]*
excellent ADJ अच्छा *[acchā]*; बढ़िया *[baṛhiyā]*
except (apart) PP के सिवा *[ke sivā]*
exception M अपवाद *[apavād]*
exchange M आदान-प्रदान *[ādān-pradān]*
exchange (change) V.T. बदलना *[badalnā]*
exchange; dealings M लेन-देन *[len-den]*
excite, stimulate V.T. उत्तेजित करना *[uttejit karnā]*
excitement (enthusiasm) M उत्साह *[utsāh]*
exciting, thrilling ADJ रोमांचक *[romāñcak]*
exclude V.T. वर्जित करना *[varjit karnā]*
exclusive (special) ADJ विशेष *[viśeṣ]*
excuse M बहाना *[bahānā]*
excuse (forgive) V.T. माफ़ करना *[māf karnā]*

execution (hanging) F फाँसी *[phā̃sī]*
exercise (practice) M अभ्यास *[abhyās]*
exercise F कसरत *[kasrat]*
exhibition F प्रदर्शनी *[pradarśanī]*
existing ADJ मौजूद *[maujūd]*
existing; the present M वर्तमान *[vartamān]*
exit V, M निकास *[nikās]*
expand V.I. फैलना *[phailnā]*
expansion (spread) M फैलाव *[phailāv]*
expect V.T. अपेक्षा करना *[apekśā karnā]*
expectation F अपेक्षा *[apekśā]*
expense M ख़र्च *[kharc]*
expensive ADJ महँगा *[mahẽgā]*
experience M अनुभव *[anubhav]*
experienced ADJ अनुभवी *[anubhavī]*
experiment M प्रयोग *[prayog]*
expert ADJ, M विशेषज्ञ *[viśeṣajña]*
explain V.T. समझाना *[samjhānā]*
explanation F व्याख्या *[vyākhyā]*
explicit (clear) ADJ स्पष्ट *[spaṣṭ]*
explode V.I. फटना *[phaṭnā]*
exploitation M शोषण *[śoṣaṇ]*
exploration F खोज *[khoj]*
explore V.T. खोजना *[khojnā]*
explosion M विस्फोट *[visphoṭ]*
export M निर्यात *[niryāt]*
express (state) V.T. अभिव्यक्त करना *[ābhivyakt karnā]*
expression F अभिव्यक्ति *[abhivyakti]* M मुहावरा *[muhāvrā]*
extend (increase) V.T. बढ़ाना *[baṛhānā]*
extension (increase) M बढ़ावा *[baṛhāvā]*
extent (border) F सीमा *[sīmā]*
extinguish, put out V.T. बुझाना *[bujhānā]*
extort money V.T. पैसे ऐंठना *[paise aĩṭhnā]*
extra; spare; auxiliary ADJ अतिरिक्त *[atirikt]*
extraordinary ADJ असाधारण *[asādhāraṇ]*
extreme (end) M छोर *[chor]*
extremist; terrorist; radical ADJ उग्रवादी *[ugravādī]*
eye F आँख *[ā̃kh]*

eyebrow F भौंह *[bhaũh]*
eyesight F नज़र *[nazar]*

F

fabric M कपड़ा *[kaprā]*
face M मुँह *[mũh]*
face (x) V.T. (x का) सामना करना *[(x kā) sāmnā karnā]*
facility (ability) F दक्षता *[dakṣatā]*
fact M तथ्य *[tathya]*
factor (reason) M कारण *[kāraṇ]*
factory M कारख़ाना *[kārkhānā]*
fade; lose luster V.I. मुरझाना *[murjhānā]*
fail V.I. फ़ेल होना *[fel honā]*, चूकना *[cūknā]*
failed ADJ विफल *[viphal]*
failure, lack of success; futility F विफलता *[viphaltā]*
faint (light) ADJ हल्का *[halkā]*
fair M मेला *[melā]*
fair-skinned; white ADJ गोरा *[gorā]*
faith, belief, integrity M ईमान *[īmān]*
faithful, loyal ADJ वफ़ादार *[vafādār]*
fall F गिरावट *[girāvaṭ]* V.I. गिरना *[girnā]*
fall in love (with x) V.I. इश्क़ होना (x से) *[iśq honā (x se)]*: (x) to fall in love (with y) V.I. (x को) (y से) प्रेम होना *[(x ko) (y se) prem honā]*
false; fictitious ADJ झूठा *[jhūṭhā]*
falter V.I. लड़खड़ाना *[larkharānā]*
fame M यश *[yaś]*
familiar ADJ जान-पहचान का *[jān-pehcān kā]*
family M परिवार *[parivār]*
famine M अकाल *[akāl]*
famous, well known ADJ मशहूर *[maśhūr]*
fan (cooler) M पंखा *[paṅkhā]*
fanatic ADJ कट्टरपंथी *[kaṭṭarpanthī]*
fantasy (imagination) F कल्पना *[kalpanā]*
far ADV दूर *[dūr]*
fare M भाड़ा *[bhārā]*
farm M खेत *[khet]*
farm V.T. खेती-बाड़ी करना *[khetī-bārī karnā]*
farmer M किसान *[kisān]*
fashion F फ़ैशन *[faiśan]*
fast ADJ तेज़ *[tez]*

fast M व्रत *[vrat]*
fasten, bind V.T. बाँधना *[bā̃dhnā]*
fat ADJ मोटा *[moṭā]*
fat; fats and oils F वसा *[vasā]*
fatal ADJ घातक *[ghātak]*
fate M भाग्य *[bhāgya]*
father M पिता *[pitā]*
fatigue F थकान/थकावट *[thakān/thakāvaṭ]*
fatness, corpulence M मोटापा *[moṭāpā]*
fault M दोष *[doṣ]*
favor (side) M पक्ष *[pakṣ]*
favor (side) V.T. पक्ष लेना *[pakṣ lenā]*
favorite ADJ मनपसंद *[manpasand]*
fear M डर *[ḍar]*
fear V.I. डरना *[ḍarnā]*
fearful, dreadful, terrible ADJ ख़ौफ़नाक *[khaufnāk]*
feast F दावत *[dāvat]*
feather M पंख *[paṅkh]*
feature (trait) M गुण *[guṇ]*
February (month) F फ़रवरी *[farvarī]*
feeble ADJ कमज़ोर *[kamzor]*
feed food, treat V.T. खाना खिलाना *[khānā khilānā]*
feel V.T. टटोलना *[ṭaṭolnā]*: महसूस करना *[mehsūs karnā]*: (x) to feel at home, happy, engaged; (x) to feel easy V.I. (x का) मन लगना *[(x kā) man lagnā]*; (x) to feel hot V.I. (x को) गर्मी लगना *[(x ko) garmī lagnā]*; (x) to feel hungry V.I. (x को) भूख लगना *[(x ko) bhūkh lagnā]*; (x) to feel sleepy V.I. (x को) नींद लगना *[(x ko) nī̃d lagnā]*; (x) to feel sorrow V.I. (x को) अफ़सोस होना *[(x ko) afsos honā]*; (x) to feel/perceive V.I. (x को) महसूस होना *[(x ko) mahsūs honā]*; feel like (x); (x) to feel like V.I. (x का) मन होना *[(x kā) man honā]*
feel grateful V.I. एहसानमंद होना *[ehsānmand honā]*
feel nauseous V.I. घिन लगना *[ghin lagnā]*, मचली आना *[maclī ānā]*
feel obliged V.T. एहसान मानना *[ehsān mānnā]*
feel the pulse of V.T. नाड़ी देखना *[nāṛī dekhnā]*, नब्ज़ टटोलना/देखना *[nabz ṭaṭolnā/dekhnā]*

feeling M एहसास *[ehsās]*

female (woman) F औरत *[aurat]*

female F स्त्री *[strī]*

fence F बाड़ *[bāṛ]*

fennel F सौंफ़ *[saũf]*

fenugreek F मेथी *[methī]*

festival M उत्सव *[utsav]*

fever M बुख़ार *[bukhār]*: (x) **to have a fever** V.I. (x को) बुख़ार होना *[(x ko) bukhār honā]*

few, some ADJ कुछ *[kuch]*

fewer (less) ADJ कम *[kam]*

fiancé or fiancée (betrothed) ADJ, F, M मँगेतर *[mãgetar]*

fiber M रेशा *[reśā]*

fiber, chord ADJ, M तार *[tār]*

fickle ADJ चंचल *[cañcal]*

fiction (story) F कथा *[kathā]*

fidelity F वफ़ा *[vafā]*

field M खेत *[khet]*; मैदान *[maidān]*

field (area) M क्षेत्र *[kṣetra]*

fierce ADJ भीषण *[bhīṣaṇ]*

fifteen ADJ पंद्रह *[pandrah]*

fifth ADJ पाँचवाँ *[pãcvã]*

fifty ADJ पचास *[pacās]*

fifty-eight ADJ अट्ठावन *[aṭṭhāvan]*

fifty-five ADJ पचपन *[pacpan]*

fifty-four ADJ चौवन *[cauvan]*

fifty-nine ADJ उनसठ *[unsaṭh]*

fifty-one ADJ इक्यावन *[ikyāvan]*

fifty-seven ADJ सत्तावन *[sattāvan]*

fifty-six ADJ छप्पन *[chappan]*

fifty-two ADJ बावन *[bāvan]*

fight V.I., V.T. लड़ना *[laṛnā]*

fight F लड़ाई *[laṛāī]*

fight an election V.T. चुनाव लड़ना *[cunāv laṛnā]*

fighter ADJ लड़ाकू *[laṛākū]*

figure (number) F संख्या *[saṅkhyā]*

fill V.I., V.T. भरना *[bharnā]*

film F फ़िल्म *[film]*

filter V.T. छानना *[chānnā]*

filthy ADJ गंदा *[gandā]*

final ADJ अंतिम *[antim]*

finally ADV अंत में *[ant mẽ]*

find V.T. पाना *[pānā]*

find out, discover V.T. पता करना *[patā karnā]*; पता लगाना *[patā lagānā]*: (x) to find out/discover V.I. (x को) पता चलना *[(x ko) patā calnā]*

finding (conclusion) M निष्कर्ष *[niṣkarṣ]*

fine ADJ अच्छा *[acchā]*
finger F उँगली *[ũglī]*
finish (terminate) V.T. ख़त्म करना *[khatm karnā]*
finish (end) M अंत *[ant]*
fire F आग *[āg]*
fire (sack) V.T. नौकरी से निकालना *[naukrī se nikālnā]*
fire a bullet V.T. गोली चलाना *[golī calānā]*
fire brigade; fire engine M दमकल *[damkal]*
fireplace; hearth F चूल्हा *[cūlhā]*
firewood; timber F लकड़ी *[lakṛī]*
firm ADJ दृढ़ *[dṛṛh]*
firm (hard) ADJ सख़्त *[sakht]*
firm (company) F कंपनी *[kampanī]*
first ADJ पहला *[pehlā]*
fish F मछली *[machlī]*
fish V.T. मछली पकड़ना *[machlī pakaṛnā]*
fisherman M मछुआ *[machuā]*
fist M मुक्का *[mukkā]*
fit ADJ दुरुस्त *[durust]*
fit (suit) V.I. फबना *[phabnā]*
fit (sit well) V.I. ठीक बैठना *[ṭhīk baiṭhnā]*
fit (worthy) ADJ योग्य *[yogya]*
fitness F योग्यता *[yogyatā]*
five ADJ पाँच *[pā̃c]*
fix V.T. ठीक करना *[ṭhīk karnā]*
fixed (settled) ADJ निश्चित *[niścit]*
flag M झंडा *[jhaṇḍā]* F ध्वजा *[dhvajā]*
flame F आँच *[ā̃c]*
flash F कौंध *[kaũdh]*
flash V.I. कौंधना *[kaũdhnā]*
flat ADJ सपाट *[sapāṭ]*
flatter (x) V.T. (x की) ख़ुशामद करना *[(x kī) khuśāmad karnā]*
flavor M स्वाद *[svād]*
flee V.I. भागना *[bhāgnā]*
fleet (navy) F नौसेना *[nausenā]*
flesh (meat) M मांस *[māns]*
flexible ADJ लचीला *[lacīlā]*
flight; sortie F उड़ान *[uṛān]*
fling, hurl, cast, toss; waste; emit V.T. फेंकना *[phẽknā]*
flip (upturn) V.T., V.I. उलटना *[ulaṭnā]*
float V.I. तिरना *[tirnā]*
flock M झुंड *[jhuṇḍ]*
flood F बाढ़ *[bāṛh]*
floor M फ़र्श *[farś]*
flour M आटा *[āṭā]*

flourish, prosper V.I. पनपना *[panapnā]*
flow M प्रवाह *[pravāh]*
flow V.I. बहना *[behnā]*
flower M फूल *[phūl]*
flower V.I. फूलना *[phūlnā]*
fluid ADJ तरल *[taral]*
fly V.I. उड़ना *[uṛnā]*
fly F मक्खी *[makkhī]*
focus (center) M केंद्र *[kendra]*
fog M कुहरा *[kuhrā]*
fold; roll up V.T. लपेटना *[lapeṭnā]*
folk, person M जन *[jan]*
follow V.T. पीछा करना *[pīchā karnā]*
following ADJ अगला *[aglā]*
food M भोजन *[bhojan]*; खाना *[khānā]*
fool ADJ मूर्ख *[mūrkh]*
fool; to make a fool of V.T. उल्लू बनाना *[ullū banānā]*
foolish ADJ बेवकूफ़ *[bevaqūf]*
foot M पाँव *[pā̃v]*; पैर *[pair]*
footstep M क़दम *[qadam]*
for (x), in order to (x) [if x is a verb] PP (x) के लिये *[(x) ke liye]*
for sale, salable ADJ बिकाऊ *[bikāū]*
forbid V.T. मना करना *[manā karnā]*
forbidden ADJ मना *[manā]*
force F ज़बरदस्ती *[zabardastī]* M ज़ोर *[zor]*
force (compel) V.T. विवश करना *[vivaś karnā]*
forehead; forepart M माथा *[māthā]*
foreign country M विदेश *[videś]*
foreigner ADJ विदेशी *[videśī]*
forest, wood M जंगल *[jaṅgal]*
forever (always) ADV हमेशा *[hameśā]*
forget V.I. भूलना *[bhūlnā]*, भूल जाना *[bhūl jāna]*
forget, force out of mind V.T. बिसारना *[bisārnā]*
forgive V.T. माफ़ करना *[māf karnā]*
forgiveness F माफ़ी *[māfī]*
fork; hook M काँटा *[kā̃ṭā]*
form M रूप *[rūp]*
formal ADJ औपचारिक *[aupcārik]*
formality F औपचारिकता *[aupcāriktā]*
former ADJ पूर्व *[pūrv]*
formerly ADV पहले *[pehle]*

formula M फ़ार्मुला *[fārmulā]*
fort M क़िला *[qilā]*
forth ADV आगे *[āge]*
fortunately ADV सौभाग्यवश *[saubhāgyavaś]*
fortune, lot, luck F क़िस्मत *[qismat]*
forty ADJ चालीस *[cālīs]*
forty-eight ADJ अड़तालीस *[arṭālīs]*
forty-five ADJ पैंतालीस *[paĩṭālīs]*
forty-four ADJ चवालीस *[cavālīs]*; चौवालीस *[cauvālīs]*
forty-nine ADJ उनचास *[uncās]*
forty-one ADJ इकतालीस *[iktālīs]*
forty-seven ADJ सैंतालीस *[saĩtālīs]*
forty-six ADJ छियालीस *[chiyālīs]*
forty-three ADJ तैंतालीस *[taĩtālīs]*
forty-two ADJ बयालीस *[bayālīs]*
forward (ahead) ADV आगे *[āge]*
foster (rear) V.T. पालना *[pālnā]*
found V.T. स्थापित करना *[sthāpit karnā]*
foundation; basis M आधार *[ādhār]*
founder M संस्थापक *[sansthāpak]*
four ADJ चार *[cār]*
fourteen ADJ चौदह *[caudah]*
fourth ADJ चौथा *[cauthā]*
fraction (portion) M अंश *[anś]*
fragment M अंश *[anś]*
fragile (delicate) ADJ सुकुमार *[sukumār]*
fragrance, aroma; perfume, scent F ख़ुशबू *[khuśbū]*
frame M ढाँचा *[ḍhā̃cā]*
frankly (openly) ADV खुलेआम *[khuleām]*
fraud F कपट *[kapaṭ]*
free ADJ आज़ाद *[āzād]*; फ़ारिग़ *[fārigh]*; स्वाधीन *[svādhīn]*
free of charge ADJ मुफ़्त *[muft]*
freedom F आज़ादी *[āzādī]*
freeze V.I. जमना *[jamnā]*
French ADJ फ़्रांसीसी *[frānsīsī]*
frequently ADV अक्सर *[aksar]*
fresh ADJ ताज़ा *[tāzā]*
freshness F ताज़गी *[tāzagī]*
Friday M शुक्रवार *[śukravār]*
friend M, F दोस्त *[dost]*

friendly (outgoing) ADJ मिलनसार *[milansār]*
friendship F दोस्ती *[dostī]*
frighten V.T. डराना *[ḍarānā]*
frightful ADJ भयंकर *[bhayaṅkar]*
from PP से *[se]*
from the other side ADV उधर से *[udhar se]*
front, before, in the future ADV आगे *[āge]*
front (battle) M मोर्चा *[morcā]*
frozen ADJ जमा हुआ *[jamā huā]*
fruit M फल *[phal]*
frustrate (bother) V.T. परेशान करना *[pareśān karnā]*
frustration (bother) F परेशानी *[pareśānī]*
fry V.I. तलना *[talnā]*
fry, to broil V.T. भूनना *[bhūnnā]*
frying pan (small) F कड़ाही *[kaṛāhī]*
fuck V.T. चोदना *[codnā]*
fuel F ईंधन *[īndhan]*
full ADJ भरा हुआ *[bharā huā]*
fully (completely) ADV पूरी तरह *[pūrī tarah]*
fun M मज़ा *[mazā]*
function (event) M समारोह *[samāroh]*
function (task) M काम *[kām]*
functional ADJ काम का *[kām kā]*
fund M फ़ंड *[fand]*
funeral (cremation) M दाह-संस्कार *[dāh-sanskār]*
funeral (procession, Hindu) F शव-यात्रा *[śav-yātrā]*
funeral (procession, Muslim) M जनाज़ा *[janāzā]*
funny ADJ हास्यास्पद *[hāsyāspad]*
furnish V.T. सजाना *[sajānā]*
furniture M फरनिचर *[farnicar]*
furthermore CONJ ऊपर से *[ūpar se]*
future M भविष्य *[bhaviṣya]*

G

gaiety F रौनक़ *[raunaq]*
gain M लाभ *[lābh]*
game M खेल *[khel]*
gang M गिरोह *[giroh]*
Ganges (name of a river in India) F गंगा *[gaṅgā]*
garbage M कूड़ा *[kūṛā]*
garden M बग़ीचा *[baghīcā]*
garden, park M बाग़ *[bāgh]*
gardener M माली *[mālī]*

garlic M लहसुन *[lehsun]*
gas F गैस *[gais]*
gasoline M तेल, पेट्रोल *[tel, peṭrol]*
gate, entrance M फाटक *[phāṭak]*
gather V.I. इकट्ठा होना *[ikaṭṭhā honā]*
gather up (as in clouds); converge V.I. घुमड़ना *[ghumaṛnā]*
gathering (crowd) F भीड़ *[bhīṛ]*
gay (homosexual) ADJ समलैंगिक *[samlaiṅgik]*
gaze, watch intently, view V.T. ताकना *[tāknā]*
gear (stuff) M सामान *[sāmān]*
gender M लिंग *[liṅg]*
generally ADV आम तौर पर *[ām taur par]*
generation F पीढ़ी *[pīṛhī]*
generous ADJ उदार *[udār]*
genre F विधा *[vidhā]*
gentle ADJ नरम *[naram]*
gentleman ADJ, M सज्जन *[sajjan]*
gently, softly ADV आहिस्ता *[āhistā]*
genuine (real) ADJ असली *[aslī]*
German; German (language) ADJ, M जर्मन *[jarman]*
germinate; spring up V.I. उगना *[ugnā]*
gesture M इशारा *[iśārā]*
get stuck; be held up V.I. अटकना *[aṭaknā]*
get up, make rise; raise; wake up V.T. उठाना *[uṭhānā]*
get up; pass away, expire V.I. उठना *[uṭhnā]*
get wet V.I. भीगना *[bhīgnā]*
ghee M घी *[ghī]*
ghost M भूत *[bhūt]*
gift M तोहफ़ा *[tohfā]*
gift, grant F बख़्शीश *[bakhśīś]*
girl F लड़की *[laṛkī]*
give V.T. देना *[denā]*
give a bribe V.T. घूस देना *[ghūs denā]*, रिश्वत देना *[riśvat denā]*
give a command V.T. आदेश देना *[ādeś denā]*
give a kiss V.T. चुम्मा देना *[cummā denā]*
give a present/gift V.T. उपहार देना *[upahār denā]*
give a sermon; preaching M उपदेश देना *[updeś denā]*

give advice, counsel V.T. सलाह देना *[salāh denā]*
give an examination (teacher) V.T. इम्तहान लेना *[imtahān lenā]*
give an order V.T. हुक्म देना *[hukm denā]*
give back; send back V.T. लौटाना *[lauṭānā]*
give blessings V.T. आशीर्वाद देना *[āśīrvād denā]*
give evidence V.T. गवाही देना *[gavāhī denā]*
give solace V.T. ढाढ़स देना *[ḍhāṛhas denā]*
glad ADJ ख़ुश *[khuś]*
glance F निगाह *[nigāh]*
glass M काँच *[kāc]*
glass bottle F शीशी *[śiśī]*
glimpse F झलक *[jhalak]*
global (extensive) ADJ व्यापक *[vyāpak]*
globe M भूमंडल *[bhūmaṇḍal]*
glorious ADJ शानदार *[śāndār]*
glory (fame) M यश *[yaś]*
glove M दस्ताना *[dastānā]*
go V.I. जाना *[jānā]*
go astray, meander V.I. भटकना *[bhaṭaknā]*
go bad, break, be spoiled V.I. ख़राब होना *[kharāb honā]*
go to the toilet; defecate V.T. टट्टी करना *[ṭaṭṭī karnā]*
go up V.I. चढ़ना *[caṛhnā]*
goal M लक्ष्य *[lakṣya]*
goat M बकरा *[bakrā]*
God M ईश्वर/ईश्वर *[īśvar]*
gold M सोना *[sonā]*
golden ADJ सुनहरा *[sunharā]*
golden temple (Amritsar) M स्वर्ण मंदिर *[svarṇ mandir]*
good ADJ अच्छा *[acchā]*
good wishes F शुभकामनाएँ *[śubhkāmnāẽ]*
goodness F अच्छाई *[acchāī]*
goods M माल *[māl]*; सामान *[sāmān]*
gossip; chit-chat F गपशप *[gapśap]*
govern V.T. शासन करना *[śāsan karnā]*
government F सरकार *[sarkār]*
grab V.T. पकड़ना *[pakaṛnā]*
grace (kindess) M अनुग्रह *[anugrah]*
grade (rank) F कोटि *[koṭi]*
grain M अनाज *[anāj]*
grand ADJ शानदार *[śāndār]*
grandeur; pomp F शान *[śān]*
grandfather (paternal) M दादा *[dādā]*

grandfather (maternal) M नाना *[nānā]*
grandmother (paternal) M दादी *[dādī]*
grandmother (maternal) M नानी *[nānī]*
grandson; testicle M पोता *[potā]*
grant M अनुदान *[anudān]*
grape M अंगूर *[aṅgūr]*
grasp (understand) V.T., V.I. समझना *[samajhnā]*
grasp (grab) V.T. पकड़ना *[pakaṛnā]*
grass F घास *[ghās]*
grateful; indebted ADJ आभारी *[ābhārī]*
gratis, for free ADV मुफ़्त में *[muft mẽ]*
grave (serious) ADJ गंभीर *[gambhīr]*
grave F क़ब्र *[qabra]*
gravity (seriousness) F गंभीरता *[gambhīrtā]*
gravity (heaviness) M गुरुत्व *[gurutva]*
gray ADJ धूसर *[dhūsar]*
great; big ADJ महान *[mahān]*
greatness F महानता *[mahāntā]*
greed M लालच *[lālac]*
greedy ADJ लालची *[lālcī]*
Greek ADJ यूनानी *[yūnānī]*
green ADJ हरा *[harā]*
greenery, vegetation F हरियाली *[hariyālī]*
greet V.T. स्वागत करना *[svāgat karnā]*
grief M शोक *[śok]*
grievance; accusation F शिकायत *[śikāyat]*
grieve V.T. शोक मनाना *[śok manānā]*
grin (smile) V.I. मुस्कराना *[muskarānā]*
grind V.T. पीसना *[pīsnā]*
grip F पकड़ *[pakaṛ]*
groan V.I. कराहना *[karāhnā]*
grocery M परचून *[parcūn]*
grope; probe; sound; reconnoiter V.T. टटोलना *[ṭaṭolnā]*
gross ADJ स्थूल *[sthūl]*
ground F ज़मीन *[zamīn]*, भूमि *[bhūmi]*
group M दल *[dal]*
grow V.I. उगना *[ugnā]*, बढ़ना *[baṛhnā]* V.T. बढ़ाना *[baṛhānā]*
grow a beard V.T. दाढ़ी रखना *[dāṛhī rakhnā]*
grow up V.I. बड़ा होना *[baṛā honā]*

growth (development) M विकास *[vikās]*
grumble V.T. बड़बड़ाना *[baṛbaṛānā]*
guarantee F गारंटी *[gāranṭī]*
guard V.T. रक्षा करना *[rakṣā karnā]*
guardian M अभिभावक *[abhibhāvak]*
guess M अनुमान *[anumān]*
guest M अतिथि *[atithi]*, मेहमान *[mehmān]*
guidance M मार्गदर्शन *[mārgdarśan]*
guide V.T. मार्गदर्शन करना *[mārgdarśan karnā]*
guide M गाइड *[gāiḍ]*
guilt M गुनाह *[gunāh]*
guilty ADJ गुनहगार *[gunahgār]*
gulp V.I. निगलना *[nigalnā]*
gun F बंदूक़ *[bandūq]*
Gurdwara (Sikh temple) M गुरुद्वारा *[gurudvārā]*
gust (of wind) M झोंका *[jhõkā]*
gusto, zeal F उमंग *[umaṅg]*
gut (stomach) M पेट *[peṭ]*
guy M आदमी *[ādmī]*

H

habit F आदत *[ādat]*
habituated ADJ आदी *[ādī]*
hair; young one M, F बाल *[bāl]*
half ADJ आधा *[ādhā]*
hall M हॉल *[hāl]*
halt V.I. ठहरना *[ṭheharnā]*
hand M हाथ *[hāth]*
hand over V.T. सौंपना *[saũpnā]*
handkerchief M रूमाल *[rūmāl]*
handle (steady) V.T. संभालना *[sambhālnā]*
handsome ADJ सुंदर *[sundar]*
hang V.I. लटकना *[laṭaknā]* V.T. लटकाना *[laṭkānā]*; टाँगना *[ṭã̄gnā]*
happen V.I. होना *[honā]*
happiness F ख़ुशी *[khuśī]* M सुख *[sukh]*
happily ADV सुख से *[sukh se]*
happy ADJ ख़ुश *[khuś]*; सुखी *[sukhī]*: (x) to be happy, happiness to occur (to x) V.I. (x को) ख़ुशी होना *[(x ko) khuśī honā]*
harass V.T. सताना *[satānā]*
hard ADJ सख़्त *[sakht]*
hard (difficult) ADJ मुश्किल *[muśkil]*
hard work F मेहनत *[mehnat]*

hardness F सख़्ती *[sakhtī]*
hardworking ADJ मेहनती *[mehnatī]*
harm M हर्ज *[harj]*
harsh ADJ सख़्त *[sakht]*
harshness, stiffness, rigorousness F सख़्ती *[sakhtī]*
harvest (crop) F फ़सल *[fasal]*
hat F टोपी *[ṭopī]*
hatred F नफ़रत *[nafrat]*
haul (carry) V.T. ढोना *[ḍhonā]*
have access, enter, penetrate V.I. पैठना *[paiṭhnā]*
hawker, street vendor ADJ फेरीवाला *[pherīvālā]*
hay F सूखी घास *[sūkhī ghās]*
hazard M संकट *[saṅkaṭ]*
hazy ADJ धुँधला *[dhũdhlā]*
he/she/that/it (far from the speaker) PRO वह *[vah (vo)]*
he/she/this/it (close to the speaker) PRO यह *[yeh]*
head M सिर *[sir]*
headache M सरदर्द *[sardard]*
headline (newspaper) M शीर्षक *[śīrṣak]*
heal V.T. इलाज करना *[ilāj karnā]*
health, state of physical and mental wellbeing F तबियत (तबीयत) *[tabiyat/tabīyat]*
healthy ADJ तंदुरुस्त *[tandurust]*
hear V.T. सुनना *[sunnā]*
heart M दिल *[dil]*; मन *[man]*
heat F गरमी/गर्मी *[garmī]* V.T. तापना *[tāpnā]*
heated V.I. तपना *[tapnā]* ADJ गरमागरम *[garmāgarm]*
heaven M स्वर्ग *[svarg]*
heavy ADJ भारी *[bhārī]*
heel F एड़ी *[eṛī]*
height F लंबाई *[lambāī]*
height; altitude, elevation; loftiness F ऊँचाई *[ũcāī]*
height M क़द *[qad]*
hell M नरक *[narak]*
hello and goodbye M नमस्कार *[namaskār]*; नमस्ते *[namaste]*
help F मदद *[madad]*
help (x) V.T. (x की) मदद करना *[(x kī) madad karnā]*
helpful (helper) ADJ मददगार *[madadgār]*
helpless ADJ मजबूर *[majbūr]*
helplessness F मजबूरी *[majbūrī]*
hemp (*Cannabis sativa*) F भाँग *[bhā̃g]*

hemp plant or its leaves M गाँजा *[gā̃jā]*
hence CONJ इसलिये *[isliye]*
her POSS ADJ इसका, उसका, इनका, उनका *[iskā, uskā, inkā, unkā]*
her PRO इसे/इसको, उसे/उसको, इन्हें/इनको, उन्हें/उनको *[ise/isko, use/usko, inhẽ/inko, unhẽ/unko]*
herb F जड़ी-बूटी *[jaṛī-būṭī]*
here ADV यहाँ *[yahā̃]*
hereditary, ancestral ADJ पुश्तैनी *[puśtainī]*
heritage F विरासत *[virāsat]*
hero M नायक *[nāyak]*
hesitate V.I. ठिठकना *[ṭhiṭhaknā]*; हिचकिचाना *[hickicānā]*
hesitate; feel shy V.I. झिझकना *[jhijhaknā]*
hesitation M संकोच *[saṅkoc]*
hey! M VOC अरे *[are]*
hiccup F हिचकी *[hickī]*
hide V.I. छिपना *[chipnā]* V.T. छिपाना *[chipānā]*
hide (skin) F खाल *[khāl]*
high ADJ ऊँचा *[ū̃cā]*; बुलंद *[buland]*
him PRO इसे/इसको, उसे/उसको, इन्हें/इनको, उन्हें/उनको *[ise/isko, use/usko, inhẽ/inko, unhẽ/unko]*
Himalayas M हिमालय *[himālaya]*
Hindi (language) F हिंदी/हिन्दी *[hindī]*
Hindi script F देवनागरी *[devanāgarī]*
Hindu priest M पुरोहित *[purohit]*
hint M संकेत *[saṅket]*
hip (waist) F कमर *[kamar]*
hire (rent) V.T. किराये पर लेना *[kirāye par lenā]*
his ADJ इसका, उसका, इनका, उनका *[iskā, uskā, inkā, unkā]*
historian M इतिहासकार *[itihāskār]*
historic ADJ ऐतिहासिक *[aitihāsik]*
history M इतिहास *[itihās]*
hit (stroke) M प्रहार *[prahār]*
hobby M शौक़ *[śauq]*
hold V.T. थामना *[thāmnā]*
holiday F छुट्टी *[chuṭṭī]*
hollow ADJ खोखला *[khokhlā]*
holy ADJ पवित्र *[pavitra]*
home M घर *[ghar]*; निवास *[nivās]*

homeland, native country M वतन *[vatan]*
homeless ADJ बेघर *[beghar]*
homework M गृहकार्य *[gṛhkārya]*
honest; faithful; having integrity ADJ ईमानदार *[īmāndār]*
honesty, faithfulness, integrity F ईमानदारी *[īmāndārī]*
honey M शहद *[śahad]*
honor M आदर *[ādar]*
hop V.I. उछलना *[uchalnā]*
hope F आशा *[āśā]*; उम्मीद *[ummīd]*
hopeless ADJ नाउम्मीद *[nāummīd]*; हताश *[hatāś]*
horizon M क्षितिज *[kṣitij]*
horn M हॉर्न *[hārn]*
horrible, dangerous ADJ भयंकर *[bhayaṅkar]*
horror (fear) M भय *[bhay]*
horse M घोड़ा *[ghoṛā]*
hospital M अस्पताल *[aspatāl]*
hospitality M आतिथ्य *[ātithya]*
host M मेज़बान *[mezbān]*
host V.T. मेहमाननवाज़ी करना *[mehmānnavāzī karnā]*
hostile ADJ विरोधी *[virodhī]*
hot ADJ गरम/गर्म *[garam]*; गरमागरम *[garmāgarm]*
hotel M होटल *[hoṭal]*
hour M घंटा *[ghaṇṭā]*
house M मकान *[makān]*
household (family) M परिवार *[parivār]*
how ADJ कैसा *[kaisā]*; कैसे *[kaise]*
how much/many ADJ कितना *[kitnā]*
hug (embrace) V.T. आलिंगन करना *[āliṅgan karnā]*
huge, large, big ADJ विशाल *[vishāl]*
hum; sing to oneself in subdued tones V.I. गुनगुनाना *[gungunānā]*
human being M इंसान *[insān]*
humanity; human qualities F इंसानियत *[insāniyat]*
humble ADJ विनम्र *[vinamra]*
humidity F उमस *[umas]*
humor M हास्य *[hāsya]*
hundred ADJ, M सौ *[sau]*
hunger F भूख *[bhūkh]*
hungry, craving ADJ भूखा *[bhūkhā]*
hunt V.T. शिकार खेलना *[śikār khelnā]*
hunter M शिकारी *[śikārī]*

hurricane M तूफ़ान *[tūfān]*
hurry V.T. जल्दी करना *[jaldī karnā]*
hurt ADJ घायल *[ghāyal]*
husband M पति *[pati]*

I

I PRO मैं *[maĩ]*
ice F बर्फ़ *[barf]*
idea M ख़्याल/ख़याल *[khyāl/ khayāl]*; विचार *[vicār]*
ideal M, ADJ आदर्श *[ādarś]*
identification F पहचान *[pehcān]*
identify V.T. पहचानना *[pehcannā]*
identity F पहचान *[pehcān]*
ideology F विचारधारा *[vicārdhārā]*
idiom M मुहावरा *[muhāvrā]*
idiot ADJ बेवक़ूफ़ *[bevaqūf]*
idiot, fool M उल्लू *[ullū]*:
an absolute idiot M उल्लू का पट्ठा *[ullū kā paṭṭhā]*
idle, stupid ADJ बेकार *[bekār]*
idol F मूर्ति *[mūrti]*
ie ADV अर्थात् *[arthāt]*; यानी *[yānī]*
if CONJ अगर *[agar]*
ignorance M अज्ञान *[ajñān]*
ill ADJ बीमार *[bīmār]*
ill-fated (person) ADJ कमबख़्त *[kambakht]*
ill-luck F कमबख़्ती *[kambakhtī]*
illegal ADJ ग़ैर क़ानूनी *[ghair-qānūnī]*
illiterate; unlettered ADJ अनपढ़ *[anpaṛh]*
illness F बीमारी *[bīmārī]*
illumination; eye-sight F रोशनी *[rośnī]*
illusion F माया *[māyā]*
image M चित्र *[citra]*
imagination F कल्पना *[kalpnā]*
imagine V.T. कल्पना करना *[kalpnā karnā]*
immediately, instantly, at once ADV फ़ौरन *[fauran]*
immerse, drown V.T. डुबाना *[ḍubānā]*
immigrant M आप्रवासी *[āpravāsī]*
immigration M आप्रवासन *[āpravāsan]*
immortal, eternal ADJ अमर *[amar]*
impact M प्रभाव *[prabhāv]*
imply V.T. संकेत करना *[saṅket karnā]*

import (meaning) M आशय *[āśay]*
importance M महत्त्व *[mahattva]*
important ADJ महत्त्वपूर्ण *[mahattvapūrṇ]*
impose, thrust upon, implant; plaster V.T. थोपना *[thopnā]*
impossible ADJ असंभव *[asambhav]*
impress V.T. प्रभावित करना *[prabhāvit karnā]*
impression M प्रभाव *[prabhāv]*
impressive (influential) ADJ प्रभावशाली *[prabhāvśālī]*
imprint; stamp M छापा *[chāpā]*
imprisonment F क़ैद *[qaid]*
improper ADJ अनुचित *[anucit]*
improve V.T. सुधारना *[sudhārnā]*
improvement M सुधार *[sudhār]*
impure; desecrated, profane ADJ अपवित्र *[apa-vitra]*
in PP में *[mẽ]*
in front ADV सामने *[sāmne]*
in front of (x) PP (x) के सामने *[(x) ke sāmne]*
in place of (x) PP (x) की जगह *[(x) kī jagah]*
in reality ADV असल में *[asal mẽ]*
in the direction of (x) PP (x) की ओर *[(x) kī or]*
in this way, in this manner ADV, ADJ ऐसे *[aise]*
in what manner ADV कैसे *[kaise]*
incarnation M अवतार *[avatār]*
incense, incense stick F अगरबत्ती *[agarbattī]*
incessantly ADV, ADJ लगातार *[lagātār]*
incident F घटना *[ghaṭnā]*
include V.T. शामिल करना *[śāmil karnā]*
included ADJ शामिल *[śāmil]*
income; revenue F आमदनी *[āmdanī]*
incomplete ADJ अधूरा *[adhūrā]*
incorrect; untrue; erroneous ADJ ग़लत *[ghalat]*
increase (something) V.T. बढ़ाना *[baṛhānā]*
indeed ADV अवश्य *[avaśya]*
independence F आज़ादी *[āzādī]*

independent ADJ आज़ाद *[āzād]*
India M भारत *[bhārat]*; हिंद *[hind]*; हिंदस्तान/हिन्दुस्तान *[hindustān]*; इंडिया *[iṇḍiyā]*
Indian ADJ भारतीय *[bhāratīya]*; हिंदस्तानी/हिन्दुस्तानी *[hindustānī]*
indicate, signal, make a sign V.T. इशारा करना *[iśārā karnā]*
indication M संकेत *[saṅket]*
indigenous ADJ देसी *[desī]*
individual M व्यक्ति *[vyakti]*
individuality M व्यक्तित्व *[vyaktitva]*
indolent; lazy, idle; depressed ADJ सुस्त *[sust]*
industrial ADJ औद्योगिक *[audyogik]*
industrialization M उद्योगीकरण *[udyogīkaraṇ]*
industrious ADJ मेहनती *[mehnatī]*
industry; labor. effort M उद्योग *[udyog]*
infant M शिशु *[śiśu]*
infection M संक्रमण *[saṅkramaṇ]*
influence M प्रभाव *[prabhāv]*
influence V.T. प्रभावित करना *[prabhāvit karnā]*
influential; effective; dominant, predominant ADJ प्रभावशाली *[prabhāvśālī]*
inform V.T. सूचित करना *[sūcit karnā]*
informal ADJ अनौपचारिक *[anaupcārik]*
information F सूचना *[sūcnā]*
inhabit V.I. बसना *[basnā]*
inheritance F विरासत *[virāsat]*
initial ADJ प्रारंभिक *[prārambhik]*
initiative F पहल *[pehal]*
injured ADJ घायल *[ghāyal]*
injury F चोट *[coṭ]*
injustice F नाइंसाफ़ी *[nāinsāfī]*
inkling M आभास *[ābhās]*
innocent ADJ मासूम *[māsūm]*; निर्दोष *[nirdoṣ]*
innovation M प्रवर्त्तन *[pravarttan]*
inquiry F पूछताछ *[pūchtāch]*
insane ADJ दीवाना *[dīvānā]*
insect M कीड़ा *[kīṛā]*: a small insect M मकोड़ा *[makoṛā]*
inside ADV अंदर *[andar]*
inspection M निरीक्षण *[nirīkṣaṇ]*

inspector M निरीक्षक *[nirīkṣak]*
inspiration, urge, motive F प्रेरणा *[prerṇā]*
installation F स्थापना *[sthāpnā]*
instance (example) M उदाहरण *[udāharaṇ]*
instant M क्षण *[kṣaṇ]*
instantly ADV तुरंत *[turant]*
instead of, in place of, in lieu of IND बजाय *[bajāy]*
institution F संस्था *[sansthā]*
instruct V.T. सिखाना *[sikhānā]*
instructor M शिक्षक *[śikṣak]*
instrument M यंत्र *[yantra]*
instrument (musical) M बाजा *[bājā]*
insult M अपमान *[apamān]*
insult, disgrace, humilate V.T. इज़्ज़त उतारना/बिगाड़ना/लेना *[izzat utārnā/bigāṛnā/lenā]*
insurance M बीमा *[bīmā]*
integrity F अखंडता *[akhaṇḍatā]*
intellect, wits F अक्ल *[aql]*
intellectual ADJ बुद्धिजीवी *[buddhijīvī]*
intelligence F बुद्धि *[buddhi]*
intelligent ADJ अक्लमंद *[aqlmand]*; होशियार *[hośiyār]*
intense ADJ तीव्र *[tīvra]*
intensity F तीव्रता *[tīvratā]*
intention M इरादा *[irādā]*
interest F रुचि *[ruci]*; दिलचस्पी *[dilcaspī]*: (x) to have the interest/hobby (of y) V.I. (x को) (y का) शौक़ होना *[(x ko) (y kā) śauq honā]*
interesting ADJ दिलचस्प *[dilcasp]*
interfere V.T. दख़ल देना *[dakhal denā]*
interior M अन्तर *[antar]*
international ADJ अंतर्राष्ट्रीय *[antarrāṣṭrīya]*
Internet M इंटरनेट *[iṇṭarnet]*
interpretation (explanation) F व्याख्या *[vyākhyā]*
interrupt V.T. टोकना *[ṭoknā]*
interval M अन्तराल *[antarāl]*
interview M साक्षात्कार *[sākṣātkār]*
intimidate V.T. धमकी देना *[dhamkī denā]*
intoxicated; carefree ADJ मस्त *[mast]*
intoxicating drug prepared from the flowers of hemp M चरस *[caras]*

intoxication M नशा *[naśā]*
intricate, complicated; inaccessible ADJ जटिल *[jaṭil]*
introduce V.T. परिचय कराना *[paricāy karānā]*
introduction M परिचय *[paricay]* F भूमिका *[bhūmikā]*
invasion M अतिक्रमण *[atikramaṇ]*
invent V.T. आविष्कार करना *[āviṣkār karnā]*, ईजाद करना *[ījād karnā]*
invention M आविष्कार *[āviṣkār]*
invest V.T. निवेश करना *[niveś karnā]*
investigate, test (x) V.T. (x की) जाँच करना *[(x kī) jā̃c karnā]*
investigate, verify, test V.T. जाँचना *[jā̃cnā]*
investigation, examination, test F जाँच *[jā̃c]*
investment (M) निवेश *[niveś]*
invisible ADJ अंतर्धान *[antardhān]*
invitation M निमंत्रण *[nimantraṇ]*
invite V.T. बुलाना *[bulānā]*
involve (include) V.T. शामिल करना *[śāmil karnā]*
involved V.I. उलझना *[ulajhnā]*
involvement (partnership) F भागीदारी *[bhāgīdārī]*
Iran M इरान *[irān]*
Irani ADJ इरानी *[irānī]*
Iraq M इराक़ *[irāq]*
Iraqi ADJ इराक़ी *[irāqī]*
iron M लोहा *[lohā]*
iron; press F इस्तिरी *[isitrī]*
iron V.T. इस्तिरी करना *[istirī karnā]*
irrigate V.T. सींचना *[sĩcnā]*
irritate; meddle (in); disturb V.T. छेड़ना *[cheṛnā]*
irritated V.I. चिढ़ना *[ciṛhnā]*
irritated/petulant/peeved V.I. झुँझलाना *[jhũjhlānā]*
irritation; strong aversion F चिढ़ *[ciṛh]*
is/are V.I., PL हैं *[haĩ]*; V.I., SING है *[hai]*
Islam M इसलाम *[islām]*
Islamic ADJ इसलामी *[islāmī]*
island M टापू *[ṭāpū]*
isolate ADJ अलग-थलग *[alag-thalag]*
issue V.T. जारी करना *[jārī karnā]*
issue M मामला *[māmlā]*

issue a citation V.T. चालान काटना *[cālān kāṭnā]*
issue a sharp rebuke V.T. डपटना *[ḍapaṭnā]*
it PRO यह/वह *[yeh/voh]*
itch F खुजली *[khujlī]* V.T. खुजलाना *[khujlānā]*
item (thing) F चीज़ *[cīz]*
its ADJ इसका/उसका *[iskā/ uskā]*

J

jackel M गीदड़ *[gīdaṛ]*
jacket F जाकेट *[jāket]*
jail, prison F जेल *[jel]*
Jain, follower of Jainism M जैन *[jain]*
January (month) F जनवरी *[janvarī]*
Japan M जापान *[jāpān]*
Japanese ADJ जापानी *[jāpānī]*
jar M जार *[jār]*
jaw M जबड़ा *[jabṛā]*
jealousy F जलन *[jalan]*
jerk off V.T. झटकना *[jhaṭaknā]*
jerk violently V.T. झँझोड़ना *[jhā̃jhoṛnā]*
jet (stream) F धार *[dhār]*
jewelry M गहना *[gehnā]*
jingle, tinkle V.I. छनकना *[chanaknā]*
job M कार्य *[kārya]*
join V.T. जोड़ना *[joṛnā]*
joint M जोड़ *[joṛ]*
joke M मज़ाक़ *[mazāq]*
jolt M झटका *[jhaṭkā]*
journal F पत्रिका *[patrikā]*
journalism F पत्रकारिता *[patrakāritā]*
journalist M पत्रकार *[patrakār]*
journey F यात्रा *[yātrā]*
joy M हर्ष *[harṣ]*
judge M जज *[jaj]*
judgment (decision) M निर्णय *[nirṇay]*
juice M रस *[ras]*
juiceless, dry; flat; insipid ADJ नीरस *[nīras]*
July (month) F जुलाई *[julāī]*
jump F छलाँग *[chalā̃g]*
jump; skip V.I. कूदना *[kūdnā]*
jump across V.I. फाँदना *[phā̃dnā]*
June (month) M जून *[jūn]*
jungle M जंगल *[jaṅgal]*
junior ADJ कनिष्ठ *[kaniṣṭh]*
just ADV सिर्फ़ *[sirf]*
justice, justness M इंसाफ़ *[insāf]*

K

keep V.T. रखना *[rakhnā]*
keep an eye on V.T. निगाह रखना *[nigāh rakhnā]*
keep in mind V.T. याद रखना *[yād rakhnā]*
keep watch/guard V.T. निगरानी रखना *[nigrānī rakhnā]*
kettle F केतली *[ketlī]*
key (for a lock or textbook) F कुंजी *[kuñjī]*
key F चाबी *[cābī]*
kick F लात *[lāt]*
kick off; knock away V.T. ठुकराना *[ṭhukrānā]*
kid (child) M बच्चा *[bacca]*
kidnapping M अपहरण *[apaharaṇ]*
kill V.T. मारना *[mārnā]*
killer M हत्यारा *[hatyārā]*
kilogram M किलोग्राम *[kilogrām]*
kilometer M किलोमीटर *[kilomīṭar]*
kind F तरह *[tarah]*
kind (merciful) ADJ दयालु *[dayālu]*
kindness F मेहरबानी *[meharbānī]*
king M राजा *[rājā]*
kingdom M राज्य *[rājya]*
kiss (lip) V.T. चूमना *[cūmnā]*
kissing M चुंबन *[cumbam]*
kit (bag) M झोला *[jholā]*
kitchen F रसोई *[rasoī]*
knead V.T. गूँधना *[gū̃dhnā]*
knee M घुटना *[ghuṭnā]*
knife M चाकू *[cāqū]*
knit, intertwine V.T. बुनना *[bunnā]*
knock (on a door) V.T. खटखटाना *[khaṭkhaṭānā]*
knot F गाँठ *[gā̃ṭh]*
know, perceive V.T. जानना *[jānnā]*: (x) to know, find out V.I. (x को) पता होना *[(x ko) patā honā]*
knowledge F जानकारी *[jānkārī]*
knowledgeable, well-informed; having attained self-realization ADJ ज्ञानी *[jñānī]*
known ADJ मालूम *[mālūm]*: to be known (to x) V.I. (x को) मालूम होना *[(x ko) mālūm honā]*

L

labor M श्रम *[śram]*
laboratory F प्रयोगशाला *[prayogśālā]*
laborer M मज़दूर *[mazdūr]*
lace M फ़ीता *[fītā]*
lack M अभाव *[abhāv]*
ladder F सीढ़ी *[sīṛhī]*
laddu, an Indian sweet M लड्डू *[laḍḍū]*
lady F महिला *[mahilā]*
lag, be left behind, be defeated V.I. पिछड़ना *[picharṇā]*
lake F झील *[jhīl]*
lame ADJ लँगड़ा *[lãgrā]*
lamp, earthen lamp M दिया *[diyā]*
lamp; a light M चिराग़ *[cirāgh]*
land F ज़मीन *[zamīn]*; धरती *[dhartī]*
lane (alley) F गली *[galī]*
language F ज़बान *[zabān]*; भाषा *[bhāṣā]*
lap F गोद *[god]*
large (expansive) ADJ विशाल *[viśāl]*
lassi, a yogurt drink served cold with ice and sugar F लस्सी *[lassī]*
last, final ADJ अंतिम *[antim]*
lasting, durable; firm ADJ मज़बूत *[mazbūt]*
late ADV देर से *[der se]*: **(x) to be late** V.I. (x को) देर होना *[(x ko) der honā]*
lately (recently) ADV हाल में *[hāl mẽ]*
later ADV बाद में *[bād mẽ]*
latrine M पाख़ाना *[pākhānā]*
laugh V.I. हँसना *[hãsnā]*
laughter F हँसी *[hãsī]*
law M क़ानून *[qānūn]*
lawmaker (legislator) M विधायक *[vidhāyak]*
lawyer M वकील *[vakīl]*
lay V.T. लिटाना *[liṭānā]*
layer F तह *[teh]*
laziness; slothfulness; lethargy M आलस *[ālas]*
lazy, lethargic ADJ आलसी *[ālsī]*
leader M नेता *[netā]*
leaf M पत्ता *[pattā]*
leak V.T. रिसना *[risnā]* V.I. टपकना *[ṭapaknā]*
lean V.T. टेकना *[ṭeknā]*
lean ADJ दुबला *[dublā]*
leap V.T. छलाँग लगाना/मारना *[chalãg lagānā/mārnā]*
leap, jump V.I. उछलना *[uchalnā]*

learn V.T. सीखना *[sīkhnā]*
learning F शिक्षा *[śikṣā]*
lease, lease deed M पट्टा *[paṭṭā]*
least ADJ कम से कम *[kam se kam]*
leather M चमड़ा *[camṛā]*
leave (abandon) V.T. छोड़ना *[choṛnā]*
leave (depart) V.T. प्रस्थान करना *[prasthān karnā]*
lecture M भाषण *[bhāṣaṇ]*
left ADJ बायाँ *[bāyā̃]*
left (remaining) ADJ बचा हुआ *[bacā huā]*
leg F टाँग *[ṭā̃g]*
legal, lawful ADJ क़ानूनी *[qānūnī]*
legally ADV क़ानूनन *[qānūnan]*
legislation M विधान *[vidhān]*
legislator M विधायक *[vidhāyak]*
legislature F विधान सभा *[vidhān sabhā]*
lemon M नीबू *[nībū]*
lend V.T. उधार देना *[udhār denā]*
length F लम्बाई *[lambāī]*
less, too little ADJ कम *[kam]*
lesson M सबक़ *[sabaq]*
let (rent) V.T. किराये पर देना *[kirāye par denā]*
letter F चिट्ठी *[ciṭṭhī]*
letter (of the alphabet) M अक्षर *[akṣar]*
letter of application M निवेदनपत्र *[nivedanpatra]*
liberal; magnificent ADJ उदार *[udār]*
liberated; get rid of, be free; be salvaged V.I. उबरना *[ubarnā]*
liberation; release; freedom F मुक्ति *[mukti]*
liberty (independence) F स्वतंत्रता *[svatantratā]*
library M पुस्तकालय *[pustakālay]*
lick V.T. चाटना *[cāṭnā]*
lid M ढक्कन *[ḍhakkan]*
lie M झूठ *[jhūṭh]* V.I. झूठ बोलना *[jhūṭh bolnā]*
lie (down) V.I. लेटना *[leṭnā]*
life F ज़िंदगी *[zindagī]* M जीवन *[jīvan]*
life, stamina F जान *[jān]*
lifestyle F जीवनशैली *[jīvanśailī]*
lift V.T. उठाना *[uṭhānā]*
light F रोशनी *[rośnī]*
light (shed light) V.T. प्रकाश डालना *[prakāś ḍālnā]*

light (not heavy) ADJ हल्का *[halkā]*
lightning F बिजली *[bijlī]*
like REL ADJ जैसा *[jaisā]*: **(x) to like** V.I. (x को) अच्छा लगना *[(x ko) acchā lagnā]*
like (x) PP (x) की तरह *[(x) kī tarah]*
like, similar to, resembling (a suffix) ADJ सा *[sā]*
liked ADJ, F पसंद *[pasand]*
likelihood (possibility) F संभावना *[sambhāvnā]*
likely (possible) ADJ संभव *[sambhav]*
liking, choice, taste, preference ADJ, F पसंद *[pasand]*
limb; a member M अंग *[aṅg]*
limit F सीमा *[sīmā]*
limit V.T. सीमित करना *[sīmit karnā]*
line F पंक्ति *[paṅkti]*; रेखा *[rekhā]*
link (chain) F कड़ी *[kaṛī]*
link, unite; collect, accumulate V.T. जोड़ना *[joṛnā]*
lion M शेर *[śer]*
lip M होंठ *[hõṭh]*
liquid M द्रव *[drav]*
liquor; medical treatment F दारू *[dārū]*
list F सूची *[sūcī]*
listen V.T. सुनना *[sunnā]*
literary ADJ साहित्यिक *[sāhityik]*
literature M साहित्य *[sāhitya]*
little ADJ छोटा *[choṭā]*
little, some ADJ थोड़ा *[thoṛā]*
live V.I. रहना *[rehnā]*
live, be alive V.I. जीना *[jīnā]*
live ADJ जीवित *[jīvit]*
liver M कलेजा *[kalejā]*
living, ways M रहन-सहन *[rehan-sehan]*
load (burden) M बोझ *[bojh]*
load V.T. लादना *[lādnā]*
loafer ADJ, M लफ़ंगा *[lafaṅgā]*
loan M कर्ज़ *[karz]*
local ADJ स्थानीय *[sthānīya]*
locality, territory M इलाक़ा *[ilāqā]*
location (place) M स्थान *[sthān]*
lock M ताला *[tālā]*
lock V.T. ताला लगाना *[tālā lagānā]*
logic M तर्क *[tark]*
loneliness, solitude F तनहाई *[tanhāī]*
lonely, solitary ADJ तनहा *[tanhā]*

long ADJ लंबा *[lambā]*
long (yearn) V.I. तड़पना *[taṛapnā]*
look (see) V.T. देखना *[dekhnā]*
loose ADJ ढीला *[ḍhīlā]*
lord M ठाकुर *[ṭhākur]*
Lord (God) M भगवान् *[bhagvān]*
lose v.i., v.t. खोना *[khonā]*
lose; be wearied V.I. हारना *[hārnā]*
lose hope V.I. आशा टूटना *[āśā ṭūṭnā]*
lose one's way V.I. भटकना *[bhaṭaknā]*
loss M नुक़सान *[nuqsān]* F हार *[hār]*
lots ADJ बहुत *[bahut]*
loud (high) ADJ ऊँचा *[ū̃cā]*
love M प्यार *[pyār]*
lovely, pleasing, liked; lover, husband ADJ, M प्रिय *[priya]*
lover M यार *[yār]*
low ADV नीचे *[nīce]* ADJ नीचा *[nīcā]*
lower (reduce) V.T. कम करना *[kam karnā]*
loyal ADJ वफ़ादार *[vafādār]*
loyalty F वफ़ा *[vafā]*
luck M भाग्य *[bhāgya]*
lucky ADJ भाग्यशाली *[bhāgyaśālī]*
luggage, stuff M सामान *[sāmān]*
lukewarm ADJ गुनगुना *[gungunā]*
lunch M दिन का खाना *[din kā khānā]*
lung M फेफड़ा *[phephṛā]*

M

machine F मशीन *[maśīn]*
mad ADJ पागल *[pāgal]*
madness F दीवानगी *[dīvāngī]*
magazine F पत्रिका *[patrikā]*
magic, charm M जादू *[jādū]*
magnet M चुम्बक *[cumbak]*
mail F डाक *[ḍāk]*
main ADJ मुख्य *[mukhya]*
mainstream F मुख्यधारा *[mukhyadhārā]*
maintain; take care of V.T. संभालना *[sambhālnā]*
maintenance (caretaking) F देख-भाल *[dekh-bhāl]*
major ADJ प्रमुख *[pramukh]*
majority ADJ बहुसंख्यक *[bahusaṅkhyak]*
make V.T. बनाना *[banānā]*

make (something) fall V.T. गिराना *[girānā]*
make (something or someone) move V.T. चलाना *[calānā]*
make a guess V.T. अटकल लगाना *[aṭkal lagānā]*
make a note or comment V.T. टिप्पणी करना *[ṭippaṇī karnā]*
make a sacrifice V.T. क़ुर्बानी देना *[qurbānī denā]*
make a sudden swoop V.I. झपटना *[jhapaṭnā]*
make a wry face; look displeased; sour V.T. मुँह बनाना *[mũh banānā]*
make an allegation V.T. आरोप लगाना *[ārop lagānā]*
make an announcement V.T. एलान करना *[elān karnā]*
make an excuse V.T. बहाना बनाना *[bahānā banānā]*
make chutney; thoroughly beat up V.T. चटनी बनाना *[caṭnī banānā]*
make disappear V.T. ग़ायब करना *[g͟hāyab karnā]*
make ends meet; get by V.T. गुज़ारा करना *[guzārā karnā]*
make flow V.T. बहाना *[bahānā]*
make fly; squander; steal or kidnap; explode; blow away V.T. उड़ाना *[uṛānā]*
make revolve; make wander; take around V.T. घुमाना *[ghumānā]*
make someone lie down V.T. लिटाना *[liṭānā]*
maker (creator) M विधाता *[vidhātā]*
makeup (beautification) M शृंगार *[śṛṅgār]*
male M पुरुष *[puruṣ]*
man M आदमी *[ādmī]*; मर्द *[mard]*
manage V.T. प्रबंध करना *[prabandh karnā]*
manage, make do with V.T. काम चलाना *[kām calānā]*
management M प्रबंध *[prabandh]*
manager M प्रबंधक *[prabandhak]*
mandarin M संतरा *[santarā]*
mango M आम *[ām]*
manifest, reveal V.T. प्रकट करना *[prakaṭ karnā]*
manner M ढंग *[ḍhaṅg]*
manner, technique M तरीक़ा *[tarīqā]*

mansion F हवेली *[havelī]*
manual (guide) F पुस्तिका *[pustikā]*
manufacturer (maker) M निर्माता *[nirmātā]*
manufacturing M निर्माण *[nirmāṇ]*
many ADJ बहुत *[bahut]*
map M नक़्शा *[naqśā]*
marble M संगमरमर *[saṅgmarmar]*
March (month) M मार्च *[mārc]*
margin (border) M किनारा *[kinārā]*
mark; landmark; scar; impression; trace; clue M निशान *[niśān]*
market M बाज़ार *[bāzār]*
marketplace M बाज़ार *[bāzār]*
marriage F शादी *[śādī]*
marriage party F बरात *[barāt]*
married ADJ शादीशुदा *[śādīśudā]*
marry (x) V.T. (x से) शादी करना *[(x se) śādī karnā]*
martial ADJ फ़ौजी *[faujī]*
mask M मुखौटा *[mukhauṭā]*
mass (amount) F राशि *[rāśi]*
massage V.T. मालिश करना *[māliś karnā]*
master M उस्ताद *[ustād]*
master, employer M मालिक *[mālik]*
match M खेल *[khel]*; मैच *[maic]*
mate M दोस्त *[dost]*
maternal grandfather M नाना *[nānā]*
maternal grandmother F नानी *[nānī]*
maternal grandparents M नाना-नानी *[nānā-nānī]*
maternal uncle M मामा *[māmā]*
mathematics M गणित *[gaṇit]*
matter M द्रव्य *[dravya]* F बात *[bāt]*
May (month) F मई *[maī]*
maybe (perhaps) CONJ शायद *[śāyad]*
me PRO मुझे/मुझको *[mujhe/mujhko]*
meal M भोजन *[bhojan]*; खाना *[khānā]*
mean ADJ क्रूर *[krūr]*
mean (average) F औसत *[ausat]*
meaning M मतलब *[matlab]*
meaning; import, sense; wealth, money M अर्थ *[arth]*

means, medium, instrument M ज़रीया *[zarīyā]*
means; equipment M साधन *[sādhan]*
meanwhile CONJ इतने में *[itne mẽ]*
measure V.T. नापना *[nāpnā]*
measurement F नाप *[nāp]*
meat M मांस *[māns]*
mechanic M मिस्तरी *[mistarī]*
mechanical ADJ मशीनी *[maśīnī]*
medal M पदक *[padak]*
media M मीडिया *[mīḍiyā]*
medication (treatment) M इलाज *[ilāj]*
medicine F दवा *[davā]*
meditation M ध्यान *[dhyān]*
medium M माध्यम *[mādhyam]*
medium; middle ADJ मध्यम *[madhyam]*
meet V.I. मिलना *[milnā]*: (y) to meet (with x), (y's) meeting to take place (with x) V.I. (x से) (y की) मुलाक़ात होना *[(x se) (y kī) mulāqāt honā]*
meeting M मिलन *[milan]* F मुलाक़ात *[mulāqāt]*
melody F लय *[lay]*
melt V.I. पिघलना *[pighalnā]*; गलना *[galnā]*
member M सदस्य *[sadasya]*
membership F सदस्यता *[sadasyatā]*
memorize V.T. रटना *[raṭnā]*
memory F याद *[yād]*
menstruation F माहवारी *[māhvārī]*
mental ADJ मानसिक *[mānsik]*
mention, make reference to (x) V.T. (x का) ज़िक्र करना *[(x kā) zikra karnā]*
mentor M, ADJ गुरु *[guru]*
menu M मेन्यू-कार्ड *[menyū-kārḍ]*
merchant M सौदागर *[saudāgar]*
mercy F दया *[dayā]*
mere ADJ मात्र *[mātra]*
merely ADJ महज़ *[mehaz]*
mess F गड़बड़ *[gaṛbaṛ]*
message M संदेश *[sandeś]*
metal F धातु *[dhātu]*
metaphor M रूपक *[rūpak]*
method M तरीक़ा *[tarīqā]*
midday F दोपहर *[dopahar]*
middle M मध्य *[madhya]*
middle class M मध्यवर्ग *[madhyavarg]*
might F शक्ति *[śakti]*

mild ADJ नरम *[naram]*
military F सेना *[senā]*
milk M दूध *[dūdh]*
million ADJ दस लाख *[das lākh]*
millionaire; very wealthy person M लखपती *[lakhpatī]*
mind M दिमाग़ *[dimāg]*; मन *[man]*
mine F खान *[khān]*
mineral F धातु *[dhātu]*
minimum M न्यूनतम *[nyūntam]*
minister M मंत्री *[mantrī]*
ministry M मंत्रालय *[mantrālay]*
minority ADJ अल्पसंख्यक *[alpasaṅkhyak]*
minute M मिनट *[minaṭ]*
miracle M कमाल *[kamāl]*
mirror M आइना *[āinā]*
mischievous, rowdy ADJ, M बदमाश *[badmāś]*
miserly, miser ADJ कंजूस *[kañjūs]*
mislead V.T. बहकाना *[behkānā]*; गुमराह करना *[gumrāh karnā]*
miss V.I. चूकना *[cūknā]*: **(x) to miss (y)** V.I. (x को) (y की) याद आना *[(x ko) (y kī) yād ānā]*
missing ADJ लापता *[lāpatā]*
mission M मिशन *[miśan]*
mistake F ग़लती *[ghaltī]*
misty, foggy; faded; blurred ADJ धुँधला *[dhũdhlā]*
misunderstanding, misgiving F ग़लतफ़हमी *[ghalatfehmī]*
mix V.T. मिलाना *[milānā]*
mixture M मिश्रण *[miśraṇ]*
moan, cry in pain V.I. कराहना *[karāhnā]*
mobile (phone) M मोबाइल *[mobāil]*
mode M प्रकार *[prakār]*; तरीक़ा *[tarīqā]*
model (pattern) M नमूना *[numūnā]*
model, norm; pattern M आदर्श *[ādarś]*
modern ADJ आधुनिक *[ādhunik]*
modernity F आधुनिकता *[ādhuniktā]*
modest ADJ विनयी *[vinayī]*
modify (change) V.T. बदलना *[badalnā]*
moist ADJ गीला *[gīlā]*
moment, a measure of time equal to twenty-four seconds M पल *[pal]*

moment M लमहा *[lamhā]*; क्षण *[kṣaṇ]*
Monday M सोमवार *[somvār]*
money M पैसा *[paisā]*; रुपया *[rupayā]*
monkey; harbor M बंदर *[bandar]*
monsoon M मानसून *[mānsūn]*
monster (demon) M राक्षस *[rākṣas]*
month; menses M महीना *[mahīnā]*
monthly ADJ मासिक *[māsik]*
mood M मिज़ाज *[mizāj]*
moon M चंद्र *[candra]*; चाँद *[cā̃d]*
moonlight F चाँदनी *[cā̃dnī]*
moral ADJ नैतिक *[naitik]*
morale M हौसला *[hauslā]*
more ADJ, AD, CONJ और *[aur]*
more, much ADJ, INVAR ज़्यादा *[zyādā]*
morning M सवेरा *[saverā]* F सुबह *[subah]*
mortality (death) F मौत *[maut]*; मृत्यु *[mṛtyu]*
mortgage F गिरवी *[girvī]*
mosque F मस्जिद *[masjid]*
mosquito; gnat M मच्छड़ /मच्छर *[macchaṛ/macchar]*
mosquito net/curtain F मसहरी *[masharī]*
most ADJ अधिकांश *[adhikānś]*
mother F माँ *[mā̃]*; माता *[mātā]*
motion F गति *[gati]*
motivation M प्रोत्साहन *[protsāhan]*
motive M उद्देश्य *[uddeśya]*
motor M मोटर *[moṭar]*
motorcycle F मोटरसाइकिल *[moṭarsāikil]*
mountain M पर्वत *[parvat]*; पहाड़ *[pahāṛ]*
mounted; rider ADJ, M सवार *[savār]*
mouse M चूहा *[cūhā]*
mouth, opening M मुँह *[mũh]*
move V.I. चलना *[calnā]*; हिलना *[hilnā]*
move, go away V.I. हटना *[haṭnā]*
move away V.I. चला जाना *[calā jānā]*
move forward V.I. आगे बढ़ना *[āge baṛhnā]*
movement F गति *[gati]*
movie F फ़िल्म *[film]*
Mr M श्री *[śrī]*
Mrs F श्रीमती *[śrīmatī]*
much ADJ बहुत *[bahut]*
mud M कीचड़ *[kīcaṛ]*

munch; masticate V.T. चबाना *[cabānā]*
municipality F नगरपालिका *[nagarpālikā]*
murder F हत्या *[hatyā]*
murder (x) V.T. (x का) ख़ून करना *[(x kā) khūn karnā]*
murderer M हत्यारा *[hatyārā]*
muscle F मांसपेशी *[mānspeśī]*
museum M संग्रहालय *[saṅgrahālay]*
music M संगीत *[saṅgīt]*
musical intrument; band M बाजा *[bājā]*
musician M संगीतकार *[saṅgītkār]*
Muslim M मुसलमान *[musalmān]*
mustache F मूँछ *[mū̃ch]*
mustard (seed and plant) F सरसों *[sarsõ]*
mustard, black mustard F राई *[rāī]*
mute, unable to talk ADJ गूँगा *[gū̃gā]*
mutual, reciprocal ADJ आपसी *[āpasī]*
mutually, with one another ADV आपस में *[āpas mẽ]*
my PRO मेरा *[merā]*
mysterious ADJ रहस्यमय *[rahasyamay]*
mystery; secrecy M रहस्य *[rahasya]*
myth M मिथ *[mith]*

N

nail M नाख़ून *[nākhūn]*
naked ADJ नंगा *[naṅgā]*
name M नाम *[nām]*
name V.T. नाम रखना *[nām rakhnā]*
narrow (as in a lane), scarce, troubled, harassed ADJ तंग *[taṅg]*
nation M राष्ट्र *[rāṣṭra]*
national ADJ राष्ट्रीय *[rāṣṭrīya]*
nationality; nationalism F राष्ट्रीयता *[rāṣṭrīyatā]*
native M देसी *[desī]*
natural ADJ प्राकृतिक *[prākṛtik]*
nature M स्वभाव *[svabhāv]*
nature; temper M मिज़ाज *[mizāj]*
naughty ADJ शरारती *[śarārtī]*
near (x) PP (x) के पास *[(x) ke pās]*

near; close by; about, approximately, almost ADV क़रीब *[qarīb]*
near ADV नज़दीक *[nazdīk]*
nearby ADV आसपास *[āspās]*
nearly ADV क़रीब क़रीब *[qarīb qarīb]*
neat (tidy) ADJ साफ़-सुथरा *[sāf-suthrā]*
necessary ADV ज़रूरी *[zarūrī]*
necessity F ज़रूरत *[zarūrat]*: (the) necessity of (x) to happen V.I. (x की) ज़रूरत होना *[(x kī) zarūrat honā]*
neck F गर्दन *[gardan]*
need F ज़रूरत *[zarūrat]*; आवश्यकता *[āvaśyaktā]*
needle F सुई *[suī]*
negative ADJ नकारात्मक *[nakārātmak]*
neglect; ignore V.T. उपेक्षा करना *[upekṣā karnā]*
negligent; heedless ADJ लापरवाह *[lāparvāh]*
negotiate (compromise) V.T. समझौता करना *[samjhautā karnā]*
neighbor M पड़ोसी *[paṛosī]*
neighborhood M मुहल्ला *[muhallā]*
neither CONJ न तो *[na to]*
nerve F नस *[nas]*
nervous V.I. घबराना/घबड़ाना *[ghabrānā/ghabṛānā]*
nest M घोंसला *[ghõslā]*
net M जाल *[jāl]*
never ADV कभी नहीं *[kabhī nahī̃]*
nevertheless CONJ फिर भी *[phir bhī]*
new ADJ नया *[nayā]*
newly (afresh) ADV नये सिरे से *[naye sire se]*
news F ख़बर *[<u>kh</u>abar]*
newspaper M अख़बार *[a<u>kh</u>bār]*
next ADJ अगला *[aglā]*
night F रात *[rāt]*
nine ADJ नौ *[nau]*
nineteen ADJ उन्नीस *[unnīs]*
nineteenth ADJ उन्नीसवाँ *[unnīsvā̃]*
ninety ADJ नब्बे *[nabbe]*
ninety-eight ADJ अट्ठानवे/अट्ठानबे *[aṭṭhānve/aṭṭhānbe]*
ninety-four ADJ चौरानबे *[caurānbe]*
ninety-nine ADJ निन्यानबे *[ninyānabe]*
ninety-one ADJ इक्यानवे *[ikyānve]*
ninety-seven ADJ सत्तानवे

[sattanve]
ninety-six ADJ छियानबे *[chiyānabe]*
ninety-three ADJ तिरानबे *[tirānbe]*
ninety-two ADJ बानबे *[bānbe]*
no ADV जी नहीं *[jī nahī̃]*; न *[na]*
no, not ADV नहीं *[nahī̃]*
no (a word denoting negation) ADV ना *[nā]*
nobody PRO कोई नहीं *[koī nahī̃]*
nod V.T. सिर हिलाना *[sir hilānā]*
noise F आवाज़ *[āvāz]*
nonsense F बकवास *[bakvās]*
noon F दोपहर *[dopehar]*
nor CONJ न *[na]*
normal (ordinary) ADJ साधारण *[sādhāraṇ]*
normally (generally) ADV आम तौर पर *[ām taur par]*
north M उत्तर *[uttar]*
northern ADJ उत्तरी *[uttarī]*
nose; (a symbol of) prestige and honor F नाक *[nāk]*
not ADV मत *[mat]*
not, isn't it? ADV न *[na]*
note F टिप्पणी *[ṭippaṇī]*; M नोट *[noṭ]*
note down, record V.T. लिखना *[likhnā]*
notebook F कापी *[kāpī]*
nothing PRO कुछ नहीं *[kuch nahī̃]*
notice V.T. ध्यान देना *[dhyān denā]*
notice (information) F सूचना *[sūcnā]*
notion M विचार *[vicār]*
novel M उपन्यास *[upanyās]*
November (month) M नवंबर/नवम्बर *[navambar]*
now ADV अब *[ab]*
nowhere ADV कहीं नहीं *[kahī̃ nahī̃]*
nude ADJ नंगा *[naṅgā]*
number M नंबर *[numbar]*
numerous; several ADJ अनेक *[anek]*
nurture; tame, domesticate V.T. पालना *[pālnā]*
nutrition F पुष्टि *[puṣṭi]*
nutritious ADJ पौष्टिक *[pauṣṭik]*

O

o'clock ADV बजे *[baje]*
oath F क़सम *[qasam]*
oath, swearing F शपथ *[śapath]*
object F चीज़ *[cīz]* M मक़सद *[maqsad]*
objection, exception M एतराज़ *[etrāz]*
objective M लक्ष्य *[lakṣya]*
obligation M आभार *[ābhār]*
obliged ADJ आभारी *[ābhārī]*; मजबूर *[majbūr]*
oblique; skew; difficult ADJ टेढ़ा *[ṭeṛhā]*
obstacle F रुकावट *[rukāvaṭ]*
obstinate ADJ ज़िद्दी *[ziddī]*
obtain; be able to V.I., V.T. पाना *[pānā]*: (x) to obtain V.I. (x को) प्राप्त होना *[(x ko) prāpt honā]*
obtain deliverance V.T. छुटकारा पाना *[chuṭkārā pānā]*
obvious, evident ADJ ज़ाहिर *[zāhir]*
obviously ADV स्पष्ट रूप से *[spaṣṭ rūp se]*
occasion M अवसर *[avsar]*
occasionally ADV कभी-कभार *[kabhī-kabhār]*
occupation; business; work M धंधा *[dhandhā]*
occur V.I. होना *[honā]*
ocean M समुद्र *[samudra]*
odd ADJ विषम *[viṣam]*
oddity F विषमता *[viṣamtā]*
odor, foul smell F बू *[bū]*
off (closed) ADJ बंद *[band]*
off (stale) ADJ बासी *[bāsī]*
offender (criminal) M अपराधी *[aprādhī]*
offense (crime) M अपराध *[aprādh]*
offer (present) V.T. पेश करना *[peś karnā]*
offer (proposal) M प्रस्ताव *[prastāv]*
office M दफ़्तर *[daftar]*
officer M अफ़सर *[afsar]*
official; a servant M कर्मचारी *[karmcārī]*
official ADJ आधिकारिक *[ādhikārik]*
offspring F संतान *[santān]*
often ADV अक्सर *[aksar]*
oh INTR ओह *[oh]*
oil M तेल *[tel]*
okay ADJ ठीक *[ṭhīk]* INVAR, M बस *[bas]*
old ADJ बूढ़ा *[būṛhā]*

old (said of things, not people) ADJ पुराना *[purānā]*
old age F बुढ़ापा *[buṛhāpā]*
old-fashioned ADJ पुराने विचारों का *[purāne vicārõ kā]*
on PP पर *[par]*
on foot ADV पैदल *[paidal]*
on the contrary, on the other hand IND बल्कि *[balki]*
once ADV एक बार *[ek bār]*
one ADJ एक *[ek]*
one-and-a-half ADJ डेढ़ *[ḍeṛh]*
one-and-a-quarter ADJ, INVAR सवा *[savā]*
one-fourth ADJ चौथाई *[cauthāī]*
one-half ADJ आधा *[ādhā]*
one hundred ADJ सौ *[sau]*
one-quarter ADJ एक चौथाई *[ek cauthāī]*
one-sided ADJ एकतरफ़ा *[ektarafā]*
one-third ADJ एक तिहाई *[ek tihāī]*
one-way ADJ एकतरफ़ा *[ektarafā]*
one's own ADJ निजी *[nijī]*; अपना *[apnā]*
onion M प्याज़ *[pyāz]*
only ADV सिर्फ़ *[sirf]* INVAR ही *[hī]*
open ADJ खुला हुआ *[khulā huā]*
open V.T. खोलना *[kholnā]* V.I. खुलना *[khulnā]*
openly ADV खुलेआम *[khuleām]*
operate (make move) V.T. चलाना *[calānā]*
operation (activity) F कारवाई *[kārvāī]*
opinion F, M राय *[rāy]*
opponent (opposed) ADJ, M विरोधी *[virodhī]*
opportunity M मौक़ा *[mauqā]*
oppose; encounter V.T. मुक़ाबला करना *[muqāblā karnā]*
opposed ADJ ख़िलाफ़ *[khilāf]*
opposite; inverted ADJ उलटा *[ulṭā]*
opposition M विरोध *[virodh]*
optimistic ADJ M आशावादी *[āśāvādī]*
or CONJ या *[yā]*
oral ADJ मौखिक *[maukhik]*
orange M संतरा *[santarā]* F नारंगी *[nāraṅgī]*
order F आज्ञा *[ājñā]*; व्यवस्था *[vyavasthā]*

order V.T. ऑर्डर देना *[ārḍar denā]*
ordinary ADJ आम *[ām]*
ordinary, simple, common ADJ साधारण *[sādhāraṇ]*
ordinary, so-so ADJ मामूली *[māmūlī]*
organism M जीव *[jīv]*
organization M संगठन/संघटन *[saṅgaṭhan/saṅghaṭan]*
organize V.T. आयोजन करना *[āyojan karnā]*
origin M मूल *[mūl]*
originally ADV मूल रूप से *[mūl rūp se]*
ornament M गहना *[gehnā]*
orphan M अनाथ *[anāth]*
other, another ADJ दूसरा *[dūsrā]*
other ADJ अन्य *[anya]*
otherwise CONJ नहीं तो *[nahĩ to]*
our ADJ हमारा *[hamārā]* ADV बाहर *[bāhar]*
outcome (result) M नतीजा *[natījā]*
outdoor ADV बाहर *[bāhar]*
outfit (attire) F पोशाक *[pośāk]*; **(uniform)** F वर्दी *[vardī]*
outline M रूपरेखा *[rūprekhā]*
output (production) M उत्पादन *[utpādan]*
outside ADV बाहर *[bāhar]*
outsider (foreigner) ADJ M विदेशी *[videśī]*
outstanding (excellent) ADJ बढ़िया *[baṛhiyā]*
oven M तंदूर *[tandūr]*
over ADV ऊपर *[ūpar]*
over here ADV इधर *[idhar]*
over there; that side ADV उधर *[udhar]*
overall (in total) ADV कुल मिलाकर *[kul milākar]*
overcome (defeat) V.T. पराजित करना *[parājit karnā]*
overhang; be suspended V.I. लटकना *[laṭaknā]*
oversee V.T. निगरानी करना *[nigrānī karnā]*
overturn; overthrow; convert; upset; reverse V.T., V.I. पलटना *[palaṭnā]*
overturned V.I., V.T. उलटना *[ulaṭnā]*
owl M उल्लू *[ullū]*
own V.I. मालिक होना *[mālik honā]*
owner M मालिक *[mālik]*

P

pace F रफ़्तार *[raftār]*
package M पार्सल *[pārsal]*
page M पन्ना *[pannā]*
pain M दर्द *[dard]*
painful ADJ दर्दनाक *[dardnāk]*
paint (color) M रंग *[raṅg]*
painter M चित्रकार *[citrakār]*
painting (picture) F तसवीर *[tasvīr]*
pair F जोड़ी *[joṛī]*
pajamas M पायजामा *[pāyjāmā]*
palace M महल *[mahal]*
pale ADJ ज़र्द *[zard]*; पीला *[pīlā]*
palm of the hand F हथेली *[hathelī]*
palpitate, pulsate V.I. फड़कना *[phaṛaknā]*
pan F कड़ाही *[kaṛāhī]*
pancake-like preparation of kneaded flour fried in ghee M पराँठा *[parā̃ṭhā]*
panic F दहशत *[dehśat]*
pants F पैंट *[paiṭ]*
papa M पापा *[pāpā]*
papaya M पपीता *[papītā]*
paper M काग़ज़ *[kāghaz]*
parade M जुलूस *[julūs]*
pardon V.T. माफ़ करना *[māf karnā]*
parents M, PL माँ-बाप *[mā̃-bāp]*
parents; mother and father M, PL माता-पिता *[mātā-pitā]*
park M पार्क *[pārk]*
park V.T. खड़ा करना *[khaṛā karnā]*
parking F पार्किंग *[pārkiṅg]*
part M भाग *[bhāg]*; हिस्सा *[hissā]*
part, share M अंश *[anś]*
participate V.T. भाग लेना *[bhāg lenā]*
participate V.I. (x में) शरीक होना *[(x mẽ) śarīk honā]*
particular ADJ विशेष *[viśeṣ]*
particularly ADV विशेष रूप से *[viśeṣ rūp se]*
partition M बँटवारा *[bā̃ṭvārā]*; विभाजन *[vibhājan]*
partner M भागीदार *[bhāgīdār]*
partnership F भागीदारी *[bhāgīdārī]*
party M दल *[dal]* F पार्टी *[pārṭī]*
pass V.I. बीतना *[bītnā]*
pass (an exam) V.I. पास होना *[pās honā]*
pass (by); pass away V.I. गुज़रना *[guzarnā]*

pass (time) V.T. बिताना *[bitānā]*; गुज़ारना *[guzārnā]*
pass away V.T. सिधारना *[sidhārnā]*
passage (path) M मार्ग *[mārg]*
passenger; procession F सवारी *[savārī]*
passion F कामना *[kāmnā]*
past M अतीत *[atīt]*
pat V.T. थपथपाना *[thapthapānā]*
paternal grandfather M दादा *[dādā]*
paternal grandmother F दादी *[dādī]*
paternal grandparents M दादा-दादी *[dādā-dādī]*
path M मार्ग *[mārg]*; रास्ता *[rāstā]*
patience M धैर्य *[dhairya]*
patient ADJ, M मरीज़ *[marīz]*
patient ADJ धैर्यवान् *[dhairyavān]*
patrol V.T. गश्त लगाना *[gaśt lagānā]*
pattern M नमूना *[namūnā]*
pause; stay; wait V.I. ठहरना *[ṭheharnā]*
pawn(ed) F, ADJ गिरवी *[girvī]*
pay; wages M वेतन *[vetan]*
pay (give money) V.T. पैसा देना *[paisā denā]*
pay off, defray V.T. चुकाना *[cukānā]*
payment M भुगतान *[bhugtān]*
pea M मटर *[maṭar]*
peace M चैन *[cain]* F शांति *[śānti]*
peaceful ADJ शांत *[śānt]*
peach M आड़ू *[āṛū]*
peacock M मयूर *[mayūr]*
peak (apex) F चोटी *[coṭī]*
peanut F मूँगफली *[mū̃gphalī]*
pear F नाशपाती *[nāśpātī]*
pearl M मोती *[motī]*
peasant M किसान *[kisān]*
peculiar; uncommon; strange ADJ निराला *[nirālā]*
peculiar ADJ अजीब *[ajīb]*
peel V.T. छीलना *[chīlnā]*
peep in or out V.T. झाँकना *[jhā̃knā]*
peer V.T. ताकना *[tāknā]*
peg M खूँटा *[khū̃ṭā]*
pen M पेन *[pen]* F क़लम *[qalam]*
penalty, fine; staff, rod, beam, shaft, stalk दंड *[daṇḍ]*
pencil F पेंसिल *[pensil]*
penetrate, thrust into V.T.

भौंकना *[bhaũknā]*
penetrate V.I. घुसना *[ghusnā]*
penis M लंड *[laṇḍ]*
pepper F काली मिर्च *[kālī mirc]*
people M PL लोग *[log]*
percentage M प्रतिशत *[pratiśat]*
perfect ADJ संपूर्ण *[sampūrṇ]*
perforation; opening M छेद *[ched]*
perform V.T. करना *[karnā]*
performance (acting) M अभिनय *[abhinay]*
performer (actor) M अभिनेता *[abhinetā]*
perfume; scent M इत्र *[itra]*
perhaps; probably CONJ शायद *[śāyad]*
period M अरसा *[arsa]*
permanent ADJ स्थायी *[sthāyī]*
permission F इजाज़त *[ijāzat]*
permit V.T. अनुमति देना *[anumati denā]*
permit M परमिट *[parmiṭ]*
perplexity F उलझन *[uljhan]*
Persian F फ़ारसी *[fārsī]*
persist (stand firm) V.I. डटना *[ḍaṭnā]*
person M व्यक्ति *[vyakti]*: a **fair-skinned person** M गोरा *[gorā]*; a stingy person M कंजूस मक्खीचूस *[kañjūs makkhīcūs]*
personal ADJ निजी *[nijī]*
personality M व्यक्तित्व *[vyaktitva]*
perspective; angle M नज़रिया *[nazriyā]*
persuade V.T. मनाना *[manānā]*
pet M पालतू जानवर *[pāltū jānvar]*
petition F अर्ज़ी *[arzī]*
pharmacy M दवाख़ाना *[davākhānā]*
phase M दौर *[daur]*; चरण *[caraṇ]*
philosopher ADJ, M दार्शनिक *[dārśanik]*
philosophy M दर्शन *[darśan]*
phone M फ़ोन *[fon]* V.T. फ़ोन करना *[fon karnā]*
photograph M फ़ोटो *[foṭo]*
photograph V.T. फ़ोटो खींचना *[foṭo khīcnā]*
photographer M फ़ोटोग्राफ़र *[foṭogrāfar]*
photography F फ़ोटोग्राफ़ी *[foṭogrāfī]*
physician M डॉक्टर *[ḍākṭar]*

pick, prick V.T. गोदना *[godnā]*
pick up, pluck; choose V.T. बीनना *[bīnnā]*
pick up the phone V.T. फ़ोन उठाना *[fon uṭhānā]*
pickles M अचार *[acār]*
pickpocket M जेबकतरा *[jebkatrā]*
picture F तस्वीर *[tasvīr]*
piece M टकड़ा *[ṭukṛā]*
pig M सुअँर *[sūar]*
pigeon M कबूतर *[kabūtar]*
pilaf, rice mixed with vegetables and/or meat and spices M पुलाव *[pulāv]*
pile M ढेर *[ḍher]*
pill F गोली *[golī]*
pillar M खंभा *[khambhā]*
pillow M तकिया *[takiyā]*
pilot M पायलट *[pāylaṭ]*
pin F पिन *[pin]*
pinch, snapping with the finger F चुटकी *[cuṭkī]*
pine tree M चीड़ *[cīṛ]*
pineapple tree and its fruit M अनन्नास *[anannās]*
pink ADJ गुलाबी *[gulābī]*
pipe M नल *[nal]*
pistachio M पिस्ता *[pistā]*
pistol F पिस्तौल *[pistaul]*
pit M गड्ढा *[gaḍḍhā]*
pitcher (earthen) M गागर *[gāgar]*
pity F दया *[dayā]*
place F जगह *[jagah]* V.T. रखना *[rakhnā]*
place a step V.T. क़दम रखना *[qadam rakhnā]*
place (put down) the phone V.T. फ़ोन रखना *[fon rakhnā]*
plain ADJ सादा *[sādā]*
plait V.T. गूँथना *[gū̃thnā]*
plan F योजना *[yojnā]*
plan V.T. योजना बनाना *[yognā banānā]*
plane M हवाई जहाज़ *[havāī jahāz]*
planet M ग्रह *[greh]*
planning F योजना *[yojnā]*
plant M पौदा *[paudā]* V.T. बोना *[bonā]*
plate F तश्तरी *[taśtarī]*; प्लेट *[pleṭ]*
platform M प्लेटफ़ार्म *[pleṭfārm]*
play V.I., V.T. खेलना *[khelnā]* M नाटक *[nāṭak]*
play a musical instrument V.T. बाजा बजाना *[bājā bajānā]*
play music V.T. गाना बजाना *[gānā bajānā]*

player M खिलाड़ी *[khilāṛī]*
plaything M खिलौना *[khilaunā]*
please; kindly ADV कृपया *[kṛpayā]*
please (become happy) V.I. खुश होना *[khuś honā]*
pleased (happy) ADJ खुश *[khuś]*
pleasing, lovely; dear one, beloved ADJ, M प्यारा *[pyārā]*
pleasing; likable ADJ सुहावना *[suhāvnā]*
pleasure M सुख *[sukh]*
plenty (much) ADJ बहुत *[bahut]*
plot (conspiracy) F साज़िश *[sāziś]*
plow, till V.T. जोतना *[jotnā]*
plump ADJ मोटा *[moṭā]*
plumpness M मोटापा *[moṭāpā]*
plunder V.T. लूटना *[lūṭnā]*
plus (and, more) CONJ, ADJ और *[aur]*
plus one half (from three and one half onwards) ADJ साढ़े *[sāṛhe]*
PM (afternoon, evening, night) ADV दोपहर को, शाम को, रात को *[dopehar ko, śām ko, rāt ko]*
pocket F जेब *[jeb]*
poem F कविता *[kavitā]*
poet M कवि *[kavi]*
poetry M काव्य *[kāvya]*
point F नोक *[nok]*
point, dot; zero, cipher M बिंदु *[bindu]*
point (indicate) V.T. इशारा करना *[iśārā karnā]*
poison M ज़हर *[zehar]*
poisonous, venomous, full of poison ADJ ज़हरी *[zehrī]*
pole M खंभा *[khambhā]*
police F पुलिस *[pulis]*
politician M नेता *[netā]*
politics F राजनीति *[rājnīti]*
pollution, stigma; defect, flaw M प्रदूषण *[pradūṣaṇ]*
pomegranate M अनार *[anār]*
pond F पोखर *[pokhar]*
poor ADJ ग़रीब *[gharīb]*
popular ADJ लोकप्रिय *[lokpriya]*
popularity F लोकप्रियता *[lokpriyatā]*
population F जनसंख्या *[jansaṅkhyā]*
pork M सुअर का मांस *[suar kā māns]*
port (harbor) M बंदरगाह *[bandargāh]*

portion M भाग *[bhāg]*
portrait F तसवीर *[tasvīr]*
pose F मुद्रा *[mudrā]*
position (state) F स्थिति *[sthiti]*
position M स्थान *[sthān]*
positive ADJ सकारात्मक *[sakārātmak]*
possession M कब्ज़ा *[kabzā]*
possibility F संभावना *[sambhāvnā]*
possible ADJ संभव *[sambhav]*
possibly ADV सम्भवतः *[sambhavataḥ]*
post F डाक *[ḍāk]*
post (position) M पद *[pad]*
post a letter V.T. चिट्ठी डालना *[ciṭṭhī ḍālnā]*
post office M डाकख़ाना *[ḍākkhānā]*
postpone; put off V.T. टालना *[ṭālnā]*
postponed ADJ स्थगित *[sthagit]*
potato M आलू *[ālū]*
pounce V.I. झपटना *[jhapaṭnā]*
pound V.T. पीसना *[pīsnā]*
pour V.T. उँडेलना *[ũḍelnā]*
pour out (as in liquor) V.T. ढालना *[ḍhālnā]*
poverty F ग़रीबी *[gharībī]*
power F शक्ति *[śakti]*
power, sway, authority F सत्ता *[sattā]*
powerful ADJ शक्तिशाली *[śaktiśālī]*
practical ADJ व्यावहारिक *[vyāvahārik]*
practice M अभ्यास *[abhyās]*
practice V.T. अभ्यास करना *[abhyās karnā]*
praise F तारीफ़ *[tārīf]* V.T. सराहना *[sarāhnā]*; प्रशंसा करना *[praśansā karnā]*
pray V.T. प्रार्थना करना *[prārthnā karnā]*; दुआ माँगना *[duā mā̃gnā]*; नमाज़ पढ़ना *[namāz paṛhnā]*
prayer F प्रार्थना *[prārthnā]*; दुआ *[duā]*; नमाज़ *[namāz]*
preach V.T. प्रवचन करना *[pravacan karnā]*
precious ADJ बेशक़ीमती *[beśqīmti]*; अनमोल *[anmol]*
precise ADJ ठीक-ठीक *[ṭhīk-ṭhīk]*
prefer V.T. पसंद करना *[pasand karnā]*
preference (liking) F पसंद *[pasand]*
pregnant ADJ गर्भवती *[garbhvatī]*

preparation F तैयारी *[taiyārī]*
prepare V.T. तैयार करना *[taiyār karnā]* V.I. तैयारी करना *[taiyārī karnā]*
prepared ADJ तैयार *[taiyār]* V.I. तैयार होना *[taiyār honā]*
prescription M नुसख़ा *[nuskhā]*
presence F मौजूदगी *[maujūdagī]*
present M तोहफ़ा *[tohfā]* V.T. प्रस्तुत करना *[prastut karnā]* ADJ मौजूद *[maujūd]*
preserve (maintain) V.T. बनाए रखना *[banāe rakhnā]*
president M राष्ट्रपति *[rāṣṭrapati]*
press M प्रेस *[pres]*
press (printing) M छापाख़ाना *[chāpākhānā]*
press, press down V.T. दबाना *[dabānā]*
pressed V.I. दबना *[dabnā]*
pressure M दबाव *[dabāv]*
pretend (imagine) V.T. कल्पना करना *[kalpanā karnā]*
pretty ADJ सुंदर *[sundar]*
prevent, ban, repress, curb V.T. रोकना *[roknā]*
prevention (ban) M प्रतिबंध *[pratibandh]* F रोक *[rok]*
previous ADJ पिछला *[pichlā]*
previously ADV पहले *[pehle]*
price M दाम *[dām]*
pride; elation M गर्व *[garv]*
priest (Hindu) M पुजारी *[pujārī]*
primary ADJ प्राथमिक *[prāthamik]*
prime ADJ प्रधान *[pradhān]*
Prime Minister M प्रधान मंत्री *[pradhān mantrī]*
principal, main; president, chairman ADJ, M प्रधान *[pradhān]*
principle M सिद्धांत *[siddhānt]*
print V.T. छापना *[chāpnā]*
prior ADJ पिछला *[pichlā]*; पूर्व *[pūrv]*
priority F प्राथमिकता *[prāthamiktā]*
prison, jail M कारागार *[kārāgār]*, क़ैदख़ाना *[qaidkhānā]*
prisoner M क़ैदी *[qaidī]*
prize M इनाम *[inām]*
pro (in favor) ADV पक्ष में *[pakṣ mẽ]*
probably CONJ शायद *[śāyad]*
problem F समस्या *[samasyā]*
proceed V.I. आगे बढ़ना *[āge baṛhnā]*

process F प्रक्रिया *[prakriyā]*
proclamation F घोषणा *[ghoṣṇā]*
produce V.T. बनाना *[banānā]*
produce; create; procreate V.T. उत्पन्न करना *[utpanna karnā]*
produce, give birth V.T. पैदा करना *[paidā karnā]*
producer M निर्माता *[nirmātā]*
product M पदार्थ *[padārth]*
production M उत्पादन *[utpādan]*
profession M पेशा *[peśā]*
professional ADJ पेशेवर *[peśevar]*
professor M प्रोफ़ेसर *[profesar]*
profile (picture) M चित्र *[citra]*; F तसवीर *[tasvīr]*
profit M मुनाफ़ा *[munāfā]*
profound; intimate ADJ गहरा *[gehrā]*
program M कार्यक्रम *[kāryakram]*; प्रोग्राम *[progrām]*
progress F प्रगति *[pragati]*
prohibit V.T. मना करना *[manā karnā]*
prohibited ADJ मना *[manā]*
project (throw) V.T. फेंकना *[phẽknā]*
promise M वायदा *[vāydā]* V.T. वायदा करना *[vāydā karnā]*
promising; the inevitable, destiny ADJ, M होनहार *[honhār]*
proof M प्रमाण *[pramāṇ]*; सबूत *[sabūt]*
proper ADJ उचित *[ucit]*
proper, appropriate ADJ ठीक *[ṭhīk]*
property F जायदाद *[jāyadād]*
proposal M प्रस्ताव *[prastāv]*
propose V.T. सुझाना *[sujhānā]*
prospect (possibility) F संभावना *[sambhāvnā]*
prosperous ADJ समृद्ध *[samṛddh]*
protect (x) V.T. (x की) रक्षा करना *[(x kī) rakṣā karnā]*
protect (one's) honor V.T. लाज रखना *[lāj rakhnā]*
protection F सुरक्षा *[surakṣā]*
protest (demonstration) M प्रदर्शन *[pradarśan]*
protest (demonstrate) V.T. प्रदर्शन करना *[pradarśan karnā]*
proud (haughty) ADJ घमंडी *[ghamaṇḍī]*
prove V.T. साबित करना *[sābit karnā]*

proverb F कहावत *[kahāvat]*
provide V.T. प्रदान करना *[pradān karnā]*
province M प्रदेश *[pradeś]*; प्रांत *[prānt]*
provoke V.T. भड़काना *[bhaṛkānā]*
provoke; molest; tease V.T. छेड़छाड़ करना *[cheṛchāṛ karnā]*
psychological ADJ मनोवैज्ञानिक *[manovaijñānik]*
psychology M मनोविज्ञान *[manovijñān]*
public ADJ सार्वजनिक *[sārvajanik]*
public (people) F जनता *[jantā]*
publication M प्रकाशन *[prakāśan]*
publicity M प्रचार *[pracār]*
publish V.T. प्रकाशित करना *[prakāśit karnā]*
published; brought to light, manifest, obvious; resplendent ADJ प्रकाशित *[prakāśit]*
publisher M प्रकाशक *[prakāśak]*
puff M झोंका *[jhõkā]*
puff; burn, ignite, set on fire; waste, squander away V.T. फूँकना *[phū̃knā]*
pull V.T. खींचना *[khī̃cnā]*
pulse (heartbeat) F नब्ज़ *[nabz]*
pump M पम्प *[pamp]*
pungent ADJ चटपटा *[caṭpaṭā]*
punish V.T. दंड देना *[daṇḍ denā]*; सज़ा देना *[sazā denā]*
punishment F सज़ा *[sazā]*
pupil (of the eye) F पुतली *[putlī]*
purchase (buy) V.T. ख़रीदना *[k͟harīdnā]*
pure ADJ खरा *[kharā]*; शुद्ध *[śuddh]*
pure vegetarian ADJ शुद्ध शाकाहारी *[śuddh śākāhārī]*
purity F शुद्धि *[śuddhi]*
purple ADJ बैंगनी *[baiganī]*
purpose M मक़सद *[maqsad]*
purse M बटआ *[baṭuā]*
pursue (follow) V.T. पीछा करना *[pīchā karnā]*
push M धक्का *[dhakkā]*
push; thrust ahead V.T. धकेलना *[dhakelnā]*
put V.T. रखना *[rakhnā]*
put, place V.T. डालना *[ḍālnā]*
puzzle (riddle) F पहेली *[pahelī]*

puzzle (become mystified) V.I. हैरान होना *[hairān honā]*

Q

qualified, able ADJ योग्य *[yogya]*
quality M गुण *[guṇ]*
quantity F मात्रा *[mātrā]*
quarrel M झगड़ा *[jhagṛā]*
quarrel; collide V.I., V.T. लड़ना *[laṛnā]*
quarter ADJ चौथाई *[cauthaī]*
quarter to (less a quarter) ADJ पौने *[paune]*
queen F रानी *[rānī]*
quench, slake V.T. बुझाना *[bujhānā]*
quenched V.I. बुझना *[bujhnā]*
quest (search) F तलाश *[talāś]*
question M सवाल *[savāl]*
quickly ADV जल्दी *[jaldī]*
quiet ADJ चुप *[cup]*
quiet, calm ADJ प्रशांत *[praśānt]*
quilt M लिहाफ़ *[lihāf]* F रज़ाई *[razāī]*
quit V.T. छोड़ना *[choṛnā]*
quite ADJ काफ़ी *[kāfī]*
quiver; shiver V.I. काँपना *[kā̃pnā]*
quota M कोटा *[koṭā]*
quote M उद्धरण *[uddharaṇ]*

R

race F दौड़ *[dauṛ]*
race V.I. दौड़ना *[dauṛnā]*
racism M जातिवाद *[jātivād]*
rage, fury M ग़ुस्सा *[ghussā]*
rail F रेल *[rel]*
railway F रेलवे *[relve]*
rain F बारिश *[bāriś]* V.I. बारिश होना *[bāriś honā]*
raise V.T. उठाना *[uṭhānā]*; उकसाना *[uksānā]*
raisin F किशमिश *[kiśmiś]*
rally (march) M जुलूस *[julūs]*
range (reach) F पहुँच *[pahũc]*
range (limit) F सीमा *[sīmā]*
rank, gradation, status, category, quality, order M दर्जा *[darjā]*
rape M बलात्कार *[balātkār]*
rape; disgrace, take one's honor V.T. इज़्ज़त लूटना *[izzat lūṭnā]*
rapid (fast) ADJ तीव्र *[tīvra]*
rapidly ADV जल्दी *[jaldī]*

rat M चूहा *[cūhā]*
rate F दर *[dar]*
rather CONJ आपितु *[āpitu]*, बल्कि *[balki]*
raw ADJ कच्चा *[kaccā]*
razor (blade) M उस्तरा *[ustarā]*
reach (arrive) V.I. पहुँचना *[pahũcnā]*
reach F पहुँच *[pahũc]*
reaction F प्रतिक्रिया *[pratikriyā]*
read V.T. पढ़ना *[paṛhnā]*
reader M पाठक *[pāṭhak]*
readily (happily) ADV ख़ुशी से *[<u>kh</u>uśī se]*
reading and writing, study F लिखाई-पढ़ाई *[likhāī-paṛhāī]*
ready ADJ तैयार *[taiyār]*
real ADJ असल *[usal]*
reality F असलियत *[asaliyat]*
realize; collect V.T. वसूल करना *[vasūl karnā]*
really ADV सचमुच *[sacmuc]*
realm (area) M क्षेत्र *[kṣetra]*
rear V.T. पालना *[pālnā]*
reason M कारण *[kāraṇ]*
reasonable ADJ उचित *[ucit]*
rebate F छूट *[chūṭ]*
rebel M विद्रोही *[vidrohī]*
rebel V.T. विद्रोह करना *[vidroh karnā]*
recall (remember) V.T. याद करना *[yād karnā]*
recede V.I. हटना *[haṭnā]*
receipt F रसीद *[rasīd]*
receive V.I. मिलना *[milnā]*
recent ADJ हाल का *[hāl kā]*
recently ADV हाल में *[hāl mẽ]*
reception M स्वागत समारोह *[svāgat samāroh]*; रिसेप्शन *[risepśan]*
recipe M नुसख़ा *[nus<u>kh</u>ā]*
recognition F पहचान *[pehcān]*
recognize V.T. पहचानना *[pehcānnā]*
recommend V.T. सिफ़ारिश करना *[sifāriś karnā]*
recommendation F सिफ़ारिश *[sifāriś]*
record V.T दर्ज करना *[darj karnā]*
record M कीर्तिमान *[kīrtimān]*
recover (return to health) V.I. स्वस्त होना *[svast honā]*
recover (realize) V.T. वसूल करना *[vasūl karnā]*
recovery (realization) F वसूली *[vasūlī]*
recreation M मनोरंजन *[manorañjan]*
red ADJ लाल *[lāl]*

reduce V.T. कम करना *[kam karnā]*
reduction (discount) F छूट *[chūṭ]*
reference M उल्लेख *[ullekh]*
refine V.T. शोधना *[śodhnā]*
reflect V.T. ग़ौर करना *[ghaur karnā]*
reflection M प्रतिबिंब *[pratibimb]*
reform V.T. सुधारना *[sudhārnā]*
refugee M शरणार्थी *[śaraṇārthī]*
refuse; sweepings M कूड़ा *[kūṛā]*
refuse, deny (x) V.T. इनकार करना (x से) *[inkār karnā (x se)]*
regard V.T. मानना *[mānnā]*
regard V.I., V.T. समझना *[samajhnā]*
regret V.T. पछताना *[pachtānā]*
regret M खेद *[khed]*
regulate (control) V.T. नियंत्रण करना *[niyantraṇ karnā]*
regulation (rule) M नियम *[niyam]*
reinforce (emphasize) V.T. ज़ोर देना *[zor denā]*
reins F लगाम *[lagām]*
reiterate, make two-fold V.T. दोहराना *[dohrānā]*
relate (a story, news, etc.) V.T. सुनाना *[sunānā]*
related ADJ संबंधित *[sambandhit]*
relation M रिश्ता *[riśtā]*; संबंध *[sambandh]*
relationship M संबंध *[sambandh]*
relative M रिश्तेदार *[riśtedār]*
relax V.T. आराम करना *[ārām karnā]*
relaxation M आराम *[ārām]*
release, liberation M छुटकारा *[chuṭkārā]*
relief F राहत *[rāhat]*
religion M धर्म *[dharm]*
religious ADJ धार्मिक *[dhārmik]*
relish V.T. चखना *[cakhnā]*
remain V.I. रहना *[rehnā]*
remain quiet V.I. चुप रहना *[cup rehnā]*
remain standing V.I. खड़ा रहना *[khaṛā rehnā]*
remaining, the rest ADJ बाक़ी *[bāqī]*
remark (note) F टिप्पणी *[tippaṇī]*
remedy M इलाज *[ilāj]*

remember V.I. याद आना/याद होना *[yād ānā/yād honā]*
remember V.T. याद करना *[yād karnā]*: remember (x) V.T. (x की) याद करना *[(x kī) yād karnā]*
remind V.T. याद दिलाना *[yād dilānā]*
remorse F ग्लानि *[glāni]*
remote ADJ दूरवर्ती *[dūrvartī]*
remove V.T. दूर करना *[dūr karnā]*
rent V.T. किराये पर देना *[kirāye par denā]*
rent M किराया *[kirāya]*
rental ADJ किराये का *[kirāye kā]*
renter M किरायेदार *[kirāyedār]*
repair (x), mend (x) V.T. (x की) मरम्मत करना *[(x kī) marammat karnā]*
repair, mending F मरम्मत *[marammat]*
repeat V.T. दोहराना *[dohrānā]*
repeatedly ADV बार बार *[bār bār]*
reply V.T. जवाब देना *[javāb denā]*; उत्तर देना *[uttar denā]*
report F रिपोर्ट *[riport]*
reporter (journalist) M पत्रकार *[patrakār]*
repose, recline V.I. लेटना *[leṭnā]*
representation M निरूपण *[nirūpaṇ]*
representative; delegate M नुमाइंदा *[numāindā]*
republic M गणतंत्र *[gaṇtantra]*
reputation F प्रतिष्ठा *[pratiṣṭhā]*
request V.T. दरख़्वास्त करना *[dar<u>kh</u>vāst karnā]*
request M निवेदन *[nivedan]* V.T. फ़रमाना *[farmānā]*
require V.I. चाहिये *[cāhiye]*
required (necessary) ADJ ज़रूरी *[zarūrī]*; आवश्यक *[āvaśyak]*
requirement (necessity) F ज़रूरत *[zarūrat]*; आवश्यकता *[āvaśyaktā]*
rescue V.T. बचाना *[bacānā]*
rescue M बचाव *[bacāv]*
research M शोधकार्य *[śodhkārya]*
resembling, similar to REL ADJ जैसा *[jaisā]*
reservation M आरक्षण *[ārakṣaṇ]*
reserve V.T. आरक्षण करना *[ārakṣaṇ karnā]*

residence M निवास *[nivās]*
resident M निवासी *[nivāsī]*; बाशिंदा *[bāśindā]*: be a resident (of x) V.I. (x का) रहनेवाला होना *[(x kā) rehnevālā honā]*
resign V.T. इस्तीफ़ा देना *[istīfā denā]*
resistance M प्रतिरोध *[pratirodh]*
resolve V.T. ठानना *[ṭhānnā]*
resource M संसाधन *[sansādhan]*
respect; honor F इज़्ज़त *[izzat]*
respect V.T. इज़्ज़त करना *[izzat karnā]*: respect (x) V.T. (x का) आदर करना *[(x kā) ādar karnā]*
respond V.T. जवाब देना *[javāb denā]*
response M जवाब *[javāb]*; उत्तर *[uttar]*
responsibility F ज़िम्मेदारी *[zimmedārī]*
responsible ADJ ज़िम्मेदार *[zimmedār]*
rest M आराम *[ārām]*
rest; prop V.T. टेकना *[ṭeknā]*
restaurant M भोजनालय *[bhojanālay]*
restless ADJ चंचल *[cañcal]*
restrict (limit) V.T. सीमित करना *[sīmit karnā]*
restriction M प्रतिबंध *[pratibandh]*
result M नतीजा *[natījā]*
retailer (shopkeeper) M दुकानदार *[dukāndār]*
retain (keep) V.T. रखना *[rakhnā]*
retire V.I. रिटायर होना *[riṭāyar honā]*
return, wander, ramble; be proclaimed/circulated; undergo a change V.I. फिरना *[phirnā]*
return (something) V.T. लौटाना *[lauṭānā]*
return, come back V.I. वापस आना *[vāpas ānā]*
return; coming back F वापसी *[vāpasī]*
return, give back V.T. वापस करना *[vāpas karnā]*
return; go back V.I. लौटना *[lauṭnā]*; वापस जाना *[vāpas jānā]*
reveal V.T. प्रगट करना *[pragaṭ karnā]*
reveal (expose) a secret V.T. राज़ खोलना *[rāz kholnā]*

revenge M बदला *[badlā]*
revenue F आय *[āya]*
revere V.T. पूजना *[pūjnā]*
reverse V.T., V.I. उलटना *[ulaṭnā]*
review F समीक्षा *[samīkṣā]*
revolt M विद्रोह *[vidroh]*
revolution M चक्कर *[cakkar]* F क्रांति *[krānti]*
revolve V.I. घूमना *[ghūmnā]*
reward, award M इनाम *[inām]*
rhythm F लय *[lay]*
rib F पसली *[paslī]*
ribbon M फ़ीता *[fītā]*
rice M चावल *[cāval]*
rice pudding F खीर *[khīr]*
rich, opulent ADJ धनी *[dhanī]*
rickshaw M रिक्शा *[rikśā]*
rid V.T. मुक्त करना *[mukt karnā]*
ride V.I. सवार होना *[savār honā]*: ride on x V.I. x पर सवार होना *[x par savār honā]*
ride (conveyance) F सवारी *[savārī]*
rider (passenger) F सवारी *[savārī]*
riding ADJ, M सवार *[savār]*
rifle F बंदूक़ *[bandūq]*
right M अधिकार *[adhikār]* ADJ ठीक *[ṭhīk]*
right (as in hand) ADJ दायाँ *[dāyā̃]*
right (hand/side etc.) ADJ दाहिना *[dāhinā]*
ring F अंगूठी *[aṅgūṭhī]*
ring (encircle) V.T. घेरना *[ghernā]*
ring, range M दायरा *[dāyrā]*
riot M दंगा *[daṅgā]*
rip V.I. फटना *[phaṭnā]* V.T. फाड़ना *[phāṛnā]*
ripe ADJ पक्का *[pakkā]*
rise V.I. उठना *[uṭhnā]*; जागना *[jāgnā]*
rise; mount; launch an attack V.I. चढ़ना *[caṛhnā]*
risk (danger) M ख़तरा *[khatrā]*
risky (dangerous) ADJ ख़तरनाक *[khatarnāk]*
ritual M अनुष्ठान *[anuṣṭhān]*
river F नदी *[nadī]*
road M पथ *[path]*
roast; blast, smash; reduce to ashes V.T. भूनना *[bhūnnā]*
rob V.T. डाका डालना *[ḍākā ḍālnā]*
rock (stone) M पत्थर *[patthar]*

rogue; roguish M, ADJ लफ़ंगा *[lafaṅgā]*
roll V.I. लुढ़कना *[luṛhāknā]*
roll (wrap) V.T. लपेटना *[lapeṭnā]*
roll down; trickle down; spill V.I. ढुलकना *[ḍhulaknā]*
romance M रोमांस *[romāns]*
roof F छत *[chat]*
room M कमरा *[kamrā]*
root F जड़ *[jaṛ]*
rope F रस्सी *[rassī]*
rose M गुलाब *[gulāb]*
rotation; odd affair M चक्कर *[cakkar]*
roti F रोटी *[roṭī]*
rough ADJ रूखा *[rūkhā]*
rough (crude) ADJ स्थूल *[sthūl]*
round ADJ गोल *[gol]*
route, course, passage, approach M रास्ता *[rāstā]*
routine (daily routine) F दिनचर्या *[dincaryā]*
row, file F पंक्ति *[paṅkti]*
royal ADJ शाही *[śāhī]*
rub V.T. रगड़ना *[ragaṛnā]*
rub, efface; cloth for wiping/cleaning V.T., M पोंछना *[põchnā]*
rub; press hard; anoint V.T. मलना *[malnā]*
rub gently V.I. सहलाना *[sehlānā]*
rubbed; be worn; wear out V.I. घिसना *[ghisnā]*
rubber M रबड़ *[rabaṛ]*
rubbish M कूड़ा *[kūṛā]*
ruin F तबाही *[tabāhī]*
ruin, damage; cause to go astray V.T. बिगाड़ना *[bigāṛnā]*
ruined ADJ तबाह *[tabāh]*; बरबाद *[barbād]*
ruins, devastation; waste M नाश *[nāś]*
rule M नियम *[niyam]*
rule V.T. राज करना *[rāj karnā]*
rumor F अफ़वाह *[afvāh]*
run V.I. दौड़ना *[dauṛnā]* V.T. चलाना *[calānā]*
rupee (the Indian currency) M रुपया *[rupayā]*
rural ADJ देहाती *[dehātī]*
rush (act hastily) V.I. हड़बड़ाना *[haṛbaṛānā]*
Russian ADJ रूसी *[rūsī]*

S

sacred ADJ पवित्र *[pavitra]*
sacrifice F कुर्बानी *[qurbānī]* M बलिदान *[balidān]*
sad ADJ उदास *[udās]*; दुखी *[dukhī]*
sadness F उदासी *[udāsī]* M दुख *[dukh]*
safe ADJ सलामत *[salāmat]*
sail M पाल *[pāl]*
saint M संत *[sant]*
salary M वेतन *[vetan]*
salt M नमक *[namak]*
salted; a salty dish of snacks ADJ, M नमकीन *[namkīn]*
salvation M मोक्ष *[mokṣ]*
same ADJ एक ही *[ek hī]*
samosa, pastry filled with vegetables and/or meat M समोसा *[samosā]*
sandal F चप्पल *[cappal]*
sandalwood M चंदन *[candan]*
Sanskrit language; refined F, ADJ संस्कृत *[sanskṛt]*
sari F साड़ी *[sāṛī]*
Satan M शैतान *[śaitān]*
satellite M उपग्रह *[upagrah]*
satisfaction M संतोष *[santoṣ]*
satisfy V.T. संतुष्ट करना *[santuṣṭ karnā]*
Saturday M शनिवार/शनिश्चर *[śanivār/śaniścar]*
savage, wild ADJ जंगली *[jaṅgalī]*
save V.T. बचाना *[bacānā]*: save (x) V.T. (x का) बचाव करना *[(x kā) bacāv karnā]*
saving F बचत *[bacat]*
say (to x) V.T. (x से) कहना *[(x se) kehnā]*
saying F कहावत *[kahāvat]*
scale M पैमाना *[paimānā]*
scales F तराज़ू *[tarāzū]*
scandal (bungling) M घोटाला *[ghoṭālā]*
scare V.T. डराना *[ḍarānā]*
scary ADJ डरावना *[ḍarāvnā]*
scatter V.T. बिखरना *[bikharna]*
scent F खुशबू *[khuśbū]*; सुगंध *[sugandh]*
scene, sight ADJ, M दृश्य *[dṛśya]*
schedule F अनुसूची *[anusūcī]*
scheduled caste F अनुसूचित जाति *[anusūcit jāti]*
scheme F योजना *[yojnā]*
scholar ADJ, M विद्वान *[vidvān]*
scholarship (student grant) F छात्रवृत्ति *[chātravṛtti]*
science M विज्ञान *[vijñān]*

scientist M वैज्ञानिक *[vaijñānik]*
scissors F कैंची *[qaincī]*
scold, rebuke sharply V.T. डाँटना *[ḍā̃ṭnā]*
scope F गुंजाइश *[guñjāiś]*
scoundrel M, ADJ गुंडा *[guṇḍā]*
scour; polish V.T. माँजना *[mā̃jnā]*
scrap; scratch; chip V.T. छीलना *[chīlnā]*
scratch, bruise F खरोंच *[kharõc]*
scratch, bruise V.T. खरोंचना *[kharõcnā]*
scratch V.T. खुजाना *[khujānā]*; नोचना *[nocnā]*
scream F चीख़ *[cī<u>kh</u>]*
scream, shout V.I. चिल्लाना *[cillānā]*
scream V.I. चीख़ना *[cī<u>kh</u>nā]*
screen M परदा *[pardā]*
screen (show) V.T. दिखाना *[dikhānā]*
screw; complication, intricacy M पेच *[pec]*
script F लिपि *[lipi]*
sea M सागर *[sāgar]*; समुद्र *[samudra]*
seal F मोहर *[mohar]*
seal V.T. सील करना *[sīl karnā]*
search V.I. खोजना *[khojnā]* V.T. ढूँढना *[ḍhū̃ḍhnā]*
search, go in quest (of) V.T. तलाशना *[talāśnā]*: search for (x) V.T. (x की) तलाश करना *[(x kī) talāś karnā]*
season M मौसम *[mausam]*
seat F सीट *[sīṭ]*; **(chair)** F कुर्सी *[kursī]*
seat (someone) V.T. बिठाना/बैठाना *[biṭhānā/baiṭānā]*
second ADJ दूसरा *[dūsrā]* M सेकंड *[sekaṇḍ]*
secretary M सचिव *[saciv]*
secure V.T. सुरक्षित करना *[surakṣit karnā]*
security F सुरक्षा *[surakṣā]*
secret M भेद *[bhed]*; रहस्य *[rahasya]*
see V.T. देखना *[dekhnā]*; निहारना *[nihārnā]*
seed; origin, beginning; germ; semen; cause; nucleus M बीज *[bīj]*
seek V.T. ढूँढना *[ḍhū̃ḍhnā]*
seem V.I. लगना *[lagnā]*
seem bothered/troubled V.I. परेशान लगना *[pareśān lagnā]*
seize V.T. पकड़ना *[pakaṛnā]*
select V.T. चुनना *[cunnā]*

select, sort out; cut, trim V.T. छाँटना *[chā̃tnā]*

selection M इंतख़ाब *[intakhāb]*; चयन *[cayan]*

self M आत्म *[ātma]*

self-esteem (self-respect) M आत्मसम्मान *[ātmasammān]*

selfish ADJ मतलबी *[matlabī]*; स्वार्थी *[svārthī]*

selfishness M स्वार्थ *[svārth]*

sell V.T. बेचना *[becnā]*

send V.T. भेजना *[bhejnā]*

senior ADJ वरिष्ठ *[variṣṭh]*

senior M वयोवृद्ध *[vayovṛddh]*

sensation M एहसास *[ehsās]*

sense M होश *[hoś]*; एहसास *[ehsās]*

sensitive ADJ संवेदनशील *[samvedanśīl]*

sentence M वाक्य *[vākya]*

sentiment F भावना *[bhāvnā]*

sentimental ADJ भावुक *[bhāvuk]*

separate V.T. अलग करना *[alag karnā]*

separate, different ADJ अलग-अलग *[alag-alag]*

separation F जुदाई *[judāī]*

September M सितंबर *[sitambar]*

series M सिलसिला *[silsilā]*

serious ADJ गंभीर *[gambhīr]*

seriousness, gravity F गंभीरता *[gambhīrtā]*

servant M नौकर *[naukar]*

serve V.T. ख़िदमत करना/चाकरी करना *[khidmat karnā/ cākrī karnā]*: serve (x) V.T. (x की) सेवा करना *[(x kī) sevā karnā]*

serve food V.T. परोसना *[parosnā]*

service F सेवा *[sevā]*

session M सत्र *[satra]*

set out, despatched ADJ रवाना *[ravānā]*

set up a home V.T. घर बसाना *[ghar basānā]*

setting (arrangement) F व्यवस्था *[vyavastha]*

settle V.T. चुकाना *[cukānā]*; पटाना *[paṭānā]*; तय करना *[tay karnā]* V.I. बसना *[basnā]*

settle; make an arrangement V.T. बंदोबस्त करना *[bandobast karnā]*

settlement, satellite town, colony; inhabitation; population F बस्ती *[bastī]*

seven ADJ सात *[sāt]*

seventeen ADJ सत्रह *[satrah]*

seventeenth ADJ सत्रहवाँ *[satrahvā̃]*
seventh ADJ सातवाँ *[sātvā̃]*
seventy ADJ सत्तर *[sattar]*
seventy-eight ADJ अठहत्तर *[aṭhhattar]*
seventy-five ADJ पचहत्तर *[pachattar]*
seventy-four ADJ चौहत्तर *[cauhattar]*
seventy-nine ADJ उनासी *[unāsī]*; उन्यासी *[unyāsī]*
seventy-one ADJ इकहत्तर *[ikhattar]*
seventy-seven ADJ सतहत्तर *[sathattar]*
seventy-six ADJ छिहत्तर *[chihattar]*
seventy-three ADJ तिहत्तर *[tihattar]*
seventy-two ADJ बहत्तर *[behattar]*
several ADJ कई *[kaī]*
severe ADJ सख़्त *[sak<u>h</u>t]*
severely ADV सख़्ती से *[sak<u>h</u>tī se]*
sew V.T., M सीना *[sīnā]*
sex M संभोग *[sambhog]*
sex worker F वेश्या *[veśyā]*
sexual intercourse M संभोग *[sambhog]*
sexuality (sexual orientation) F लैंगिकता *[laiṅgiktā]*
shade M साया *[sāyā]*
shadow; shade; image; reflection; influence; resemblance F छाया *[chāyā]*
shake V.I. हिलना *[hilnā]* V.T. हिलाना *[hilānā]*
shake, jerk violently V.T. झकझोरना *[jhakjhornā]*
shallow ADJ छिछला *[chichlā]*
shalwar kameez (a loose fitting trouser and shirt) F सलवार क़मीज़ *[salvār qamīz]*
shame F शर्म *[śarm]*; शर्मिंदगी *[śarmindagī]*
shameful ADJ शर्मनाक *[śarmnāk]*
shape M रूप *[rūp]*
shape, form, appearance F शक्ल *[śakla]*
share V.T. बाँटना *[bā̃ṭnā]*
share (portion) M हिस्सा *[hissā]*
shareholder M भागीदार *[bhāgīdār]*
sharp ADJ तेज़ *[tez]*

sharpness, acridity F तेज़ी *[tezī]*
shave V.T. दाढ़ी बनाना *[dāṛhī banānā]*
shave the hair on the head V.T. मूँड़ना *[mū̃ṛnā]*
shawl M शाल *[śāl]*
she PRO वह/वे *[voh/vo]*
shed; drop or fall; be discharged V.I. झड़ना *[jhāṛnā]*
sheep F भेड़ *[bheṛ]*
sheet F चादर *[cādar]*
shelf M ख़ाना *[khānā]*
shift (move) V.T. हटाना *[haṭānā]*
shine V.I. चमकना *[camaknā]*
ship M जहाज़ *[jahāz]*
ship (send) V.T. भेजना *[bhejnā]*
shirt F क़मीज़ *[qamīz]* M कुरता *[kurtā]*
shit F टट्टी *[ṭaṭṭī]*
shit V.T. हगना *[hagnā]*
shiver V.I. सिहरना *[siharnā]*
shock V.I. झटका लगना *[jhaṭkā lagnā]*
shock; lurch; beheading an animal with one stroke M झटका *[jhaṭkā]*
shoe M जूता *[jūtā]*
shoot V.T. गोली मारना *[golī mārnā]*
shop F दुकान *[dukān]*
shopkeeper M दुकानदार *[dukāndār]*
shopping F ख़रीदारी *[kharīdārī]*
shore M किनारा *[kinārā]*
short; younger ADJ छोटा *[choṭā]*
shortage F कमी *[kamī]*
shoulder M कंधा *[kandhā]*
shout V.I. चिल्लाना *[cillānā]*
shove V.T. धकेलना *[dhakelnā]*
shove; push; give a push/impetus V.T. धक्का देना *[dhakkā denā]*
show M तमाशा *[tamāśā]* F दिखावट *[dikhāvaṭ]*
show V.T. दिखाना *[dikhānā]*
show one's face V.T. मुँह दिखाना *[mũh dikhānā]*
shower (rain) F बौछार *[bauchār]*
shrewd ADJ होशियार *[hośiyār]*
shriek; screech F चीख़ *[cīkh]*
shrink V.I. सिकुड़ना *[sikuṛnā]*; सिमटना *[simaṭnā]*
shut (the eyes etc.) V.T. मूँदना *[mū̃dnā]*
shy ADJ शर्मीला *[śarmīlā]*

siblings M PL भाई-बहन *[bhāī-behan]*
sick ADJ बीमार *[bīmār]*
sickness F बीमारी *[bīmārī]*
side ADV, F तरफ़ *[taraf]* M पहलू *[pehlū]*
sidewalk M पैदलपथ *[paidalpath]*
sieve F चलनी *[calnī]*
sigh F आह *[āh]*
sight M दर्शन *[darśan]*
sight, view F दृष्टि *[dṛṣṭi]*
sign M इशारा *[iśārā]*; निशान *[niśān]*; संकेत *[saṅket]*
sign V.T. दस्तख़त करना *[dastak͟hat karnā]*
signal V.T. इशारा करना *[iśārā karnā]*
signal, indication; rendezvous M संकेत *[saṅket]*
signal; hint M इशारा *[iśārā]*
signature M हस्ताक्षर *[hastākṣar]*
significance; greatness M महत्त्व *[mahattva]*
significant ADJ महत्त्वपूर्ण *[mahttvapūrṇ]*
silence F चुप्पी *[cuppī]*; ख़ामोशी *[k͟hāmośī]*
silent ADJ ख़ामोश *[k͟hāmoś]*; चुप *[cup]*
silently; quietly; stealthily ADV चुपचाप *[cupcāp]*
silk M रेशम *[reśam]*
silk ADJ रेशमी *[reśmī]*
silver F चाँदी *[cā̃dī]*
similar ADJ एक सा *[ek sā]*
simple ADJ सहज *[sehaj]*
simple, right, erect ADJ सीधा *[sīdhā]*
simple; convenient ADJ आसान *[āsān]*
simplicity, plainness F सादगी *[sādagī]*
simultaneously ADV एक ही समय *[ek hī samay]*
sin M पाप *[pāp]*
since PP से *[se]*
since when, for how long कब से *[kab se]*
sing V.T. गाना *[gānā]*
sing a song V.T. गीत गाना *[gīt gānā]*
singer; musician M गायक *[gāyak]*
single (alone) ADJ अकेला *[akelā]*
sink V.I. डूबना *[dūbnā]*
sip; a gulp M घूँट *[ghū̃ṭ]*
sip; exploit V.T. चूसना *[cūsnā]*
sir M साहब *[sāhab]*
sister F बहन *[behan]*

sit V.I. बैठना *[baiṭhnā]*
sit for (take) an exam V.T. परीक्षा देना *[parīkṣā denā]*
site M स्थल *[sthal]*
sitting room F बैठक *[baiṭhak]*
situation F स्थिति *[sthiti]*
six ADJ छै/छह/छ: *[chai/chah/chaḥ]*
sixteen ADJ सोलह *[solah]*
sixth ADJ छठा *[chaṭhā]*
sixty ADJ साठ *[sāṭh]*; षष्टि *[ṣaṣṭi]*
sixty-eight ADJ अड़सठ *[aṛsaṭh]*
sixty-five ADJ पैंसठ *[paĩsaṭh]*
sixty-four ADJ चौंसठ *[caũsaṭh]*
sixty-nine ADJ उनहत्तर *[unhattar]*
sixty-one ADJ इकसठ *[iksaṭh]*
sixty-seven ADJ सरसठ *[sarsaṭh]*
sixty-three ADJ तिरसठ/तिरेसठ *[tirsaṭh/tiresaṭh]*
size F नाप *[nāp]*
skeleton, physical frame M कंकाल *[kaṅkāl]*
skid; fall for, be fascinated V.I. फिसलना *[phisalnā]*
skill M कौशल *[kauśal]*
skillful ADJ कुशल *[kuśal]*
skin F खाल *[khāl]*; त्वचा *[tvacā]*
skin; husk M छिलका *[chilkā]*
skull F खोपड़ी *[khopṛī]*
sky M आकाश *[ākāś]*; आसमान *[āsmān]*
slack; sluggish; soft ADJ ढीला *[ḍhīlā]*
slap M चपत *[capat]*
slap V.T. चपत झाड़ना *[capat jhāṛnā]*; चाँटा जड़ना/देना/लगाना/रसीद करना *[cā̃ṭā jaṛnā/denā/lagānā/rasīd karnā]*
slave M ग़ुलाम *[ghulām]*
slavery; servility F ग़ुलामी *[ghulāmī]*
sleep F नींद *[nīd̃]* V.I. सोना *[sonā]*
sleeve F आस्तीन *[āstīn]*
slender, narrow ADJ पतला *[patlā]*
slender, subtle ADJ बारीक *[bārīk]*
slide V.I. फिसलना *[phisalnā]* V.T. खिसकाना *[khiskānā]*
slide, creep V.I. सरकना *[saraknā]*
slight (insult) M अपमान *[apamān]*

slight (light) ADJ हलका *[halkā]*
slip V.I. फिसलना *[phisalnā]*; सरकना *[saraknā]*
slope F ढलान *[ḍhalān]*
slot (hole) M छेद *[ched]*
slow ADJ धीमा *[dhīmā]*
slowly ADV आहिस्ता *[āhistā]*; धीरे *[dhīre]*
slowly ADV धीरे-धीरे *[dhīre-dhīre]*
slowly, gently, gradually ADV आहिस्ता-आहिस्ता *[āhistā-āhistā]*
small ADJ छोटा *[choṭā]*; थोड़ा *[thoṛā]*
smallness, pettiness M छोटापन *[choṭāpan]*
smart ADJ होशियार *[hośiyār]*
smell F बू *[bū]*
smell, scent V.T. सूँघना *[sū̃ghnā]*
smile F मुस्कान *[muskān]*
smile V.I. मुस्कराना/मुस्कुराना *[muskarānā/muskurānā]*
smoke M धुआँ *[dhuā̃]*
smoke (a cigarette) V.T. सिगरेट पीना *[sigreṭ pīnā]*
smoking M धूम्रपान *[dhūmrapān]*
smooth ADJ चिकना *[ciknā]*
smuggler M तस्कर *[taskar]*
snake M साँप *[sā̃p]*
snap (break) V.T. तोड़ना *[toṛnā]*
snatch, grab; seize V.T. छीनना *[chīnnā]*
sneeze F छींक *[chī̃k]* V.I. छींकना *[chī̃knā]*
sniff V.T. सूँघना *[sū̃ghnā]*
snore M खर्राटा *[kharraṭā]*
snore V.T. खर्राटा भरना *[kharraṭā bharnā]*
snow F बर्फ़ *[barf]* M हिम *[him]*
snow V.I. बर्फ़ पड़ना *[barf paṛnā]*
snowy ADJ बर्फ़ीला *[barfīlā]*
so, then CONJ, PART [ALSO EMPHATIC PARTICLE] तो *[to]*
soak, moisten V.T. भिगोना *[bhigonā]*
soap M साबुन *[sābun]*
soar (fly) V.I. उड़ना *[uṛnā]*
sob V.I. सिसकना *[sisaknā]*
sobbing F सिसकी *[siskī]*
sociable ADJ मिलनसार *[milansār]*
society M समाज *[samāj]*
sock M मोज़ा *[mozā]*
sofa M सोफ़ा *[sofā]*
soft ADJ कोमल *[komal]*

softly (quietly) ADV धीरे धीरे *[dhīre dhīre]*
soil F मिट्टी *[miṭṭī]*
solace, assurance M दिलासा *[dilāsā]*
soldier M सैनिक *[sainik]*
sole (alone) ADJ अकेला *[akelā]*
sole (of a shoe), base, floor; keel (of a boat); lower/underside M तला *[talā]*
sole (of the foot) F तलवा *[talvā]*
solid ADJ दृढ़ *[dṛṛh]*
solid; sound ADJ ठोस *[ṭhos]*
solidify, clot V.I. जमना *[jamnā]*
solution M सुलझाव *[suljhāv]*
solution (to a problem) M समाधान *[samādhān]*; हल *[hal]*
solve V.T. सुलझाना *[suljhānā]*
some PRO, ADJ कुछ *[kuch]*
some, any; someone, anyone ADJ, PRO कोई *[koī]*
someday ADV किसी दिन *[kisī din]*
somehow ADV किसी तरह *[kisī tarah]*
something PRO कुछ *[kuch]*
sometime ADV कभी *[kabhī]*
sometimes ADV कभी कभी *[kabhī kabhī]*
somewhere ADV कहीं *[kahı̃]* (कहाँ + ही)
son (sometimes used affectionately as a mode of address for a girl) M बेटा *[beṭā]*
song M गाना *[gānā]*
soon (quickly) ADV जल्दी *[jaldī]*
sorrow M दुख *[dukh]*; शोक *[śok]*
sort V.T. छाँटना *[chā̃ṭnā]*
sort, manner F तरह *[tarah]*
soul, inner self F अंतरात्मा *[antarātmā]*
sound M स्वर *[svar]*
source M स्रोत *[srot]*
south M दक्षिण *[dakṣiṇ]*
sow V.T. बोना *[bonā]*
space M अंतरिक्ष *[antarikṣ]*; आकाश *[ākāś]*
spare time F फ़ुरसत *[fursat]*
spark F चिनगारी *[cingārī]*
sparkle; flash V.I. चमकना *[camaknā]*
speak (to x) V.I., V.T. (x से) बोलना *[(x se) bolnā]*
special ADJ विशेष *[viśeṣ]*; ख़ास *[k͟hās]*

specialist M विशेषज्ञ *[viśeṣajña]*
specialty F विशेषता *[viśeṣtā]*
species F जाति *[jāti]*
specific ADJ विशेष *[viśeṣ]*
specimen; model M नमूना *[namūnā]*
spectacle, entertainment M तमाशा *[tamāśā]*
spectacles M चश्मा *[caśmā]*
spectator, visitor M दर्शक *[darśak]*
spectulate (estimate) V.T. अंदाज़ा लगाना *[andāzā lagānā]*
speech M भाषण *[bhāṣaṇ]*
speed F रफ़्तार *[raftār]*
spend V.T. बिताना *[bitānā]*
spending (expenditure) M व्यय *[vyay]*
spice M मसाला *[masālā]*
spicy ADJ चटपटा *[caṭpaṭā]*; तीखा *[tīkhā]*
spider F मकड़ी *[makṛī]* M मकड़ा *[makṛā]*: a large spider M मकड़ा *[makṛā]*
spill (make fall) V.T. गिराना *[girānā]*
spinach M पालक *[pālak]*
spine F, M पीठ *[pīṭh]*; रीढ़ *[rīṛh]*
spirit (soul) F आत्मा *[ātmā]*
spiritual ADJ आध्यात्मिक *[ādhyātmik]*
spit; reproach, treat with contempt V.T. थूकना *[thūknā]*
splendor F शान *[śān]*
split, burst, erupt, explode; shoot, sprout; (secret) be revealed; (eyes) go blind V.I. फूटना *[phūṭnā]*
spokesman M प्रवक्ता *[pravaktā]*
spoil V.T. बिगाड़ना *[bigāṛnā]*
sponsor M प्रयोजक *[prayojak]*
sponsor V.T. प्रयोजन करना *[prayojan karnā]*
spontaneously ADJ अनायास *[anāyās]*
spoon M चम्मच *[cammac]*: a large spoon M चमचा *[camcā]*
sport; show M खेल *[khel]*
sports M खेल-कूद *[khel-kūd]*
sportsman M खिलाड़ी *[khilāṛī]*
sprain F मोच *[moc]*
spread V.T. फैलाना *[phailānā]*
spread out; strike down V.T. बिछाना *[bichānā]*

spread, be diffused V.I. फैलना *[phailnā]*
spring (season) M वसंत *[vasant]*
spring (season); bloom F बहार *[bahār]*
spring; flow forth; fall V.I. झरना *[jharnā]*
sprinkle V.T. छिड़काना *[chiṛkānā]*
sprinkle; a splash; bespattering M छींटा *[chĩṭā]*
spy M गुप्तचर *[guptacar]*
spy or detective M खुफ़िया *[khufiyā]*
square M चौक *[cauk]*
squat V.I. उकड़ू बैठना *[ukṛū baiṭhnā]*
squeeze V.T. निचोड़ना *[nicoṛnā]*
stab V.T. भोंकना *[bhõknā]*
stab with a knife V.T. चाकू घोंपना/भोंकना *[cāqū ghõpnā/bhõknā]*
stable ADJ स्थिर *[sthir]*
stack M चट्टा *[caṭṭā]*
stadium (field) M मैदान *[maidān]*
staff (stick) F लाठी *[lāṭhī]*
stage; platform M मंच *[mañc]*
stage a play V.T. नाटक खेलना *[nāṭak khelnā]*
stagger V.I. लड़खड़ाना *[laṛkhaṛānā]*
stain M दाग़ *[dāgh]*
stairs, staircase F सीढ़ी *[sīṛhī]*
stale ADJ बासी *[bāsī]*
stamina M दम *[dam]*
stamp F मोहर *[mohar]*
stamp; put a stamp on V.T. मुहर लगाना *[muhar lagānā]*
stance (position) F स्थिति *[sthiti]*
stand M अड्डा *[aḍḍā]*
stand V.I. डटना *[ḍaṭnā]*
standard ADJ मानक *[mānak]*
standard M मापदंड *[māpdaṇḍ]*
standing ADJ खड़ा *[khaṛā]*
star M तारा *[tārā]*
stare V.T. ताकना *[tāknā]*
start V.T. शुरू करना *[śurū karnā]*
startle, alarm (someone) V.T. चौंकाना *[caũkānā]*
startled, alarmed V.I. चौंकना *[caũknā]*
state F दशा *[daśā]*; हालत *[hālat]* M प्रदेश *[pradeś]*; हाल *[hāl]*

statement M बयान *[bayān]*
statement, utterance M कथन *[kathan]*
station M स्टेशन *[sṭeśan]*
statistics (figures) M आँकड़े *[ā̃kṛe]*
statue; image F मूर्ति *[mūrti]*
status F हैसियत *[haisiyat]*
stay (tarry) V.I. ठहरना *[ṭheharnā]*
stay V.I. रहना *[rehnā]*
steadily ADV धीरे धीरे *[dhīre dhīre]*
steady V.T. संभालना *[sambhālnā]* ADJ स्थिर *[sthir]*
steal V.T. चुराना *[curānā]*: steal (x) V.T. (x की) चोरी करना *[(x kī) corī karnā]*
steam F भाप *[bhāp]*
steel M इस्पात *[ispāt]*
step V.T. क़दम रखना *[qadam rakhnā]*
stick F लाठी *[lāṭhī]*
stick, wand M डंडा *[ḍaṇḍā]*
stiff ADJ कड़ा *[kaṛā]*
still (until now) ADV अब तक *[ab tak]*
stilled; stunned ADJ स्तब्ध *[stabdh]*
stimulate V.T. उत्तेजित करना *[uttejit karnā]*
stimulating ADJ उत्तेजक *[uttejak]*
stimulation M उत्तेजन *[uttejan]*
stimulus F उत्तेजना *[uttejnā]*
sting V.T. डँसना *[ḍã̄snā]*
stipend M वज़ीफ़ा *[vazīfā]*
stir (commotion) F हलचल *[halcal]*
stock (goods) M माल *[māl]*
stomach M पेट *[peṭ]*
stone M पत्थर *[patthar]*
stony, littered with stones ADJ पथरीला *[pathrīlā]*
stop V.I. ठहरना *[ṭheharnā]*, रुकना *[ruknā]* V.T. रोकना *[roknā]*
storage M भंडार *[bhaṇḍār]*
store (shop) F दुकान *[dukān]*
store (keep) V.T. रखना *[rakhnā]*
storehouse M भंडार *[bhaṇḍār]*
storm, dust-storm F आँधी *[ā̃dhī]*
story, floor F मंज़िल *[manzil]*
story, tale F कथा *[kathā]*; कहानी *[kahānī]*
stove M चूल्हा *[cūlhā]*
straight ADJ सीधा *[sīdhā]*
straight (honest) ADJ ईमानदार *[īmāndār]*

straighten V.T. सीधा करना *[sīdhā karnā]*
strain; percolate V.T. छानना *[chānnā]*
strainer F छलनी *[chalnī]*
strange ADJ अजीब *[ajīb]*; विचित्र *[vicitra]*
stranger M अजनबी *[ajnabī]*
stream (flow) F धारा *[dhārā]*
street F सड़क *[saṛak]*
strength M बल *[bal]* F मज़बूती *[mazbūtī]*; शक्ति *[śakti]*
strengthen V.T. मज़बूत बनाना *[mazbūt banānā]*
stress M तनाव *[tanāv]*
stress/strain; suppression; compression; compulsion, coercion M दबाव *[dabāv]*
stretch V.T. तानना *[tānnā]*
strict ADJ सख़्त *[sakht]*
strike F हड़ताल *[haṛtāl]*
strike V.T. बजाना *[bajānā]*
strike, kill V.T. मारना *[mārnā]*
strip F पट्टी *[paṭṭī]*
strip (make naked) V.T. नंगा करना *[naṅgā karnā]*
stroke (blow) M आघात *[āghāt]*
stroke (caress) V.T. सहलाना *[sehlānā]*
stroll V.I. टहलना *[ṭehalnā]*
strong ADJ पक्का *[pakkā]*; मज़बूत *[mazbūt]*
strong, harsh ADJ तेज़ *[tez]*
strong, mighty ADJ ताक़तवर *[tāqatvar]*
strongly ADV ज़ोर से *[zor se]*
struggle M संघर्ष *[saṅghars̩]*
struggle, combat V.T. जूझना *[jūjhnā]*
student M छात्र *[chātra]*:
 student hostel M छात्रावास *[chātrāvās]*
studies F पढ़ाई *[paṛhāī]*
study V.T. पढ़ना *[paṛhnā]*; पढ़ाई करना *[paṛhāī karnā]*
stuff (goods) M सामान *[sāmān]*
stuff in, thrust in V.T. खोंसना *[khõsnā]*
stumble; wobble V.I. लड़खड़ाना *[laṛkhaṛānā]*
stupid ADJ बेवकूफ़ *[bevaqūf]*
stupidity F बेवकूफ़ी *[bevaqūfī]*
style M अंदाज़ *[andāz]*
subcontinent M उपमहाद्वीप *[upamahādvīp]*
subject M विषय *[viṣay]*
submit; be subdued; be repressed; be covered, be concealed, be hushed up; cool down V.I. दबना *[dabnā]*

substance (essence) M सार *[sār]*
subtract; deduct V.T. घटाना *[ghaṭānā]*
suburb (neighborhood) M मुहल्ला *[muhallā]*
succeed V.I. सफल होना *[saphal honā]*
success F सफलता *[saphaltā]*; कामयाबी *[kāmyābī]*
successful ADJ सफल *[saphal]*
such, of this type ADJ ऐसा *[aisā]*
suck, suck dry V.T. चूसना *[cūsnā]*
suddenly ADV अचानक *[acānak]*
suffer V.T. भोगना *[bhognā]*
sufficient ADJ पर्याप्त *[paryāpt]*
sugar F चीनी *[cīnī]* M शक्कर/शकर *[śakkar/śakar]*
suggest V.T. सुझाना *[sujhānā]*
suggestion M सुझाव *[sujhāv]*
suicide V.T. आत्महत्या करना *[ātmahatyā karnā]*
suit M सूट *[sūṭ]*
suitable (appropriate) ADJ उपयुक्त *[upayukt]*
suitable, reasonable, fair ADJ उचित *[ucit]*
sulk, be displeased V.I. रूठना *[rūṭhnā]*
sum (total) M कुल *[kul]*
summary M सार *[sār]*; सारांश *[sārāns]*
summer F गरमी/गर्मी *[garmī]*
summer season F ग्रीष्म ऋतु *[grīṣma ṛtu]*
sun M सूरज *[sūraj]*; सूर्य *[sūrya]*: sun to rise V.I. सूरज निकलना *[sūraj nikalnā]*; sun to set V.I. सूरज ढलना *[sūraj ḍhalnā]*
Sunday M रविवार *[ravivār]*; इतवार *[itvār]*
sunlight F धूप *[dhūp]*
sunny (light) ADJ रोशनीदार *[rośnīdār]*
sunshine F धूप *[dhūp]*
super (excellent) ADJ बढ़िया *[baṛhiyā]*
superfluous; useless, worthless ADJ फ़ालतू *[fāltū]*
superstitious ADJ अंधविश्वासी *[andhviśvāsī]*
supervision; guard, watch F निगरानी *[nigrānī]*
supervisor (inspector) M निरीक्षक *[nirīkṣak]*
support V.T. टेकना *[ṭeknā]* M समर्थन *[samarthan]*; सहारा

[sahārā]
support (assistance) F सहायता *[sahāytā]*
supporter M समर्थक *[samarthak]*
Supreme Spirit M परमात्मा *[paramātmā]*
suppress V.T. दबाना *[dabānā]*
sure ADJ पक्का *[pakkā]*
surface F सतह *[sateh]*
surge V.I. उमड़ना *[umarṇā]*
surprise M आश्चर्य *[āścarya]*; विस्मय *[vismay]*
surprised; flabbergasted ADJ चकित *[cakit]*
surprising ADJ आश्चर्यजनक *[āścaryajanak]*
surround V.T. घेरना *[ghernā]*
surrounded V.I. घिरना *[ghirnā]*
surrounding ADV आसपास *[āspās]*
surveillance F निगरानी *[nigrānī]*
survey M सर्वेक्षण *[sarvekṣaṇ]*
survive V.I. बचना *[bacnā]*
suspect V.T. संदेह करना *[sandeh karnā]*
suspect (suspicious individual) M संदिग्ध व्यक्ति *[sandigdh vyakti]*
suspend V.T. निलंबित करना *[nilambit karnā]*
suspend (hang) V.T. लटकाना *[laṭkānā]*
suspicion M शक *[śak]*; संदेह *[sandeh]*
suspicion; false notion M वहम *[vaham]*
suspicious ADJ संदिग्ध *[sandigdh]*
swallow V.I. निगलना *[nigalnā]* V.T. हड़पना *[haṛapnā]*
swan M हंस *[hans]*
sway V.I. झूमना *[jhūmnā]*
swear (abuse) V.T. गाली देना *[gālī denā]*
swearing F क़सम *[qasam]*
sweat M पसीना *[pasinā]*
sweater M स्वेटर *[sveṭar]*
sweep with a broom V.T. झाड़ू लगाना *[jhāṛū lagānā]*
sweet ADJ मधुर *[madhur]*; मीठा *[mīṭhā]*
sweetmeat F मिठाई *[miṭhāī]*
sweetness F मधुरता *[madhurtā]*
swim V.I. तैरना *[tairnā]*
swimming F तैराकी *[tairākī]*
swing V.I. डोलना *[ḍolnā]*;

झूलना *[jhūlnā]*; V.I. झूमना *[jhūmnā]*
swing; suspended scaffold M झूला *[jhūlā]*
swing; get very familiar V.I. हिलना *[hilnā]*
switch (button) M बटन *[baṭan]*
switch (change) V.T. बदलना *[badalnā]*
sword F तलवार *[talvār]*
symbol M प्रतीक *[pratīk]*
sympathy F सहानुभूति *[sahānubhūti]*
symptom M लक्षण *[lakṣaṇ]*
system F व्यवस्था *[vyavasthā]*

T

table F मेज़ *[mez]*
tablespoon M चम्मच *[cammac]*
tablet F गोली *[golī]*
tail, rear part; hanger-on F पूँछ *[pū̃ch]*
take V.T. लेना *[lenā]*
take a breath V.T. साँस लेना *[sā̃s lenā]*
take a bribe V.T. घूस लेना *[ghūs lenā]*; रिश्वत लेना *[riśvat lenā]*
take a dip डुबकी मारना/लगाना *[ḍubkī mārnā/lagānā]*
take a loss; suffer a loss V.T. घाटा खाना *[ghāṭā khānā]*
take a picture V.T. तस्वीर खींचना *[tasvīr khī̃cnā]*
take a photograph V.T. फ़ोटो खींचना *[foṭo khī̃cnā]*
take aim V.T. निशाना साधना *[niśānā sādhanā]*
take an examination (student) V.T. इम्तहान देना *[imtahān denā]*
take an oath V.T. शपथ लेना *[śapath lenā]*
take an oath, swear V.T. क़सम खाना *[qasam khānā]*
take away V.I. ले जाना *[le jānā]*
take cover/shelter V.T. ओट लेना *[oṭ lenā]*
take initiative V.T. पहल करना *[pehal karnā]*
take out V.T. निकालना *[nikālnā]*
take possession of; confiscate V.T. क़ब्ज़ा करना *[qabzā karnā]*
take time/delay (x to) V.I. देर लगना (x को) *[der lagnā (x ko)]*

take trouble, be bothered तकलीफ़ उठाना *[taklif uṭhānā]*
tale F कथा *[kathā]*
talent (skill) M कौशल *[kauśal]*
talented (skilled) ADJ कुशल *[kuśal]*
talk F बात *[bāt]*, बातचीत *[bātcīt]* V.T. (x से) बात करना *[(x se) bāt karnā]*: (x) to talk (to y) V.I. (x) की बात (y से) होना *[(x) kī bāt (y se) honā]*
talk openly V.T. खोलकर बात करना *[kholkar bāt karnā]*
tall ADJ लंबा/लम्बा *[lambā]*
tame V.T., F साधना *[sādhnā]*
tame, tamed ADJ पालतू *[pāltū]*
tank; rhythm M ताल *[tāl]*
tap M नल *[nal]*
tape M फ़ीता *[fītā]*
target; butt; mark M निशाना *[niśānā]*
tarry V.I. रुकना *[ruknā]*
tarry; stand one's ground V.I. टिकना *[ṭiknā]*
task M काम *[kām]*
taste V.T. चखना *[cakhnā]* M स्वाद *[svād]*
tasteless ADJ फीका *[phīkā]*
tasty ADJ मज़ेदार *[mazedār]*; लैज़ीज़ *[lazīz]*
tax M टैक्स *[ṭaiks]*
taxi F टैक्सी *[ṭaiksī]*
tea F चाय *[cāy]*
teach V.T. सिखाना *[sikhānā]*
teach, make read V.T. पढ़ाना *[paṛhānā]*
teacher M आचार्य *[ācārya]*; अध्यापक *[adhyāpak]*; उस्ताद *[ustād]*; शिक्षक *[śikṣak]* M, ADJ गुरु *[guru]*
teaching F शिक्षा *[śikṣā]*
team; swarm M दल *[dal]*
tear M आँसू *[ā̃sū]*
tear (rip) V.T. फाड़ना *[phāṛnā]*
tease V.T. चिढ़ाना *[ciṛhānā]*; छेड़ना *[cheṛnā]*
teaspoon F छोटी चम्मच *[choṭī cammac]*
technique M तेकनीक *[teknīk]*
teenage ADJ किशोर *[kiśor]*
telephone M टेलीफ़ोन *[ṭelīfon]*
telescope M दूरबीन *[dūrbīn]*
television M दूरदर्शन *[dūrdarśan]*; टेलीविज़न *[ṭelīvizan]*
tell V.T. बताना *[batānā]*
temperature M तापमान *[tāpmān]*

temple M मंदिर *[mandir]*
ten ADJ दस *[das]*
ten million ADJ करोड़ *[karoṛ]*
tend (look after) V.T. देखभाल करना *[dekhbhāl karnā]*
tender ADJ कोमल *[komal]*
tension M तनाव *[tanāv]*
tent M खेमा *[khemā]*
tepid ADJ गुनगुना *[gungunā]*
term (condition) F शर्त *[śart]*
terrain (ground) F ज़मीन *[zamīn]*
terrible ADJ डरावना *[ḍarāvnā]*; भयंकर *[bhayaṅkar]*
terrifying ADJ भयानक *[bhayānak]*
terrorism M आतंकवाद *[ātaṅkvād]*
terrorist M आतंकवादी *[ātaṅkvādī]*
test V.T. परखना *[parakhnā]*
test (exam) F परीक्षा *[parīkṣā]*
testify (bear witness) V.T. गवाही देना *[gavāhī denā]*
text F इबारत *[ibārat]*
textbook F पाठ्यपुस्तक *[paṭhyapustak]*
than PP से *[se]*
thank V.T. शुक्रिया अदा करना *[śukriyā adā karnā]*
thank you! M शुक्रिया *[śukriyā]*
that PRO वह *[voh]*
that, for CONJ कि *[ki]*
theater M थिएटर *[thieṭar]*; सिनेमाहाल *[sinemāhāl]*
their ADJ इनका *[inkā]*; उनका *[unkā]*
them PRO इन्हें/इनको *[inhẽ/inko]*; उन्हें/उनको *[unhẽ/unko]*
then CONJ फिर *[phir]*
then, at that time ADV तब *[tab]*
theory M सिद्धांत *[siddhānt]*
there ADV उधर *[udhar]*; वहाँ *[vahā̃]*
therefore, for this reason, so CONJ इसलिये *[isliye]*
these days ADV आजकल *[ājkal]*
these/he/she/they PL PRO ये *[ye]*
they/those/he/she PRO वे *[vo]*
thick; intensive ADJ घना *[ghanā]*
thicket F झाड़ी *[jhāṛī]*
thief M चोर *[cor]*
thigh F जाँघ *[jā̃gh]*
thin ADJ दुबला *[dublā]*; पतला

[patlā]; बारीक [bārīk] ADJ, M हलका [halkā]
thing F बात [bāt]; चीज़ [cīz]; वस्तु [vastu]
think V.T. सोचना [socnā]
thinking F सोच [soc]
third ADJ तीसरा [tīsrā]
thirst F प्यास [pyās]
thirsty ADJ प्यासा [pyāsā]: (x) to be thirsty V.I. (x को) प्यास लगना [(x ko) pyās lagnā]
thirteen ADJ तेरह [terah]
thirty-eight ADJ अड़तीस [aṛtīs]
thirty-five ADJ पैंतीस [paĩtīs]
thirty-four ADJ चौंतीस [caũtīs]
thirty-nine ADJ उनतालीस [untālīs]
thirty-one ADJ इकत्तीस [ikattīs]
thirty-seven ADJ सैंतीस [saĩtīs]
thirty-six ADJ छत्तीस [chattīs]
thirty-three ADJ तैंतीस [taĩtīs]
thirty-two ADJ बत्तीस [battīs]
thirty ADJ तीस [tīs]
this PRO यह [yeh]
thorn M काँटा [kā̃ṭā]
those PRO वे [vo]
though IND हालाँकि [hālā̃ki]
thought M ख़्याल/ख़याल [khyāl/khayāl]; विचार [vicār]
thousand ADJ हज़ार [hazār]
thrash V.T. पीटना [pīṭnā]
thread M धागा [dhāgā]
thread V.T. गूँथना [gū̃thnā]
threat, bluster F धमकी [dhamkī]
threaten V.T. धमकी देना [dhamkī denā]
three-quarters, quarter to one ADJ पौन [paun]
three-quarters ADJ तीन चौथाई [tīn cauthāī]
three ADJ तीन [tīn]
threshold F दहलीज़ [dehlīz]
thrift F किफ़ायत [kifāyat]
thrifty, frugal ADJ मितव्ययी [mitvyayī], किफ़ायती [kifāyatī]
thrive V.I. पनपना [panapnā]
throat M गला [galā]
throb V.I. धड़कना [dhaṛaknā]
throbbing (of heart) F धड़कन [dharkan]
throttle; strangle V.T. गला घोटना [galā ghoṭnā]
through, through the medium of PP द्वारा [dvārā]
throw V.T. फेंकना [phẽknā]
throw down, dash down V.T. पटकना [paṭaknā]

throw in; thrust in V.T. झोंकना *[jhõknā]*
thrust V.T. ठाँसना *[ṭhā̃snā]*
thrust into, pierce through V.T. भोंकना *[bhõknā]*
thumb M अँगूठा *[ãgūṭhā]*
thunder F गरज *[garaj]*
thunderbolt; ear ornament F बिजली *[bijlī]*
Thursday M गुरुवार *[guruvār]*
thus ADJ यूँ *[yū̃]*
ticket M, F टिकट *[ṭikaṭ]*: **a return ticket** M वापसी टिकट *[vāpasī ṭikaṭ]*
tie V.T. बाँधना *[bā̃dhnā]*
tiger M शेर *[śer]*
tight ADJ तंग *[taṅg]*
tighten V.T. कसना *[kasnā]*
till PP तक *[tak]*
timber (wood) F लकड़ी *[lakṛī]*
time M वक़्त *[vaqt]*; समय *[samay]*; टाइम *[ṭāim]*
time and again ADV बार-बार *[bār-bār]*
tip F बख़्शीश *[bakhśīś]*
tip; end; forepart F नोक *[nok]*
tire V.T. थकना *[thaknā]*
tired, fatigued V.I. थकना *[thaknā]*: (x) to be/ become tired V.I. (x को) थकान होना *[(x ko) thakān honā]*
title, heading M शीर्षक *[śīrṣak]*
to PP को *[ko]*
today M, ADV आज *[āj]*
toe F पैर की उँगली *[pair kī ũglī]*
together ADV एक साथ *[ek sāth]*; साथ साथ *[sāth sāth]*
toilet M शौचालय *[śaucālay]*
tolerate V.T. सहना *[sehnā]* बरदाश्त करना *[bardāśt karnā]*
toll F चुंगी *[cuṅgī]*
tomato M टमाटर *[ṭamāṭar]*
tomb M मक़बरा *[maqbarā]*; मज़ार *[mazār]*
tomorrow M कल *[kal]*
tone M लहजा *[lehjā]*
tongue F ज़बान *[zabān]*
tonight F आज रात *[āj rāt]*
too PART भी *[bhī]*
tool M यंत्र *[yantra]*; औजार *[aujār]*
tooth M दाँत *[dā̃t]*
top (summit) F चोटी *[coṭī]*; M शिखर *[śikhar]*
top (chief) ADJ मुख्य *[mukhya]*
topic M विषय *[viṣay]*
torch M टार्च *[ṭārc]*

torture, trouble V.T. सताना *[satānā]*
toss, roll about restlessly uneasily; writhe in pain V.I. तड़पना *[taṛapnā]*
toss, throw up V.T. उछालना *[uchālnā]*
total M कुल *[kul]*
touch, contact; feel M स्पर्श *[spārś]*
touch, feel V.T. छूना *[chūnā]*
toughness, strength; rigidity, tenacity F दृढ़ता *[dṛṛhtā]*
tour; fit M दौरा *[daurā]*
tourism M पर्यटन *[paryaṭan]*
tourist M पर्यटक *[paryaṭak]*
tournament (competition) F प्रतियोगिता *[pratiyogitā]*
towards ADV, F तरफ़ *[taraf]*
towel F, M तौलिया *[tauliyā]*
tower F मीनार *[mīnār]*
town M नगर *[nagar]*
toy M खिलौना *[khilaunā]*
toxic ADJ विषैला *[viṣailā]*
trace F सुराग़ *[surāgh]*
trace (search) V.T. खोजना *[khojnā]*
track F पगडंडी *[pagḍaṇḍī]*
trackway; pavement; ruler, wooden strip F पटरी *[paṭrī]*
trade (business) M व्यापार *[vyāpār]*
trader, merchant M व्यापारी *[vyāpārī]*
tradition F परंपरा *[paramparā]*
traditional, orthodox ADJ परंपरागत *[paramparāgat]*
tragedy M दुर्भाग्य *[durbhāgya]*
tragic ADJ दुःखमय *[duḥkhmay]*
trail (walking path) F पगडंडी *[pagḍaṇḍī]*
train F गाड़ी *[gāṛī]*; रेलगाड़ी *[relgāṛī]*; ट्रेन *[ṭren]*
train V.T., F साधना *[sādhnā]*; ट्रेन *[ṭren]*
trainer M प्रशिक्षक *[praśikṣak]*
training M प्रशिक्षण *[praśikṣaṇ]*
trait (sign) M लक्षण *[lakṣaṇ]*
tranquil ADJ शांत *[śānt]*
tranquillity F शांति *[śānti]*
transaction M सौदा *[saudā]*
transfer; cloudiness, stray cloud; substitution F बदली *[badlī]*
transform V.I., V.T. बदलना *[badalnā]*
transformation M परिवर्तन *[parivartan]*
transit (in) ADV रास्ते में *[rāste mẽ]*

translation M अनुवाद *[anuvād]*
transmission (broadcast) M संचारण *[sañcāraṇ]*
transmit V.T. संचारण करना *[sañcāraṇ karnā]*
transmit, remit V.T. भेजना *[bhejnā]*
transport V.T. ढोना *[ḍhonā]*
transportation M परिवहन *[parivahan]*
trap M फंदा *[phandā]*
trap V.T. फँसाना *[phãsānā]*
trash M कूड़ा *[kūṛā]*
trash can M कूड़ेदान *[kūṛedān]*
travel F यात्रा *[yātrā]* M सफ़र *[safar]*
travel V.T. यात्रा करना *[yātrā karnā]*; सफ़र करना *[safar karnā]*
traveler M मुसाफ़िर *[musāfir]*; यात्री *[yātrī]*
trauma (emotional blow) M सदमा *[sadmā]*
treasure M ख़ज़ाना *[khazānā]*
treat (x) V.T. (x का) इलाज करना *[(x kā) ilāj karnā]*
treatment M इलाज *[ilāj]*; उपचार *[upcār]*
treatment M सुलूक *[sulūk]*
treaty; junction, union F संधि *[sandhi]*
tree M पेड़ *[peṛ]*
tremble V.I. काँपना *[kā̃pnā]*
tremor M कंपन *[kampan]*
trend (tendency) F प्रवृत्ति *[pravṛtti]*
trial (court) M मुक़दमा *[muqadmā]*
trial (test) F परीक्षा *[parīkṣā]*
tribe F जनजाति *[janjāti]*
trick (fraud) M कपट *[kapaṭ]*
trifling, of no consequence ADJ ऐसा-वैसा *[aisā-vaisā]*
trigger M घोड़ा *[ghoṛā]*
trim V.T. कतरना *[katarnā]*
trip F यात्रा *[yātrā]*
triumph F विजय *[vijay]*
trivial ADJ तुच्छ *[tucch]*
trolly; cart; truck; barrow M ठेला *[ṭhelā]*
troop F टोली *[ṭolī]*
trouble F तकलीफ़ *[taklīf]*
trouble (someone) तकलीफ़ देना *[taklīf denā]*
trouble V.T. दिक़ करना *[diq karnā]*
troubled ADJ परेशान *[pareśān]*
truck F ट्रक *[ṭrak]*
true ADJ ठीक *[ṭhīk]*
true; truth, veracity ADJ, M सत्य *[satya]*

truly ADV वाक़ई *[vāqaī]*; सचमुच *[sacmuc]*
trunk M ट्रंक *[ṭraṅk]*
trunk (elephant) F सूँड़ *[sū̃ṛ]*
trust M भरोसा *[bharosā]*
trust, believe (x) V.T. (x पर) भरोसा करना *[(x par) bharosā karnā]*
trust, faith, reliance M विश्वास *[viśvās]*
truth F सच्चाई *[saccāī]*
truth, veracity M सत्य *[satya]*
try F कोशिश *[kośiś]*
try V.T. कोशिश करना *[kośiś karnā]*
tube; pipe; barrel of a gun F नली *[nalī]*
tuck in V.T. खोंसना *[khõsnā]*
Tuesday M मंगलवार *[maṅgalvār]*
tune F लय *[lay]*; धुन *[dhun]*
tune; fusion; merging; disappearance F लय *[lay]*
tunnel F सुरंग *[suraṅg]*
turban F पगड़ी *[pagṛī]*
turmeric F हल्दी *[haldī]*
turn V.I. फिरना *[phirnā]*
turn M मरतबा *[martabā]* F बारी *[bārī]*
turn back V.T., V.I. पलटना *[palaṭnā]*
turn, return; invert; repeat again and again; change the order, shuffle; proclaim, pronounce V.T. फेरना *[phernā]*
turn; be twisted; bend V.I. मुड़ना *[muṛnā]*
turn; turn in another direction V.T. मोड़ना *[moṛnā]*
T.V. F टी० वी० *[ṭī. vī.]*
twelve ADJ बारह *[bārah]*
twentieth ADJ बीसवाँ *[bīsvā̃]*
twenty ADJ बीस *[bīs]*
twenty-eight ADJ अट्ठाईस *[aṭṭhāīs]*
twenty-first ADJ इक्कीसवाँ *[ikkīsvā̃]*
twenty-five ADJ पच्चीस *[paccīs]*
twenty-four ADJ चौबीस *[caubīs]*
twenty-fourth ADJ चौबीसवाँ *[caubīsvā̃]*
twenty-nine ADJ उनतीस *[untīs]*
twenty-one ADJ इक्कीस *[ikkīs]*
twenty-second ADJ बाईसवाँ *[bāīsvā̃]*
twenty-seven ADJ सत्ताईस *[sattāīs]*

twenty-six ADJ छब्बीस *[chabbīs]*
twenty-third ADJ तेईसवाँ *[teīsvā̃]*
twenty-three ADJ तेईस *[teīs]*
twenty-two ADJ बाईस *[bāīs]*
twice, a second time ADV दोबारा *[dobārā]*
twin ADJ जुड़वाँ *[juṛvā̃]*
twinkle V.I. झिलमिलाना *[jhilmilānā]*
twist F मरोड़ *[maroṛ]*; मोच *[moc]* V.T. मरोड़ना *[maroṛnā]*
two ADJ दो *[do]*
two-and-a-half ADJ ढाई *[ḍhāī]*
two days after tomorrow; two days before yesterday ADV नरसों *[narsõ]*
two-fold; equivocal; stoutish ADJ दोहरा *[dohrā]*
two-thirds ADJ दो तिहाई *[do tihāī]*
type F क़िस्म *[qism]*; तरह *[tarah]*; भाँति *[bhā̃ti]* M प्रकार *[prakār]*
type; solder V.T. टंकण करना *[ṭaṅkaṇ karnā]*
typical ADJ ठेठ *[ṭheṭh]*
typically ADV आम तौर पर *[ām taur par]*
tyranny, outrage M ज़ुल्म *[zulm]*
tyre, tire M टायर *[ṭāyar]*

U

ugly, unsightly ADJ कुरूप *[kurūp]*
uh VOC उफ़ *[uf]*
ulcer, tumor M फोड़ा *[phoṛā]*
ultimate ADJ अंतिम *[antim]*
ultimately ADV अंत में *[ant mẽ]*
umbrella M छाता *[chātā]*
unable (incapable) ADJ असमर्थ *[asamarth]*
unacquainted; ignorant ADJ अनजान *[anjān]*
unarmed ADJ निहत्था *[nihatthā]*
unbreakable ADJ अटूट *[aṭūṭ]*
unceasing ADJ अथक *[athak]*
uncertain ADJ अनिश्चित *[aniścit]*
unclaimed ADJ लावारिस *[lāvāris]*
uncle (mother's brother) M मामा *[māmā]*
uncle (father's older brother) M ताऊ *[tāū]*

uncle (father's younger brother) M चाचा *[cācā]*
uncomfortable ADJ असहज *[asahaj]*
uncontaminated ADJ ख़ालिस *[khālis]*
uncooked, unboiled; raw, unripe; green; crude; incomplete, unfinished; rough; imperfect, immature; inauthentic; doubtful; vague; weak ADJ कच्चा *[kaccā]*
uncover V.T. पोल खोलना *[pol kholnā]*
undefeated ADJ अजित *[ajit]*
under ADV नीचे *[nīce]*
under pressure, being compelled/forced ADV मजबूरन *[majbūran]*
undergo V.T. भुगतना *[bhugatnā]*
undergo, experience; derive sexual pleasure V.T. भोगना *[bhognā]*
undergraduate M स्नातक *[snātak]*
undermine V.T. जड़ काटना *[jaṛ kāṭnā]*
understand V.I., V.T. समझना *[samajhnā]*: (x) to understand (lit: to come into x's understanding) V.I. (x की) समझ में आना *[(x kī) samajh mẽ ānā]*
understand, make out; solve; enquire, ask V.T. बूझना *[būjhnā]*
understanding F समझ *[samajh]*
undertake (begin) V.T. शुरू करना *[śurū karnā]*
underwear (esp for children) F चड्डी *[caḍḍī]*
undivided ADJ अखंड *[akhaṇḍ]*
uneducated; unlettered ADJ अशिक्षित *[aśikṣit]*
unemployment F बेरोज़गारी *[berozgārī]*
uneven ADJ ऊबड़-खाबड़ *[ūbaṛ-khābaṛ]*
unexpectedly; all at once ADV एकाएक *[ekāek]*
unfair ADJ नाइनसाफ़ *[nāinsāf]*
unfaithful ADJ बेवफ़ा *[bevafā]*
unfamiliar; alien ADJ अजनबी *[ajnabī]*
unfinished ADJ अधूरा *[adhūrā]*
unfold (happen) V.I. होना *[honā]*

unfortunate ADJ कमबख़्त *[kambakht]*
unfortunately ADV दुर्भाग्यवश *[durbhāgyavaś]*
unhappy ADJ दुखी *[dukhī]*; नाख़ुश *[nākhuś]*
unholy ADJ अपवित्र *[apavitra]*
uniform ADJ एकरूप *[ekrūp]* F वरदी *[vardī]*
uninterrupted, incessant ADV निरंतर *[nirantar]*
union, league M संघ *[saṅgh]*
unique ADJ अनोखा *[anokhā]*; निराला *[nirālā]*; लाजवाब *[lājavāb]*
unit F इकाई *[ikāī]*
unite V.T. मिलाना *[milānā]*
united ADJ संयुक्त *[sanyukt]*
unity F एकता *[ektā]*
universal (extensive) ADJ व्यापक *[vyāpak]*
universe M विश्व *[viśva]*
university M विश्वविद्यालय *[viśvavidyālay]*
unknowingly ADV अनजाने *[anjāne]*; अनजाने में *[anjāne mẽ]*
unknown (stranger) ADJ अजनबी *[ajnabī]*; अनजान *[anjān]*
unlike ADJ असमान *[asamān]*
unlikely ADV शायद ही/थोड़े ही *[śāyad hī/thoṛe hī]*
unload; take across V.T. उतारना *[utārnā]*
unowned, heirless (used for both things and people) ADJ लावारिस *[lāvāris]*
unpleasant ADJ अप्रिय *[apriya]*
unravel V.T. सुलझाना *[suljhānā]*
unripe, raw ADJ अपक्व *[apa-kva]*
unsew; unravel; open up; unroll; untwist; excoriate V.T. उधेड़ना *[udheṛnā]*
unskilled; a novice M, ADJ अनाड़ी *[anāṛī]*
unsuccessful; vain ADJ विफल *[viphal]*
untangle V.T. सुलझाना *[suljhānā]*
untie V.T. खोलना *[kholnā]*
until PP तक *[tak]*
untrue; sham; mock; feigned ADJ झूठा *[jhūṭhā]*
unusual ADJ असाधारण *[asādhāraṇ]*
unwanted ADJ अनचाहा *[ancāhā]*
unworthy ADJ नालायक़

[nālāyaq]
up ADV ऊपर *[ūpar]*
update V.T. ख़बर देना *[khabar denā]*
upheaval M हंगामा *[haṅgāmā]*
upon PP पर *[par]*
upper ADJ ऊपरी *[ūparī]*
upper class M, PL ऊँचे तबक़े के लोग *[ũce tabqe ke log]*
upper undergarment F बनियाइन *[baniyāin]*
uproar M हंगामा *[haṅgāmā]*
uproot V.T. उखाड़ना *[ukhāṛnā]*
uprooted, be dislodged; be out of spirits, be out of sorts V.I. उखड़ना *[ukhaṛnā]*
ups and downs, rise and fall, fluctuation; vicissitude M उतार-चढ़ाव *[utār-caṛhāv]*
upset ADJ व्याकुल *[vyākul]*
upset (sad) ADJ दुखी *[dukhī]*
upset (spoil) V.T. बिगाड़ना *[bigāṛnā]*
upstairs ADV ऊपरी मंज़िल *[ūparī manzil]*
urban ADJ शहरी *[śehrī]*
urge (desire) F इच्छा *[icchā]*
urine M, F पेशाब *[peśāb]*
urinate; piss V.T. मूतना *[mūtnā]*
us PL, PRO हमें/हमको *[hamẽ/hamko]*
use M इस्तेमाल *[istemāl]*; प्रयोग *[prayog]*: **use (x)** V.T. (x का) सेवन करना *[(x kā) sevan karnā]*
use V.T. (x का) प्रयोग करना *[(x kā) prayog karnā]*
use; apply V.T. (x का) इस्तेमाल करना *[(x kā) istemāl karnā]*
use, put to use; deal with V.T. बरतना *[baratnā]*
used; secondhand ADJ इस्तेमालशुदा *[istemālśudā]*
useful ADJ उपयोगी *[upyogī]*; मुफ़ीद *[mufīd]*
useless ADJ फ़ज़ूल *[fuzūl]*, बेकार *[bekār]*
useless, worthless, futile ADJ फ़ज़ूल *[fazūl]*
uselessly, for no reason; without any purpose IND ख़्वाहमख़्वाह *[khvāhamkhvāh]*
usual (ordinary) ADJ आम *[ām]*
usually (ordinarily) ADV आम तौर पर *[ām taur par]*
utensil, vessel M बरतन *[bartan]*

V

vacation (holiday) F छुट्टी *[chuṭṭī]*
vaccination M टीका *[ṭīkā]*
vagina; for of existence or station fixed at birth F योनि *[yoni]*
valid (current) ADJ जारी *[jārī]*
valley F घाटी *[ghāṭī]*
valuable; precious; costly ADJ क़ीमती *[qīmtī]*
value F क़ीमत *[qīmat]* M मूल्य *[mūlya]*
van M वान *[vān]*
vanish V.I. ग़ायब होना *[g̲hāyab honā]*
vanished ADJ ग़ायब *[g̲hāyab]*
vanquish V.T. हराना *[harānā]*
variety F विविधता *[vividhatā]*
various, miscellaneous ADJ विविध *[vividh]*
vase M गुलदान *[guldān]*
vast (expansive) ADJ विशाल *[viśāl]*
vegetable F सब्ज़ी *[sabzī]*
vegetable, greens M साग *[sāg]*
vegetarian M शाकाहारी *[śākāhārī]*
vehicle F गाड़ी *[gāṛī]*
veil V.T. घूँघट करना *[ghū̃ghaṭ karnā]*
vein F रग *[rag]*
venerable, respected; forefathers, elderly people ADJ, M बुज़ुर्ग *[buzurg]*
verandah M बरामदा *[barāmdā]*
versus ADV बनाम *[banām]*
vertical (erect) ADJ खड़ा *[khaṛā]*
very, a lot ADJ बहुत *[bahut]*
very little ADJ लेश *[leś]*
vessel (container) M पत्र *[patra]*
via ADV के रास्ते *[ke rāste]*
vice, flaw, fault, defect F बुराई *[burāī]*
victim M शिकार *[śikār]*
victory F जीत *[jīt]*; विजय *[vijay]*
video M विडियो *[viḍiyo]*
view M दर्शन *[darśan]*; मत *[mat]*
view, opinion M ख़्याल/ख़याल *[k̲h̲yāl/k̲h̲ayāl]*
viewer M दर्शक *[darśak]*
vigilant ADJ सावधान *[sāvdhān]*
vigorous, fit ADJ तंदुरुस्त *[tandurust]*
village M गाँव *[gā̃v]*

village; a gram M ग्राम *[grām]*
vinegar M सिरका *[sirkā]*
violence F हिंसा *[hinsā]*
violent ADJ, M हिंसक *[hinsak]*
virtue F अच्छाई *[acchāī]* ADJ, M पुण्य *[puṇya]*
virtuous (noble) ADJ शरीफ़ *[śarīf]*
virus F विषाणु *[viṣāṇu]*
vision F नज़र *[nazar]*
vision, glance F दृष्टि *[dṛṣṭi]*
visit (trip) F यात्रा *[yātrā]*
visitor ADJ, M यात्री *[yātrī]*; अतिथि *[atithi]*, मेहमान *[mehmān]*
vocation, occupation M पेशा *[peśā]*
voice F आवाज़ *[āvāz]*
voice; tone M स्वर *[svar]*
volume (of a book) M खंड *[khaṇḍ]*
voluntary ADJ स्वैच्छिक *[svaicchik]*
volunteer M स्वयंसेवक *[svayamsevak]*
vote M वोट *[voṭ]*; मतदान *[matdān]*
vote V.T. मतदान देना *[matdān denā]*; वोट देना *[voṭ denā]*
voter M मतदाता *[matdātā]*

W

wage (salary) M वेतन *[vetan]*
wager F शर्त *[śart]* V.T. शर्त लगाना *[śart lagānā]*
wail V.T. बिलखना *[bilakhnā]*
waist F कमर *[kamar]*
wait V.I. रुकना *[ruknā]*
wait (for x) V.T. (x का) इंतज़ार करना *[(x kā) intazār karnā]*
waiting M इंतज़ार *[intazār]* F प्रतीक्षा *[pratīkṣā]*
wake V.T. जगाना *[jagānā]*
wake V.I. जागना *[jāgnā]*
wake up, awaken V.I. जगना *[jagnā]*
wake up, be alert V.I. जागना *[jāgnā]*
walk (move) V.I. चलना *[calnā]*
walk V.I. पैदल जाना/चलना *[paidal jānā/calnā]*
wall F दीवार *[dīvār]*
wallet M बटआ *[baṭuā]*
walnut M अँखरोट *[akhroṭ]*
wander V.I. घूमना *[ghūmnā]* V.T. सैर करना *[sair karnā]*
want V.T. चाहना *[cāhnā]*
wanted/needed (subject takes को) INVAR चाहिये/चाहिए *[cāhiye/cāhie]*
war M युद्ध *[yuddh]*

war, battle F जंग *[jaṅg]*
warehouse M गोदाम *[godām]*
warm ADJ गर्म *[garm]*
warm V.T. गर्म करना *[garm karnā]*
warmth; passion; anger F गरमी/गर्मी *[garmī]*
warning F चेतावनी *[cetāvanī]*
warrior M योद्धा *[yoddhā]*
wash V.T. धोना *[dhonā]*
washed V.I. धुलना *[dhulnā]*
washerman M धोबी *[dhobī]*
wasp M ततैया *[tataiyā]*
waste V.T. गँवाना *[gãvānā]*
waste (trash) M कूड़ा *[kūṛā]*
waste, ruin V.T. ज़ाया करना *[zāyā karnā]*
watch F घड़ी *[ghaṛī]* V.T. देखना *[dekhnā]*
watch; guarding; office or job of a watchman F चौकीदारी *[caukīdārī]*
watch; guard V.T. निगरानी करना *[nigrānī karnā]*
watchman; guard M चौकीदार *[caukīdār]*
water M पानी *[pānī]*
wave F तरंग *[taraṅg]*; लहर *[lehar]* V.T. हिलाना *[hilānā]*
wave; fluctuate V.I. लहराना *[lehrānā]*
waver, pause and ponder V.I. ठिठकना *[ṭhiṭhaknā]*
wax F मोम *[mom]*
way M तरीक़ा *[tarīqā]*; मार्ग *[mārg]*; रास्ता *[rāstā]*
way, measure M उपाय *[upāy]*
we PRO, PL हम *[ham]*
weak ADJ कमज़ोर *[kamzor]*
weakness F कमज़ोरी *[kamzorī]*
wealth F दौलत *[daulat]*
wealthy ADJ अमीर *[amīr]*
weapon M हथियार *[hathiyār]*
wear, put on V.T. पहनना *[pehannā]*
wear clothes V.T. कपड़े पहनना *[kapṛe pehannā]*
weather M मौसम *[mausam]*
weave V.T. बुनना *[bunnā]*
web F जाली *[jālī]*
(the) web of worldy illusion M मायाजाल *[māyājāl]*
wedding F शादी *[śādī]*
wedding party F बारात *[bārāt]*
Wednesday M बुधवार (बुध) *[budhvār (budh)]*
week/Saturday M हफ़्ता *[haftā]*
weekend M वीकेंड *[vīkeṇḍ]*

weekly ADV हर हफ़्ते *[har hafte]*
weep bitterly, lament V.T. बिलखना *[bilakhnā]*
weigh V.T. तोलना *[tolnā]* M वज़न *[vazan]*
weighty ADJ भारी *[bhārī]*
weird ADJ अजीब *[ajīb]*
welcome (x) V.T. (x का) स्वागत करना *[(x kā) svāgat karnā]*
Welcome! ADV स्वागतम् *[svāgatam]*
welfare M कल्याण *[kalyāṇ]*
Well! All right! F ख़ैर *[khair]*
well M कुआँ *[kuā̃]*
well-being M कल्याण *[kalyāṇ]*
Well done!; Excellent! INT शाबाश *[śābāś]*
well, in a good manner ADV अच्छी तरह *[acchī tarah]*
well-known (famous) ADJ मशहूर *[maśhūr]*
west M पश्चिम *[paścim]*
western ADJ पाश्चात्य *[pāścātya]*
wet ADJ गीला *[gīlā]* V.T. भिगोना *[bhigonā]*
what (also marks a question) PRO क्या *[kyā]*
what kind of ADJ कैसा *[kaisā]*
whatever, whichever, whoever REL PRO जो भी *[jo bhī]*
wheat M गेहूँ *[gehū̃]*
wheel M पहिया *[pahiyā]*
when ADV कब *[kab]* REL ADV जब *[jab]*
where REL ADV जहाँ *[jahā̃]*; जिधर *[jidhar]* INTER कहाँ *[kahā̃]*
whereas ADV जब कि *[jab ki]*
wherever ADV जहाँ भी *[jahā̃ bhī]*
whether IND चाहे *[cāhe]*
which INTER ADJ कौन-सा *[kaun-sā]*
whisper, speak in a low or hushed voice V.T. फुसफुसाना *[phusphusānā]*
whisper, whispering sound F फुसफुसाहट *[phusphusāhaṭ]*
whistle F सीटी *[sīṭī]* V.T. सीटी देना *[sīṭī denā]*
white ADJ श्वेत *[śvet]*; सफ़ेद *[safed]*
who PRO कौन *[kaun]* REL PRO जो *[jo]*
whoever PRO जो भी *[jo bhī]*
whole ADJ अखंड *[akhaṇḍ]*
whole, entire ADJ तमाम *[tamām]*; समग्र *[samagra]*; समूचा *[samūcā]*

whole, full ADJ भर *[bhar]*
whom PRO किसे/किसको *[kise/ kisko]*
whose ADJ किसका *[kiskā]*
why INTER क्यों *[kyõ]*
wicked, lewd ADJ बदमाश *[badmāś]*
wickedness, lewdness, mischievousness, rowdiness, hooliganism F बदमाशी *[badmāśī]*
wide ADJ चौड़ा *[cauṛā]*
widespread ADJ व्यापक *[vyāpak]*
widow F विधवा *[vidhvā]*
width; breadth F चौड़ाई *[cauṛāī]*
wife F पत्नी *[patnī]*
wild ADJ जंगली *[jaṅgalī]*
will F मर्ज़ी *[marzī]*; वसीयत *[vasīyat]*
willing, approving ADJ राज़ी *[rāzī]*
win V.I. V.T. जीतना *[jītnā]*
win (victory) F विजय *[vijay]*
wind F हवा *[havā]*
wind V.T. घुमाना *[ghumānā]*
window F खिड़की *[khiṛkī]*
wine F शराब *[śarāb]*; मदिरा *[madirā]*
wing M पंख *[paṅkh]*
winner (victor) ADJ, M विजेता *[vijetā]*
winter F सर्दी *[sardī]* M जाड़ा *[jāṛā]*
wipe V.T., M पोंछना *[põchnā]*
wire ADJ, M तार *[tār]*
wisdom; mind, sense F बुद्धि *[buddhi]*
wisdom M ज्ञान *[jñān]*
wise ADJ ज्ञानी *[jñānī]*
wise, prudent, sensible; brilliant ADJ बुद्धिमान *[buddhimān]*
wish; will F इच्छा *[icchā]*
witch F चुड़ैल *[cuṛail]*
with ADV साथ *[sāth]* PP से *[se]*: with (x) PP (x) के साथ *[(x) ke sāth]*; with attention ADV ध्यान से *[dhyān se]*; with ease ADV आसानी से *[āsānī se]*
withdraw V.I. हटना *[haṭnā]*
wither V.I. मुरझाना *[murjhānā]*; सकुचना *[sakucnā]*
wither; dwindle V.I. सूखना *[sūkhnā]*
without (x) PP (x) के बग़ैर *[(x) ke baghair]*, (x) के बिना *[(x) ke binā]*
witness M गवाह *[gavāh]*

witness V.T. देखना *[dekhnā]*
witticism M लतीफ़ा *[latīfā]*
wolf M भेड़िया *[bheṛiyā]*
woman F औरत *[aurat]*; महिला *[mahilā]*
womb M गर्भ *[garbh]*
wonder M आश्चर्य *[āścarya]*; चमत्कार *[camatkār]*; विस्मय *[vismay]*
wonder; excellence M कमाल *[kamāl]*
wonderful ADJ आश्चर्यजनक *[āścaryajanak]*
wood M काठ *[kāṭh]* F लकड़ी *[lakṛī]*
wooden ADJ लकड़ी का *[lakṛī kā]*
wool M ऊन *[ūn]*
wuulen, woolly ADJ ऊनी *[ūnī]*
word M शब्द *[śabd]*
work M काम *[kām]* F नौकरी *[naukrī]*: a work (of art or literature) F कृति *[kṛti]*
work V.T. काम करना *[kām karnā]*
work (for money) V.T. नौकरी करना *[naukrī karnā]*
work M कामकाज *[kāmkāj]*
work hard V.T. मेहनत करना *[mehnat karnā]*
workable ADJ कामचलाऊ *[kāmcalāū]*
worker M कर्मचारी *[karmcārī]*; मज़दूर *[mazdūr]*
workplace (office) M दफ़्तर *[daftar]*
world F धरती *[dhartī]*; दुनिया *[duniyā]* M संसार *[sansār]*
world peace F विश्वशांति *[viśvaśānti]*
worried ADJ फ़िक्रमंद *[fikramand]*; चिंतित *[cintit]*
(the) world, universe M जगत *[jagat]*
worry F चिंता *[cintā]*: **(x) to worry** V.I. (x को) फ़िक्र होना *[(x ko) fikra honā]*; worry (about x) V.T. (x की) फ़िक्र करना *[(x kī) fikra karnā]*
worship V.T. पूजना *[pūjnā]* F पूजा *[pūjā]*: worship (x) V.T. (x की) पूजा करना *[(x kī) pūjā karnā]*
worth (value) M मूल्य *[mūlya]*
worth (worthy) ADJ लायक़ *[lāyak]*
worthless; unfit; incompetent ADJ नालायक़ *[nālāyaq]*

worthy ADJ क़ाबिल *[qābil]*; योग्य *[yogya]*; लायक़ *[lāyaq]*: worthy of (x) PP (x) के क़ाबिल *[(x) ke qābil]*; (x) के लायक़ *[(x) ke lāyaq]*
wound V.T. घायल करना *[ghāyal karnā]*
wound, blow, stroke F चोट *[coṭ]*
wounded ADJ घायल *[ghāyal]*
wow! VOC वाह! *[vāh!]*
wrap up V.T. समेटना *[sameṭnā]*
wrestle V.T. कुश्ती लड़ना *[kuśtī laṛnā]*
wrinkle F झुर्री *[jhurrī]*
wrist F कलाई *[kalāī]*
write V.T. लिखना *[likhnā]*
write a prescription V.T. नुसख़ा लिखना *[nuskhā likhnā]*
writer M लेखक *[lekhak]*
writhe in pain, be restless, toss and turn; long/yearn impatiently for V.I. छटपटाना *[chaṭpaṭānā]*
writing system F लिपि *[lipi]*
written ADJ लिखित *[likhit]*
wrong ADJ ग़लत *[ghalat]*

Y

yawn V.T. जम्हाई लेना *[jamhāī lenā]* V.I. जम्हाना *[jamhānā]*
yawning F जम्हाई *[jamhāī]*
year M बरस *[baras]*; वर्ष *[varṣ]*; साल *[sāl]*
year (of the Christian calendar) M सन् *[san]*
yearly ADJ सालाना *[sālānā]*; वार्षिक *[vārṣik]*
yearn for V.I. तड़पना *[taṛapnā]*
yearning, desire F तलब *[talab]*
yell V.I. चिल्लाना *[cillānā]*
yellow ADJ पीला *[pīlā]*
yes F हाँ *[hā̃]*; जी हाँ *[jī hā̃]*
yet ADJ अब तक *[ab tak]*
yesterday M कल *[kal]*
yield F पैदावार *[paidāvār]*
yoga M योगासन *[yogāsan]*
yogurt M दही *[dahī]*
you (FAMILIAR, PL) PRO तुम *[tum]*
you (INTIMATE, SING) PRO तू *[tū]*
you (PLURAL POLITE) PRO आप *[āp]*
young ADJ, M जवान *[javān]*: **young woman** F युवती *[yuvatī]*
your ADJ आपका *[āpkā]*; तुम्हारा *[tumhārā]*; तेरा *[terā]*

yours, yours sincerely, yours faithfully IND भवदीय *[bhavadīya]*

youth, young age, youthfulness F जवानी *[javānī]*

youth, young man M युवक *[yuvak]*

youthful; a youth, soldier ADJ, M जवान *[javān]*

Z

zeal M उत्साह *[utsāh]*

zero M शून्य *[śūnya]*; सिफ़र *[sifar]*

zone M क्षेत्र *[kṣetra]*

zoo M चिड़ियाघर *[ciṛiyāghar]*

Published by Tuttle Publishing, an imprint of Periplus Editions (HK) Ltd.

www.tuttlepublishing.com

ISBN 978-0-8048-4291-4

Distributed by:

North America, Latin America and Europe
Tuttle Publishing
364 Innovation Drive, North Clarendon,
VT 05759-9436 USA.
Tel: 1(802) 773-8930 Fax: 1(802) 773-6993
info@tuttlepublishing.com; www.tuttlepublishing.com

Asia Pacific
Berkeley Books Pte. Ltd.
3 Kallang Sector #04-01, Singapore 349278
Tel: (65) 6741-2178 Fax: (65) 6741-2179
inquiries@periplus.com.sg; www.periplus.com

22 21 20 19 5 4 3 2 1 1908CM
Printed in China